Special Issue of
Language and Cognitive Processes

LEXICAL REPRESENTATIONS AND SENTENCE PROCESSING

Edited by

Maryellen C. MacDonald
University of Southern California, U.S.A.

Psychology Press
Taylor & Francis Group
HOVE AND NEW YORK

Psychology Press
Taylor & Francis Group
27 Church Road
Hove
East Sussex BN3 2FA

Psychology Press
Taylor & Francis Group
711 Third Avenue
New York, NY 10017

First issued in paperback 2015

Psychology Press is an imprint of the Taylor and Francis Group, an informa business

ISBN 13: 978-1-138-87732-0 (pbk)
ISBN 13: 978-0-8637-7962-6 (hbk)

Cover designed by Joyce Chester

Contents*

*This book is also a special issue of the journal *Language and Cognitive Processes* which forms issue 2/3 of Volume 12 (1997). The page numbers are taken from the journal and so begin with p. 121.

LANGUAGE AND COGNITIVE PROCESSES, 1997, *12* (2/3), 121–136

Lexical Representations and Sentence Processing: An Introduction

Maryellen C. MacDonald

University of Southern California, Los Angeles, CA, USA

This introduction reviews some history of how lexical representations have come to play an important role in sentence processing research. It discusses a number of issues related to lexical representations and sentence processing, including the importance of timecourse information in theorising, the importance of frequency information in theories of sentence processing and the question of the grain of frequency information.

INTRODUCTION

Most psycholinguists think of lexical representations as including a rich array of information about the individual words in a language. For example, the lexical representation of *race* includes information about its phonology, spelling, lexical categories (both noun and verb), semantics (a contest of speed, a genetic subgroup within the human species) and other item-specific information. The process of language comprehension relies heavily on this information, but it also goes well beyond it, in that the comprehender must understand entire sentences and discourses, where critical additional information is conveyed by syntactic structure and non-linguistic information, such as the fact that the speaker is pointing to an object while speaking. Language comprehension is clearly a process of integrating multiple levels of information together, and a major focus of comprehension research concerns questions of precisely how the different levels are represented and how integration within and across levels takes place.

Requests for reprints should be addressed to Maryellen C. MacDonald, Hedco Neuroscience Building, University of Southern California, Los Angeles, CA 90089-2520, USA. E-mail: mcm@gizmo.usc.edu

During the preparation of this introduction, the author was supported by NSF Grant SBR-9511270 and by NIA Grant R01-AG11773. I would like to thank Mark Seidenberg and Robert Thornton for helpful comments on this introduction and thanks are also due to the many reviewers who provided extremely insightful and helpful comments on the papers contained in this special issue.

Researchers who study sentence processing, the part of comprehension in which a syntactic representation is recovered from the input as a comprehender listens or reads, have become increasingly interested in how lexical and syntactic information is represented and integrated. Much recent work in sentence processing assumes that lexical information has a substantial role in the syntactic interpretation of a sentence, in contrast to the position often taken in previous research. This change in status reflects several different developments in two neighbouring fields. First, the status of lexical representations has changed in theories of syntax. Much of the early work within generative theories of syntax (Chomsky, 1957, 1965) assumed that lexical information was peripheral to syntactic structure. An important model of sentence processing, the *garden path* model (Frazier, 1979, 1987), was originally developed with this generative theory as its linguistic underpinning. The garden path model is an example of a "structural" model, in that the construction of a syntactic representation for the input is thought to be guided by strategies that refer to the structure of the sentence rather than to the individual words in the sentence. This model reflected the generative approach to lexical information and relegated lexical information to a second stage of processing, following an initial syntactic analysis that ignored lexical information. This distinction between syntactic and lexical information has become less clear in recent linguistic research, however. Several syntactic theories have long given substantial importance to lexical representations (see Sells, 1985, for a review), as does more recent work within the generative approach (Chomsky, 1981, 1995). Reflecting these developments, many researchers in sentence processing have used insights from the linguistic theories in investigations of sentence processing.[1]

A second source of the shift in the role of lexical representations in sentence processing lies in connnectionist (or parallel distributed processing) research (Rumelhart & McClelland, 1986). This framework offers an approach to lexical representations in which lexical information is not stored as items in a list for each word, as was commonly assumed in earlier linguistic and psycholinguistic work. In the connectionist approach, there are no atomic lexical "entries". Instead, phonological, semantic, morphological and orthographic information is represented in a distributed fashion in a network, in which the processing units in the network all contribute to the representations of many words. In a system employing this

[1]The garden path model of sentence processing is something of an exception to this trend to adopt a larger role for lexical representations in syntax (Frazier, 1990). However, lexical information is now assumed in this model to influence the early stages of interpretation of a restricted range of syntactic structures (Frazier & Clifton, 1996).

type of knowledge structure, the representations of words are not stored as separate entries and therefore cannot be "accessed"; rather, they are computed, perhaps with different patterns activated in different contexts (Kawamoto, 1993; Seidenberg & McClelland, 1989). These models do not preserve a strong distinction between "accessing" a lexical entry and "constructing" a syntactic structure, and thus they do not maintain a central distinction between lexical and syntactic representations that embody structural approaches to syntactic processing, such as the garden path model. A major alternative approach to sentence processing, often called the *constraint-based* or *contraint-satisfaction* approach, embraces this alternative view of lexical representation and suggests that syntactic processing has the same general properties as lexical processing (for reviews, see MacDonald, Pearlmutter, & Seidenberg, 1994; Tanenhaus & Trueswell, 1995).

Given these dramatic shifts in the status of lexical representations in sentence processing, it is appropriate to take stock of this new research. This issue of *Language and Cognitive Processes* contains six papers investigating the role of lexical representations in sentence processing. The authors start from several different theoretical perspectives and view the field quite differently, yet they all share a focus on lexical representations that was essentially non-existent only a few years ago. This introduction is designed to set the stage for these papers by reviewing some of the major issues that arise with the increased attention to lexical representations during sentence processing.[2]

ORGANISATION OF THIS ISSUE

It will be clear from the discussion below that the papers in this special issue approach the role of lexical information in sentence comprehension from a variety of directions. The diversity of approaches and issues defies any neat groupings into specific categories, but there is a general organisation to the issue. The first three papers investigate the role of lexical information within

[2]One theme in current research that is not represented in this volume, largely owing to the lexical focus here, is the number of new constraints on sentence processing that have been investigated recently. These investigations include studies of how information from the visual world is integrated with linguistic information during language comprehension (Tanenhaus, Spivey-Knowlton, Eberhard, & Sedivy, 1995), and how prosodic information affects language comprehension (see the special issues on prosodic information of the journals *Language and Cognitive Processes*, 1996, and the *Journal of Psycholinguistic Research*, 1996). The very clever work in both the visual and prosodic domains is due not only to the ingenuity of the investigators, but also to recent advances in technology that permit the complex manipulations and analyses required in these domains.

a constraint-based approach to sentence processing, whereas the second group of three papers operate within more structural accounts. Within each of these two groups, the more empirical papers precede the more computational ones.

In the first paper, McRae, Ferretti and Amyote draw on research concerning the nature of conceptual representations to investigate sentence processing. Whereas most work on conceptual structure has previously focused on noun representations, McRae et al. extend the work to the study of verbs. They suggest that the thematic roles that verbs can assign are not abstract categories such as "agent" and "patient", but are tightly linked to individual verbs—that is, thematic roles are verb-specific concepts. This verb-based approach has implications for the way in which verbs and their arguments are integrated during on-line language processing as well as for linguistic accounts of thematic roles.

Burgess and Lund also investigate the role of combinatorial information. They investigate the relationship between the lexical properties of a word and the linguistic context in which the word appears. The major focus of the paper is whether a word's linguistic environment is informative about the lexical and contextual properties of the word, and whether this lexical information constrains sentence processing. Burgess and Lund address these questions using HAL, a multi-dimensional space that encodes co-occurrences between words, based on a very large sample of text. They review psycholinguistic research in several areas and ask whether particular outcomes obtained in a number of experiments could be due to particular stimulus choices, as evidenced by the "context vectors" developed in the HAL representation.

Tabor, Juliano and Tanenhaus draw on theories of dynamical systems for insight into sentence processing. They investigate the hypothesis that syntactic ambiguity resolution can be treated like the process of settling into an "attractor" in a metric space corresponding to one versus other syntactic interpretations of an ambiguous sentence. Tabor et al. explore attractor dynamics and sentence processing with connectionist stimulations of reading times at key points of ambiguity resolution in several experiments. They consider their experimental and simulation results in light of questions about the role of lexical and contextual information in sentence processing, and the extent to which both human comprehenders and the connectionist networks can extract higher-level generalisations from the linguistic input.

The next three papers in the issue address the role of lexical representations from a very different perspective, in that they pursue structural accounts. In the first of these, Ferreira and McClure investigate the role of reciprocal verbs such as *hug* in the interpretation of syntactic ambiguities such as *After Mary and John hugged the woman left*, in which it is temporarily ambiguous whether *the woman* is the direct object of *hug* or the subject of a new clause. According to the garden path model, comprehenders should initially interpret *the woman* as the direct object of the preceding verb, following the structural principle called "late closure". Ferreira and McClure found instead that the interpretation of the post-verbal noun was strongly guided by the verb, so that comprehenders were more likely to interpret the post-verbal noun as a direct object when the verb was not a reciprocal verb. These authors suggest that neither the garden path model nor constraint-based models form a completely satisfying account of their data, and they propose that a maximal arguments principle guides comprehenders' interpretation of these and other ambiguities.

Konieczny, Hemforth, Scheepers and Strube investigate several syntactic ambiguities in German which shed light on how the presence or absence of lexical information can guide parsing. One ambiguity is analogous to PP attachment ambiguities in English, as in *The spy saw the cop with the binoculars*, in which the prepositional phrase *with the binoculars* could modify either the verb *saw* or the noun phrase *the cop* (Rayner, Carlson, & Frazier, 1983; Spivey-Knowlton & Sedivy, 1995; Taraban & McClelland, 1988). Variations in verb placement in German permit a contrast between a situation in which the verb precedes the ambiguous PP, as above, and one where it follows—roughly the German equivalent of *The spy has the cop with the binoculars seen*. Konieczny et al. find the interpretation of the PP to be dependent on the availability of the lexical information from the verb. They interpret these results within a structural approach in which lexical information constrains the earliest stages of sentence processing, in contrast to both the garden path model and to constraint-based models. The paper focuses on experimental results, but the authors also discuss their computational work, the SOUL architecture, as an algorithmic instantiation of the parsing principles they advocate.

No current collection addressing syntactic ambiguity resolution would be complete without some attention to the main verb/reduced relative ambiguity that has been the testing ground for so much theorising in the field (MacDonald et al., 1994; Rayner et al., 1983; Tanenhaus & Trueswell, 1995). Stevenson and Merlo investigate the effect of various verbs on interpretation of this classic ambiguity. They ask why some reduced relative sentences, such as *The horse raced past the barn fell*, are nearly impossible to parse, whereas others, such as *The butter melted in the microwave was lumpy*, are much easier. They suggest that important properties of a verb's semantics influence the extent to which reduced relatives containing these verbs are acceptable, and they reject the account of these structures offered by the constraint-based approach (e.g. Trueswell, Tanenhaus, & Garnsey, 1994). Stevenson and Merlo use Stevenson's (1994) hybrid symbolic/connectionist parser to illustrate how a verb's lexical representation constrains interpretation of this ambiguity.

ISSUES IN LEXICAL REPRESENTATIONS AND SENTENCE PROCESSING

Constraint-based *vs* Structural Accounts

As the review of the papers in this issue should make clear, the distinction between constraint-based and structural approaches has been at the heart of recent research in sentence processing (for reviews, see Frazier, 1995; MacDonald et al., 1994; Tanenhaus & Trueswell, 1995; in this volume, Konieczny et al. and Ferreira & McClure also review some of these issues). Constraint-based models hold that language comprehension, including syntactic processing, is accomplished through the satisfaction of multiple probabilistic constraints. Lexical constraints, for example the preference for a verb to have a particular argument structure, or the frequency with which several words co-occur within a phrase, tend to provide stronger constraints on processing than discourse level constraints (Garnsey, Pearlmutter, Myers, & Lotocky, in press; Spivey-Knowlton, Trueswell, & Tanenhaus, 1993; Spivey-Knowlton & Sedivy, 1995). The heavy reliance on lexical level information stems from the nature of the input and the nature of the learning process—individual words are encountered more frequently than are complex combinations of words, and thus local (lexical) information will tend to be more informative than more combinatorial (e.g. discourse) information (see Kawamoto, 1993, for related arguments). This balance is expected to change with the amount of exposure to the language, so that combinatorial information may become more constraining with more experience (Pearlmutter & MacDonald, 1995). Essentially all major questions within the constraint-based approach concern lexical representations to some degree—the nature of these representations, how they come to constrain syntactic processing, and how lexical constraints are weighed against other constraints such as structural and discourse level constraints. The three papers in this volume that report work within the constraint-based framework (McRae et al., Burgess and Lund, and Tabor et al.) each address these issues in various ways.

The approach to lexical information is both different and more varied within structural processing frameworks. The unifying theme of structural models is that syntactic processing is accomplished via the application of parsing principles or heuristics that make reference to structural aspects of sentences (such as lexical categories like *noun phrase*), instead of, or in addition to, lexical and pragmatic information. The best known structural approach, the garden path model (Frazier, 1987), has as a central tenet that lexical information does not affect the initial interpretation of a sentence but only has its effect at a later stage (though a restricted range of structures are influenced by some lexical information; Frazier & Clifton, 1996). Investigation of the nature of lexical effects is therefore rare within the garden path framework. Ferreira and McClure's study of the effect of reciprocal verbs is therefore something of an exception to this trend, and they offer some suggestions of how the garden path approach might incorporate slightly more lexical information. Other structural accounts do not define the timecourse of lexical information to such a strong degree, and the papers by Konieczny et al. and Stevenson and Merlo both suggest a major and immediate role for lexical information during sentence processing. Thus lexical information always shares the stage with strong structural principles in the structural models, but there is still substantial variation among alternative proposals concerning the nature of the role that lexical information plays in the syntactic interpretation of sentences.

Cross-linguistic Studies

Claims within structurally based theories for the universal nature of parsing principles has sparked interest in sentence processing in languages other than English (e.g. Mitchell, Cuetos, Corley, & Brysbaert, 1995). Cross-linguistic work is equally important to constraint-based theories, as it can illuminate questions of how constraints at different levels of representation are weighed during language comprehension. The paper by Konieczny et al. is an example of this research, and it is clear that the German structures studied in that paper are far better suited to address the questions they investigate than are the English equivalents. The remaining papers in the volume focus on English, which still reflects the general distribution in the field. Though studies of languages other than English are happily increasing, they are still in the minority. A notable exception to the general scarcity of non-English work is the long tradition of cross-linguistic research within Bates and MacWhinney's (1989) competition model, which is related to the constraint-based approach. The competition model has been largely ignored in much of sentence processing research, in part because it did not focus on issues of the timecourse of processing and ambiguity resolution that have been so central to the field. As we will see in the next section, however, the status of the timecourse issues in theory development is undergoing some important changes.

The Role of Timecourse in Theorising

Although all sentence processing researchers have as their ultimate goal an understanding of the nature of the human language comprehension system, most sentence processing studies have in recent years focused on the narrower issue of the timecourse of information use during syntactic ambiguity resolution. The field was drawn in this direction by the strong theoretical account provided by the garden path model (Frazier, 1987), which posited two distinct stages of syntactic processing: the operation of the parser followed by operation of the thematic processor. The parser was thought to be governed only by syntactic rules of the language and by two structure-based heuristics (minimal attachment and late closure) to cope with syntactic ambiguities, while access to lexical, semantic and discourse information was not available until a second stage when the thematic processor began to operate on the input. Tests of the garden path model by both its proponents and critics focused on the extent to which these two stages were isolable; that is, the extent to which non-syntactic information, claimed to be limited to the second stage, could affect the operations of the first-stage parser. The modal experiment therefore has been a 2×2 design in which one factor was some kind of non-syntactic information such as discourse context or plausibility of alternative interpretations of an ambiguity, and the second factor was the presence or absence of syntactic ambiguity. A main effect of ambiguity, in which ambiguous sentences were more difficult than unambiguous controls, favoured the garden path model, in that the manipulated non-syntactic context did not appear to affect parsing. An interaction between ambiguity and context, however, argued against the garden path model, in that it suggested that non-syntactic information was influencing parsing.

This description is actually a bit simplistic, in that the garden path model's claim was that *initial* parsing was autonomous from non-syntactic information, not that such information never affected the interpretation of ambiguities. Precise timecourse information was therefore necessary to evaluate alternative claims. Researchers have looked primarily to reading measures for timecourse information, as they provide information about reading times, and thus processing difficulty, at different points in a sentence. Most useful in this regard are eyetracking methodologies, in which a reader's behaviour can be divided into various stages. The common division into stages has included first-pass reading, which is the reader's initial left-to-right eye fixations on a region of text (possibly including any regressive eye movements within the region), and total or second-pass reading, which also includes the reader's refixations on a region of text following regressive eye movements back to this region from later points in the text (Rayner et al., 1989). A number of studies suggested that whereas second-pass reading times clearly reflected the use of non-syntactic information, first-pass reading times reflected evidence only of the parser's use of the two ambiguity resolution heuristics (e.g. Frazier & Rayner, 1982; Ferreira & Clifton, 1986). Thus the state of the field was that a two-stage model focused interest on issues of timecourse to distinguish the stages of processing, which in turn promoted the use of methods, such as eyetracking, that permitted data to be collected at different points in time.

Several developments have begun to change this research tradition. First, constraint-based models have provided a different view of how various kinds of information may be used during sentence processing (MacDonald et al., 1994; Tanenhaus & Trueswell, 1995). Within the constraint-based approach, language comprehension is conceived as a constraint satisfaction process over multiple levels of probabilistic information. The extent to which a particular kind of information (lexical, syntactic, pragmatic, etc.) is used, and when it is used, is not governed by two stages of parsing, but rather by the extent to which the information constrains the interpretation. The focus then shifts from timecourse issues to issues concerning what the nature of the interactions are and how the constraints arise. Second, driven in part by research within the constraint-based approach, a number of careful eyetracking studies have strongly challenged the belief that eyetracking can provide a window into two distinct stages of parsing. These studies have shown clear evidence of the use of non-syntactic information in first-pass reading measures (e.g. Garnsey et al., 1996; Trueswell et al., 1994) and even in the first fixation durations on words (Speer & Clifton, in press), a measure that has often been taken as evidence for the earliest processing evidence obtainable with eyetracking (Rayner et al., 1989). Thus at the same time that new theoretical developments have shifted the focus of research, new empirical findings have suggested that there is no transparent mapping between certain patterns of reading data and hypothesised stages of processing. As a result, the interpretation of timecourse data is much less straightforward than it once was thought to be.

This is not to say that researchers should throw away their eyetrackers. Issues concerning the timecourse of processing still continue to be extremely interesting, even if they do not distinguish between theories as clearly as we once thought. That is, we can still investigate the relative timecourse of different sorts of information, and a result that information A has an earlier effect than B is certainly informative, even though this result does not guarantee that A and B are processed in two distinct stages. Indeed, timecourse issues are inherent to all aspects of language comprehension, in that information arrives over time as the comprehender listens or reads, and a major question concerns how the comprehender integrates all of this temporally asynchronous input. Most of the papers in this issue deal with questions concerning the timecourse of use of lexical information, even when these issues are not always framed in the classic contrast between structural and constraint-based models.

The Role of Frequency in Theorising

Frequency information has been a crucial part of psycholinguistic studies of lexical representation, at least since Cattel's (1886) investigation of the word superiority effect. The increased role for lexical representations in sentence processing will necessarily bring more attention to the role of frequency information, its origin and the "grain" or specificity with which frequency information is encoded and used by the comprehender. Previously, the focus on structural accounts tended to direct attention away from frequency information, as this information was thought to be irrelevant to the generation of syntactic structures during parsing, and lexical information (which was assumed to be affected by frequency) was not available to the parser during the initial parse.

By contrast, the constraint-based framework places tremendous importance on distributional information—that is, the frequency with which a word, collocation or syntactic structure tends to occur in the language. Frequency in these models is thought to drive the activation levels of representations, in that frequently encountered inputs are more highly activated, and have a larger effect on processing, than do rarely encountered inputs. Together with other assumptions about processing (e.g. that activation is non-linear; McClelland, 1987), predictions can be made about the kinds of information that will tend to dominate processing. These models have been criticised for the important role that frequency plays in the theory (e.g. Frazier, 1995; Gibson, Schütze, & Salomon, 1996; Stevenson & Merlo, this issue), and it is worth examining the debate more closely.

Drawing an analogy to research in word recognition is useful for understanding the role of frequency in constraint-based models of sentence processing. In the field of word recognition, there are literally hundreds of papers that manipulate or control the frequencies of relevant processing units such as words, syllable onsets, graphemes and phonemes. The interest in frequency is motivated by the fact that this factor has powerful effects on the recognition process, and interactions between frequency and other factors, such as the regularity of spelling and the complexity of semantic representations, have played a central role in theorising about the architecture of the cognitive system. It is notable that frequency has this critical role in theorising largely independent of questions concerning why frequency asymmetries exist. That is, everyone knows that there are reasons why some words, phonemes, graphemes, etc., are more frequent than others, and there are phoneticians, historical linguists and others who are actively investigating these reasons. Within research on word recognition, however, issues about the origin of frequencies can be largely separated from questions about the effects of frequency on the recognition process.

The situation in constraint-based syntactic processing is remarkably similar. The claim that frequency information is an important constraint in syntactic processing has clear implications for the architecture of the processing system. As in the case of word recognition, the investigation of the effects of frequency information is driving much of the theorising about the nature of syntactic processing, and this research can be largely separated from questions concerning where these frequency asymmetries come from.

Of course these frequency asymmetries have an origin, and questions about the source of preferences for argument structures, word orders, syntactic structures, etc., have long been a topic of study among typological linguists and others. As with word recognition, however, sentence processing researchers can make a great deal of headway towards understanding language comprehension without having a complete answer to the origin questions in hand.

The place where the analogy to word recognition breaks down is in how frequency is perceived in the broader sentence processing field. Whereas the role of frequency information has long been part of investigations of word recognition and other lexical processes, it is a relative newcomer in syntactic processing.[3] Until very recently, syntactic parsing was generally assumed to be guided by strict adherence to syntactic rules and ambiguity resolution principles; an explanatory account was thought to be one that invoked heuristics or parsing principles such as late closure (Frazier, 1987). From this perspective, the attention to frequency information appears "unprincipled", and common complaints about constraint-based approaches include the claims that merely counting the frequencies of things is uninteresting, that reliance on frequency information as an explanation of behaviour is circular, and invoking frequency information without an explanation of its origin cannot constitute a satisfying theory of sentence processing (Frazier, 1995; Stevenson & Merlo, this issue).

This critique of the role of frequency misses two important points. First, the constraint-based model's claims about frequency are part of a larger claim about the architecture of the language comprehension system—that is, that it has a particular architecture that encodes and uses frequency information. Part of this account is the claim that frequency information over multiple levels of representation affects the activation of these representations, and that sentence interpretation is accomplished through constraint satisfaction over these partially activated representations. Another part of the claim is that the learning and processing mechanisms that humans possess include the ability to build up representations (via weight changes during processing, in connectionist accounts) of distributional properties of the language through exposure. Certainly, details of the theory have yet to be fully specified, but it is clear that frequency is only part of a broader theory about how learning and comprehension take place. The basic principles that guide the operation of

[3]This is not to say that no-one had mentioned the importance of frequency information in sentence processing. Bever (1970), in a paper that launched a substantial amount of work in syntactic ambiguity resolution, suggested that frequencies of syntactic structures were a driving force in syntactic interpretation. The fact that the field took about 20 years to return to this idea would appear to be due, at least in part, to the views about distinctions between syntactic and lexical processes discussed here.

the system are a major focus of research (e.g. McClelland, 1994; Seidenberg, 1994).

Indeed, the role of frequency in the constraint-based theory is remarkably parallel to the role of parsing principles in structural theories. Just as frequency is not a theory in the constraint-based approach, the principles, such as late closure within the garden path model, are not the theory themselves. Rather, parsing principles are part of a larger claim that the parser has a particular architecture—one that uses the principles, does not use frequency information, etc. Second, in the same way in which frequency asymmetries are assumed to be due to other factors within the constraint-based approach, parsing principles such as minimal attachment must be assumed to be due to deeper properties of the linguistic or cognitive systems, such as limitations of short-term memory. Several researchers have observed that parsing principles are not the ultimate primitives in structural theories (Frazier & Fodor, 1978; Gibson, 1991); but the source of parsing principles is not a major focus of research within structural theories. Instead, as we saw in the case of frequency, structural parsing research has chosen to pursue the effects of the principles and their implications for parsing architecture separately from the question of the principles' origin. Thus the research strategy in both structural and constraint-based theories has more parallels than the critiques by structural proponents would suggest.

The Origin Question

The fact that it is extremely profitable to view questions of effects of frequency or parsing principles separately from questions of their origin does not imply that the latter sort of questions are not extremely interesting ones. Indeed, several of the authors address these issues here. Within the constraint-based approach, McRae et al. suggest that the origin of some frequency effects can be traced to the nature of conceptual representations. They argue that verbs have a conceptual structure similar to the structure of noun concepts, and this structure affects the nature of thematic role representations and parsing operations. From the structural approach, Stevenson and Merlo draw on current linguistic theory for an account of the lexical structure of several different classes of verbs, and they argue that these lexical representations affect both frequency distributions and how the parser interprets some syntactic ambiguities.

Weighing Constraints and "Grain" Issues

Closely related to questions of frequency, lexical representations and the origin of frequency asymmetries are issues of the "grain" of frequency information that constrains sentence processing. Mitchell et al. (1995), who applied the term "grain" to this issue, have suggested that lexical frequency information is not used immediately during sentence processing, but that comprehenders are instead sensitive to the frequency with which various syntactic structures have previously been used. Gibson et al. (1996) have argued against this and other frequency grains. Reflecting the important relationship between frequency and the architecture of the processing architecture, researchers' different approaches to the grain question are intimately connected with their positions on the broader question of the architecture of the language processing system. For example, Mitchell and co-workers' (1995) claims about the feasibility of using information of different grains in sentence processing are firmly grounded in their view that comprehenders can encode and store information at only relatively coarse grains.

Constraint-based models make very different assumptions about the grain issue. Within this approach, there is not a question of which single kind of frequency information guides sentence processing and which others are ignored, but rather how the many kinds of frequency information might be acquired during experience with the language, how they are weighed, and whether there are temporal and/or computational limits on the kinds of combinatorial information that might be represented. The three constraint-based papers in this issue address questions relating to the grain issue. McRae et al. investigate the extent to which thematic roles assigned by individual verbs are unique to each verb, and they discuss how verb-specific roles relate to previous claims for a coarser grain—generic thematic roles like agent and patient. Burgess and Lund use the multidimensional context space they developed to suggest how combinatorial information is gleaned from linguistic input and how co-occurrence information constrains sentence processing. Finally, Tabor et al. address the grain issue directly. They suggest that their simulations show how constraints over multiple levels of "grain" could arise from experience comprehending language, and how different grains could tend to dominate different computations. It is clear from their discussion that questions concerning the emergence of various grains of representation from exposure to instances of language input, as well as questions concerning the complex processes with which various kinds of information are weighed, will increasingly require exploration using computational models, to which we now turn.

Computational Modelling

Until recently, the relationship between psycholinguistic models of sentence processing and computational models was an uneasy one. The garden path model and other models that were developed to account for particular patterns of comprehension difficulty (reading time) through the sentence have never been instantiated as computational models. By contrast, models that were discussed or implemented as computational parsers (e.g. Gibson, 1991; Pritchett, 1988; Stevenson, 1994) often seemed to bear little relationship to the timecourse issues that were the focus of the psycholinguistic work, in that most of these models were designed to capture ultimate success or failure in interpreting ambiguity rather than precise patterns of processing difficulty through the sentence. Connectionist models of parsing (e.g. Christiansen, 1994; Elman, 1990; St. John & McClelland, 1990) have also not been transparently related to the psycholinguistic studies, for several reasons. First, the error measures that have been used to evaluate these models have not always had a clear relationship to reading times in psycholinguistic experiments. Second, these models have tended to focus on parsing difficulties associated with unambiguous syntactic structures of varying complexities rather than on the processes of ambiguity resolution (St. John & McClelland, 1990, is an exception). Third, these parsing models typically have had a limited scale and have incorporated little semantic information, making them poor candidates for questions concerning the integration of syntactic and semantic information during language comprehension.

Several papers in this issue point to some new directions that may change the relationship between theoretical, experimental and modelling work. For example, Stevenson and Merlo draw on Stevenson's (1994) hybrid parser to illustrate their claims for particular effects of verb representations on ambiguity resolution. The result is not new simulations, but rather a merging of a linguistic analysis with a previously tested parsing architecture.

Within the constraint-based approach, Burgess and Lund present simulations suggesting how rich contextual information can be gleaned from exposure to the language, and how this information could be used during sentence processing. The result is not a parsing model *per se*, but a set of contextual representations that the authors argue form an important constraint on language comprehension. Finally, Tabor et al. present a new modelling approach combining recurrent networks and a dynamical system. Their use of the outputs of the dynamical system to model comprehenders' reading times in ambiguous and unambiguous sentences is quite novel in sentence processing modelling and suggests that there is exciting potential in this direction.

CONCLUSIONS

These are interesting times in sentence processing research. The growing role of lexical representations in sentence processing is an important part of a larger set of changes in the field. The six papers in this special issue approach the question of how lexical information is represented and comes to constrain syntactic processes from several distinct perspectives and methodologies. There are clearly points on which some authors strongly disagree, yet they all share a commitment to a detailed account of syntactic processing and language comprehension and a firm belief in the importance of lexical information in that account.

REFERENCES

Bates, E., & MacWhinney, B. (1989). *Functionalism and the competition model.* Cambridge: Cambridge University Press.

Bever, T.G. (1970). The cognitive basis for linguistic structure. In J.R. Hayes (Ed.), *Cognitive development of language*, pp. 279–362. New York: John Wiley.

Cattel, J.M. (1886). The inertia of the eye and brain. *Brain, 8*, 295–312.

Chomsky, N. (1957). *Syntactic structure.* The Hague: Mouton.

Chomsky, N. (1965). *Aspects of the theory of syntax.* Cambridge, MA: MIT Press.

Chomsky, N. (1981). *Rules and representations.* New York: Columbia University Press.

Chomsky, N. (1995). *The minimalist program.* Cambridge, MA: MIT Press.

Christiansen, M.H. (1994). *Infinite languages, finite minds: Connectionism, learning, and linguistic structure.* Unpublished PhD dissertation, University of Edinburgh, Edinburgh.

Elman, J.L. (1990). Finding structure in time. *Cognitive Science, 14*, 179–211.

Ferreira, F., & Clifton, C. (1986). The independence of syntactic processing. *Journal of Memory and Language, 25*, 348–368.

Frazier, L. (1979). *On comprehending sentences: Syntactic parsing strategies.* PhD dissertation, University of Connecticut, Storrs, CT. Distributed by Indiana University Linguistics Club.

Frazier, L. (1987). Sentence processing: A tutorial review. In M. Coltheart (Ed.), *Attention and performance XII: The psychology of reading*, pp. 559–586. Hillsdale, NJ: Lawrence Erlbaum Associates Inc.

Frazier, L. (1990). Parsing modifiers: Special-purpose routines in the human sentence processing mechanism? In G.B. Flores d'Arcais, D.A. Balota, & K. Rayner (Eds), *Comprehension processes in reading*, pp. 303–330. Hillsdale, NJ: Lawrence Erlbaum Associates Inc.

Frazier, L. (1995). Constraint satisfaction as a theory of sentence processing. *Journal of Psycholinguistic Research, 24*, 437–468.

Frazier, L., & Clifton, C. (1996). *Construal.* Cambridge, MA: MIT Press.

Frazier, L., & Fodor, J. (1978). The sausage machine: A new two-stage parsing model. *Cognition, 6*, 291–328.

Frazier, L., & Rayner, K. (1982). Making and correcting errors during sentence comprehension: Eye movements in the analysis of structurally ambiguous sentences. *Cognitive Psychology, 14*, 178–210.

Garnsey, S., Pearlmutter, N.J., Myers, E., & Lotocky, M. (in press). The contributions of verbs and plausibility to the comprehension of temporarily ambiguous sentences. *Journal of Memory and Language.*

Gibson, E. (1991). *A computational theory of human linguistic processing: Memory limitations and processing breakdown.* Unpublished PhD dissertation, Carnegie Mellon University, Pittsburgh, PA.

Gibson, E., Schütze, C.T., & Salomon, P. (1996). The relationship between the frequency and the processing complexity of linguistic structure. *Journal of Psycholinguistic Research, 25*, 59–92.

Kawamoto, A. (1993). A model of lexical ambiguity resolution. *Journal of Memory and Language, 32*, 474–516.

MacDonald, M.C., Pearlmutter, N.J., & Seidenberg, M.S. (1994). The lexical nature of syntactic ambiguity resolution. *Psychological Review, 101*, 676–703.

McClelland, J.L. (1987). The case for interactionism in language processing. In M. Coltheart (Ed.), *Attention and performance XII: Reading*, pp. 3–36. London: Lawrence Erlbaum Associates Ltd.

McClelland, J.L. (1994). Toward a theory of information processing in graded, random, and interactive networks. In C. Umilta & M. Moscovitch (Eds), *Attention and performance XV: Conscious and nonconscious information processing*, pp. 655–688. Cambridge, MA: MIT Press.

Mitchell, D.C., Cuetos, F., Corley, M.M.B., & Brysbaert, M. (1995). Exposure-based models of human parsing: Evidence for the use of coarse-grained (nonlexical) statistical records. *Journal of Psycholinguistic Research, 24*, 469–488.

Pearlmutter, N.J., & MacDonald, M.C. (1995). Individual differences and probabilistic constraints in syntactic ambiguity resolution. *Journal of Memory and Language, 34*, 521–542.

Pritchett, B. (1988). Garden path phenomena and the grammatical basis of language processing. *Language, 64*, 539–576.

Rayner, K., Carlson, M., & Frazier, L. (1983). The interaction of syntax and semantics during sentence processing. *Journal of Verbal Learning and Verbal Behavior, 22*, 358–374.

Rayner, K., Sereno, S.C., Morris, R.K., Schmauder, A.R., & Clifton, C. (1989). Eye movements and on-line language comprehension processes. *Language and Cognitive Processes, 4*, SI21–50.

Rumelhart, D.E., & McClelland, J.L. (1986). On learning the past tenses of English verbs. In J.L. McClelland & D. Rumelhart (Eds), *Parallel distributed processing: Explorations in the microstructure of cognition*, Vol. 2, pp. 216–271. Cambridge, MA: MIT Press.

Seidenberg, M.S. (1994). Language and connectionism: The developing interface. *Cognition, 50*, 385–401.

Seidenberg, M.S., & McClelland, J.L. (1989). A distributed, developmental model of word recognition and naming. *Psychological Review, 96*, 523–568.

Sells, P. (1985). *Lectures on contemporary syntactic theories: An introduction to Government-Binding Theory, Generalized Phrase Structure Grammar, and Lexical-Functional Grammar.* Center for the Study of Language Information, Stanford University, Stanford, CA.

Speer, S., & Clifton, C.E. Jr. (in press). Plausibility and argument structure in sentence comprehension. *Memory and Cognition.*

Spivey-Knowlton, M.J., & Sedivy, J.C. (1995). Resolving attachment ambiguities with multiple constraints. *Cognition, 55*, 227–267.

Spivey-Knowlton, M.J., Trueswell, J.C., & Tanenhaus, M.K. (1993). Context and syntactic ambiguity resolution. *Canadian Journal of Experimental Psychology, 47*, 276–309.

St. John, M., & McClelland, J.L. (1990). Learning and applying contextual constraints in sentence comprehension. *Artificial Intelligence, 46*, 217–257.

Stevenson, S. (1994). *A competitive attachment model for resolving syntactic ambiguities in natural language parsing.* PhD dissertation, Department of Computer Science, University of Maryland.

Tanenhaus, M.K., & Trueswell, J.C. (1995). Sentence comprehension. In J.L. Miller & P.D. Eimas (Eds), *Speech, language, and communication*, pp. 217–262. San Diego, CA: Academic Press.

Tanenhaus, M.K., Spivey-Knowlton, M.J., Eberhard, K.M., & Sedivy, J.C. (1995). Integration of visual and linguistic information in spoken language comprehension. *Science, 268*, 1632–1634.

Taraban, R., & McClelland, J. (1988). Constituent attachment and thematic role assignment in sentence processing: Influences of content-based expectations. *Journal of Memory and Language, 27*, 285–318.

Trueswell, J.C., Tanenhaus, M.K., & Garnsey, S.M. (1994). Semantic influences on parsing: Use of thematic role information in syntactic disambiguation. *Journal of Memory and Language, 33*, 285–318.

LANGUAGE AND COGNITIVE PROCESSES, 1997, *12* (2/3), 137–176

Thematic Roles as Verb-specific Concepts

Ken McRae, Todd R. Ferretti and Liane Amyote

University of Western Ontario, London, Ontario, Canada

Thematic roles are typically viewed as slot and filler mechanisms in which the slots are devoid of content, or the content is limited to a few syntactically relevant features. This traditional view excludes important knowledge that people possess about who tends to do what to whom in specific situations. Thus it was extended here by treating thematic roles as verb-specific, feature-based concepts. In Experiment 1, subjects produced features for agent and patient roles such as "someone who is frightened". Role/filler typicality ratings, in which subjects provided judgements for questions such as "How common is it for a monster to frighten someone?" (i.e. monster as an agent of frighten), were collected in Experiment 2A. In Experiment 2B, different subjects were presented with the role features from Experiment 1 and the typical agents and patients from Experiment 2A. They were asked to rate how central each of the role features was to the nominal concepts, and role/filler featural similarity was calculated from these ratings. Analogous to studies of object concepts, role/filler featural similarity predicted role/filler typicality, thus suggesting that thematic roles and nominal concepts are represented in similar forms. Experiment 3 was a self-paced reading study in which adjectival features were used to bias an initial noun concept towards being a good agent or patient of the past participle of a reduced relative clause ("The shrewd heartless/young naive gambler manipulated by the dealer had bid more than he could afford to lose"). Featural bias modulated ambiguity resolution. The present work, in conjunction with other recent results, suggests that thematic roles might best be viewed as verb-specific concepts, and that this conceptual/world knowledge is computed and used immediately in on-line language processing. Results are discussed in relation to other recent treatments of thematic roles as well as constraint-based and garden path models.

Requests for reprints should be addressed to Ken McRae, Department of Psychology, Social Science Centre, University of Western Ontario, London, Ontario N6A 5C2, Canada. E-mail: kenm@sunrae.sscl.uwo.ca

This work was supported by NSERC Grant OGP0155704 to the first author. A subset of this research formed part of T.R.F.'s Master's thesis. Parts of this research were presented at the 1994 Meeting of the Psychonomic Society and the 1995 CUNY Sentence Processing Conference. We are indebted to Michael Spivey-Knowlton, Mike Tanenhaus, Amit Almor and two anonymous reviewers for illuminating discussions and/or helpful comments on earlier drafts. The complete set of feature norms from Experiments 2 and 3 can be obtained from K.M.

INTRODUCTION

It is well known that people typically understand language with little if any delay (Marslen-Wilson, 1975). Consistent with this observation, recent research has demonstrated that on-line language comprehension involves quickly combining a number of informational constraints to arrive at an interpretation that best satisfies them. Some of the constraints that have been investigated to date are syntactic principles (Frazier & Rayner, 1982), lexically specific syntactic knowledge, including both the relative frequency of verb forms (MacDonald, Pearlmutter, & Seidenberg, 1994) and subcategorisation frames (Trueswell, Tanenhaus, & Kello, 1993), accrued information about the discourse (Altmann, Garnham, & Dennis, 1992; Spivey-Knowlton & Sedivy, 1995) and relevant aspects of the visual environment (Tanenhaus, Spivey-Knowlton, Eberhard, & Sedivy, 1995). The aim of this paper is to further this line of research by focusing on an important lexical-conceptual constraint, namely thematic roles (sometimes called case roles, thematic relations or semantic case, although these terms can refer to slightly different notions). There exists a considerable body of evidence demonstrating that people's thematic role knowledge is used quickly to constrain sentence interpretation. Evidence has been found in studies of the main clause/reduced relative clause ambiguity (McRae, Spivey-Knowlton, & Tanenhaus, in prep.; Pearlmutter & MacDonald, 1992; Trueswell, Tanenhaus, & Garnsey, 1994), the prepositional phrase ambiguity (Taraban & McClelland, 1988), the clause boundary ambiguity (Clifton, 1993; Stowe, 1989) and filler–gap constructions (Boland, Tanenhaus, Garnsey, & Carlson, 1995). Consequently, thematic role knowledge is a central component of most current theories of on-line sentence comprehension (Carlson & Tanenhaus, 1988; Frazier, 1987; MacDonald et al., 1994) and language comprehension in general (Graesser, Singer, & Trabasso, 1994). The present work outlines and tests a conceptually based theory of thematic roles that has direct implications for on-line sentence interpretation and the relationship between linguistic and world knowledge.

Thematic roles have been defined as the "semantic roles that may be played by the subcategorized complements (or arguments) of a verb" (Tanenhaus, Carlson, & Trueswell, 1989, p. 212). Roughly, they represent the roles that participants (widely defined) play in the events described by verbs. Linguists have proposed numerous thematic taxonomies that typically include roles such as agent, patient, theme, goal, instrument and location (e.g. Cook, 1979; Dowty, 1991; Fillmore, 1968). Three of these are illustrated in the sentence, "Mary ate the pizza with her hands". In this sentence, "Mary" is the agent because she is performing the event, "the pizza" is the patient because the event is being performed on it, and "her hands" are the instruments because they are being used to perform the event.

The research reported below examined thematic roles by focusing on agents and patients. The precise definition of the agent and patient roles differs widely across researchers. Our choice of nomenclature was influenced by Jackendoff (1987, p. 378), who stated that "thematic relations are to be reduced to structural configurations in conceptual structure; the names for them are just convenient mnemonics for particularly prominent configurations" (see Ladusaw & Dowty, 1988, for a similar view). In other words, because the particular labels given to roles are not crucial in our framework, "agent" and "patient" are used simply as convenient mnemonics for the entity performing the event and the entity having the event performed on it, respectively. Note that this differs from theories in which roles or cases are hypothesised to be conceptual primitives, so that special significance is attached to the labels, as in Fillmore (1968).

THE CONTENT OF A THEMATIC ROLE

Thematic roles have been studied intensively in linguistics and psycholinguistics for about 30 years. During this time, a number of viewpoints have been expressed concerning whether they are syntactic, semantic or conceptual in nature (e.g. Dowty, 1991; Fillmore, 1968; Jackendoff, 1972; Schlesinger, 1995). Some theorists claim that the content of a thematic role is limited to a few syntactically relevant selectional restrictions (e.g. ⟨animacy⟩; Caplan, Hildebrandt, & Waters, 1994; Chomsky, 1965), whereas others have defined a role as a set of a small number of general features (Dowty, 1991) or conceptually primitive dimensions such as ⟨cause⟩ and ⟨control⟩ (Schlesinger, 1995).[1] The main issue addressed in this paper concerns the amount and type of content allotted to thematic roles. This issue is important because theoretical differences in thematic role content have direct implications for the on-line assignment of noun phrases (NPs) to possible roles, a process that is viewed as central to language comprehension. In addition, this issue has direct implications for the relationship between linguistic and world knowledge. For example, theories from the Chomskyan perspective draw sharp boundaries between syntax and semantics, so that thematic roles are viewed as syntactically specified slot and filler mechanisms with minimal conceptual content (e.g. Caplan et al., 1994; Schlesinger, 1995). Consequently, on-line thematic assignment is

[1] In this paper, a feature is enclosed in angled brackets, a concept name is printed in upper case when it is meant to denote the mental representation of the concept, experimental examples are in upper case also, and experimental sentences or sentence fragments are enclosed by quotes when they occur in the text (in contrast to being set off by themselves and numbered).

primarily driven by syntactic factors such as word order or the phrase's position in a phrase-structure tree or subcategorisation frame. World knowledge, such as the fact that judges typically convict other people but are rarely convicted themselves, is viewed as stored separately from linguistic knowledge and is used for checking the accuracy of thematic assignments, but not for guiding them. In contrast, in this paper, we explore the notion that thematic roles are primarily conceptual, reflecting world knowledge about specific events and the entities and objects that participate in such events. Furthermore, we claim that this type of world knowledge is organised in a manner that allows it to be computed and used immediately in language processing. Predictions derived from these notions are tested in three experiments.

The present view borrows from a number of treatments of thematic roles. For example, Tanenhaus et al. (1989) argued that thematic roles are lexical-conceptual entities with close ties to syntactic information. They also claimed that the act of recognising a verb makes available information about the sense of the verb (i.e. its core meaning), its thematic roles, the types of constituents that can be complements, and information concerning how the roles and constituents are interconnected. Thus, as in Jackendoff (1987), thematic role knowledge is viewed as lexical, in that it is part of a verb's meaning, and this knowledge is assumed to be automatically made available when a verb is read or heard. Along these lines, Gentner (1981) has argued that verbs are relational concepts and the present emphasis on thematic role concepts can be construed as a claim that an important aspect of a verb's meaning is its relation to the entities and objects that commonly participate in the events described by that verb. In other words, the meaning of many verbs is carried by the specification of the action taking place in conjunction with information about the common participants. In contrast, a number of theories of thematic roles (particularly in the form of case or theta roles) have treated them as part of the grammar—that is, as syntactic knowledge (e.g. Cullicover, 1988). This is particularly evident in theories that treat them as slot and filler mechanisms with minimal content (i.e. most treatments from the Chomskyan tradition), a position that often includes the view that roles are innately specified, non-decomposable primitives. For example, Schlesinger (1995, p. 5) espouses a view of this sort, claiming that cases are regarded as fuzzy categories that are "linguistic constructs that function in the grammar". Schlesinger was careful to distinguish them from cognitive "notions" about what types of people and things might be good fillers for roles. Finally, in the artificial intelligence literature, where thematic roles have played an important part in a number of implemented parsing models, this issue has been handled in a number of ways. Perhaps Cottrell (1988, p. 171) said it best when he asked "what counts as 'syntactic' and what 'semantic'? The answer is usually a matter of taste".

The present work also takes a lead from Fillmore (1968), who claimed that cases exist in cognition and somewhat independently of language, and that this knowledge is used efficiently during language processing. In addition, we draw no sharp distinctions among lexical, semantic, conceptual and episodic knowledge, as in Jackendoff (1983), but contrary to Schlesinger (1995). Verbs describe episodes; that is, one way to view them is as labels for sets of similar events (i.e. event categories; Kersten & Billman, 1995). Thus a verb's semantic representation is computed from the set of episodes that have been linked to the verb's word (i.e. spelling or sound). In what can be take as support for these claims, McKoon, Ratcliff and Dell (1986) have persuasively argued that there is little if any evidence to support Tulving's (1972, 1983) distinction between semantic and episodic memory, arguing instead that word meaning and general world knowledge is stored in the same form as episodes, and presumably constructed on-line from them. The next section provides a description of one aspect of verb meaning, namely, the notion of a thematic role concept.

Computed Prototypes

In a recent treatment of thematic roles, Dowty (1991) claimed that the search for the optimal taxonomy of roles was at an impasse, and thus concluded that it was time to discard the view that roles are discrete and categorical. To remedy this situation, he borrowed from prototype theories of concepts and categorisation to propose that thematic roles consist of lists of features (Rosch and Mervis, 1975). Dowty posited two basic roles, proto-agent and proto-patient. He described the proto-patient role, for example, as having the following general features: ⟨undergoes change of state⟩; ⟨incremental theme⟩; ⟨causally affected by another subject⟩; ⟨stationary relative to movement of another subject⟩; and ⟨does not exist independently of the event or not at all⟩. According to Dowty, the patient role for a specific verb constitutes a proper subset of these features. It should be noted that other linguists such as Schlesinger (1995) have stressed that role features of this type are innate and/or conceptually primitive, although Dowty did not. We took Dowty's lead and moved a step further. Our view resembles Dowty's in that each role of each verb is a concept. However, rather than being a proper subset of Dowty's general features, role concepts are formed through the everyday experiences during which people learn about the entities and objects that tend to play certain roles in certain events. This knowledge then serves as an important constraint in on-line language comprehension and production. For example, a person's representation of the agent role of ACCUSE is a result of her experiences with people who accuse others in everyday occurrences and in linguistic descriptions of them.

Via a computed role concept, this knowledge is made available when ACCUSE is read or heard, and hence is a key factor in driving on-line thematic assignment. (A discussion of the implications for on-line thematic assignment is deferred until the introduction to Experiment 3, an on-line reading study.)

What form might these role concepts take? When dealing with lexical concepts, it is important to distinguish between the information that is laid down in memory and the representation that is formed on-line when word meaning is computed. For example, some researchers have claimed that specific instances or episodes are encoded in memory (e.g. Hintzman, 1986), whereas others have stressed that knowledge is an abstraction over those instances (e.g. Posner & Keele, 1968). In distributed connectionist models such as that of McClelland and Rumelhart (1985), specific episodes are encoded in a superimposed memory system. In a system such as this, whether a computed representation corresponds to a prototype versus a specific episode depends on the amount and quality of relevant context that is included in the memory probe; that is, the better the probe context matches the context of a specific episode, the greater is the likelihood of recalling it. Given a memory system like that of Hintzman or McClelland and Rumelhart, when a word is read or heard, the resultant representation that is computed on-line is akin to a feature-based prototype. For example, when someone reads or hears a word like DOG in the absence of distinguishing context, she computes a representation that consists of the features typically possessed by the dogs that she has encountered and encoded (e.g. ⟨has paws⟩, ⟨barks⟩, ⟨wags tail⟩, etc.). Likewise, a computed role concept can be viewed as a set of features that is typically possessed by the fillers of that role. Take, for example, the agent role of ACCUSE. Most people have been accused of something or have witnessed others being accused. Although a wide range of individuals may be accusers at different times, they often possess certain features, such as being ⟨mean⟩, ⟨judgemental⟩ or ⟨insecure⟩, and it is features like these that are most likely computed as part of the agent role representation of the verb.

Note that prototype theory is not being advocated here in its most restricted sense. In the type of system envisioned, the features and their relative saliences that comprise a computed role concept differ over time as a result of experience with events and ones similar to it. Barsalou (1987) has conducted a series of studies to illustrate that the internal structure of categories (as operationalised by typicality ratings) differs between individuals as well as within individuals over time. Furthermore, the computed representation differs with context, so Barslou's (1982) notions of context-dependent and context-independent features are relevant here. Finally, analogous to the claims of Rosch (1978), Malt and Smith (1984) and McRae, de Sa and Seidenberg (1997), as in the realm of object concepts, it is believed that a complete understanding of thematic role concepts necessitates an exploration of how features correlate both within and across roles, a factor that is excluded from basic prototype theories (and is not investigated in this paper).

A theory that posits computed prototype-style representations is advantageous for a number of reasons. First, prototype theory is pertinent to language processing in that reading or hearing a word appears to result in the activation of some sort of prototype (see Hintzman, 1986, for a particularly enlightening demonstration of this). This is particularly true in psycholinguistic experiments, in which context is typically absent or impoverished. Second, prototype theory has successfully been used to account for human performance in numerous studies of lexical concepts (e.g. Rosch & Mervis, 1975; Tversky, 1977). Third, prototype theory entails that concepts have fuzzy boundaries and internal structure. Fuzzy boundaries for role concepts are necessary to capture the fact that it is not always clear whether or not a filler is appropriate for a role. Although there are cases where the boundaries are quite clear (e.g. the agent role of EAT must be filled by an animate being or the meaning becomes metaphorical, as in "That photocopier ate my memo"), there are many verbs for which people would disagree about the appropriateness of boundary examples (see McCloskey & Glucksberg, 1978, for corresponding experiments with concrete nouns). Even more central to the experiments presented below is the fact that prototype theory directly implies that concepts have internal structure (e.g. a chair is a better example of a piece of FURNITURE than is a lamp or a rug). When applied to thematic roles, it leads to the prediction that some nouns fill a role better than others. For example, a waiter is a great agent of SERVE, whereas a nurse is a good one. Furthermore, although a reporter is far from a prototypical agent, a reporter can plausibly bring someone their lunch or a cup of coffee. Finally, prototype theory is attractive because a prototype need not correspond to any single lexical concept. Thus this notion automatically entails the view that activating a thematic role concept is *not* akin to activating a set of words, but instead is a process of activating features that overlap more or less with a number of lexical concepts.

Verb-specific Features

The type of feature employed differentiates our approach from previous ones. Experiment 1 investigated role concepts by using a norming procedure similar to those used in numerous studies of object concepts (e.g. Rosch & Mervis, 1975). Specifically, subjects listed features for agent and patient roles such as "someone who is served", thus providing detailed information about the roles of specific events. This approach contrasts with those of Schlesinger (1995) and Dowty (1991), who used their intuition to derive sets of conceptual primitives or general features. Note that no subject listed this type of feature in Experiment 1. The empirically derived features can also be compared and contrasted with selectional restrictions that have been incorporated into a number of theories of thematic and case roles (e.g. Chomsky, 1965; Fillmore, 1968). Theories vary in terms of the number and complexity of selectional restrictions used. Some incorporate a small number of syntactically relevant restrictions such as ⟨animacy⟩ (Caplan et al., 1994), whereas other theories, particularly artificial intelligence parsers, incorporate a large number of rather elaborate ones (e.g. Cottrell, 1988). In a sense, the present work could be viewed as positing elaborate, empirically derived, event-specific selectional restrictions. There is a key difference, however. Selectional restrictions have a categorical feel to them that can be viewed as roughly corresponding to a classical theory of concepts (see Smith & Medin, 1981, for a description). Thus a selectional restriction specifies a condition that a filler *must* satisfy to avoid creating an anomalous or metaphorical sentence. This property clashes directly with a central tenet of prototype theory; namely, that features are characteristic rather than defining.

HIGHER-LEVEL GENERALISATIONS

It should be noted that our aim is to elaborate, rather than replace, theories that treat roles as slot and filler mechanisms or those that use general features. A verb-general notion of thematic roles has played an important part in discovering linguistic generalisations and specifying rules that link roles to grammatical positions like subject and direct object (Fillmore, 1968; Jackendoff, 1972), although the utility of linking rules has recently come under attack (Gropen, Pinker, Hollander, & Goldberg, 1991). Furthermore, verb-specific thematic role concepts might relate to higher-level verb-general roles in systematic ways. Most theories of object concepts rely in some way on the notion of a hierarchical structure of categories, as illustrated by the following set of concepts: robin → bird → animal → living thing. An analogous hierarchical structure of role categories is envisioned that is based on semantic neighbourhoods of verbs (e.g. "smash" at the basic level → break-type verbs → verbs of aggression → action verbs). Presumably, the general features discussed by Dowty (1991) and others are important to describing generalisations that are related to the higher levels in a hierarchy of this sort. To illustrate this, consider the effects of various levels when someone attempts to understand a sentence such as "The pencil kicked the cow". Because English word order strongly constrains interpretation, to make sense of it, the comprehender must contract features from the agent role concept to PENCIL. That is, the comprehender must imagine that the pencil is ⟨alive⟩ and ⟨can move⟩ (verb-general), that it ⟨has legs⟩ (probably verb-specific), and that maybe it is ⟨mean⟩ or ⟨angry⟩ (verb-specific). A further verb-specific aspect is revealed by contrasting KICKED with PUNCHED; understanding the above sentence does not require imagining that the pencil ⟨has arms⟩, although it would if KICKED was replaced by the related verb PUNCHED.

PREDICTIONS

The experiments presented below tested five main hypotheses derived from our view of thematic roles as feature-based, verb-specific, computed prototypes. In Experiment 1, subjects listed features for specific roles such as "someone who is convicted" and these featural descriptions were used to create first-order approximations to 20 role concepts that served as the basis for Experiment 2. The representations were used to test whether some roles are better defined than others (presumably because there are key differences in the regularities among the entities or objects that form the basis of the role concept). In Experiment 2A, subjects rated role/filler typicality. This involved indicating on a 7-point scale how common it is for some concept, such as CRIMINAL or JUROR, to be an agent or patient in an event described by a verb (e.g. "How common is it for a criminal to convict someone?"). These data were used to test the second hypothesis; namely, whether role concepts have internal structure, as predicted by prototype theory. Experiment 2B tested the hypothesis that this internal structure might be accounted for by role/filler featural similarity, thus testing whether thematic roles are like nominal concepts in at least one important respect. In Experiment 2B, subjects were presented with the features from Experiment 1 and rated their importance to concepts that Experiment 2A had established as either good agents or patients. Using a variation on the logic that has been applied to studies of object concepts (e.g. Malt & Smith, 1984; Rosch & Mervis, 1975), role/filler featural similarity was used to account for role/filler typicality. Finally, Experiment 3 tested two further hypotheses. First, it tested whether the thematic role knowledge studied in Experiments 1 and 2 is linguistically relevant in the sense that it is computed and used immediately and automatically in on-line language processing. In so doing, it tested whether a subtle featural manipulation would have an early effect on syntactic ambiguity resolution, a prediction relevant to the current debate between constraint-based and garden path theories of sentence comprehension. In Experiment 3, features (in the form of adjectives) were used to bias the initial NP of a sentence towards being a good filler for either the agent or patient role of the verb, and this featural information modulated resolution of the main clause/reduced relative clause ambiguity.

EXPERIMENT 1

Subjects' knowledge of role concepts was tapped by asking them to generate features that were then used to construct conceptual representations. This feature-listing method has been used in many previous studies (e.g. Barsalou, Olseth, & Wu, 1995; Rosch & Mervis, 1975; Smith, Osherson, Rips, & Keane, 1988). The resulting norms are assumed to provide valid information not because they yield a literal record of semantic representations, but rather because such representations are systematically used to generate features. Thus feature norms provide a window into important aspects of concepts without necessarily being definitive (Medin, 1989). The agent and patient roles of 20 verbs were normed. Subjects were given a form containing one role per verb (e.g. "someone who is convicted") and were asked to list features for them (e.g. ⟨is guilty⟩, ⟨has broken the law⟩).

There were three purposes of Experiment 1. The first was to test whether subjects would be able to provide coherent lists of features for roles such as "someone who is convicted". The working assumption was that they would. Thus the second purpose was to use the feature lists to construct representations of role concepts in terms of independent feature lists. Although role concepts are undoubtedly more complex than lists of individual features, this representation was used as a starting point for our investigation. The third purpose was to test whether differences existed among roles in terms of the ease with which subjects could produce features for them. Roles differ in terms of the distribution of exemplars that fill them, and these differences may have implications for the corresponding computed representations. Three aspects of the distribution of exemplars in a thematic role category may have important repercussions for the featural representation of that role: the number of exemplars that commonly fill the role; shared features among the common exemplars (inter-exemplar featural similarity); and the number of exemplars that can plausibly fill the role. Consider the agent roles of the verbs CONVICT and ACCUSE. There are only a few common agents of convicting events in our society, and these same agents are also the only plausible ones (basically judges of different types, jurors, the government and tribunals). Because these exemplars share many features, it should be easy for subjects to list features of people who convict others and there should be substantial inter-subject consistency. In contrast, there are many plausible exemplars for the agent role of ACCUSE; basically any person can accuse someone else. On the other hand, the people who commonly accuse others seem to share some attributes that are relevant to the role. Thus it should be more difficult for people to list features for "someone who convicts others", but still be easier than for many other roles (e.g. the agent role of SIT). A similar observation has been made in the realm of object concepts. For example, in McRae et al. (1997), subjects found it easy to produce features for basic level concepts such as DOG, presumably because the features of individual dogs are densely correlated and/or overlap substantially. On the other hand, subjects found it difficult to produce coherent feature lists for heterogeneous, ambiguously bounded superordinate concepts such as FURNITURE. In summary, it was predicted that there would be variability among roles in terms of the consistency of listed features across subjects.

Method

Subjects. Thirty-two native English-speaking psychology undergraduates from the University of Western Ontario participated for course credit.

Materials. The stimuli consisted of 20 transitive verbs. These verbs were chosen because the experimenters intuitively felt they took animate agents and patients, thus holding animacy constant. The verbs also have reasonably restricted agent and patient roles, thus increasing the probability that subjects would find this to be a coherent task; that is, verbs like SIT were not included. In the two test packages, subjects were asked to list agent features for 10 of the verbs (e.g. "someone who frightens people") and patient features for the other 10 (e.g. "someone who is arrested"). No subject listed features for the agent and patient roles of the same verb. Four verbs, each followed by 10 blank lines, were presented on each page. The agent roles were presented on the left side and the patient roles on the right. Packages were constructed to ensure that the subjects did not list features for the same role of two semantically similar verbs. For example, if a test package contained "someone who lectures people", it contained "someone who is taught" rather than "someone who teaches people", under the assumption that the agent concepts of LECTURE and TEACH are similar.

Procedure. Subjects were run in small groups in 45 minute sessions. Instructions were read and then left visible on a projector screen for the duration of the experiment. The instructions are included below because this is the first study in which subjects have been asked to list features for thematic roles. They were as follows.

> Most verbs describe actions (e.g. hit, run). Much of the time, in an event described by a verb, someone is doing something to someone else. For many events (verbs), a variety of people or things can be involved. However, we are interested in the fact that there are certain types of people that are commonly associated with specific events. For example, certain people (e.g. hypnotist or Freudian psychologist) typically hypnotize others (e.g. their patient or a volunteer from the crowd). The types of people that commonly participate in

an action or event are often similar in some respects in that they tend to share certain features. For example, some features that might be shared by the kind of person who typically carries people are: [example here]. In this experiment, you will be asked to list features like those shown above. In addition to listing features for the type of people who tend to perform the action, you will be asked to list features for those who tend to have the action done to them. For example, below are listed some features that are common to people who are carried by other people: [example here]. Note that we did not list names of the individuals that commonly participate in these actions (e.g. baby or invalid for someone who is carried). Rather, we listed features that these individuals tend to share. Please list as many features as you can in the 10 spaces provided. You may list more than 10 features if you can think of them. You will have two minutes per item. Please do not move on to the next item until you are instructed to do so. Please do not exceed the two minute time limit.

Results and Discussion

A separate file was created for each role to catalogue and organise the responses. Features were recorded with their production frequency, that is the number of subjects who listed the feature for that particular role (maximum of 16). When recording the features, care was taken to record synonyms under a single label. For example, the features ⟨is large⟩ and ⟨is big⟩ were recorded under a single label, ⟨is big⟩. Many subjects also listed single-word features (e.g. ⟨wise⟩, ⟨brave⟩, ⟨big⟩). These one-word features were given the prefix *is* to ensure a consistent presentation in Experiment 2. Care was also taken to ensure that features with different meanings were recorded using distinct labels. For example, both ⟨is guilty⟩ and ⟨may be guilty⟩ were listed for "someone who is accused". These features were recorded separately because it was felt that their meanings differ in an important way. Decisions concerning feature meaning were made with the assistance of three naive colleagues.

Subjects had no trouble providing features for the roles. Individual subjects listed an average of 5.5 features per role (5.7 per agent role, 5.3 per patient role). There were 3530 total responses, 1838 for agent roles, 1692 for patient roles. Of the 3530 responses, 1573 different features were listed, 800 for the agent roles and 773 for the patient roles. Thus each feature was listed by an average of 2.2 subjects, 2.3 for agent roles and 2.2 for patient roles. Of the 1573 features, 46% (721) were listed by at least 2 of the 16 subjects and 28% (445) by at least 3. The corresponding numbers were 48% (383/800) and 30% (237/800) for the agent roles and 44% (338/773) and 27% (208/773) for the patient roles. Similar statistics for consistency of responses were found in a recent feature norming experiment in which common object concepts such as DOG and CHAIR served as stimuli (McRae et al., 1997). In McRae and co-workers' study, 42% of features were listed by 2 or more subjects and 27% by 3 or more (out of a possible 30 subjects).

The main purpose of Experiment 1 was to create agent and patient feature-based role representations for Experiment 2B. These representations included the features listed by at least 3 of 16 subjects for a role. Table 1 provides a flavour for these representations by presenting the role features for FRIGHTEN (the entire set of norms can be obtained from K.M.). Note that none of the features for these 40 roles resembled the conceptual primitives of Schlesinger (1995), nor the proto-agent or proto-patient features of Dowty (1991), and that this was true for all 40 role concepts. Rather, like those in Table 1, the features were specific to common participants in the events to which the verbs referred.

To investigate the variability in the ease with which subjects could produce features for specific roles, between-subject response consistency was computed. Consistency was first measured in terms of the number of features per role representation (i.e. features listed by at least 3 of 16 subjects), which was non-significantly greater for agent ($\bar{x} = 11.9$, range $= 8$–18) than for patient roles ($\bar{x} = 10.4$, range $= 6$–15) [$t(19) = 1.66$, $P > 0.1$]. A second measure was computed by dividing the number of features listed by three or more subjects by the number of semantically distinct features listed for that role. Table 2 presents the 20 verbs in decreasing order of the percentage of features listed by at least three subjects, averaged across the two roles. Again, response consistency was non-significantly greater for agent ($\bar{x} = 30\%$, range $= 20$–47%) than for patient roles ($\bar{x} = 28\%$, range $= 14$–41%) [$t(19) = 1.18$, $P > 0.2$]. However, it is clear that some roles are more well-defined than others. For example, there is substantial consistency across subjects for the agent roles of RESCUE (47%), ENTERTAIN (45%) and CONVICT (41%), and the patient roles of CONVICT (41%) and TEACH (40%). In contrast, the lack of response consistency in the patient roles of ACCUSE (14%), SERVE (14%) and TERRORISE (15%) reflects the fact that basically anyone can be accused, served or terrorised. In

TABLE 1
Role Features and Production Frequencies for FRIGHTEN

Agent Feature	*Production Frequency*	*Patient Feature*	*Production Frequency*
is mean	10	is scared	10
is scary	10	is small	7
is ugly	8	is weak	7
is big	7	is helpless	4
is sadistic	6	is jumpy	4
has problems	4	is nervous	4
is insensitive	4	is not knowledgeable	4
is heartless	3	is insecure	3
is unfriendly	3	is in trouble	3
		is shuddering	3

TABLE 2
Number (and Percentage) of Features Listed by at Least Three Subjects in Experiment 1

Verb	*Agent Role*		*Patient Role*	
	Number of Features	*Number Listed by ≥ 3 Subjects*	*Number of Features*	*Number Listed by ≥ 3 Subjects*
convict	37	15 (41%)	32	13 (41%)
teach	41	14 (34%)	25	10 (40%)
rescue	38	18 (47%)	33	9 (27%)
entertain	29	13 (45%)	38	11 (29%)
fire	42	12 (29%)	34	14 (41%)
cure	28	11 (39%)	38	11 (29%)
punish	45	12 (27%)	37	12 (32%)
hire	40	12 (30%)	46	14 (30%)
evaluate	30	9 (30%)	34	10 (29%)
arrest	46	15 (33%)	47	12 (26%)
lecture	45	9 (20%)	42	15 (36%)
frighten	39	10 (26%)	35	10 (29%)
instruct	33	9 (27%)	35	9 (26%)
terrorise	43	15 (35%)	39	6 (15%)
investigate	47	11 (23%)	34	8 (24%)
worship	40	9 (22%)	46	12 (26%)
interview	46	10 (22%)	44	10 (23%)
accuse	46	13 (28%)	49	7 (14%)
serve	44	12 (27%)	42	6 (14%)
interrogate	41	8 (20%)	43	9 (21%)

summary, there were clear differences among verbs in terms of consistency of responses, but the agent and patient roles did not differ reliably.

EXPERIMENT 2

Experiment 2 investigated whether the role representations created in Experiment 1 capture some basic aspects of people's knowledge about the roles that certain entities play in events, and whether this knowledge is reflected by a view of thematic roles as verb-specific computed prototypes. In Experiment 2A, role/filler typicality was normed for the agent and patient roles of the Experiment 1 verbs. In this task, subjects provided ratings for questions such as, "How common is it for a hostage to rescue someone?", or "How common is it for a hostage to be rescued by someone?" A 7-point scale was used, where 1 corresponded to very uncommon and 7 to very common. In Experiment 2B, different subjects were presented with the role features from Experiment 1 but were not informed of their source, and were asked to rate the importance/centrality of these features for a specific nominal filler concept. Each noun used in Experiment 2B was either a good agent or a good patient of its corresponding verb, as established by Experiment 2A. For example, a subject might rate the importance of the features of the agent role of FRIGHTEN to the concept MONSTER. The mean featural importance rating was used as a measure of role/filler featural similarity. This measure was then used to predict role/filler typicality. The logic of Experiment 2 mirrored that of previous studies in which feature-based concept similarity has been used to predict typicality ratings (e.g. Malt & Smith, 1984; Rosch & Mervis, 1975). However, this is the first time that it has been used in the context of thematic roles.

EXPERIMENT 2A

There were two aims. The first was to demonstrate that thematic roles have internal structure by showing that some nominal concepts are rated as better fillers than others (see Schlesinger, 1995, for similar rating experiments). The second was to use the agenthood and patienthood ratings to select nominal concepts that were relatively polarised for Experiment 2B. An effort was made to design a questionnaire that would reflect people's judgements about events in the world, rather than about language *per se*. Therefore, instead of using, for example, a sentence acceptability judgement or a fragment completion task, subjects were asked how common they perceive certain events to be.

Method

Subjects. One hundred and forty-eight native English-speaking psychology undergraduates from the University of Southern California volunteered to participate. Note that no subject was involved in more than one of the experiments reported in this paper.

Materials. The items were 96 verbs, each paired with 3–7 nouns. These verbs included the 20 from Experiment 1, as well as those used by McRae et al. (in prep.), Pearlmutter and MacDonald (1992) and Trueswell et al. (1994).[2] Nouns that the experimenters intuitively felt were either good agents or patients were chosen for each verb, or were taken from previously conducted experiments. To encourage subjects to use the middle of the scale, a small number of filler nouns were added to many of the verbs. Because there were a large number of verbs, they were divided into two lists of 48 to decrease the number of ratings required of each subject. Furthermore, each subject rated the nouns for either agenthood or patienthood, but not both. Thus four lists were created.

---

[2] We wish to thank Michael Spivey-Knowlton, Maryellen MacDonald, Mike Tanenhaus and Neal Pearlmutter, who worked together with the first author in the collection of these role/filler typicality norms.

Procedure. Questionnaires were administered in a paper and pen format. Subjects were asked to rate on a 7-point scale how common it is for some type of person or animal to play a specific role in an event. Agenthood questions resembled example (1a) and patienthood questions resembled example (1b):

1a. How common is it for a
snake ______
nurse ______
monster ______
baby ______
cat ______
to **frighten** someone/something?

1b. How common is it for a
snake ______
nurse ______
monster ______
baby ______
cat ______
to **be frightened by** someone/something?

Examples were provided before subjects began the task. No time limit was imposed.

Results and Discussion

A good agent and a good patient were chosen from the 20 verbs of Experiment 1 based on two considerations. First, they were chosen to be near the ends of the continuum to facilitate analyses of variance in Experiment 2B, in which it was tested whether the featural importance ratings distinguished between good agents and patients. Second, they were chosen so that there was variation in the agenthood and patienthood ratings to facilitate regression analyses in Experiment 2B that tested whether role/filler featural similarity predicts role/filler typicality. Agenthood and patienthood ratings for the 20 good agents did not overlap [agenthood: $\bar{x} = 6.4$, range = 4.5–7.0; patienthood: $\bar{x} = 2.5$, range = 1.3–4.1; $t(19) = 20.68$, $P < 0.0001$]. The same was true for the good patients [agenthood: $\bar{x} = 1.9$, range = 1.2–3.5; patienthood: $\bar{x} = 6.1$, range = 5.2–7.0; $t(19) = 23.26$, $P < 0.0001$]. The good agents and patients are listed in Table 3, together with some statistics from Experiment 2B that are described as part of that experiment.

Although the majority of items in Experiment 2A were relatively polarised, there was a definite internal structure to the roles, as prototype theory would predict. Table 4 shows some example ratings to make this fact

TABLE 3
Role/Filler Featural Similarity from Experiment 2

Verb	*Agent Role*					*Patient Role*				
	Good Agent		*Good Patient*		*A – P*	*Good Patient*		*Good Agent*		*P – A*
accuse	witness	3.2	suspect	2.4	0.8*	suspect	4.5	witness	3.3	1.3
arrest	cop	5.4	crook	2.6	2.8	crook	5.1	cop	2.2	2.9
convict	juror	4.6	criminal	2.7	1.9	criminal	4.5	juror	2.7	1.8
cure	doctor	6.0	patient	1.3	4.7	patient	4.3	doctor	3.2	1.1*
entertain	stripper	4.4	audience	2.2	2.2	audience	5.0	stripper	2.5	2.5
evaluate	committee	4.8	applicant	2.7	2.1	applicant	5.1	committee	3.6	1.5
fire	employer	4.3	employee	2.4	1.9	employee	2.7	employer	2.4	0.3
frighten	monster	5.2	baby	2.0	3.2	baby	3.7	monster	2.0	1.7
hire	boss	4.8	applicant	3.2	1.6	applicant	4.9	boss	5.3	–0.4*
instruct	coach	5.4	novice	2.3	3.0	novice	4.8	coach	2.9	1.9
interrogate	inspector	4.4	suspect	1.8	2.6	suspect	4.1	inspector	2.4	1.7
interview	reporter	5.4	candidate	4.1	1.3	candidate	4.5	reporter	4.2	0.3*
investigate	auditor	4.8	gangster	3.0	1.8	gangster	4.3	auditor	2.1	2.2
lecture	policeman	4.9	freshman	2.0	2.9	freshman	3.6	policeman	2.5	1.1
punish	babysitter	2.9	child	2.0	0.9	child	3.0	babysitter	2.1	0.9
rescue	knight	5.8	hostage	2.5	3.3	hostage	4.7	knight	2.1	2.6
serve	waitress	5.0	customer	2.0	3.0	customer	4.1	waitress	2.2	1.9
teach	professor	5.1	trainee	4.0	1.1	trainee	5.0	professor	4.1	0.9*
terrorise	pirate	4.1	victim	1.9	2.2	victim	5.0	pirate	1.8	3.2
worship	priest	3.9	goddess	1.8	2.0	goddess	4.7	priest	3.8	0.9*

* A non-significant difference.

TABLE 4
Some Example Role/Filler Typicality Ratings

Verb	*Noun Filler*	*Agenthood Rating*	*Patienthood Rating*
frighten	monster	6.4	1.8
	snake	6.2	3.9
	nurse	3.8	3.0
	cat	3.1	5.5
	baby	2.0	5.5
hire	manager	6.7	3.6
	boss	6.7	2.9
	chairman	4.5	2.7
	employee	1.9	5.6
	applicant	1.3	5.6

apparent. Presumably, a judiciously chosen large sample of nouns would result in a more complete and relatively smooth gradient, although this was not fully tested in this experiment. It is concluded that the conceptual categories corresponding to agent and patient roles are not classical in nature, as theories that incorporate selectional restrictions might suggest.

EXPERIMENT 2B

The purpose was to test whether the internal structure of agent and patient roles could be captured by a measure of the similarity between role concepts and nominal fillers, henceforth referred to as role/filler featural similarity. The experiment used a good agent and patient for each verb selected on the basis of Experiment 2A role/filler typicality.

Method

Subjects. Forty native English-speaking psychology undergraduates from the University of Western Ontario participated for course credit.

Materials. Stimuli were constructed by crossing the good agents and patients from Experiment 2A with the role features of the 20 verbs from Experiment 1 (2 roles × 2 fillers × 20 verbs = 80 items). Four lists were created, each containing 20 items. Each verb was represented once on each list. For example, agent features for RESCUE appeared in one list with KNIGHT and another with HOSTAGE. The other two lists paired KNIGHT and HOSTAGE with the patient features for RESCUE. A 7-point scale was presented at the top of each test page, ranging from "not at all important/central" to "very important/central". Four items were presented on each page and the pages were randomly ordered.

Procedure. Subjects were run in small groups. Each subject received one list. The instructions were read to subjects and remained on a projector screen throughout. Subjects were asked to rate on a 7-point scale how important/central each feature was to their concept of the noun in question. The source of the features was not divulged. No time limit was imposed. On average, the study took about 15 min to complete.

Results and Discussion. Mean feature centrality rating across subjects was computed for each feature and an example (FRIGHTEN) is presented in Table 5. Role/filler featural similarity was computed as the mean feature centrality rating for each filler and is presented in Table 3 above.

The first analyses were designed to demonstrate that role/filler featural similarity captured basic aspects of the relationship between the roles and fillers. They tested whether role/filler featural similarity is greater when the filler matches the role. For example, it was predicted that role/filler featural similarity would be greater for MONSTER/FRIGHTEN's agent role features than for BABY/FRIGHTEN's agent role features, but less when the features come from FRIGHTEN's patient role. Analyses of variance were conducted using role (agent *vs* patient features) and congruency (whether the filler matches the role) as independent variables and role/filler featural similarity as the dependent variable. As predicted, role/filler featural similarity was significantly higher for congruent ($\bar{x}=4.5$, SE$=0.1$) than for incongruent fillers ($\bar{x}=2.7$, SE$=0.1$) [$F_1(1,38)=166.94$, $P<0.0001$; $F_2(1,38)=100.36$, $P<0.0001$]. Interestingly, role and congruency interacted [$F_1(1,38)=9.73$, $P<0.004$; $F_2(1,38)=8.11$, $P<0.008$]. Planned comparisons showed that the source of the interaction was a greater difference between congruent and incongruent fillers for agent roles [congruent: $\bar{x}=4.7$, SE$=0.1$; incongruent: $\bar{x}=2.4$, SE$=0.2$; $F_1(1,38)=128.75$, $P<0.0001$; $F_2(1,38)=36.63$, $P<0.0001$] than for patient roles [congruent: $\bar{x}=4.3$, SE$=0.1$; incongruent: $\bar{x}=2.9$, SE$=0.2$; $F_1(1,38)=34.58$, $P<0.0001$; $F_2(1,38)=20.41$, $P<0.0001$]. Differences between roles are discussed below. Finally, there was no main effect of role ($F<1$ in both analyses).

To complement the analyses of variance, regression analyses were conducted in which role/filler featural similarity was used to predict role/filler typicality that had been measured in Experiment 2A. Regressions were conducted on the set of data as a whole, and on the two roles separately. First, collapsed across the two roles, role/filler featural similarity predicted 59% of the variance in role/filler typicality [$r=0.77$; $F(1,78)=111.90$, $P<0.0001$]. Figure 1 graphically depicts this strong correlation. The second analysis investigated the typicality gradient of the agent role. Role/filler featural similarity between the agent concepts and the good agents and patients predicted 75% of the variance in role/filler typicality [$r=0.87$; $F(1,38)=114.32$, $P<0.0001$]. For the patient role, role/filler featural

TABLE 5
Role Features for FRIGHTEN with Featural Importance Ratings

Role	Feature	Importance Rating Good Agent	Importance Rating Good Patient
Agent		monster	baby
	is mean	5.5	2.3
	is scary	6.3	1.1
	is ugly	5.7	1.2
	is big	5.9	1.8
	is sadistic	3.7	1.2
	has problems	3.2	3.5
	is insensitive	5.0	1.9
	is heartless	5.2	4.6
	is unfriendly	6.1	1.2
Patient		monster	baby
	is scared	2.5	3.5
	is small	2.3	5.7
	is weak	2.2	4.4
	is helpless	1.5	5.6
	is jumpy	2.9	2.7
	is nervous	1.3	3.1
	is not knowledgeable	1.2	4.4
	is insecure	2.0	2.6
	is in trouble	2.3	2.3
	is shuddering	2.0	2.2

similarity predicted 39% of the variance in role/filler typicality [$r = 0.62$; $F(1,38) = 23.84$, $P < 0.0001$]. A test of the difference between correlations revealed that role/filler featural similarity better captured role/filler typicality for the agent role than for the patient role ($z = 2.53$, $P < 0.02$).

To explore potential differences between agent and patient roles further, additional analyses tested for a congruency effect within each role of each verb; that is, paired t-tests determined whether role/filler featural similarity differed for congruent versus incongruent fillers for each role (rather than overall, as was investigated above). These analyses revealed that 34 of the 40 roles followed the general pattern; that is, role/filler featural similarity was higher for the congruent filler ($P < 0.05$). The results are presented in Table 3. Asterisks designate the six non-significant differences, those being the agent role of ACCUSE and the patient roles of CURE, HIRE, INTERVIEW, TEACH and WORSHIP. Thus this set of analyses again showed that role/filler featural similarity better captured role/filler typicality for the agent roles than for the patient roles. Insight into this result might be gained by considering the patient roles of the five verbs for which role/filler featural similarity did not adequately capture role/filler typicality. The main

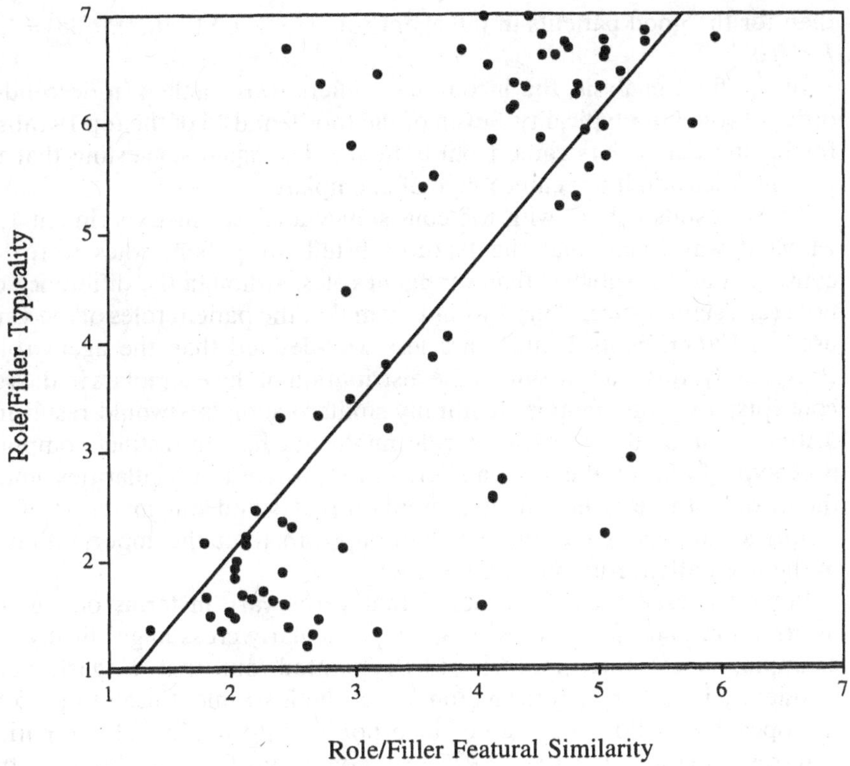

FIG. 1. Scatter plot with regression line showing that role/filler featural similarity predicts role/filler typicality ($r^2 = 0.59$). The figure includes all 80 fillers from the 40 roles. ● = one role/filler pair (e.g. cop as patient of arrest).

factor appears to be that these role categories sensibly admit many examplars; that is, almost everyone has been cured, hired, interviewed and taught (although this does not extend as well to being worshipped). Thus, in these cases, the good agents actually fit the patient features quite well, whereas this was not the case for more restricted patient roles like that of ARREST.

Further support for the possibility that the patient roles generally admit a wider range of fillers was obtained by considering the role/filler typicality of the incongruent fillers (role/filler featural similarity was not included in these analyses). A *t*-test was conducted to contrast the roles in terms of the role/filler typicality of their incongruent fillers. Note that these ratings should be low for both roles precisely because the fillers were incongruent. Although role/filler typicality was relatively low in both cases, it was significantly higher for the good agents in the patient role ($\bar{x} = 2.5$, SE = 0.2) than for the good patients in the agent role ($\bar{x} = 1.9$, SE = 0.2) [$t(38) = 2.46$, $P < 0.02$].

In the final analysis, the incongruent fillers were ranked in descending order of role/filler typicality. Seven of the top 10 and 15 of the top 19 ratings for incongruent fillers came from patient roles, again suggesting that the patient roles admit a greater range of exemplars.

These results cohere with the consistency analyses in Experiment 1, in which it was found that the features listed for patient roles were less consistent across subjects than for agent roles, although the difference did not reach significance. Thus it would seem that the patient roles of the verbs used in Experiments 1 and 2 are less well-defined than the agent roles. Presumably, this is a function of the distribution of the exemplars in the role concepts; a set of common, featurally similar exemplars would result in a distinct computed prototype. A role might not have a distinct computed prototype if the set of common fillers have few featural regularities among them, or if there is no set of exemplars that stand out in terms of the frequency of playing the role. The latter appears to be the important factor in the five patient roles mentioned above.

Previous researchers have noted that verbs vary in terms of the role information that they carry with them, particularly cross-linguistically. For example, Nagy and Gentner (1990) pointed out that English verbs frequently incorporate information about the instrument used to perform the specified action, but rarely incorporate information about patient features. In contrast, Talmy (1975) has noted that German differs in that there is a greater tendency for verbs to specify patient features. The differences between agent and patient role concepts presented above indicate a tendency in English for verbs to carry more information about their agents than their patients. It is possible, however, that the tendencies in English might vary systematically. For instance, the verbs used in Experiments 1 and 2 were chosen to favour animate patients and one fact about the world is that many things that happen to people can happen to many types of people; thus producing indistinct patient role concepts in these verbs. However, it is easy to think of verbs for which the patient role has a distinct prototype, particularly those that favour inanimate patients. For example, only air is breathed (although one can breathe pure oxygen or other components of air) and only a few things are raked, such as lawns, gardens and flower beds. Thus it is possible that the distinctiveness of role prototypes varies across verbs according to such general semantic principles.

In summary, in accord with many studies of natural concepts (e.g. Rosch & Mervis, 1975), thematic role concepts exhibit a typicality gradient, with category/exemplar (role/filler) typicality being predictable from a measure of featural similarity. Thus these experiments taken together demonstrate that certain aspects of event concepts act like nominal concepts. Due to the focus on nominal concepts in the concepts literature, this is the first time that this link has been made.

EXPERIMENT 3

Experiments 1 and 2 demonstrated that the notion of feature-based role concepts can be used to capture important aspects of people's knowledge about events and their common participants. Experiment 3 tested the claim that this knowledge should be viewed as a primary component of thematic roles by showing that it is computed and used quickly in on-line language comprehension. Although a number of linguists and psycholinguists have recognised that the knowledge studied in Experiments 1 and 2 is important to language processing, they have retained the distinction between it and grammatical knowledge, of which they assume thematic roles are a part (Schlesinger, 1995). For example, Schlesinger was explicit in stating that conceptual primitives relevant to thematic roles such as ⟨cause⟩ and ⟨change⟩ are part of the lexical representation of the verb, but features of the type studied above become active only through a delayed inference process (i.e. world knowledge is stored somewhere else in the system and it takes time to access it). Likewise, in the garden path theory of Frazier and colleagues (e.g. Frazier, 1987; Rayner, Carlson, & Frazier, 1983), this information is part of the "thematic processor" and influences language comprehension only after a delay. In direct contrast, the present claim is that a verb automatically and immediately makes available thematic role concepts. Furthermore, these role concepts immediately influence on-line comprehension and production, primarily because of the constraint-based nature of sentence processing. In the remainder of this introduction, some recent evidence is presented suggesting that this is so, and an on-line reading experiment is introduced that further tested these claims.

Immediately Available

McRae, Ferretti and Airey (1996) presented three automatic priming studies to demonstrate that verb-specific thematic role concepts become available immediately and automatically. In the first experiment, verbs (e.g. CONVICTING) were used to prime their typical agents and patients (e.g. JUROR and CRIMINAL). Verbs such as LOVING that tend to be used with animate agents and patients were used as primes in the unrelated control condition. A significant overall priming effect was obtained in a semantic decision task when primes and targets were presented visually with a stimulus onset asynchrony of 250 msec. When analysed by role, however, the priming effect was significant for patients (33 msec), but not for agents (9 msec). Presumably, this difference was due to the fact that in English, agents usually precede the verb and patients follow it, whereas in the priming experiment, both agents and patients directly followed their verb prime. Therefore, in a subsequent experiment, the same verbs were placed in short sentence fragments so as to have both agents and patients follow the verb in a natural manner (e.g. "The man convicted the" or "The man was convicted by the"). When subjects heard a fragment and then cross-modally named a good agent or patient, priming was found for both agents (19 msec) and patients (25 msec). Finally, McRae et al. tested for automatic activation of role features by priming adjectival patient features (e.g. gullible) with verbs presented in isolation (e.g. TRICKING). A significant 33 msec priming effect was found in a lexical decision task when verb primes and feature targets were presented visually with a stimulus onset asynchrony of 250 msec. These three experiments demonstrate that verb-specific thematic role knowledge is activated immediately and automatically, and that this activation is influenced by structural factors.

Immediately Used

Given that this information is available, the next issue is how quickly it influences sentence interpretation. On-line experiments designed to investigate this question actually test two related hypotheses simultaneously. First, if this type of knowledge is used immediately to aid the assignment of noun fillers to their roles, then it is appropriate to view it as thematic role knowledge. This conclusion would contrast with Schlesinger (1995) and others, who claim that information about events and their participants is a product of inferencing and comes into play only at a later stage. Second, if thematic role concepts immediately influence comprehension, then this stands as evidence against sentence processing theories that highlight a front-end syntactic module, the most prominent of which is the garden path theory of Frazier and colleagues (Ferreira & Clifton, 1986; Frazier, 1987; Rayner et al., 1983). In principle, a theory of thematic roles as verb-specific concepts can be integrated with either the constraint-based theory of sentence processing (e.g. MacDonald et al., 1994), or with the garden path theory as part of the thematic processor (Rayner et al., 1983). However, given our claims concerning the automaticity and speed with which this conceptual knowledge is assumed to influence comprehension, it is a better fit with the constraint-based theory in which all information is computed as quickly as possible and used as soon as it is available, than with the garden path theory, in which syntactic processing is given temporal priority over conceptual processing.

The on-line process of designating local NPs to a verb's thematic roles is known as thematic assignment. We assume that assignment is based on a number of cues, including structural regularities, conceptual knowledge and discourse context. The present work focused on conceptual knowledge, remaining agnostic as to the form in which structural regularities are represented and implemented (for contrasting views on this issue, see Frazier, 1995; MacDonald et al., 1994), as well as the precise mechanism that allows for the interaction between structural and conceptual cues (see Gropen et al., 1991, for one account). Thematic fit was operationalised in Experiment 3 as role/filler typicality (as it was in McRae et al., in prep.; Pearlmutter & MacDonald, 1992; Tabossi, Spivey-Knowlton, McRae, & Tanenhaus, 1994), which presumably reflects role/filler featural similarity, as shown in Experiment 2. Thus it was assumed that thematic assignment depends on the on-line activation of a role concept, which is akin to activating a set of features that may or may not match a single lexical concept, and may overlap to varying degrees with a number of lexical concepts. Thematic assignment is then a form of speeded categorisation, in which a candidate noun filler concept can be compared to a role concept, resulting in a judgement of varying certainty (Hampton, 1993; Smith, 1978). Note that this contrasts sharply with another possible view in which a list of words (i.e. possible fillers) is searched and assignment is based on whether or not the candidate filler is found (as in verification models of word recognition, such as Becker, 1980). Importantly, thematic fit is assumed to be a primary determinant of assignment, particularly when syntactic cues underdetermine role assignments, as in cases of local structural ambiguity.

McRae et al. (in prep.), Pearlmutter and MacDonald (1992) and Tabossi et al. (1994) have demonstrated verb-specific effects of thematic fit on the resolution of the main clause/reduced relative clause ambiguity. McRae et al. is described below because it is the clearest demonstration of immediate effects and is most related to the present work. McRae et al. contrasted people's ability to resolve a main clause/reduced relative clause ambiguity when the initial NP, which was always animate, was either a good patient/poor agent such as CUSTOMER (2a) or a good agent/poor patient such as WAITRESS (2b), as established by role/filler typicality norms:

2a. The customer (who was) served by the trainee was displeased with his attitude.
2b. The waitress (who was) served by the trainee was displeased with his attitude.

In English, a sentence-initial "NP verbed" sequence usually signals a main clause construction (Tabossi et al., 1994). Furthermore, sentence-initial "NP verbed" sequences typically translate to "agent verbed" (Bever, 1970). Because sentences like (2a) and (2b) violate this regularity, correctly interpreting them requires the reader or listener to make the less preferred assignments. In a self-paced reading experiment, McRae et al. found that readers made immediate use of thematic fit information in that thematic fit and reduction interacted in the verb + by region, where reduction refers to the difference between unreduced ("who was" present) versus reduced ("who was" absent). Furthermore, sentences like (2a) that began with a good patient were resolved more quickly than ones like (2b) that began with a good agent. In addition, ambiguity resolution was simulated by a competition model in which thematic fit played a major role and was not delayed. These experiments indicate that the knowledge explored in Experiments 1 and 2 is best conceived of as thematic role knowledge and that this information is computed and used immediately, contrary to researchers who make a temporal distinction between structural and conceptual processing, such as Schlesinger (1995) and Frazier (1987).

Biasing On-line with Features

The goal of Experiment 3 was to add to both the thematic role and structural ambiguity resolution literatures by determining whether role feature information could modulate the processing difficulty associated with reading temporarily ambiguous reduced relative clauses. Just as features can be reported linguistically as adjectives, they can be presented in sentences as adjectives. Thus to bias the initial NP towards being a good agent or patient, features were used that were associated with verb-specific agent and patient roles. The items had the following structure (the complete set is listed in the Appendix).

3a. The shrewd heartless gambler (who was) manipulated by the dealer had bid more than he could afford to lose.
3b. The young naive gambler (who was) manipulated by the dealer had bid more than he could afford to lose.

For the thematic fit manipulation to be effective in this case, the reader needs to perform a number of computations. First, she must interpret the complex initial NP (adjective adjective noun). If the entire NP is not understood, no effect of thematic fit can arise because the base noun ("gambler") is identical in both conditions. Murphy (1990) and Smith et al. (1988) have discussed some ways in which adjective–noun NPs might be computed on the fly. In addition, Murphy has shown that sensible NPs consisting of a noun modified by predicting adjectives are understood quite quickly and easily, and all NPs used in Experiment 3 were of this type. (A predicating adjective is one that can be used in a "The noun is adjective" construction, such as "The gambler is young"). The reader must then compute the fit between the complex NP and the agent and patient roles of the initial verb. Thus a substantial amount of semantic processing must be completed quickly if the manipulation is to have an early influence on ambiguity resolution.

There are a number of constraints other than thematic fit at work in these sentences, each of which was held constant within a pair like (3a) and (3b). Three of the constraints were available at the past participle ("manipulated"). The strongest was a general structural bias in favour of a main clause; in a recent analysis of text, it was found that a sentence-initial sequence of "NP verbed" begins a main clause 92% of the time (Tabossi et al., 1994). In addition, a referential bias worked against finding an immediate effect of thematic fit. Referential theory suggests that the more that a noun is modified, the less felicitous it is to further modify it with a relative clause (Altmann & Steedman, 1988). This notion is pertinent to Experiment 3, in which two adjectives served as pre-nominal modifiers, then a post-nominal (reduced) relative clause followed. Third, the initial nouns were either relatively balanced or favoured a main clause reading, depending on one's perspective. According to a role/filler typicality rating norming study reported below, the initial nouns were good agents and patients, although they were better patients than agents. However, according to a theory in which thematic roles contain only a few selectional restrictions, the nouns would be agent-biased because all of them were animate and paired with verbs that prefer animate agents.

In addition to the constraints available at the verb, post-verbal constraints combined to provide support for a reduced relative reading. The post-verbal by-phrase probabilistically cued readers that they were in a reduced relative clause (MacDonald, 1994). However, a by-phrase can also indicate manner, location, time or amount, but these interpretations were largely blocked by two additional factors. First, the experimenters judged the verbs (actually, past participles) as transitive-biased (i.e. are usually used with a direct object), thus increasing the probability that the by-phrase contained its agent. Second, the noun in the by-phrase was a good agent, but a very poor manner, location, time and amount (e.g. "dealer" in 2a and 2b), further biasing the reader towards a reduced relative interpretation.

It was predicted that sentences like (3a), which used patient-biasing features, would be easier to read than those like (3b), which used agent-biasing features. As a slight qualification, it should also be noted that because of the subtlety of the featural manipulation, the complexity of the initial NP, and the referential bias, it seemed unlikely that an immediate effect of thematic fit would be found. This is important in terms of the way in which Experiment 3 bears on the debate between constraint-based and garden path theories. The critical difference between the empirical predictions of these theories hinges on whether a non-structural or lexically specific constraint influences interpretation at the earliest possible moment. Because early effects do not categorically distinguish between the theories, it was expected that this experiment would not provide definitive evidence, but instead would contribute to the debate by showing that this information can be computed and used rapidly.

Method

Subjects. Forty-eight native English-speaking psychology undergraduates from the University of Western Ontario received course credit for their participation.

Materials. Twenty noun–verb combinations were created with the constraint that the noun was both a good agent and patient of the verb (e.g. GAMBLER MANIPULATED). Note that we were able to use only a few of the verbs and features from Experiments 1 and 2 because of the difficulty in devising nouns for those verbs that both sounded natural and were approximately balanced in terms of their agenthood and patienthood. The newly created set of items was normed in two ways. First, 20 subjects provided role/filler typicality ratings for the nouns. Although the nouns were rated as good agents and patients, they were rated as better patients ($\bar{x} = 5.1$, range = 3.6–6.7) than agents ($\bar{x} = 4.4$, range = 2.7–6.2) for their respective verbs [$t(19) = 2.24$, $P < 0.04$].

Each of the 20 noun–verb combinations was combined with two pairs of adjectival features; one pair biased the noun towards being a good agent but a poor patient of the verb, and the other biased the noun towards being a good patient but a poor agent. Because we were unable to use the verbs from Experiments 1 and 2, the adjectives were selected on the basis of an independent norming study in which 30 subjects rated how common it is for a particular noun concept that is modified by two adjectives to fill either the agent or patient role of a particular verb, as in the following:

4. How common is it for a
   friendly witty ______
   shrewd heartless ______
   gullible sensitive ______
   mean talented ______
   young naive ______
   gambler to manipulate someone?

Subjects rated either the agenthood or patienthood of each item on a 7-point scale, where 1 corresponded to very uncommon and 7 to very common. Agent-biased NPs received significantly higher agenthood ($\bar{x} = 6.3$, range = 4.5–7.0) than patienthood ratings ($\bar{x} = 3.8$, range = 1.8–6.0) [$t(19) = 10.18$, $P < 0.0001$]. Similarly, patient-biased NPs received significantly higher patienthood ($\bar{x} = 5.3$, range = 2.8–5.8) than agenthood ratings ($\bar{x} = 2.0$, range = 1.1–4.5) [$t(19) = 14.30$, $P < 0.0001$].

Each of the resulting 20 noun–verb combinations was treated as an item (see Appendix). Four target sentences were constructed from each item by crossing featural bias (agent *vs* patient) and reduction ("who was" present *vs* absent). A second sentence was added to each target to increase the meaningfulness of the narrative. The following is an example.

5a. The shrewd heartless gambler who was manipulated by the dealer had bid a lot more money than he could afford to lose. Fortunately for him, he won.

5b. The young naive gambler who was manipulated by the dealer had bid a lot more money than he could afford to lose. Fortunately for him, he won.

The four versions were placed in separate lists to ensure that no subject saw any target verb or NP more than once. All of the noun–verb combinations were contained in each list, so that each contained five agent-biased unreduced, five agent-biased reduced, five patient-biased unreduced and five patient-biased reduced sentences. To dampen order effects, two versions of each of the four lists were formed by reversing the order of the target items. Sixty sentence pairs not containing a relative clause were included so that targets never occurred consecutively nor appeared first in a list. Fourteen additional sentence pairs without relative clauses were used for practice. Adjectives were included in many of the filler sentences.

Procedure. Sentences were displayed on a 16 inch Sony Trinitron monitor controlled by a Macintosh LCIII. They were presented using PsyScope (Cohen, MacWhinney, Flatt, & Provost, 1993) in a two-word-at-a-time moving window format. Two-word-at-a-time presentation, in contrast to one-word-at-a-time, was used because it more accurately mimics key elements of reading reduced relative clauses that contain a post-verbal by-phrase (Burgess, 1991). Thus sentence pairs were initially presented on the screen with each non-space character replaced by a dash. Subjects pressed a button to reveal the first two words of the sentence. Each subsequent button press revealed the next two words and replaced the previous two with dashes. Subjects read each sentence pair in this manner and then answered a "yes/no" comprehension question. Testing sessions began with 14 practice items. Subjects then read the remaining 80 experimental trials, taking a break after every 20 trials. They were instructed to read at a pace that resembled how they would typically read a magazine or newspaper. A testing session lasted approximately 30 min. Two-word-at-a-time reading latencies were recorded with millisecond accuracy via a CMU button box and measured as the time interval between successive button presses.

Results. Reading latencies were analysed based on the word pairs presented to subjects. The three critical regions are shown below:

6. The young naive gambler / manipulated by / the dealer / had bid /
   verb + by agent NP main verb
   more than he could afford to lose.

Analyses of variance were conducted for the three regions using two-word reading latency as the dependent variable. There were two factors, each with two levels: featural bias (agent *vs* patient) and reduction (unreduced *vs* reduced). Both featural bias and reduction were within subjects and items. Planned comparisons were conducted to investigate the reduction effect separately for agent-biased and patient-biased items in all three regions. Reduction effects for the three critical regions are presented graphically in Fig. 2.

Verb + by. Featural bias showed little or no influence on reading latencies in this region. Bias and reduction did not interact ($F<1$ in both analyses). Planned comparisons revealed that subjects experienced difficulty with both agent-biased [451 *vs* 512 msec: $F_1(1,47)=15.04$, $P<0.0004$; $F_2(1,19)=18.95$, $P<0.0004$] and patient-biased sentences [464 *vs* 530 msec: $F_1(1,47)=17.42$, $P<0.0001$; $F_2(1,19)=22.12$, $P<0.0003$]. Overall, reading latencies for patient-biased sentences were a non-significant 15 msec longer [$F_1(1,47)=1.92$, $P>0.1$; $F_2<1$]. Finally, the average reading latency for unreduced sentences was 63 msec shorter than their reduced counterparts [$F_1(1,47)=24.09$, $P<0.0001$; $F_2(1,19)=13.86$, $P<0.002$].

Agent NP. Featural bias influenced reading latencies in the "determiner + noun" region (the actual agent of the past participle). The interaction between bias and reduction failed to reach significance [$F_1(1,47)=2.52$, $P>0.1$; $F_2(1,19)=2.09$, $P>0.1$]. However, Fig. 2 and planned comparisons show that subjects had no difficulty with patient-biased reduced relatives (478 *vs* 479 msec: $F<1$ in both analyses), but reading difficulty was evident with agent-biased reduced relatives [458 *vs* 500 msec: $F_1(1,47)=5.43$, $P<0.03$; $F_2(1,19)=4.42$, $P<0.05$]. Finally, there was no main effect of bias (1 msec effect: $F<1$ in both analyses) nor of reduction [22 msec effect: $F_1(1,47)=2.11$, $P>0.1$; $F_2(1,19)=1.32$, $P>0.2$].

Main Verb. In this region, reading difficulty for a reduced relative clause had been basically eliminated for both types of sentences; however, patient-biased sentences were read faster overall. Bias and reduction did not interact ($F<1$ in both analyses). Planned comparisons revealed that

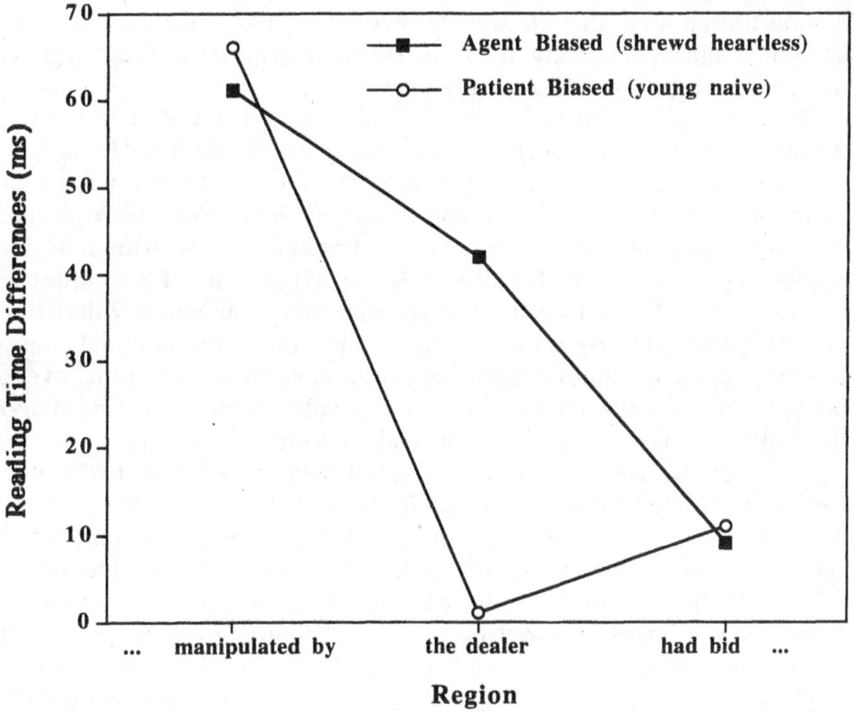

FIG. 2. Reduction effects for the critical regions in the four sentence types. Note that the reading difficulty in the agent NP region ("the dealer") was substantial for sentences with agent-biased featural adjectives ("shrewd heartless") but negligible for patient-biased ones ("young naive").

subjects had little difficulty reading reduced relatives, regardless of whether the features were patient-biasing (458 *vs* 469 msec) or agent-biasing (483 *vs* 492 msec) ($F < 1$ in all analyses). There was, however, a 23 msec main effect of featural bias that was significant by items [$F_2(1,19) = 6.03$, $P < 0.03$] and marginal by subjects [$F_1(1,47) = 3.50$, $P < 0.07$]. Finally, the 11 msec reduction effect was non-significant ($F < 1$ in both analyses).

Discussion

Experiment 3 showed that manipulating the fit between readers' role concepts and complex NPs rapidly influenced their ability to resolve a main clause/reduced relative clause ambiguity. When the initial noun was preceded by patient-biasing features, readers used the thematic information to minimise the difficulty associated with a sentence-initial reduced relative clause. This experiment adds to those of McRae et al. (1996; in prep.), Pearlmutter and MacDonald (1992) and Tabossi et al. (1994) in demonstrating that the knowledge studied in Experiments 1 and 2 is computed and used quickly in on-line language processing, thus suggesting that role concepts are linguistically relevant.

The influence of featural bias found in Experiment 3 was not as strong as the effects of McRae et al. (in prep.) nor the animacy effects of Trueswell et al. (1994).[3] However, the present manipulation was somewhat weaker and more complex. Trueswell et al. contrasted inanimates that were virtually impossible as agents of the verb (e.g. "The bricks lifted") with animate good agents (e.g. "The workers lifted"). McRae et al., as well as Pearlmutter and MacDonald (1992), contrasted strongly agent-biased animates with strongly patient-biased ones. By using different nouns, the entire nominal concept was manipulated, although there was presumably some conceptual overlap between good agent and patient. This is equivalent to manipulating many of the features of the entity, as well as making salient the relevant ones (e.g. "The cop/crook arrested"). In contrast, in Experiment 3, only two features were manipulated at a time (plus perhaps features that were strongly correlated with them), with the initial noun remaining constant for the agent- versus patient-biased sentences. Thus even though thematic fit influenced ambiguity resolution quite rapidly (at the "determiner + noun" region), Experiment 3 cannot be taken as definitive evidence against the garden path model of Frazier and colleagues (Frazier, 1987; Rayner et al., 1983). However, it does provide yet another example of a rapid effect of non-structural information on on-line language comprehension and seems better suited to the principles of constraint-based models (MacDonald et al., 1994).

We have claimed that there is a verb-specific component to thematic role knowledge in addition to their verb-general aspects that are typically studied. An interesting question concerns the degree to which the manipulation in Experiment 3 should be considered as reflecting verb-specific role concepts. The answer depends on the rival theory. Given a theory in which the conceptual content of a thematic role is limited to syntactically relevant features such as ⟨animacy⟩ (e.g. Caplan et al., 1994), the answer is unequivocally "yes". Because animacy was equated in Experiment 3, the results demand an explanation in which additional information is being computed and used rapidly. Furthermore, McRae et al. (in prep.) have found immediate effects of thematic fit using solely animate nouns.

On the other hand, a well-articulated theory that is more similar to the present one is that of Dowty (1991), which is weakly verb-specific. Dowty postulates five proto-agent and proto-patient features. Although the

[3]Note that Ferreira and Clifton (1986) failed to find an effect of initial NP animacy. However, Trueswell et al. (1994) corrected a number of problems with Ferreira and Clifton's experiment and found a strong and immediate effect of animacy when those problems were alleviated.

features are general in nature, such as ⟨volitional involvement in the event or state⟩ and ⟨undergoes change of state⟩, the theory is verb-specific in that a verb's role might consist of any number of these features. It is weakly verb-specific because many verbs within broad semantic classes would be expected to have identical role representations. In contrast, the present theory incorporates features that more subtly differentiate among verbs. The pertinent question here is whether the features used in Experiment 3 biased readers generally towards agenthood or patienthood (i.e. in a Dowty way) or towards agent and patient role concepts of the specific verb. We attempted to answer this question by conducting role/filler typicality rating experiments in which the verb was omitted. In these experiments, subjects provided ratings for questions such as "How common is it for a shrewd heartless person to do something to someone?", or "How common is it for a shrewd heartless person to have something done to them?" Both the agent-biased [agenthood: $\bar{x}=4.9$, range $=2.2$–6.6; patienthood: $\bar{x}=3.8$, range $=2.7$–5.3; $t(19)=3.28$, $P<0.004$] and patient-biased [agenthood: $\bar{x}=2.9$, range $=1.0$–6.8; patienthood: $\bar{x}=4.9$, range $=2.6$–6.1; $t(19)=4.39$, $P<0.0004$] adjective pairs received significantly higher ratings for their congruent general role. Similar results were obtained when the noun was included, as in "How common is it for a shrewd heartless gambler to have something done to them?": agent-biased [agenthood: $\bar{x}=4.6$, range $=2.2$–6.4; patienthood: $\bar{x}=3.8$, range $=2.5$–5.3; $t(19)=2.37$, $P<0.03$]; patient-biased [agenthood: $\bar{x}=2.6$, range $=1.1$–6.3; patienthood: $\bar{x}=4.1$, range $=2.4$–5.7; $t(19)=5.27$, $P<0.0001$]. Finally, the three types of ratings were significantly correlated: verb-specific features *vs* verb-general features ($r=0.77$, $P<0.0001$ for agent-biased; $r=0.36$, $P<0.03$ for patient-biased); verb-specific versus verb-general features plus noun ($r=0.72$, $P<0.0001$ for agent-biased; $r=0.43$, $P<0.01$ for patient-biased); verb-general features only versus verb-general features plus noun ($r=0.91$, $P<0.0001$ for agent-biased; $r=0.18$, $P>0.2$ for patient-biased). Thus the stimuli did not differ substantially on the basis of these ratings.

One method that might empirically distinguish between Dowty-type effects and those of the present theory is to shuffle the adjectives and/or nouns among the sentences. If the information that gave rise to the effect of thematic fit in Experiment 3 was indeed at the level of Dowty's features, then the precise pairings of the nouns, adjectives and verbs were irrelevant. Therefore, the same results should be obtained if the adjectives were randomly recombined with different nouns and the noun–verb combinations were retained. The results should also be obtained if the NPs were kept together and recombined with different verbs. Although these experiments have not been conducted, it is highly unlikely that effects of thematic fit would be found with random recombinations, even if care was taken to avoid nonsensical sentences.

GENERAL DISCUSSION

The experiments presented above, particularly when considered in conjunction with those of McRae et al. (1996; in prep.), Pearlmutter and MacDonald (1992) and Tabossi et al. (1994), outline and provide evidence for a novel view of thematic roles; namely, the notion of thematic roles as verb-specific concepts. In Experiment 1, subjects listed features for roles such as "someone who is convicted" and these featural descriptions were used to create approximations to computed role concepts. Experiment 1 also showed that some roles are better defined than others, presumably because there are important differences in the regularities among the exemplars that form their bases. In Experiment 2A, subjects' ratings of role/filler typicality showed that role concepts have internal structure, as predicted when roles are viewed as computed prototypes. Experiment 2B demonstrated that thematic roles share characteristics with nominal concepts in that role/filler featural similarity predicted role/filler typicality, analogous to studies of object concepts (Rosch & Mervis, 1975). This was the first demonstration of this sort with event concepts. Finally, Experiment 3 demonstrated an on-line influence of role features, also a novel empirical result. Resolution of a main clause/reduced relative clause ambiguity was modulated by the presence of adjectives that biased the sentence-initial nominal concept towards being a good agent or patient. This experiment adds to the expanding list of early effects of thematic information on syntactic ambiguity resolution. By so doing, it bears on the issue of how linguistic and extralinguistic knowledge sources are combined and coordinated during on-line comprehension, and provides an additional empirical result that appears to be better suited to the constraint-based model of language processing than to the garden path model.

A major contribution of this paper is that it provides a principled way to capture verb-specific aspects of thematic roles that have apparently been previously considered as linguistically insignificant idiosyncrasies of individual verbs. It does so by claiming that world knowledge of events and their common participants is organised so that it is linguistically relevant, rather than being outside of the knowledge that is directly relevant to language processing. This view is in direct opposition to Chomskyan syntactic modularists (Frazier, 1987; Schlesinger, 1995), but is in accord with the views of cognitive linguists (e.g. Langacker, 1987). In our view, the question of where the knowledge is stored is irrelevant; the relevant questions concern what prompts its computation and how quickly this computation is performed. The claim here is that role knowledge is organised in an efficient manner that promotes its automatic computation whenever a verb is read or heard. Note that the claim is not that every instance of an event is brought to consciousness when the verb is encountered. In other words, a reader's consciousness is not flooded with memories of accusing events when she reads ACCUSE. Rather, the claim is that memory is organised in a manner akin to a matrix memory model such as that of Hintzman (1986), or related models such as that of McClelland and Rumelhart (1985), so that one consequence of hearing or reading ACCUSE is the computation of a representation that corresponds to a prototypical accuser. Note that memory models of these types also enable computed representations to be shaded by context. Thus hearing ACCUSE during a movie about a squabbling family might produce somewhat different role representations than during a courtroom drama.

We have described a framework for thinking about how the conceptual aspect of thematic roles might be computed and used in on-line language comprehension. There are, however, a large number of further questions to be addressed. For example, how do role concepts function in conjunction with multiple thematic grids, ambiguous verbs, and obligatory versus optional roles? What is the timecourse of activation and decay of role concepts? Are, for example, patient role concepts more highly activated for transitive- than intransitive-biased verbs? What is the relationship between role concepts and linking rules? We do not attempt to answer these questions here, but instead conceive of them as important questions to investigate in the near future.

Finally, one interesting aspect of thematic processing concerns the distinction between computing thematic fit and contracting features. There are key differences between the features that a filler of a role would be expected to possess (i.e. the features used to compute thematic fit) and those that are contracted to the filler as a result of the event described by the verb. For example, according to the results of Experiment 1, the patient of SERVE should be someone who has characteristics such as ⟨needs help⟩, ⟨is rich⟩, ⟨is powerful⟩, ⟨is important⟩ and ⟨is hungry⟩. The act of serving that person, however, may change a number of those characteristics; that is, some features like ⟨is satisfied⟩ or ⟨is full⟩ might be contracted out (see Schlesinger, 1995, for a detailed description of contracting features). The experiments described above were designed to tap the features that a verb expects a filler to possess, and thematic fit is assumed to be computed over that type of feature. An interesting issue concerns the processes and representations that control the contracting of new features to someone who has been SERVED or CURED.

In conclusion, the present work stands as an example of the potential advantages of combining theoretical notions and empirical techniques from areas of research that are typically treated as distinct. In particular, importing ideas from research in concepts and categorisation into sentence processing provided us with a way to shed new light on an old issue, namely the nature of thematic roles.

REFERENCES

Altmann, G., & Steedman, M. (1988). Interaction with context during human sentence processing. *Cognition*, *30*, 191–238.

Altmann, G., Garnham, A., & Dennis, Y. (1992). Avoiding the garden path: Eye movements in context. *Journal of Memory and Language*, *31*, 685–712.

Barsalou, L.W. (1982). Context-independent and context-dependent information in concepts. *Memory and Cognition*, *10*, 82–93.

Barsalou, L.W. (1987). The instability of graded structure in concepts. In U. Neisser (Ed.), *Concepts and conceptual development: Ecological and intellectual factors in categorization*, pp. 101–140. Cambridge: Cambridge University Press.

Barsalou, L.W., Olseth, K.L., & Wu, L. (1995). *Producing features for concepts*. Work in progress, University of Chicago, Chicago, IL.

Becker, C.A. (1980). Semantic context effects in visual word recognition: An analysis of semantic strategies. *Memory and Cognition*, *8*, 493–512.

Bever, T.G. (1970). The cognitive basis for linguistic structure. In J.R. Hayes (Ed.), *Cognitive development of language*, pp. 279–363. New York: John Wiley.

Boland, J.E., Tanenhaus, M.K., Garnsey, S.M., & Carlson, G. (1995). Verb argument structure in parsing and interpretation: Evidence from wh-questions. *Journal of Memory and Language*, *34*, 774–806.

Burgess, C. (1991). *The interaction of syntactic, semantic, and visual factors in syntactic ambiguity resolution*. Unpublished doctoral dissertation, University of Rochester, Rochester, NY.

Caplan, D., Hildebrandt, H., & Waters, G.S. (1994). Interaction of verb selectional restrictions, noun animacy and syntactic form in sentence processing. *Language and Cognitive Processes*, *9*, 549–585.

Carlson, G.N., & Tanenhaus, M.K. (1988). Thematic roles and language comprehension. In W. Wilkins (Ed.), *Syntax and semantics, Vol. 21: Thematic relations*, pp. 263–288. New York: Academic Press.

Chomsky, N. (1965). *Aspects of the theory of syntax*. Cambridge, MA: MIT Press.

Clifton, C. (1993). Thematic roles in sentence parsing. *Canadian Journal of Experimental Psychology*, *47*, 222–246.

Cohen, J.D., MacWhinney, B., Flatt, M., & Provost, J. (1993). PsyScope: A new graphic interactive environment for designing psychology experiments. *Behavioral Research Methods, Instruments and Computers*, *25*, 257–271.

Cook, W.A. (1979). *Case grammar: The development of the matrix model (1970–1978)*. Washington: Georgetown University Press.

Cottrell, G.W. (1988). *A connectionist approach to word sense disambiguation*. San Mateo, CA: Morgan Kaufmann.

Cullicover, P.W. (1988). Autonomy, prediction, and thematic relations. In W. Wilkins (Ed.), *Syntax and semantics, Vol. 21: Thematic relations*, pp. 37–61. New York: Academic Press.

Dowty, D.R. (1991). Thematic proto-roles and argument selection. *Language*, *67*, 547–619.

Ferreira, F., & Clifton, C. (1986). The independence of syntactic processing, *Journal of Memory and Language*, *25*, 348–368.

Fillmore, C. (1968). The case for case. In E. Bach & R.T. Harms (Eds), *Universals in linguistic theory*, pp. 1–90. New York: Holt, Rinehart and Winston.

Frazier, L. (1987). Theories of syntactic processing. In J. Garfield (Ed.), *Modularity in knowledge representation and natural language processing*, pp. 559–586. Cambridge, MA: MIT Press.

Frazier, L. (1995). Constraint satisfaction as a theory of sentence processing. *Journal of Psycholinguistic Research, 24*, 437–468.

Frazier, L., & Rayner, K. (1982). Making and correcting errors during sentence comprehension: Eye movements in the analysis of structurally ambiguous sentences. *Cognitive Psychology, 14*, 178–210.

Gentner, D. (1981). Some interesting differences between nouns and verbs. *Cognition and Brain Theory, 4*, 161–178.

Graesser, A.C., Singer, M., & Trabasso, T. (1994). Constructing inferences during narrative text comprehension. *Psychological Review, 101*, 371–395.

Gropen, J., Pinker, S., Hollander, M., & Goldberg, R. (1991). Affectedness and direct objects: The role of lexical semantics in the acquisition of verb argument structure. *Cognition, 41*, 153–195.

Hampton, J.A. (1993). Prototype models of concept representation. In I. van Mechelen, J.A. Hampton, R.S. Michalski, & P. Theuns (Eds), *Categories and concepts: Theoretical views and inductive data analysis*, pp. 67–95. London: Academic Press.

Hintzman, D.L. (1986). "Schema abstraction" in a multiple-trace memory model. *Psychological Review, 93*, 411–428.

Jackendoff, R. (1972). *Semantic interpretation in generative grammar*. Cambridge, MA: MIT Press.

Jackendoff, R. (1983). *Semantics and cognition*. Cambridge, MA: MIT Press.

Jackendoff, R. (1987). The status of thematic relations in linguistic theory. *Linguistic Inquiry, 18*, 369–411.

Kersten, A.W., & Billman, D. (1995). The roles of motion and moving parts in noun and verb meanings. In *Proceedings of the Seventeenth Annual Conference of the Cognitive Science Society*, pp. 498–503. Hillsdale, NJ: Lawrence Erlbaum Associates Inc.

Ladusaw, W.A., & Dowty, D.R. (1988). Toward a nongrammatical account of thematic roles. In W. Wilkins (Ed.), *Syntax and semantics, Vol. 21: Thematic relations*, pp. 62–74. New York: Academic Press.

Langacker, R.W. (1987). *Foundations of cognitive grammar, Vol. 1: Theoretical prerequisites*. Stanford, CA: Stanford University Press.

MacDonald, M.C. (1994). Probabilistic constraints and syntactic ambiguity resolution. *Language and Cognitive Processes, 9*, 157–201.

MacDonald, M.C., Pearlmutter, N.J., & Seidenberg, M.S. (1994). The lexical nature of syntactic ambiguity resolution. *Psychological Review, 101*, 676–703.

Malt, B.C., & Smith, E.E. (1984). Correlated features in natural categories. *Journal of Verbal Learning and Verbal Behavior, 23*, 250–269.

Marslen-Wilson, W.D. (1975). Sentence perception as an interactive parallel process. *Science, 189*, 226–228.

McClelland, J.L., & Rumelhart, D.E. (1985). Distributed memory and the representation of general and specific information. *Journal of Experimental Psychology: General, 114*, 159–188.

McCloskey, M.E., & Glucksberg, S. (1978). Natural categories: Well defined or fuzzy sets? *Memory and Cognition, 6*, 462–472.

McKoon, G., Ratcliff, R., & Dell, G.S. (1986). A critical evaluation of the semantic–episodic distinction. *Journal of Experimental Psychology: Learning, Memory and Cognition, 12*, 295–306.

McRae, K., Ferretti, T.R., & Airey, M. (1996). Automatic activation of typical fillers of thematic roles. Poster presented at the *Ninth Annual CUNY Conference on Human Sentence Processing*, New York, NY, March.

McRae, K., de Sa, V.R., & Seidenberg, M.S. (1977). On the nature and scope of featural representations of word meaning. *Journal of Experimental Psychology: General, 126*, 99–130.

McRae, K., Spivey-Knowlton, M.J., & Tanenhaus, M.K. (in prep). Modeling the influence of thematic fit (and other constraints) in on-line sentence comprehension.

Medin, D.L. (1989). Concepts and conceptual structure. *American Psychologist*, *44*, 1469–1481.

Murphy, G.L. (1990). Noun phrase interpretation and conceptual combination. *Journal of Memory and Language*, *29*, 259–288.

Nagy, W., & Gentner, D. (1990). Semantic constraints on lexical categories. *Language and Cognitive Processes*, *5*, 169–201.

Pearlmutter, N.J., & MacDonald, M.C. (1992). Plausibility and syntactic ambiguity resolution. In *Proceedings of the Fourteenth Annual Conference of the Cognitive Science Society*, pp. 498–503. Hillsdale NJ: Lawrence Erlbaum Associates Inc.

Posner, M.I., & Keele, S.W. (1968). On the genesis of abstract ideas. *Journal of Experimental Psychology*, *77*, 353–363.

Rayner, K., Carlson, M., & Frazier, L. (1983). The interaction of syntax and semantics during sentence processing: Eye movements in the analysis of semantically biased sentences. *Journal of Verbal Learning and Verbal Behavior*, *22*, 358–374.

Rosch, E. (1978). Principles of categorization. In E. Rosch & B.B. Lloyd (Eds), *Cognition and categorization*, pp. 27–48. Hillsdale, NJ: Lawrence Erlbaum Associates Inc.

Rosch, E., & Mervis, C.B. (1975). Family resemblances: Studies in the internal structure of categories. *Cognitive Psychology*, *7*, 573–605.

Schlesinger, I.M. (1995). *Cognitive space and linguistic case*. Cambridge: Cambridge University Press.

Smith, E.E. (1978). Theories of semantic memory. In W.K. Estes (Ed.), *Handbook of learning and cognitive processes*, Vol. 6, pp. 1–56. Hillsdale, NJ: Lawrence Erlbaum Associates Inc.

Smith, E.E., & Medin, D.L. (1981). *Categories and concepts*. Cambridge, MA: Harvard University Press.

Smith, E.E., Osherson, D.N., Rips, L.J., & Keane, M. (1988). Combining prototypes: A selective modification model. *Cognitive Science*, *12*, 485–527.

Spivey-Knowlton, M.J., & Sedivy, J.C. (1995). Resolving attachment ambiguities with multiple constraints. *Cognition*, *55*, 227–267.

Stowe, L.A. (1989). Thematic structures and sentence comprehension. In G.N. Carlson & M.K. Tanenhaus (Eds), *Linguistic structure in language processing*, pp. 319–357. Boston, MA: Kluwer Academic.

Tabossi, P., Spivey-Knowlton, M.J., McRae, K., & Tanenhaus, M.K. (1994). Semantic effects on syntactic ambiguity resolution: Evidence for a constraint-based resolution process. In C. Umilta & M. Moscovitch (Eds), *Attention and performance XV*, pp. 589–616. Cambridge, MA: MIT Press.

Talmy, L. (1975). Semantics and the syntax of motion. In J.P. Kimball (Ed.), *Syntax and semantics*, Vol. 4, pp. 181–238. New York: Academic Press.

Tanenhaus, M.K., Carlson, G.N., & Trueswell, J.T. (1989). The role of thematic structures in interpretation and parsing. *Language and Cognitive Processes*, *4*, SI 211–234.

Tanenhaus, M.K., Spivey-Knowlton, M.J., Eberhard, K.M., & Sedivy, J.C. (1995). Integration of visual and linguistic information in spoken language comprehension. *Science*, *268*, 1632–1634.

Taraban, R., & McClelland, J.L. (1988). Constituent attachment and thematic role assignment in sentence processing: Influences of content-based expectations. *Journal of Memory and Language*, *27*, 597–632.

Trueswell, J.C., Tanenhaus, M.K., & Kello, C. (1993). Verb-specific constraints in sentence processing: Separating effects of lexical preference from garden paths. *Journal of Experimental Psychology: Learning, Memory and Cognition*, *19*, 528–553.

Trueswell, J.C., Tanenhaus, M.K., & Garnsey, S.M. (1994). Semantic influences on parsing: Use of thematic role information in syntactic ambiguity resolution. *Journal of Memory and Language*, *33*, 285–318.
Tulving, E. (1972). Episodic and semantic memory. In E. Tulving & W. Donaldson (Eds), *Organization of memory*, pp. 381–403. New York: Academic Press.
Tulving, E. (1983). *Elements of episodic memory*. New York: Oxford University Press.
Tversky, A. (1977). Features of similarity. *Psychological Review*, *84*, 327–352.

APPENDIX

The 20 items used in Experiment 3. Feature pairs are separated by a backslash, with agent-biasing presented before patient-biasing.

1. The shrewd heartless / young naive gambler (who was) manipulated by the dealer had bid a lot more money than he could afford to lose.
2. The honest efficient / dishonest lazy worker (who was) replaced by a computer was forced to find another job.
3. The rude outspoken / thoughtful sensitive student (who was) offended by the comment walked out of the room.
4. The big strong / frail little kid (who was) protected by his brother was never bothered by the bully at school.
5. The persistent intimidating / polite timid beggar (who was) harassed by the police moved to a new location.
6. The respected veteran / young inexperienced employee (who was) trained by the specialist quickly learned how to operate the new equipment.
7. The mean and devious / harmless and gullible college student (who was) tricked by his buddies was upset by their practical joke.
8. The angry aggressive / preoccupied unsuspecting teenager (who was) attacked by the mugger had foolishly tried to cut through the park.
9. The calm quiet / violent unpredictable child (who was) feared by his classmates sometimes fought out on the schoolyard.
10. The large hungry / small defenseless animal (who was) devoured by the lion had been on its own looking for food.
11. The wealthy and generous / penniless and sick old man (who was) supported by his daughter decided that it was time to go to the hospital.
12. The loud screaming / quiet peaceful baby (who was) disturbed by the noise refused to lie back down.
13. The ugly scary / nervous timid man (who was) frightened by the gunshot believed that he was going to die.
14. The daring courageous / helpless injured mother (who was) rescued by the fireman was taken to the hospital for smoke inhalation.
15. The ruthless sadistic / unconscious bleeding spy (who was) tortured by the CIA had thought that he would not be discovered.
16. The young playful / frightened fleeing cat (who was) chased by the dog climbed the neighbour's tree.
17. The young and aspiring / famous and respected hockey player (who was) idolized by his brother decided that it was time to teach him how to play.
18. The talented artistic / beautiful nude woman (who was) sketched by her friend was happy with how it looked.

19. The dominant authoritative / vulnerable submissive husband (who was) controlled by his wife fooled himself into thinking he was in charge.
20. The obnoxious vulgar / quiet hardworking secretary (who was) annoyed by her boss was constantly complaining and swearing about her work.

LANGUAGE AND COGNITIVE PROCESSES, 1997, *12* (2/3), 177–210

Modelling Parsing Constraints with High-dimensional Context Space

Curt Burgess and Kevin Lund

University of California Riverside, Riverside, CA, USA

Deriving representations of meaning has been a long-standing problem in cognitive psychology and psycholinguistics. The lack of a model for representing semantic and grammatical knowledge has been a handicap in attempting to model the effects of semantic constraints in human syntactic processing. A computational model of high-dimensional context space, the Hyperspace Analogue to Language (HAL), is presented with a series of simulations modelling a variety of human empirical results. HAL learns its representations from the unsupervised processing of 300 million words of conversational text. We propose that HAL's high-dimensional context space can be used to (1) provide a basic categorisation of semantic and grammatical concepts, (2) model certain aspects of morphological ambiguity in verbs, and (3) provide an account of semantic context effects in syntactic processing. We propose that the distributed and contextually derived representations that HAL acquires provide a basis for the subconceptual knowledge that can be used in accounting for a diverse set of cognitive phenomena.

INTRODUCTION

All accounts of syntactic processing, language comprehension and memory posit a role for semantic representations. An important aspect of any model of language comprehension is to specify the nature of the various components of the comprehension system and to what extent these components interact. Psycholinguists have long debated the extent to which semantic information can influence syntactic processing, and at what point in the comprehension process this occurs. Two general views have

---

Requests for reprints should be addressed to Curt Burgess, Psychology Department, 1419 Life Sciences Building, University of California Riverside, Riverside, CA 92521-0426, USA. E-mail: curt@cassandra.ucr.edu

This research was supported by a NSF Presidential Faculty Fellow award SBR-9453406 to C.B. We thank Ken McRae, Nick Chater, Debra Long, Kay Livesay, Catherine Decker and two anonymous reviewers for their helpful comments and criticisms, and Maureen Keeney for bibliographic assistance.

predominated in this controversy: one is syntactically motivated, whereas the other is lexically motivated. Empirical studies in this domain have relied heavily on the resolution of syntactic ambiguity to marshall evidence for either view.

The syntactically motivated theories presume that syntactic ambiguity is resolved in two stages. First, the syntactic processor (or parser) uses a set of parsing principles to build one or more syntactic constructions. The second stage of processing uses lexical/semantic or discourse-level information that can be used to resolve ambiguity and continue to build a mental model of the ongoing discourse. Although there are important differences in some of these models (Frazier, 1978; Frazier & Fodor, 1978; Gorrell, 1989; Kurtzman, 1985; Rayner, Carlson, & Frazier, 1983), they are in distinct contrast to the more lexically motivated models. These more lexically motivated parsing models, particularly those inspired by lexical ambiguity research (Burgess & Hollbach, 1988; Burgess & Lund, 1994; MacDonald, Pearlmutter, & Seidenberg, 1994; Tanenhaus & Carlson, 1989), allow more flexibility for communication between language subsystems and tend to incorporate more information into the lexical/semantic representations that can facilitiate making the necessary commitments that are required during on-line language comprehension. Semantics in these more constraint-based models plays a crucial role in the parsing operation, in that it can provide the parser with guidance from real-world knowledge (for reviews, see MacDonald et al., 1994; Tanenhaus & Carlson, 1989).

Though lexically motivated and syntactically motivated theories differ with respect to issues of processing modularity, they agree for the most part that there is representational modularity. For example, there is a level of semantic or discourse representation that can (or cannot) affect the behaviour of a syntactic processor. In this paper, we present a representational model that seems to mimic effects that are considered (1) semantic, (2) grammatical, or (3) show an interaction of semantic and syntactic information. We argue that the representations for words that are generated with this model are subconceptual in nature and blur the typical representational distinctions that are made.

The aims of this paper are to describe our representational model and to present a set of simulation results that bear on some of these currently debated questions, which concern semantic contraints on parsing and grammatical categorisation. In earlier papers, we have presented the Hyperspace Analogue to Language model, or HAL, as a model of semantic memory. There was good reason to make this argument. HAL provided an account of single-word priming with semantically related items whether they were associatively related (e.g. *cat–dog*) or not (e.g. *beer–ale*). Words that were not category instances, but were associatively related, using word association norms (e.g. *crater–moon*), did not show a relatedness effect using the HAL model (Lund, Burgess, & Atchley, 1995; Lund, Burgess, & Audet, 1996). Likewise, the model provided an account of semantic paralexias generated by patients with deep dyslexia, whereas word association norms did not (Buchanan, Burgess, & Lund, 1996). However, our more recent research, presented in this paper, suggests that the characterisation of HAL's representations as semantic is too specific and limiting.

HAL acquires its representations from monitoring the contexts in which words occur. HAL uses a set of these lexical co-occurrences as coordinates in a high-dimensional space that can provide a measure of similarity between lexical items. HAL's similarity measure is essentially a measure of contextuality, a notion upon which we will expand later. In brief, we will argue that this measure of contextuality can provide the various types of information that one would want in a rich memory system. The first part of the paper will describe various ways in which semantics have been modelled, followed by a description of the methodology HAL uses to generate its semantic representations. The first simulation provides a demonstration that HAL's representations can be used to make categorical distinctions among semantic categories. At this point, we will discuss the distinction between the vector elements in HAL's representations and the traditional notion of semantic features. The second simulation demonstrates that the ability of HAL's vectors to categorise information extends to basic grammatical categories as well. In the third simulation, we show that the vector representations carry sufficient information to make more fine-tuned grammatical distinctions. The final simulation demonstrates that the interword relationships, as represented by the vectors, correspond to the semantic constraints on parsing that have been investigated in a series of experiments with human subjects.

Representing Semantics

Early work in word recognition and lexical ambiguity builty heavily on localist models of semantic memory. One of the most frequently cited semantic network models is the spreading activation model introduced by Collins and Quillian (1969; see also Collins & Loftus, 1975). In this model, semantic meaning was represented by nodes which corresponded to individual words. Nodes in a spreading activation model are connected by links which represent the type of relationship shared by the nodes; the links also vary in length, reflecting the strength of the relationship. One elementary result of this model is that concepts facilitate the subsequent processing of related concepts.

Meyer and Schvaneveldt (1971) provided an early demonstration of how recognising semantically related words (*bread–butter*) can speed the lexical decision latencies as compared to seeing unrelated words (*floor–butter*).

Semantic memory research using the lexical decision (or naming) task in the last two decades has produced one of the largest bodies of cognitive psychological literature (see Neely, 1991). The presence of the semantic priming effect is one of the most robust effects in the literature, although the exact nature of the word relationships and the nature of the task and methodology can influence the magnitude and presence of priming (Fischler, 1977; Moss, Ostrin, Tyler, & Marslen-Wilson, 1995; Neely, 1991). For some of the parsing experiments that will be discussed later, it is important to note that reading one word has important consequences for the processing of a subsequent word (i.e. priming related concepts and otherwise offering various constraints).

The precise characteristics of the mental representations that underlie the semantic priming effect and the relationship of concepts to one another is an issue with a long history in cognitive science. Early approaches used psychometric techniques to compute a distance between two concepts. Osgood's semantic differential procedure (Osgood, Suci, & Tannenbaum, 1957) required subjects to rate concepts on 10–20 bipolar scales. For example, the concept LADY could be rated on the dimensions of *rough–smooth* and *fair–unfair*, among others. All words of interest would be rated on all of these dimensions. The ratings of a word on these dimensions essentially provides the coordinates of the word in a semantic space, thus making it straightforward to provide a representation for any word for which the set of ratings was collected. Similar words should be located in the same region within the space. This theory motivated the work of Smith, Shoben and Rips (1974) and the development of their semantic-feature model as an alternative to Collins and Quillian's nodal model. This approach provides a rich representation for words. Its drawbacks are that many human judgements are required for each word of interest and that the experimenter must choose the semantic dimensions upon which words are rated (see McRae, de Sa, & Seidenberg, 1997, for a similar, but more recent, normative approach to feature selection).

Semantic features have also been used by those interested in implementing more complete models of comprehension. McClelland and Kawamoto (1986) used a set of distributed representations in their model of thematic role assignment and sentence processing. Words were represented by a set of semantic microfeatures. Nouns, for instance, had features such as HUMAN, SOFTNESS, GENDER and FORM. Verbs had more complex features, such as CAUSE (whether the verb is causal), TOUCH (specifies whether the agent or instrument touches the patient) and NAT_CHNG (what kind of change takes place in the patient). This model was important in that it demonstrated that distributed semantic representations can account for case-role assignment and handle lexical ambiguity. The features selected by the authors served them well; intuitively, the features seem relevant for thematic-role assignment. Similar approaches to feature designation have frequently been used in the connectionist literature for more basic models of word recognition (Dyer, 1990; Hinton & Shallice, 1991; Plaut & Shallice, 1994). It is less than clear, though, exactly what features one would select for a more general model of semantic representation.

In the last decade, investigators using large-scale corpora have attempted to extract semantic information directly from text. Gallant (1991) has developed a methodology that extracts a distributed set of semantic microfeatures using the context in which a word is found. However, a drawback to his approach is that the features for the core meanings have to be determined by a human judge. The model that we have developed does not rely on any explicit human judgements in determining the dimensions that are used to represent a word and acquires the representations in an unsupervised fashion. Discussion of some important work similar to ours by Landauer and Dumais (1994, in press), Finch and Chater (1992) and Schutze (1992) will be included in the General Discussion, and we will now turn to how the word representations are acquired in HAL.

DEVELOPING SEMANTIC REPRESENTATIONS

Developing a plausible methodology for representing the meaning of a word is central to any serious model of memory or language comprehension. We use a large text corpus of ~300 million words to initially track lexical co-occurrence within a 10-word moving window. From the co-occurrences, we develop a 140,000 dimensional context space (for full implementational details, see Lund & Burgess, 1996; see Landauer & Dumais, in press, for a similar model). We refer to the high-dimensional space as "context" space, since each vector element represents a symbol (usually a word) in the input stream of the text. Each symbol is part of the textual context in the moving window.

Matrix Construction. The basic methodology of the simulation is to develop a matrix of word co-occurrence values for a given vocabulary. This matrix will then be divided into co-occurrence vectors for each word, which can be subjected to analysis for meaningful content. For any analysis of co-occurrence, one must define a window size; that is, the largest number of words that may occur between a pair of words such that the pair may be considered to co-occur. The smallest usable window would be a width of one, corresponding to only immediately adjacent words. At the other end of the spectrum, one may count all words within a logical division of the input text as co-occurring equally (see Landauer & Dumais, 1994, in press; Schvaneveldt, 1990). A very small window may miss constructs spanning several words (lengthy noun phrases, for instance), while large windows risk introducing large numbers of extraneous co-occurrences. Therefore, we chose a window width of 10 words to preserve locality of reference while minimising the effects of different syntactic constructions. As a further move away from dependence on syntax (or any structuring of the language under consideration other than that given by the division of words), sentence boundaries are ignored.

Within this 10-word window, co-occurrence values are inversely proportional to the number of words separating a specific pair. A word pair separated by a 9-word gap, for instance, would gain a co-occurrence strength of one, while the same pair appearing adjacently would receive an increment of 10. Cognitive plausibility was a constraint, and a 10-word window with decreasing co-occurrence strength seemed a reasonable way to mimic the span of what might be captured in working memory (Gernsbacher, 1990). The product of this procedure is an $N \times N$ matrix, where N is the number of words in the vocabulary being considered. It is this matrix which we will demonstrate contains significant amounts of information that can be used to simulate a variety of cognitive phenomena. A sample matrix is shown in Table 1. This sample matrix models the status of a matrix using only a 5-word moving window for just one sentence, *the horse raced past the barn fell.*

Text Source. The corpus analysed was approximately 300 million words of English text gathered from Usenet. All newsgroups containing English text were included. This source has a number of appealing properties. It was clear that to obtain reliable data across a large vocabulary, a large amount of text would be required. Usenet was attractive in that it could supply indefinitely about 20 million words of text per day. In addition, Usenet is conversationally diverse. Virtually no subject goes undiscussed; this allows the construction of a broadly based co-occurrence dataset. This turns out to be useful when attempting to apply the data to various stimulus sets, for there is little chance of encountering a word not in the model's vocabulary. One goal for HAL was that it would develop its representations from conversational text that was minimally preprocessed, not unlike human-concept acquisition. Unlike formal business reports or specialised dictionaries, which are frequently used as corpora, Usenet text better resembles everyday speech. That the model works with such noisy, conversational input suggests that it can deal robustly with some of the same problems that the human-language comprehender encounters.

Vocabulary. The vocabulary used for the analysis consisted of the 70,000 most frequently occurring symbols within the corpus. About half of these had entries in the standard Unix dictionary; the remaining items included

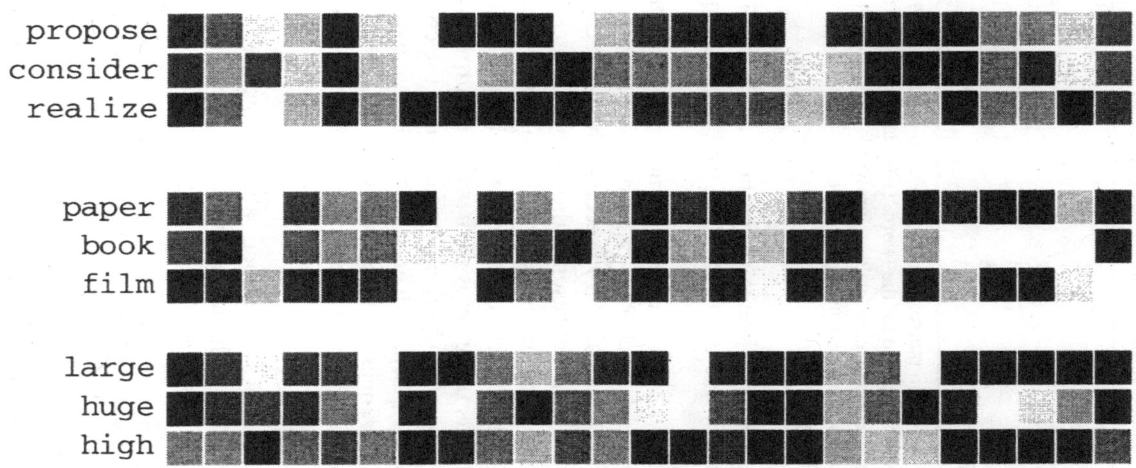

FIG. 1. Sample 25-element word vectors for three sets of verbs, nouns and adjectives. Each vector element has a continuous value (the normalised value from its matrix cell) and is grey-scaled to represent the normalised value with white corresponding to a zero.

TABLE 1
Sample Matrix, Produced by Applying a Five-word Co-occurrence Window to the Sentence *The horse ran past the barn fell*

	barn	*horse*	*past*	*raced*	*the*
barn		2	4	3	6
fell	5	1	3	2	4
horse					5
past		4		5	3
raced		5			4
the		3	5	4	2

Note: Values in matrix rows represent co-occurrence values for words which preceded the word (row label), while columns represent co-occurrence values for words following the word (column label). Cells containing zeroes have been left empty for visual clarity.

proper names, slang words, nonword symbols and misspellings. These items also presumably carry useful information for concept acquisition.

Data Extraction. The co-occurrence tabulation produces a 70,000 × 70,000 matrix. Each row of this vector represents the degree to which each word in the vocabulary preceded the word corresponding to the row, while each column represents the co-occurrence values for words following the word corresponding to the column. A full co-occurrence vector for a word consists of both the row and the column for that word. The following experiments use groups of these co-occurence vectors.

These vectors (length 140,000) can be viewed as the coordinates of points in a high-dimensional space, with each word occupying one point. Using this representation, differences between two words' co-occurrence vectors can be measured as the distance between the high-dimensional points defined by their vectors.

Vector Properties. As described above, each element of a vector represents a coordinate in high-dimensional space for a word or concept,[1] and a distance metric applied to these vectors presumably corresponds to

[1]Each vector corresponds to one lexical symbol that occurred in the input stream. We will often refer to the vectors as corresponding to words; however, it is important to bear in mind that all symbols were not words, it is just stylistically more convenient to refer to them this way. Vectors of 140,000 element length were used in the simulations reported in this paper. This is not to suggest that we think human memory is best represented in 140,000 dimensional space. At present, we think that 100–200 dimensional space is an accurate estimate of what is required for simulating human memory. For some effects, as few as 10 vector elements can account for a significant amount of variance. In connectionist models, shorter vectors would be preferable due to the training time required for learning in a network. In shortening vectors, it is important

context similarity. The vectors can also be viewed graphically, as shown in Fig. 1. Sample words (propose, film, etc.) are shown with their accompanying 25 element vectors (only 25 of the 140,000 elements are shown for viewing ease). Each vector element has a continuous numeric value (the normalised value from its matrix cell). A grey-scale is used to represent the normalised value, with black corresponding to a zero or minimal value. A word's vector can be seen as a distributed representation (Hinton, McClelland, & Rumelhart, 1986). Each word is represented by a pattern of values distributed over many elements, and any particular vector element can participate in the represenation of any word. The representations gracefully degrade as elements are removed; for example, there is only a small difference in performance between a vector with 140,000 elements and one with 1000 elements. Finally, it can be seen that words representing similar concepts have similar vectors, although this can be subtle at times. (See Lund and Burgess, 1996b, for a full description of the HAL methodology.)

The advantage of representing meaning with vectors such as these is that, since each vector element is a symbol in the input stream (typically another word), all words have as their "features" other words. This translates into the ability to have a vector representation for abstract concepts (e.g. *justice*, *reality*) as easily as one can have a representation for more basic concepts (e.g. *dog*, *book*). This is important, if not absolutely crucial, when developing a memory model that purports to be general in nature.

SIMULATION 1: DEMONSTRATING BASIC CATEGORISATION

So far, only the visual inspection of nine vectors has been offered as evidence that the most informational vector elements can be extracted from the matrix such that they provide a representation that is semantic in natue. In this first experiment, four semantic categories of words[2] are subjected to multidimensional scaling to determine if the interword distances are semantically meaningful.

---

to keep the vector elements that are most "informative". To determine this, the column and row variances for a particular word's vectors to be used in an experiment are computed. The vector elements with the smallest variances can be discarded, since they represent contexts in which the word had little experience. We find that variance drops sharply across the first 100 elements and is very low by the 200th element. Accordingly, to generate a 200 element vector, the 139,800 columns with the lowest variance would be discarded for each word. Empirically, using a long or short vector provides similar results. For the present purposes, it was more computationally straightforward to use the long vector. Further details can be found in Lund and Burgess (1996b).

[2]Word and concept will be treated as equivalent in this paper. We are mindful that it is controversial to do so (Komatsu, 1992), but do not think it detracts from our current theoretical development of the HAL model.

Methods

A number of words that represented four categories (animal types, body parts, cities and geographical locations) were used in an initial analysis of semantic content for the co-occurrence vectors. Vectors were extracted for these words and, treating each vector as a set of coordinates in a high-dimensional Euclidean space, a distance matrix was formed. Our hypothesis was that this distance matrix, representing the interword distances for the chosen set of words, would operate as a similarity matrix. Each element in the similarity matrix represented the distance between two of the chosen words in this high-dimensional space.

Results

This matrix was analysed using a multidimensional scaling algorithm (MDS) which projects points from a high-dimensional space into a lower-dimensional space in a non-linear fashion and attempts to preserve the distances between points as much as possible. The lower-dimensional projection allows for the visualisation of the spatial relationships between the co-occurrence vectors. The two-dimensional MDS solution is shown in Fig. 2. Visual inspection suggests that the four categories of words were differentiated by this procedure. Geographical regions and cities are distinct from the animals and body parts. There is some overlap among the more related categories (locations and cities; animals and body parts). Inferential statistics were computed comparing intragroup distances to intergroup distances. To do this, distances between all combinations of item pairs within a group were calculated and compared to all combinations of the group items and all other items. Animals (denoted by filled stars) were differentiated from the other three groups of items [$F(1,258) = 91.14$, $P < 0.0001$]. Likewise, body parts (denoted by open circles) were different from animals, cities and locations [$F(1,553) = 408.47$, $P < 0.0001$], and the intragroup distances for locations (denoted by open stars) differed from the other three groups [$F(1,304) = 381.45$, $P < 0.0001$]. Intragroup distances for cities (denoted by filled circles) also differed from the other three groups [$F(1,220) = 126.09$, $P < 0.0001$]. However, two pairs of categories did show some degree of overlap, so additional comparisons were conducted. Intragroup distances for animals differed from the intergroup distances to the body parts [$F(1,152) = 28.97$, $P < 0.0001$]. Intragroup distances for cities differed from the intergroup distances to the locations [$F(1,88) = 17.01$, $P < 0.0001$]. Thus the two-dimensional MDS of the 140,000 dimensional space would seem to be an accurate reduction of dimensionality.

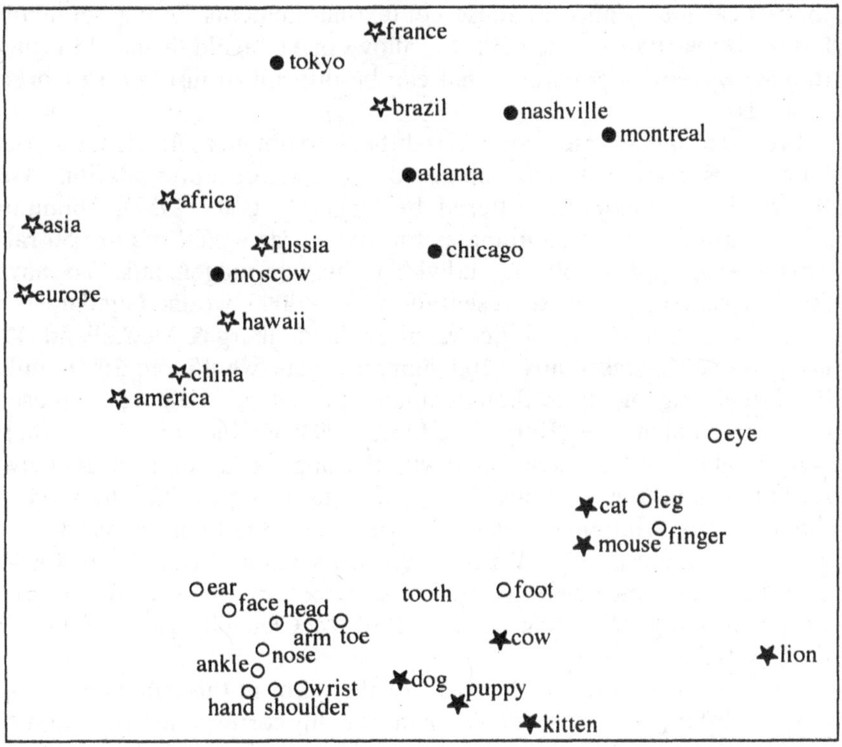

FIG. 2. Two-dimensional multidimensional scaling solution of four groups of words (geographic locations, cities, animals, body parts).

Discussion

Given that words with similar meanings tended to be close to each other in the high-dimensional space, we conclude that these vectors from the co-occurrence matrix carry information that mimics semantic knowledge. Specifically, it would appear that the distances between items reflect some aspect of the semantic relationship of those items. The MDS results presented here are very similar to the results obtained by various semantic memory investigators who employed human ratings using a semantic differential procedure (Osgood et al., 1957). There is a long history in cognitive psychology of using rating scales with some predetermined set of adjectives as bipolar anchors which essentially determine a set of "semantic features" (Smith et al., 1974). HAL does not use a set of "semantic" features; vector elements correspond to symbols that actually occurred in the learning environment. Certain of these elements contribute more heavily to the results obtained (those with the highest variance). We will argue later for the theoretical importance of these contextual elements. Using contextually based representations such as these allows one to avoid the need to commit to a set of semantic features that can be difficult to justify on theoretical grounds.

From a pragmatic viewpoint, it is difficult to obtain a sufficient number of human observations to develop an adequate set of representations. Using the minimum guidelines offered by Osgood et al. (1957), obtaining a 10-dimensional set of coordinates for 100 words would require 50 raters. This translates into 50,000 individual human judgements. To have a 20-dimensional set of representations for 3000 words (similar to the simulation without a semantic system by Seidenberg & McClelland, 1989) using a more conservative 100 human raters would require 6 million individual judgements. Although human normative data have been used in computational models (Burgess & Lund, 1994; McRae et al., 1997), there is considerable overhead associated with this approach. This is most likely the reason behind the two most frequently used approaches to modelling semantic representations: binary vectors that do not correspond to actual words (Kawamoto, 1993; Masson, 1995; Moss, Hare, Day, & Tyler, 1994), or simply constructing a set of vector features that presumably will represent a word's meaning (Hinton & Shallice, 1991; McClelland & Kawamoto, 1986; Plaut & Shallice, 1994).

The results reflected in the MDS of the items in this simulation suggest that the distances between words might roughly correspond to reaction-time latencies from single-word priming experiments. However, there has been a longstanding debate over whether word priming may, in fact, be carried by associative relationships rather than semantic similarity (Lupker, 1984; Mandler, 1962; Shelton & Martin, 1992). Elsewhere we have presented evidence that HAL's vectors are more semantic than associative in nature by looking at the correspondence between the priming effects of related and unrelated sets of item vectors and the results of experiments with human subjects (Lund et al., 1995, 1996). In addition, we have found HAL's vectors to accurately reflect human judgements made on Toglia and Battig's (1978) semantic word norms and the typicality effect (Lund & Burgess, 1994). The results of this simulation and of the experiments just cited all converge on the notion that the information carried by the vectors is more semantic than associative in nature.

Earlier, we suggested that the semantic characteristics of the vectors most likely hinge on the fact that similar words are used in similar contexts. As the 10-word window moves along the text, the matrix develops in a way that can be sensitive to the contexts in which the words occur (Lund & Burgess, 1996b). This bootstrapping procedure capitalises on the contextuality inherent in the input stream to create a set of vectors that carry this semantic, categorical knowledge reflected in the results of simulation 1. Of course, the notion that the contexts that a word occurs in results in knowledge about the word is an idea with a long history in psycholinguistics. Early models of memory recognised that one basic component of memory organisation was grammatical categorisation (Deese, 1965). Most associative responses in a word association task are of the same grammatical class (Ervin, 1963). Deese (1965, ch. 5) demonstrated that a factor analysis of word associations would produce a cluster of different grammatical classes of verb forms and types of pronouns. More recently, Slator et al. (1990) used a machine-readable dictionary analysis to categorise types of prepositions. The dictionary they used (LDOCE) includes a variety of information such as synonyms and short phrases, as well as short sample texts illustrating how a word can be used. LDOCE, however, provides a considerable amount of information to a model up front so that it may learn grammatical categorisation. Although this is a valuable way to jumpstart grammatical categorisation, it is not as satisfying as an approach that can provide the necessary representations to do this strictly from conversational text.

SIMULATION 2: SIMPLE GRAMMATICAL CATEGORISATION

Ervin (1961, 1963) and others (see Nelson, 1977, for a review) have presented considerable evidence that a child's experience with context results in both semantic and grammatical categorical knowledge. More recently, Finch and Chater (1992) demonstrated that words can be categorised according to grammatical class using a learning procedure very similar to ours. Although there is evidence that HAL's word vectors carry semantic information, Finch and Chater's results suggest that HAL's vectors may carry a broader range of categorical knowledge. One potentially important distinction between the two simulations is that Finch and Chater used a 2-word moving window, whereas we used a 10-word window. The possibility exists that the larger encoding window may not be sensitive to the more local syntactic dependencies. The goal for this experiment was to see if HAL's vector representations, generated using our 10-word window, can provide the required information to distinguish basic grammatical categories similar to that found by Finch and Chater (1992).

Method

The first analysis used vectors for items for four grammatical categories: nouns (10), verbs (10), determiners (9) and prepositions (6). The vector representations were extracted for these verbs and analysed using a MDS algorithm which projects the high-dimensional space into a lower-dimensional space while attempting to preserve the interpoint distance.

Results

The MDS solution for these four grammatical classes is shown in Fig. 3. Visual inspection suggests that the scaling procedure was able to capitalise on the information carried in the vector representations. Verbs (denoted by a triangle), for the most part, are found clustering on the right, whereas nouns (denoted by a circle) cluster on the left. Three exceptions of verbs that did not cluster with other verbs (*study*, *sketch* and *request*) are verb–noun ambiguities and clustered more closely with the nouns. The function words are all clustered between the nouns and verbs and seem to have their own independent organisation. The determiners (denoted by squares) show some substructural organisation; the plural possessive pronouns, *their* and *our*, are close, as are the singular possessive pronouns, *my*, *his* and *her*. The possessive pronoun, *your*, is ambiguous in that it can be either singular or plural, and is found between the singular and plural pronouns. The articles, *the*, *a* and *an*, were also close in proximity, with the indefinite articles closer to each other than to the definite article. Likewise, the prepositions (denoted by asterisks) show similar organisation with some correspondence to semantic similarity. At the top of Fig. 3 are *above* and *below*, and in the centre are *in*, *on*, *around* and *by*. This two-dimensional representation of this high-dimensional space is less visually compelling, however, than the results shown with the semantic categories. For example, the prepositions *above* and *below* are closer to the nouns *bed* and *roof* than they are to the other

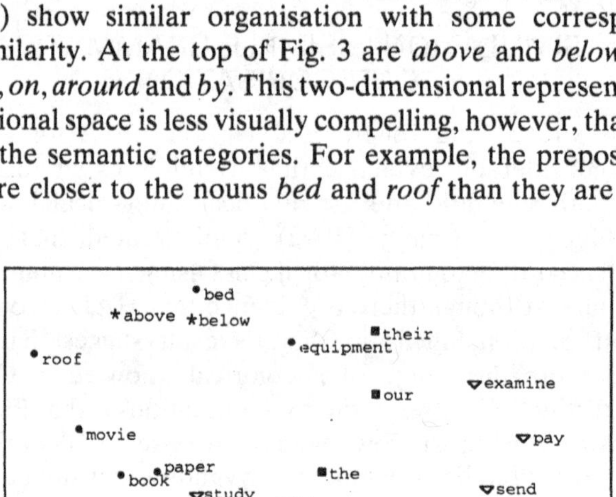

FIG. 3. Multidimensional scaling solution for verbs (inverted triangles), nouns (circles), prepositions (asterisks) and determiners (squares).

prepositions. An analysis of variance comparing each grammatical category's intragroup distances to all other intergroup distances suggests a clear separation in the high-dimensional space. Determiners are differentiated from the other three grammatical categories [$F(1,295) = 238.17$, $P < 0.0001$]. Nouns differ from the other categories [$F(1,262) = 20.36$, $P < 0.0001$], as do prepositions [$F(1,196) = 69.97$, $P < 0.0001$] and verbs [$F(1,328) = 28.75$, $P < 0.0001$]. Thus one can be reasonably confident that the high-dimensional resolution of these basic grammatical categories represents salient information carried in the word vector, and is similar to the results obtained by Finch and Chater (1992).

Discussion

These results compare favourably with the various analyses of grammatical classes by Deese (1965, ch. 5), who conducted a factor analysis of responses found in human association norms, as well as the more recent results of Finch and Chater (1992), whose vector representation procedure was similar to ours. It was important to determine that the model with the 10-word window that produced the apparent semantic categorisation in simulation 1 would also produce the grammatical categorisation found by Finch and Chater. The results from these simulations suggest that the vector representations carry important grammatical-class information sufficient to allow one to distinguish between major grammatical entities (nouns, prepositions, determiners and verbs).

It would appear plausible that the aspects of grammaticality carried in HAL's vector representations could be used by the parser as convergent information in tagging parts of speech, as well as carrying more conventional semantic information. These results are consistent with our earlier idea (Lund et al., 1995) that the categorical information carried in the vector representations emerge, in some abstract way, due to the substitutability of words in contexts. To any extent that this is true, both grammatical-categorical knowledge and semantic-categorical knowledge would seem to be an integral part of this substitutability process, as well as being implicit in a word's vector representation.

SIMULATION 3: MORPHOLOGICAL AMBIGUITY OF VERBS

The results from simulation 2 suggest that HAL's representations carry sufficient information to distinguish between discrete grammatical classes. In this simulation, we wanted to determine if a more subtle grammatical categorisation is possible. We tested this using a set of morphologically ambiguous verbs (*examined*) that were subjected to a MDS procedure, together with verbs that are unambiguously past-tense or past-participle (*threw* and *grown*, respectively). Comparing ambiguous verbs to unambiguous verbs is of particular interest, since the final simulation in this paper will focus on the contextual effects of nouns and morphologically ambiguous verbs that have been used in on-line syntactic processing experiments. As a precursor to that, it would be important to demonstrate that contextual information relevant to morphological ambiguity in verbs is carried in a word's representation.

Method

Three types of verbs were used: morphologically ambiguous verbs ($n = 26$) (past-tense or past-participle), morphologically unambiguous past-tense verbs ($n = 9$) and morphologially unambiguous past-participle verbs ($n = 9$). The ambiguous verbs were the verbs used in the study of Burgess and Tanenhaus (1996). The unambiguous past-participle verbs were items used in a previous control experiment by these authors. The unambiguous past-tense verbs were quasi-randomly selected from a list of unambiguous verbs listed in Irmscher (1972). The only constraint on the selection was that verbs that were noun–verb ambiguities (e.g. *saw*) were not used. The vector representations were extracted for these verbs and analysed using a MDS algorithm which projects the high-dimensional space into a lower-dimensional space while attempting to preserve the interpoint distance.

Results

The results of the second MDS with the morphologically ambiguous and unambiguous verbs are shown in Fig. 4. The past-tense verbs (denoted by open circles) can be seen at the bottom right of the figure, whereas the past-participle verbs (denoted by solid dark circles), at the top right of the figure, are clearly separated from the past-tense verbs. Distances were calculated between all possible items pairings allowing for intergroup and intragroup comparisons among the three types of verbs (past-tense, past-participle, ambiguous). Intragroup distances for the past-tense verbs differed from the intergroup distances of the past-tense items to the other two verb types [$F(1,292) = 82.50$, $P < 0.0001$]. Similarly, the intragroup distances for the past-participle verbs differed from the intergroup distances of the past-participle items to the other two verb types [$F(1,418) = 114.17$, $P < 0.0001$]. The exception to the close clustering of the past-participle verbs is *seen*, which can be found with the past-tense verbs. Even so, the two unambiguous verb types differ from each other and from the ambiguous verbs in the high-dimensional space. The ambiguous verbs (denoted by solid, grey-scaled circles) are dispersed throughout the high-dimensional space, as one would expect with verbs that are ambiguous, and their intragroup distances do not differ from the intergroup distances

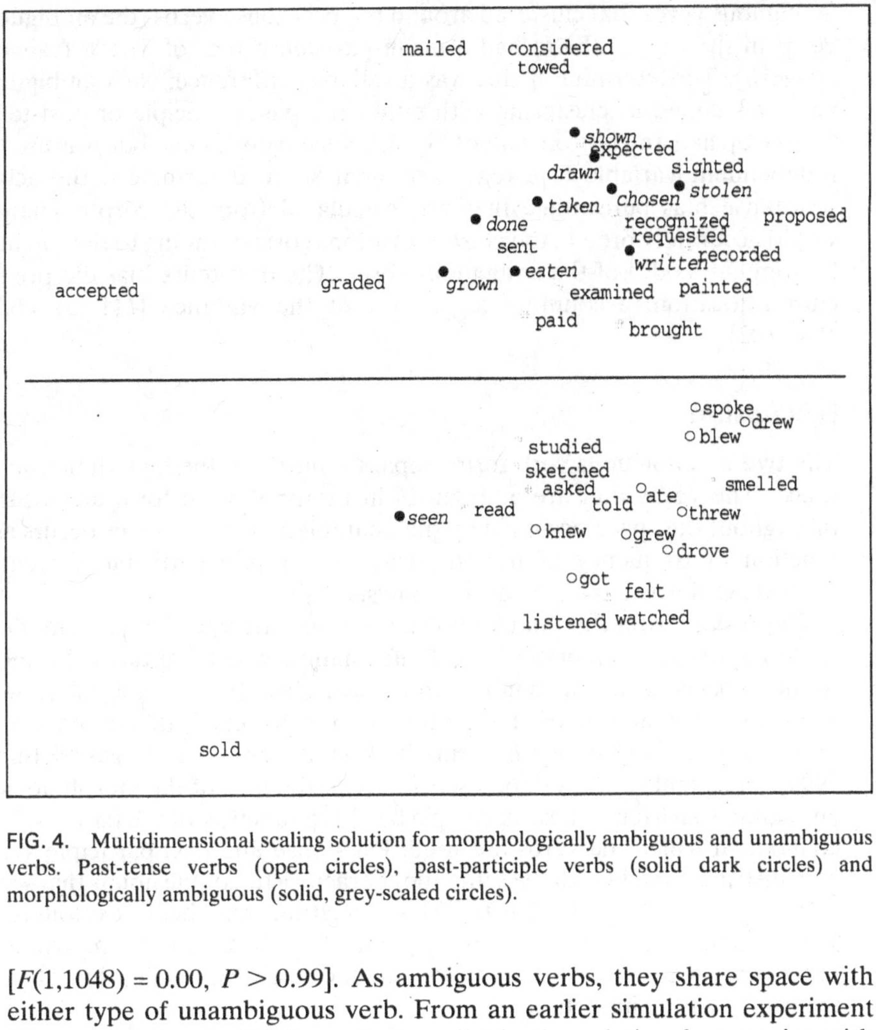

FIG. 4. Multidimensional scaling solution for morphologically ambiguous and unambiguous verbs. Past-tense verbs (open circles), past-participle verbs (solid dark circles) and morphologically ambiguous (solid, grey-scaled circles).

[F(1,1048) = 0.00, $P > 0.99$]. As ambiguous verbs, they share space with either type of unambiguous verb. From an earlier simulation experiment (Burgess & Lund, 1994), we had available the relative frequencies with which these ambiguous verbs were used in past-tense and past-participle structures (all sentences using these verbs were from the Brown corpus). One would expect a tendency for the ambiguous verbs in the top half of the figure (clustering near the past-participle verbs) to be used more frequently in past-participle constructions. Likewise, one would expect a tendency for the ambiguous verbs in the bottom half of the figure (clustering near the past-tense verbs) to be used more frequently in past-tense constructions. We conducted an analysis to determine if this was true. The ambiguous verbs that clustered around the past-participle verbs (the ambiguous verbs in the top half) had a mean past-tense bias of 70.4% (range = 33–90%); the ambiguous verbs that clustered around the past-tense verbs (the ambiguous verbs in the bottom half) had a mean past-tense bias of 87.1% (range = 50–98%). To determine if this was a reliable difference, each ambiguous verb was coded as clustering with either the past-participle or past-tense verbs (top half and bottom half of Fig. 4, respectively). This code was used as a dependent variable in a regression analysis to determine if the actual past-tense bias percentage that was calculated from the corpus analysis would accurately predict the cluster location (corresponding to the top half, bottom half code) of the ambiguous verbs. The past-tense bias did predict cluster location, accounting for 21.6% of the variance [$F(1,23) = 6.36$, $P < 0.02$].

Discussion

The two unambiguous verb forms separate nicely in the high-dimensional space. The verbs that are ambiguous in morphological form are located throughout the space occupied by the unambiguous forms. This occurs as a function of frequency of use in past-tense or past-participle sentential contexts as derived from a corpus analysis.

The results from this simulation suggest that the vector representations carry important grammatical-class information which captures the more subtle aspects within a major grammatical class (morphological forms). Moreover, the nature of this pattern of results fits with our notion of morphological verb ambiguity (Burgess & Hollbach, 1988; Burgess & Lund, 1994). Presumably, the vector's sensitivity to the bias of the morphological ambiguity (past-tense, past-participle bias) is a function of the nature of the contexts in which the verbs are used. Past-tense and past-participle verbs vary distributionally with the semantic characteristics of the nouns that serve as their subjects and objects. This variation has been exploited in psycholinguistic research investigating semantic constraints during syntactic processing. An analysis of stimuli from a set of these experiments will be the focus of the last simulation.

SIMULATION 4: SINGLE-WORD SEMANTIC CONTEXTS AND PARSING

The degree to which lexical/semantic information can assist syntactic processing during on-line sentence comprehension is determined to a large extent by the architecture of the language processor and the constraints offered by the constituents in a sentence. In this experiment, we demonstrate that the context distances which can be derived using the HAL model correspond to the constraint of the semantic contexts used in three different experiments.

Syntactically motivated theories, most notably the garden path theory of Frazier and colleagues (Ferreira & Clifton, 1986; Frazier, 1978; Rayner et al., 1983), describe a set of deterministic parsing strategies that are insensitive to contextual information, relying solely on structural cues. One of these strategies, minimal attachment, proposes that words are attached to a phrase marker using the fewest possible syntactic nodes. As a result, the parser will initially build a past-tense construction (see Fig. 5a) rather than the ultimately correct past-participle analysis (see Fig. 5b).

A series of early experiments had demonstrated that various discourse and semantic contexts were ineffective in reducing the processing load associated with the garden-pathing phenomenon (Ferreira & Clifton, 1986; Rayner et al., 1983). Ferreira and Clifton's (1986) study is probably one of the best illustrations of such an experiment. They reasoned that Rayner and co-workers' (1983) attempt may have failed due to weak pragmatic constraints expressed in the NP + V combinations. As a stronger manipulation, they varied the animacy of the sentential subject such that it was a virtually anomalous agent for the subsequent verb, so that, if the parser could use this semantic information, it would eliminate the garden path in sentence (1b) but not in (1a):

1a. The defendant examined by the lawyer turned out to be unreliable.
1b. The evidence examined by the lawyer turned out to be unreliable.

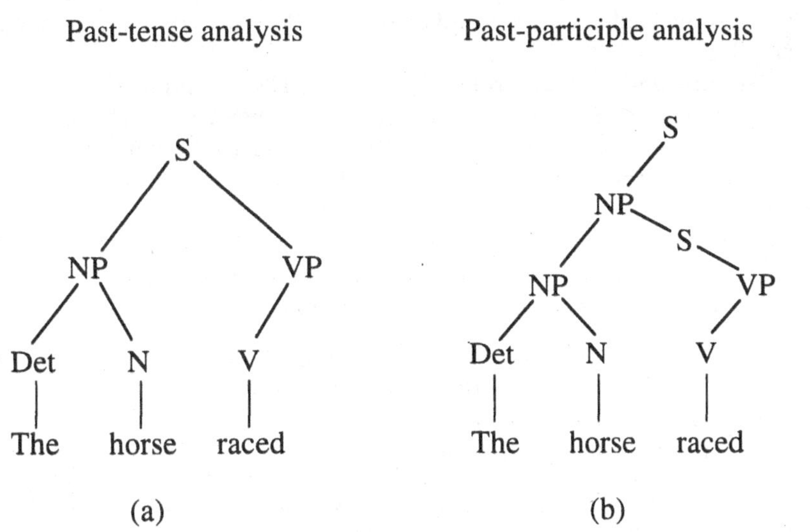

FIG. 5. Abbreviated phrase structure trees for the past-tense (a) and the past-participle (b) analyses of *the horse raced* ...

In their experiments, the animacy manipulation had no effect on first-pass reading times in the by-phrase, providing further empirical support that the minimal attachment preference results in a garden path regardless of the semantic plausibility of the noun. Considerable evidence exists suggesting that the parser is initially insensitive to pragmatic and semantic constraints and that the semantic information is used only to assist in reparsing a sentence once misassignments have been made (see Clifton & Ferreira, 1989, for a review).

Research in lexical ambiguity has motivated the development of constraint-based parsing models (Burgess & Hollbach, 1988; Burgess & Lund, 1994; MacDonald et al., 1994; Tanenhaus & Carlson, 1989). These models allow more flexibility for communication between language subsystems and suggest a larger role for lexical/semantic representations in that they can provide guidance for the necessary lexical, thematic and syntactic commitments that are required during on-line language comprehension. Semantics in these models plays a crucial role in the parsing operation. Real-world knowledge and semantic information (see MacDonald et al., 1994; Tanenhaus & Carlson, 1989) can provide immediate feedback to the parsing operation such that cognitive-processing loads (i.e. garden paths) that are obligatory on a minimal attachment view can be eliminated. There is increasing empirical evidence to support such models (Burgess & Tanenhaus, 1996; Burgess & Lund, 1994; MacDonald et al., 1994; Trueswell, Tanenhaus, & Kello, 1993; see MacDonald et al., 1994, for a review). Two of these studies will be discussed here, since their stimuli and the stimuli used in Ferreira and Clifton's (1986) study will be included in our simulation.

Burgess and Tanenhaus (1996; Burgess, 1991) conducted an experiment along the lines of Ferreira and Clifton (1986, experiment 1) using sentences similar to (1a) and (1b). However, Burgess and Tanenhaus had noted that a number of the sentences used by Ferreira and Clifton were not as constraining as might be desired (see Burgess, 1991, for details). For example, sentences with inanimate subjects, such as (2a) and (2b), presumably are biased for the past-participle interpretation because the subject noun will not make a plausible agent:

2a. The car towed from the parking lot was parked illegally.
2b. The ship sighted by the lookout probably brought bad news.
2c. The car towed the boat to the beach.
2d. The ship sighted the survivors.

It is possible, however, to continue a number of these sentences in a past-tense fashion (see 2c and 2d) which compromises the past-participle bias that was intended. Burgess and Tanenhaus conducted a norming study to construct a set of sentences that would have a more compelling past-participle constraint, and thus provide a stronger test of the semantic constraint. These items, with more constraining agent–verb relationships, showed that the processing load which Ferreira and Clifton associated with the garden-path effect could be eliminated. MacDonald (1994) conducted a similar experiment that more precisely manipulated several of these stimulus constraints. Using reduced-relative sentences (like these previous investigators), she also found that the agent–verb constraint, along with argument structure frequencies and post-ambiguity constraints, helped govern whether or not readers experienced a processing load at the point of disambiguation. The results of the studies of Burgess and Tanenhaus and of MacDonald demonstrate that with strongly enough constrained past-participle sentences, the garden path predicted by minimal attachment can be avoided. This suggests that semantic information can play a role in the initial syntactic processing during sentence comprehension.

The three syntactic processing experiments briefly reviewed here have in common a concern about the nature of the semantic/pragmatic relationships inherent in the sentence. Specifically, these three experiments all investigated the past-participle constructions in which the semantic context was posited as providing guidance to the parser via the relationship between the NP and the morphologically ambiguous verb. These experiments differed with respect to whether or not the garden path associated with the syntactic misassignment occurred. Of concern for this simulation is the extent to which the context distances between the noun–verb combinations used in these three experiments will correspond to the empirical results obtained. During the vector acquisition process, the HAL model is exposed to ~300 million words of text. As a result, verbs encounter a rich array of contexts in which they are used, and this experience is captured in the vector representations of the words. It follows, then, that the vector representations, which encode context, should reflect the probabilistic constraints of the language and that these constraints may have some correspondence to the NP–verb constraints being discussed here. Closer context distances should be an indicator of more constrained noun–verb relationships. Thus close context distances should be associated with the experiments that demonstrated the effects of context (i.e. Burgess & Tanenhaus, 1996; MacDonald, 1994), whereas the experiment that did not show a contextual effect should have noun–verb pairs with longer context distances (i.e. Ferreira & Clifton, 1986).

Method

Stimuli. Noun–verb pairs from the sentential stimuli were used from the three studies. Animate and inanimate stimuli from Ferreira and Clifton (FC) (e.g. *baby–felt*, *skin–felt*) yielded 32 noun–verb pairs (see their appendix 1).

Likewise, the animate and inanimate stimuli from Burgess and Tanenhaus (BT) (e.g. *man–paid, ransom–paid*) yielded 32 noun–verb pairs (see their appendix 1). Finally, the animate and inanimate stimuli from MacDonald (MM) (e.g. *spy–concealed, microfilm–concealed*) yielded 32 noun–verb pairs (see her appendix 3). All experiments have in common that the sentences were biased towards either a past-tense (animate) or a past-participle (inanimate) interpretation. The constraint to be evaluated by this experiment was only between the noun–verb pairs of these three stimuli sets.

Procedure. The design of the experiment was a 2 × 2 mixed factorial; both factors were between items. Bias had two levels corresponding to whether the noun–verb pairs were PTC or PPC. Study had two levels corresponding to the experiment that did not obtain an effect of context (FC) and the experiments that did show an effect of context (BT and MM). All analyses were calculated on item manipulations. Recall from the simulation methodology that the matrix develops from tracking co-occurrences using a 10-word window that slides along the text one word at a time. Earlier pilot work had demonstrated that optimal results when investigating parsing constraints are obtained with window sizes of six or eight. Therefore, for this experiment, we extracted two sets of vectors: one from a matrix using a window size of six and the other using a window size of eight. As a result, each set of stimuli from each of the three studies to be simulated has two sets of vector representations. Context distances were computed for all noun–verb pairs and are presented in RCUs (Riverside Context Units[3]), which is the distance metric used in the HAL model.

Results

The results are shown in Fig. 6. The experimental design was a 2 (bias: PTC or PPC) × 2 (study set: those showing context effects, BT & MM, and the one that did not show the effect of noun context, FC). A complete vector representation consists of 70,000 elements from the rows of the matrix and 70,000 elements from the columns of the matrix. Rows encode the information in the *n*-word moving window that occurs before the target word; columns encode the information in the *n*-word moving window that occurs after the target word. In this simulation, rows and columns were separated, since subject position nouns tend to occur before the verb in English, and thus row information might be more informative in this

[3]We refer to the distance metric used in the HAL model as Riverside Context Units (RCUs). This is an arbitrary, but normalised Euclidian distance measure (see Lund & Burgess, 1996b, for further description). To normalise a vector, we first compute its magnitude (sum the squares of its elements, take the square root of that, and divide by the number of elements). We then divide the magnitude by 666.0, and divide each vector element by the resulting number.

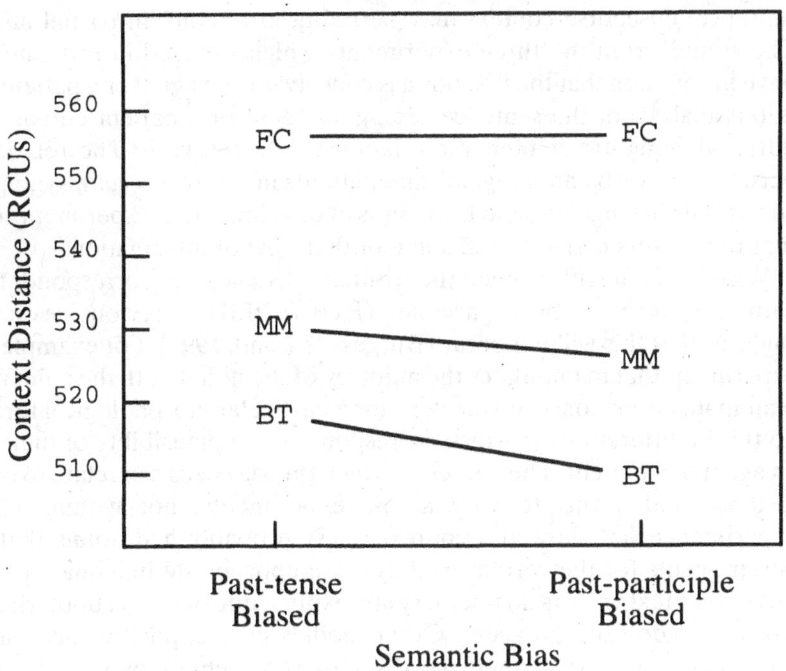

FIG. 6. Context distance as a function of simulated experiment and semantic bias.

simulation.[4] For rows, there was a main effect of study [$F(1,248) = 4.45$, $P = 0.036$] but no main effect of bias ($F < 1$), nor was the interaction reliable ($F < 1$). For columns, there was a marginal main effect of study [$F(1,246) =$ 296, $P = 0.053$] but no main effect of bias ($F < 1$), nor was the interaction reliable ($F < 1$). The two studies that showed the effect of the semantic context of the noun on parsing decisions (BT, MM) showed shorter noun–verb semantic distances than the study that did not obtain the context effect (FC). The difference between the row and column analysis was negligible.

Discussion

The more recent class of constraint satisfaction models of syntactic processing allow a role for contextual constraints that become activated during the word recognition process (Burgess & Lund, 1994; MacDonald et al., 1994; Tanenhaus & Carlson, 1989; Trueswell, Tanenhaus, & Garnsey, 1994). Modelling parsing constraints, however, offers a more serious challenge for a memory model. Generally, different syntactic alternatives will give rise to very different semantic or thematic constraints in the

[4]We want to thank Ken McRae for suggesting the comparison of the row and column results.

sentence. Discourse context may be required to confirm partial analyses. The stimuli from the three experiments which we used in this simulation have in common that the first noun is conceivably an agent or a patient in the initial analysis of the sentence. Being an agent or a patient entails a very different semantic or thematic relationship to the verb. The relationship between the verb and its agents and patients implicates certain syntagmatic constraints in language, and the results of this simulation experiment suggest that the vectors carry at least some of that type of information.

While one might expect the context distance to correspond to the within-experiment bias variable (PTB *vs* PPB), previous experience suggests that this will not occur (Burgess & Lund, 1994). For example, in an experiment that manipulates the animacy of the noun, both the animate and inanimate nouns constrain the verb for a particular morphological form, but do this in different ways which correspond to the plausibility of their being an agent or a patient. The degree to which this succeeds can relate to context distance and seems to vary across experiments, not within. That is, experiments that showed a context effect probably had nouns that were better agents for the verb as well as more appropriate inanimate patients. HAL's context vectors do not carry any explicit information about whether a word is a good or bad agent. Other models have explicitly coded agency information as part of their word-vector representations (McClelland & Kawamoto, 1986; St. John & McClelland, 1990). A model like HAL does not have agency information encoded in its vectors in any direct way (if it did, perhaps the row/column manipulation would have been more pronounced). HAL's representations are encodings of the history of the contexts in which a word has appeared. The distance between words in the high-dimensional space reflects this learning history, and the distance metric appears to predict whether the contexts were sufficiently constraining in the three parsing experiments investigated in this simulation. These vector representations are far from perfect in their predictions, however. Pearlmutter and MacDonald (1995) conducted an experiment in which sentences with morphologically ambiguous verbs (e.g. *cooked* in 3a) were contrasted with sentences with unambiguous, intransitive verbs (e.g. *bubbled* in 3b). In this case, a context distance analysis of the stimuli show that the more constraining items for their particular sentences (e.g. *soup bubbled*) have longer context distances than the less constraining items (e.g. *soup cooked*). In HAL, *soup* and *cooked* are more contextually related than are *soup* and *bubbled*. This makes intuitive sense, but it makes clear that these word vectors, as HAL is presently implemented, will not be able to capture the full constraints that are present in a sentence.

3a. The soup cooked in the pot but was not ready to eat.
3b. The soup bubbled in the pot but was not ready to eat.

Overall, the results from this experiment demonstrate that the contextual constraints that are important in determining the occurrence of a processing load during syntactic processing can be modelled using the vector representations generated by the HAL model. Although this experiment did not simulate syntactic processing *per se*, these results also lend support to the notion that contextual constraints are used during the parsing process because of the correspondence of the simulation results to this set of three psycholinguistic experiments.

GENERAL DISCUSSION

In this paper, we have attempted to demonstrate that HAL's vector representations can go a long way towards forming a useful tool for modelling contextual effects in syntactic processing. Having an adequate representational model for the meaning of a word has become crucial, as the focus on parsing constraints moves in the direction of a richer semantic system. In the first simulation we demonstrated that the representations were able to reliably differentiate four semantic categories. However, categorisability extends beyond "semantic" categorisation, and in the second simulation we showed that the vector representations carry information sufficient to categorise distinct grammatical forms (nouns, verbs, prepositions and determiners). The vectors would seem to carry a broad range of categorical information corresponding to what is typically considered to be semantic and grammatical. The third simulation with the unambiguous and ambiguous verbs demonstrates some important characteristics for representations if they are to be viable in modelling parsing constraints. HAL's vector representations for unambiguous past-tense and past-participle verbs clearly differentiated these two morphological forms. Morphologically ambiguous verbs were distributed throughout the high-dimensional space. In addition, their relative location in the space (close to the past-tense or past-participle) was related to the relative frequency of use as a past-tense or a past-participle. Models of language comprehension that posit a strong role of the lexical/semantic system require that a word's representation be rich in content. Sentence processing constraints are varied, but certainly include semantic and grammatical information and some ability to model lexical/morphological ambiguity. The results of the first three simulations suggest that HAL's vector representations have encoded information that allows for at least some basic processing along these constraint dimensions. The final simulation involved the specific constraint that a noun context has on a morphologically ambiguous verb. This type of reduced-relative structural ambiguity has a long history in psycholinguistics, since it has been used to test different models of syntactic processing. The stimuli (the noun–verb pairs) from three sets of empirical results were used to simulate the constraint of these noun–verb pairs and to determine if the original results corresponded to the context distances in the high-dimensional space. We found that the stimuli from the experiment that showed no effect of noun context on syntactic processing had longer context distances than the stimuli from the two experiments that did find the context effect. Closer context distances correspond to experiments that show context effects (at least with the three we used). We also indicated how this was not a perfect correspondence. Recall Pearlmutter and MacDonald's (1995) parsing constraint experiment that used intransitive verbs (e.g. *soup–bubbled*) and ambiguous transitive items (e.g. *soup–cooked*). HAL's context distances make the wrong prediction here (since *soup* and *cooked* are generally more contextually related). Clearly, there is linguistically relevant information that does not get captured in these word representations, possibly due to the impoverished input stream (compared to all the sensory input a human has available), or it may be that certain constraints simply cannot be captured in a word's representation. Regardless, though, it seems clear that the representations carry a considerable range of information, much of it potentially useful to a language comprehension system.

The Question of Representational Modularity

Whether or not the syntactic processor can use contextual information to guide its parsing decision has been a controversial issue; the question itself presupposes a parsing mechanism. Recent theories of parsing have been driven by lexical/semantic models of word recognition. The notion of a two-stage parser, where a syntactic structure is built without initial recourse to the available semantics, continues to be a dominant theory in psycholinguistics (Clifton & Ferreira, 1989; Frazier & Clifton, 1996). More recent models of syntactic processing have relied increasingly on the richness of the lexical/semantic system to provide the various semantic, thematic and local co-occurrence information required to correctly assign meaning to word order (Burgess & Lund, 1994; MacDonald et al., 1994; Tanenhaus & Carlson, 1989). Basic constraint satisfaction models are free to use a broad range of information and further acknowledge that these different sources of information vary in their relative contribution to the sentence comprehension process. The evidence that supports a constraint-satisfaction approach calls into question any strict notion of modularity of processing. Recent results suggest that the language processor is not modular, and that whether or not modular performance is observed, is a function of a variety of constraints that may or may not be available.

A parallel issue exists with respect to modularity of representations. Most theories of language comprehension assume that different forms of representations (e.g. syntactic, grammatical, lexical and semantic) are linguistically distinct, regardless of their position on processing modularity (Burgess & Hollbach, 1988; Burgess & Lund, 1994; Frazier, 1978; Frazier & Fodor, 1978; MacDonald et al., 1994; Tanenhaus & Carlson, 1989). Connectionist word recognition models have tended to blur this distinction by consolidating the learning from different representational sources into a single layer of hidden units (Elman, 1990; Seidenberg & McClelland, 1989). HAL's vector acquisition process simply accumulates a word's representation from the word's surrounding context. Each vector element for a particular word corresponds to a symbol (usually another word) in the input stream that was part of the contextual history for that particular word. The word's representation, then, corresponds to the complete contextual learning history that is a function of the word's context, the frequency of co-occurring symbols, and the relative weight in the moving window. The simulations reported in this paper, as well as our previous work with semantic priming, word association norms (Lund et al., 1996) and other syntactic effects (Burgess, Livesay, & Lund, 1996), suggest that HAL's representations carry a broad range of information that accounts for a variety of cognitive phenomena. This generality of HAL's representations suggests that it is possible to encode many "types" of information into a single representation and that this can be contextually driven.

With the increased reliance on contextual factors and their influence in syntactic processing, the need for a representational theory is vital. We propose that the vector representations that are acquired by the HAL model can provide such a resource. These vector representations are a product of considerable language experience (~300 million words of text in these simulations) that reflect the use of words in a highly diverse set of conversational contexts. The model does not presuppose any primitive or defining semantic features, and does not require an experimenter to commit to a particular type or set of features. Rather, the model uses as "features" (i.e. the vector elements) the other words (and symbols) that are used in language. That is, a word is defined by its use in a wide range of contexts.

Global or Local Co-occurrence?

As the lexical/semantic system increases in importance to our thinking about the language comprehension system in general, computational linguists have become increasingly interested in lexical co-occurrence as a mechanism for retrieval (Saint-Dizier & Viegas, 1995; Spence & Owens, 1990). We define local co-occurrence as the statistical likelihood of a particular word occurring in another's presence over some relatively short window. These local statistics have been useful in developing approaches to resolving syntactic ambiguity (Hindle & Rooth, 1993), in creating lexically oriented information-retrieval systems (Smadja, 1993) and in determining parts of speech (Merialdo, 1994). Juliano and Tanenhaus (1993) have shown that local co-occurrence rates of the word *that* in different syntactic contexts can predict the extent that a reader will make syntactic misassignments during reading. Burgess and Lund (1994) used as one constraint in their connectionist parsing model the probability of the disambiguating preposition *by* occurring after the morphologically ambiguous verb. Word co-occurrence may be an important source of information that a language user can use.

It is important, however, not to confuse local co-occurrence with global co-occurrence. A vector representation generated by the HAL model is a measure of global co-occurrence. Each element in a vector corresponds to a symbol (usually a word) in the input stream. Although the small window that moves along the text enters local co-occurrences into the data matrix, it is the large, sparse data matrix and the vectors that can be extracted from it that form a measure of how a word was used in a broad range of contexts. At a theoretical level, we argue that it is important not to think of these word vectors as simply the concatenation of the local co-occurrences (although it is that). It is the pattern of co-occurrences that is crucial to forming the meaning of a word in HAL. The word vector is, essentially, a contextuality vector (a measure of global co-occurrence). Similar words get used in similar contexts. Using a knowledge acquisition system that records (learns) how words were used in such a large number of diverse contexts, a representation is formed that is the result of considerable language experience. As a result, the vector representation embodies many rich semantic and grammatical aspects of the word that can be useful in modelling cognitive and psycholinguistic phenomena. Landauer and Dumais (in press) argue that their global co-occurrence model essentially exploits these local co-occurrences to induce more general knowledge representations. Their latent semantic analysis (LSA) model, Finch and Chater's (1992) bootstrapping model and our HAL model have much in common, and we agree with Landauer and Dumais' assertion that high-dimensional space models "produce sufficient enhancement of knowledge to bridge the gap between the information available in local contiguity and what people know after large amounts of experience" (p. 2).

Further Representational Issues

Symbol-grounding Problem. Glenberg (in press) raises two issues that he claims are serious problems for most memory models, the first of which is the symbol-grounding problem. The representations in a memory model do not have any extension to the real world; that is, lexical items cannot be understood with respect to just other lexical items. There also has to be a grounding of the representation of the lexical item to its physical reality in the environment (cf. Cummins, 1996). A model that represents a concept by a vector of arbitrary binary features or by some set of intuitively reasonable, but contrived, set of semantic features does not have a clear mapping onto the environment that it supposes to represent. HAL takes a very different approach to this problem. In HAL, each vector element is a coordinate in high-dimensional space for a word. What is important to realise about each vector element is that the element *is* a direct extension to the learning environment. A word's vector element represents the weighted (by frequency) value of the relationship between the part of the environment represented by that element and the word's meaning. The word's meaning is comprised of the complete vector. Symbol grounding is typically not considered a problem for abstract concepts. Abstract representations, if memory models have them, have no grounding in the environment. Again, though, HAL is different in this regard. An advantage to the representational methodology used in HAL is that abstract representations are encoded in the same way as more concrete words. The language environment (i.e. the incoming symbol stream) that HAL uses as input is special in this way. That is, abstract concepts are, in a sense, grounded.

The second problem faced by models that develop "meaningless" internal representations is that the variety of input that a human can experience does not get encoded and, therefore, the memory representation is inevitably impoverished. With the current implementation of HAL, this is certainly a limitation. The learning experience is limited to a corpus of text. This raises an important but currently unanswerable question: Are the limitations in HAL's representations due to the impoverished input or will higher-level representations be required to flesh out a complete memory system? We do think a HAL-like model that was sensitive to the same co-occurrences in the natural environment as a human-language learner (not just the language stream) would be able to capitalise on this additional information and construct more meaningful representations.

Subconceptual Representations. Since HAL's vector representations seem to carry such a board range of information (semantic, grammatical and thematic), we think that the representations are best considered subconceptual—a set of distributed units that can represent much of what one would want a mental representation to do. Much has been made of the advantages of subconceptual representations (Cussins, 1990; Smolensky, 1988; Van Orden, Pennington, & Stone, 1990). For example, the concept *bachelor* could be represented by having the features *adult*, *single* and *male* activated. However, our view is that subconceptual representation is not just some set of semantic features because such a conception begs two questions. First, how does one justify these particular features as subconceptual? Second, one can argue that microfeatures such as these are just more thinly sliced symbolic features (to paraphrase Cussins's characterisation of Fodor & Pylyshyn, 1988). The features used by HAL (the vector elements) are discrete aspects of the input stream that when encoded form a distributed representation that behaves in a variety of cognitively meaningful ways. No commitments are required to a particular set of features, and the encoding scheme is tightly tied to the actual input. This, together with how the vector representations are able to account for such a broad range of cognitive phenomena, makes this type of memory vector a good candidate for a subconceptual representation.

CONCLUSIONS

An increasing role for contextual information during comprehension is consistent with the general constraint satisfaction approach (MacDonald et al., 1994). We suspect that global co-occurrence models, more so than local co-occurrence models, will better capture the richness of cognitive and language effects that are important to the comprehension process. Landauer and Dumais (in press) have shown that their LSA model can mimic synonym vocabulary-test performance and also account for semantic context effects in lexical ambiguity. Earlier work with HAL has demonstrated that the representations can account for a broad range of cognitive effects, including semantic priming (Lund & Burgess, 1996a; Lund et al., 1995, 1996), basic categorisation (Lund & Burgess, 1994), cerebral asymmetries (Burgess & Lund, 1996) and the effects of brain damage on the semantic system (Buchanan et al., 1996). In this paper, we argue that HAL's contextual representations can provide a rich computational measure of semantic and grammatical effects.

REFERENCES

Buchanan, L., Burgess, C., & Lund, K. (1996). Overcrowding in semantic neighborhoods: Modeling deep dyslexia. *Brain and Cognition*, *32*, 111–114.

Burgess, C. (1991). *Interaction of semantic, syntactic and visual factors in syntactic ambiguity resolution*. Unpublished doctoral dissertation, University of Rochester, Rochester, NY.

Burgess, C., & Hollbach, S.C. (1988). A computational model of syntactic ambiguity as a lexical process. In *Proceedings of the Tenth Annual Meeting of the Cognitive Science Society*, pp. 263–269. Hillsdale, NJ: Lawrence Erlbaum Associates Inc.

Burgess, C., & Lund, K. (1994). Multiple constraints in syntactic ambiguity resolution: A connectionist account of pyscholinguistic data. In *Proceedings of the Sixteenth Annual Meeting of the Cognitive Science Society*, pp. 90–95. Hillsdale, NJ: Lawrence Erlbaum Associates Inc.

Burgess, C., & Lund, K. (in press). Modeling cerebral asymmetries of semantic memory using high-dimensional semantic space. In M. Beeman & C. Chiarello (Eds), *Getting it right: The cognitive neuroscience of right hemisphere language comprehension*. Hillsdale, NJ: Lawrence Erlbaum Associates Inc.

Burgess, C., & Tanenhaus, M.K. (1996). *Semantic, syntactic and visual factors in syntactic ambiguity resolution.* Unpublished manuscript, University of California Riverside.

Burgess, C., Livesay, K., & Lund, K. (1996). Modeling parsing constraints in high-dimensional semantic space: On the use of proper names. In *Proceedings of the Eighteenth Annual Meeting of the Cognitive Science Society*, p. 737. Hillsdale, NJ: Lawrence Erlbaum Associates Inc.

Clifton, C., & Ferreira, F. (1989). Ambiguity in context. *Language and Cognitive Processes, 4*, 77–103.

Collins, A.M., & Loftus, E.F. (1975). A spreading-activation theory of semantic processing. *Psychological Review, 82*, 407–428.

Collins, A.M., & Quillian, M.R. (1969). Retrieval time from semantic memory. *Journal of Verbal Learning and Verbal Behavior, 8*, 240–247.

Cummins, R. (1996). *Representations, targets, and attitudes.* Cambridge, MA: MIT Press.

Cussins, A. (1990). The connectionist construction of concepts. In M.A. Boden (Ed.), *The philosophy of artificial intelligence*, pp. 367–440. Oxford: Oxford University Press.

Deese, J. (1965). *The structure of associations in language and thought*, pp. 97–119. Baltimore, MD: Johns Hopkins Press.

Dyer, M.G. (1990). Distributed symbol formation and processing in connectionist networks. *Journal of Experimental and Theoretical Artificial Intelligence, 2*, 215–239.

Elman, J.L. (1990). Finding structure in time. *Cognitive Science, 14*, 179–211.

Ervin, S.M. (1961). Changes with age in the verbal determinants of word-association. *American Journal of Psychology, 74*, 361–372.

Ervin, S.M. (1963). Correlates of associative frequency. *Journal of Verbal Learning and Verbal Behavior, 1*, 422–431.

Ferreira, F., & Clifton, C. (1986). The independence of syntactic processing. *Journal of Memory and Language, 25*, 348–368.

Finch, S., & Chater, N. (1992). Bootstrapping syntactic categories by unsupervised learning. In *Proceedings of the Fourteenth Annual Meeting of the Cognitive Science Society*, pp. 820–825. Hillsdale, NJ: Lawrence Erlbaum Associates Inc.

Fischler, I. (1977). Semantic facilitation without association in a lexical decision task. *Memory and Cognition, 5*, 335–339.

Fodor, J., & Pylyshyn, Z. (1988). Connectionism and cognitive architecture: A critical analysis. *Cognition, 28*, 3–71.

Frazier, L. (1978). *On comprehending sentences: Syntactic parsing strategies.* PhD thesis, University of Connecticut, Storrs, CT. Distributed by Indiana University Linguistics Club.

Frazier, L., & Clifton, C. (1996). *Construal.* Cambridge, MA: MIT Press.

Frazier, L., & Fodor, J.D. (1978). The sausage machine: A new two-stage parsing model. *Cognition, 6*, 291–325.

Gallant, S.I. (1991). A practical approach for representing context and for performing word sense disambiguation using neural networks. *Neural Computation, 3*, 293–309.

Gernsbacher, M.A. (1990). *Language comprehension as structure building.* Hillsdale, NJ: Lawrence Erlbaum Associates Inc.

Glenberg, A. (in press). What memory is for. *Behavioral and Brain Sciences.*

Gorrell, P. (1989). Establishing the loci of serial and parallel effects in syntactic processing. *Journal of Psycholinguistic Research, 18*, 61–74.

Hindle, D., & Rooth, M. (1993). Structural ambiguity and lexical relations. *Computational Linguistics, 19*, 103–120.

Hinton, G.E., & Shallice, T. (1991). Lesioning an attractor network: Investigations of acquired dyslexia. *Psychological Review, 98*, 74–95.

Hinton, G.E., McClelland, J.L., & Rumelhart, D.E. (1986). Distributed representations. In D.E. Rumelhart, J.L. McClelland and the PDP Research Group (Eds), *Parallel distributed processing: Explorations in the microstructure of cognition. Vol. 1: Foundations*, pp. 77–109. Cambridge, MA: MIT Press.

Irmscher, W.F. (1972). *The Holt guide to English*. New York: Holt, Rinehart and Winston.

Juliano, C., & Tanenhaus, M.K. (1993). Contingent frequency effects in syntactic ambiguity resolution. In *Proceedings of the Fifteenth Annual Meeting of the Cognitive Science Society*, pp. 593–598. Hillsdale, NJ: Lawrence Erlbaum Associates Inc.

Kawamoto, A.H. (1993). Nonlinear dynamics in the resolution of lexical ambiguity: A parallel distributed processing account. *Journal of Memory and Language, 32*, 474–516.

Komatsu, L.K. (1992). Recent views of conceptual structure. *Psychological Bulletin, 112*, 500–526.

Kurtzman, H.S. (1985). On-line probe recognition latencies within complex sentences. *Language and Speech, 28*, 143–156.

Landauer, T.K., & Dumais, S. (1994). Memory model reads encyclopedia, passes vocabulary test. Paper presented at the *Psychonomics Society Meeting*, St. Louis, MO, November.

Landauer, T.K., & Dumais, S.T. (in press). A solution to Plato's Problem: The latent semantic analysis theory of acquisition, induction and representation of knowledge. *Psychological Review.*

Lund, K., & Burgess, C. (1994). Extraction of semantics via lexical co-occurrence: Methodology and preliminary results. Paper presented at the *NIPS*94 (Neural Information Processing Systems) Statistical and Neural Network Approaches to Natural Language Processing Post-conference Workshop*, Vail, CO, December.

Lund, K., & Burgess, C. (1996a). Hyperspace Analogue to Language (HAL): A general model of semantic representation (abstract). *Brain and Cognition, 30*, 265.

Lund, K., & Burgess, C. (1996b). Producing high-dimensional semantic spaces from lexical co-occurrence. *Behavior Research Methods, Instrumentation, and Computers, 28*, 203–208.

Lund, K., Burgess, C., & Atchley, R.A. (1995). Semantic and associative priming in high-dimensional semantic space. In *Proceedings of the Seventeenth Annual Meeting of the Cognitive Science Society*, pp. 660–665. Hillsdale, NJ: Lawrence Erlbaum Associates Inc.

Lund, K., Burgess, C., & Audet, C. (1996). Dissociating semantic and associative word relationships using high-dimensional semantic space. In *Proceedings of the Eighteenth Annual Meeting of the Cognitive Science Society*, pp. 603–608. Hillside, NJ: Lawrence Erlbaum Associates Inc.

Lupker, S.J. (1984). Semantic priming without association: A second look. *Journal of Verbal Learning and Verbal Behavior, 23*, 709–733.

MacDonald, M.C. (1994). Probabilistic constraints and syntactic ambiguity resolution. *Language and Cognitive Processes, 9*, 157–201.

MacDonald, M.C., Pearlmutter, N.J., & Seidenberg, M.S. (1994). The lexical nature of syntactic ambiguity resolution. *Psychological Review, 101*, 676–703.

Mandler, G. (1962). From association to structure. *Psychological Review, 69*, 415–427.

Masson, M.E.J. (1995). A distibuted memory model of semantic priming. *Journal of Experimental Psychology: Learning, Memory and Cognition, 21*, 3–23.

McClelland, J.L., & Kawamoto, A.H. (1986). Mechanisms of sentence processing: Assigning roles to constituents. In D.E. Rumelhart, J.L. McClelland and the PDP Research Group (Eds), *Parallel distributed processing: Explorations in the microstructure of cognition. Vol. 2: Psychological and biological models*, pp. 272–325. Cambridge, MA: MIT Press.

McRae, K., de Sa, V., & Seidenberg, M.S. (1997). On the notion and scope of featural representations of word meaning. *Journal of Experimental Psychology: General, 126*, 99–130.

Merialdo, B. (1994). Tagging English text with a probabilistic model. *Computational Linguistics, 20,* 155–171.

Meyer, D.E., & Schvaneveldt, R.W. (1971). Facilitation in recognizing pairs of words: Evidence of a dependence between retrieval operations. *Journal of Experimental Psychology, 90,* 227–235.

Moss, H.E., Hare, M.L., Day, P., & Tyler, L.K. (1994). A distributed memory model of the associative boost in semantic priming. *Connection Science, 6,* 413–427.

Moss, H.E., Ostrin, R.K., Tyler, L.K., & Marslen-Wilson, W.D. (1995). Accessing different types of lexical semantic information: Evidence from priming. *Journal of Experimental Psychology: Learning, Memory and Cognition, 21,* 863–883.

Neely, J.H. (1991). Semantic priming effects in visual word recognition: A selective review of current findings and theories. In D. Besner & G.W. Humphreys (Eds), *Basic processes in reading: Visual word recognition,* pp. 264–336. Hillsdale, NJ: Lawrence Erlbaum Associates Inc.

Nelson, K. (1977). The syntagmatic-paradigmatic shift revisited: A review of research and theory. *Psychological Bulletin, 84,* 93–116.

Osgood, C.E., Suci, G.J., & Tannenbaum, P.H. (1957). *The measurement of meaning.* Urbana, IL: University of Illinois Press.

Pearlmutter, N.J., & MacDonald, M.C. (1995). Individual differences and probabilistic constraints in syntactic ambiguity resolution. *Journal of Memory and Language, 34,* 521–542.

Plaut, D.C., & Shallice, T. (1994). *Connectionist modelling in cognitive neuropsychology: A case study.* Hove: Lawrence Erlbaum Associates Ltd.

Rayner, K., Carlson, M., & Frazier, L. (1983). The interaction of syntax and semantics during sentence processing: Eye movements in the analysis of semantically biased sentences. *Journal of Verbal Learning and Verbal Behavior, 22,* 358–374.

Saint-Dizier, P., & Viegas, E. (Eds) (1995). *Computational lexical semantics.* Cambridge: Cambridge University Press.

Schutze, H. (1992). Dimensions of meaning. In *Proceedings of Supercomputing '92,* pp. 787–796. Los Alamitos, CA: IEEE Computer Society Press.

Schvaneveldt, R.W. (Ed.) (1990). *Pathfinder associative networks: Studies in knowledge organizations.* Norwood, NJ: Ablex.

Seidenberg, M.S., & McClelland, J.L. (1989). A distributed, developmental model of word recognition and naming. *Psychological Review, 96,* 523–568.

Shelton, J.R., & Martin, R.C. (1992). How semantic is automatic semantic priming? *Journal of Experimental Psychology: Learning, Memory and Cognition, 18,* 1191–1210.

Slator, B.M., Amirsoleymani, C., Andersen, S., Braaten, K., Davis, J., Ficek, R., Hakimzadeh, H., McCann, L., Rajkumar, J., Thangiah, S., & Thureen, D. (1990). Towards empirically derived semantic classes. In *Proceedings of the Fifth Annual Rocky Mountain Conference on Artificial Intelligence,* pp. 257–262. Las Cruces, NM.

Smadja, F. (1993). Retrieving collocations from text: Xtract. *Computational Linguistics, 19,* 143–177.

Smith, E.E., Shoben, E.J., & Rips, L.J. (1974). Structure and process in semantic memory: A featural model for semantic decisions. *Psychological Review, 81,* 214–241.

Smith, F. (1971). *Understanding reading.* New York: Holt.

Smolensky, P. (1988). On the proper treatment of connectionism. *Behavioral and Brain Sciences, 11,* 1–74.

Spence, D.P., & Owens, K.C. (1990). Lexical co-occurrence and association strength. *Journal of Psycholinguistic Research, 19,* 317–330.

St. John, M.F., & McClelland, J.L. (1990). Learning and applying contextual constraints in sentence comprehension. *Artificial Intelligence, 46,* 217–257.

Tanenhaus, M.K., & Carlson, G.N. (1989). Lexical structure and language comprehension. In W. Marslen-Wilson (Ed.), *Lexical representation and process*, pp. 529–561. Cambridge, MA: MIT Press.

Toglia, M.P., & Batig, W.F. (1978). *Handbook of semantic word norms.* Hillsdale, NJ: Lawrence Erlbaum Associates Inc.

Trueswell, J.C., Tanenhaus, M.K., & Kello, C. (1993). Verb-specific constraints in sentence processing: Separating effects of lexical preference from garden-paths. *Journal of Experimental Psychology: Learning, Memory and Cognition*, *19*, 528–553.

Trueswell, J.C., Tanenhaus, M.K., & Garnsey, S.M. (1994). Semantic influences on parsing: Use of thematic role information in syntactic ambiguity resolution. *Journal of Memory and Language*, *33*, 285–318.

Van Orden, G.C., Pennington, B.F., & Stone, G.O. (1990). Word identification in reading and the promise of subsymbolic psycholinguistics. *Psychological Review*, *97*, 488–522.

LANGUAGE AND COGNITIVE PROCESSES, 1997, *12* (2/3), 211–271

Parsing in a Dynamical System: An Attractor-based Account of the Interaction of Lexical and Structural Constraints in Sentence Processing

Whitney Tabor, Cornell Juliano and Michael K. Tanenhaus

University of Rochester, Rochester, NY, USA

A dynamical systems approach to parsing is proposed in which syntactic hypotheses are associated with attractors in a metric space. These attractors have many of the properties of traditional syntactic categories, while at the same time encoding context-dependent, lexically specific distinctions. Hypotheses motivated by the dynamical system theory were tested in four reading time experiments examining the interaction of simple lexical frequencies, frequencies that are contingent on an environment defined by syntactic categories, and frequencies contingent on verb argument structure. The experiments documented a variety of contingent frequency effects that cut across traditional linguistic grains, each of which was predicted by the dynamical systems model. These effects were simulated in an implementation of the theory, employing a recurrent network trained from a corpus to construct metric representations and an algorithm implementing a gravitational dynamical system to model reading time as time to gravitate to an attractor.

INTRODUCTION

Bever's pioneering work (e.g. Bever, 1970) established that readers and listeners have strong preferences for certain syntactic sequences. For example, a noun phrase–verb–noun phrase sequence at the beginning of a sentence is typically taken to be a main clause. These preferences are revealed in garden-path effects for sentences with temporary syntactic

Requests for reprints should be addressed to Michael K. Tanenhaus, Department of Brain and Cognitive Sciences, Meliora Hall, University of Rochester, Rochester, NY 14627, USA. E-mail: mtan@bcs.rochester.edu

This research was supported in part by NIH Grant HD-27206 and by NIDCD Grant T32DC0035. Robbie Jacobs provided helpful feedback at various stages of this project. The final manuscript benefited from insightful comments by Don Mitchell, Dave Plaut and an anonymous reviewer. We did not include appendices with the materials used in Experiments 1–4 because of length constraints. These are available on request from M.K.T.

amgibuities that do not conform to these preferred syntactic configurations, as illustrated in the examples in (1):

1a. The horse raced past the barn fell.
1b. The woman warned the lawyer was misguided.

Structural preferences like these inspired a family of parsing models in which category-level structure guides the initial syntactic structuring of the linguistic input (for a review, see Tanenhaus & Trueswell, 1995). For example, in an influential proposal of this class, the two-stage, or "garden path" model, developed by Frazier and colleagues (Frazier & Rayner, 1982; Frazier, 1987), initial structure is assigned using only syntactic category information, and a small set of structurally defined parsing principles such as minimal attachment or late closure. Other information is used to evaluate, filter and, if necessary, revise the initial structure. Information excluded from initial consideration includes lexically specific syntactic and semantic information (e.g. information about the types of complements licensed by a verb and the semantic properties or thematic roles associated with these complements).[1] Evidence in support of these claims comes from numerous studies demonstrating increased processing difficulty in the form of elevated reading times when the structure that is ultimately correct is consistent with lexical constraints but inconsistent with category-based parsing principles (for reviews, see Frazier, 1987; Mitchell, 1989; Mitchell, Cuetos, Corley, & Brysbaert, 1995). Thus elevated reading times reflect syntactic misanalysis and the time it takes the reader to recover from the misanalysis.

More recently, however, a body of research has emerged demonstrating that lexically specific syntactic and semantic information, including the frequencies with which lexical items occur in different environments, can reduce, and sometimes eliminate, many strong structural preferences (for recent reviews, see MacDonald, Pearlmutter, & Seidenberg, 1994; Tanenhaus & Trueswell, 1995). For example, the sentences in (2) illustrate that, for both of the types of ambiguities in (1), there are sentences with the same structure, but with different lexical items, that are read with little or no processing difficulty (Garnsey et al., 1995; Trueswell, 1996; Trueswell, Tanenhaus, & Garnsey, 1994; Trueswell, Tanenhaus, & Kello, 1993).

2a. The land mine buried in the sand exploded.
2b. The woman said the idea was misguided.

Several classes of theoretical alternatives can be adopted to account for these lexical influences. One alternative is to retain a two-stage architecture

[1]Other two-stage models allow lexically based syntactic constraints to affect first-stage parsing, but still exclude non-syntactic lexical constraints and information such as frequency that is not incorporated into traditional grammars (e.g. Pritchett, 1992).

to capture clear cases of structural infuences. Lexical influences are then attributed to rapid revision effects (Frazier, 1989; Mitchell, 1989), with processing difficulty reflecting the time it takes to complete the revision. However, two-stage models do not have a principled way of accounting for why lexical influences are strong enough to completely mask putative first-stage effects in some syntactic environments but not others.

A second, more promising alternative is to treat structural and lexical influences as arising from a system that integrates constraints from independent levels of representation; for example, structural biases are couched in terms of sequences of categories (phrase structure rules) and lexical biases, including preferences for syntactic categories, argument structures, thematic structures, and so forth. A sensible first hypothesis is to assume that this information is combined in a probabilistic model. At each point in the sentence, the conditional probabilities of the possible continuations are computed. Processing load is then inversely related to the probability of occurrence of the actual sequence encountered; that is, low-probability sequences are relatively difficult to process.[2] Conditional probability models provide a theoretical basis for incorporating probabilistic lexical information into a model that uses syntactic rules. However, they do not provide insight into the systematic variation across contexts of the relative strengths of structural and lexical constraints. Standard conditional probability models also have a hybrid architecture in that they assume representations that are intrinsically discrete (e.g. rules in a symbolic system), and then impose probabilities on these rules. This begs important questions about how the representations in the system emerge during learning. These issues are closely related to the questions about how to define and combine information at different linguistic grains (cf. Mitchell et al., 1995).

This paper explores a third alternative, which we believe has the potential to provide revealing insights into both the nature of linguistic representations and the processing dynamics that operate on these representations. The basic idea following similar proposals by Elman (1993), Kawamoto (1993) and others is inspired by dynamical systems theory and representational ideas drawn from the connectionist learning literature. We assume that processing involves following a trajectory through a metric space, structured according to a similarity principle, such that words that are likely to lead to similar continuations are close to one another in representational space. Categorically distinct states of the language processor are associated with distinct *attractors*. Processing involves using the information provided

[2]Charniak (1993) reviews automatic parsing models along these lines; Jurafsky (1996) describes a conditional probability model which assigns preferences to ambiguous sequences that are broadly consistent with experimental results in the psycholinguistic literature.

by each successive word to place the processor somewhere in an attractor space and then letting it gravitate to whatever attractor manages to capture it. Successful parsing of each partial word sequence corresponds to arriving at, or getting very near, a single attractor (so there is no uncertainty about the current categorical status). The path followed by the trajectory through the attactors represents the syntactic structure of the sentence. Processing time is modelled as time taken to gravitate to such a state.

While this system can, in principle, be applied to both syntactic category ambiguities and attachment ambiguities, involving phrase-level structure, this paper will focus on syntactic category ambiguities. The hypothesis we are exploring is that category-based parsing preferences are embedded in representations that *emerge* within a constraint-based learning system because of similarities among lexical items in particular syntactic contexts (e.g. Juliano & Tanenhaus, 1994). The hypothesis is that an appropriate balance between lexcial and structural influences will arise as a result of (a) the nature of the lexical input, (b) the learning system that creates representations based on this input, and (c) the processing dynamics of the system.

The remainder of the paper is organised into six sections. First, we provide a brief introduction to some important constructs of dynamical systems theory, emphasising the theoretical constructs we apply to syntactic processing. The next section then presents three self-paced reading experiments that examine the interaction of contingent (i.e. conditional) frequencies at different linguistic grains to test some hypotheses derived from our approach. These experiments also serve as the empirical base for evaluating an implementation of our theory, which is presented in the following section. We implement the model with a dynamical system that uses representations developed by a recurrent neural network trained on word prediction (Elman, 1990, 1991) with inputs from small finite-state grammars. The penultimate section presents a model trained from a representative sample of a real corpus and uses it to model verb-specific variance in reading times for an experiment also reported in this section. The final section summarises our results and discusses the strengths and limitations of our models, as well as alternative approaches.

PARSING IN A DYNAMICAL SYSTEM

Dynamical systems theory is typically concerned with systems that change continuously with time (for good introductions, see Abraham & Shaw, 1984; Perko, 1991; Strogatz, 1994). Examples include: swinging pendulums; orbiting stars and planets; populations fluctuating in an ecosystem; gases swirling around in an atmosphere. It is useful to consider the trajectories of a dynamical system—that is, the paths it can follow as time progresses. In the case of the rigid-arm pendulum, some trajectories swing back and forth, others whirl around the circle, and two of them remain at one point indefinitely (hanging down and, improbably, balanced straight up). If the pendulum is damped, then all trajectories except those leading to the improbable state approach the low point-trajectory in the limit. Such a limiting trajectory is called an *attractor*. Those starting points from which the system gravitates towards a particular attractor A are collectively referred to as the *basin of attraction* of A. The basin of attraction of the pendulum's low attractor consists of every state except those that lead to the improbable state. In the case of a planetary system, each large mass is surrounded by its own basin of attraction. If a dynamical system is near one attractor and far from others, its behaviour is dominated by that attractor. By contrast, if the system is in a position intermediate between several attractors, it shows all of their influences simultaneously. We will refer to this property of attractors as the *local dominance* property. Local dominance is easy to understand intuitively in the case of a planetary system: A satellite near one large mass behaves, for all practical purposes, as though that mass is the only mass around, but a satellite roughly equidistant from several masses moves on a complex trajectory which reflects their simultaneous influences. We take advantage of the local dominance property of attractors to model the interaction of syntactic and lexical influences on sentence processing.

We hypothesise that categorically distinct states of the language processor are associated with distinct attractors in a metric space that is structured according to a similarity principle. Partial word sequences occupy nearby positions in the space if they are likely to have similar continuations. Processing involves using the information provided by each successive word to place the processor somewhere in an attractor space and then letting it gravitate to whatever attractor manages to capture it. Successful parsing of each partial word sequence corresponds to arriving at, or getting very near, a single attractor (so there is no uncertainty about the current categorical status). Processing time is modelled as the time taken to gravitate to such a state. The syntactic structure of the sentence can be represented by the succession of attractors that the processor visits during the processing of the sentence.

This similarity-based processor is closely related to a symbolic processor based on a grammar of the language. In particular, corresponding to each state, S[i], of the symbolic processor, there is a continuous (connected) region, R[i], in the metric space. Importantly, the use of regions instead of states allows the processor to be sensitive to quantitative distributional differences among elements belonging to the same lexical class. These differences give rise to small, within-region contrasts. For our current purposes, the most important property of the metric space representation is that syntactic category ambiguity is associated with *representational intermediacy*, as in Kawamoto's (1993) model of lexical ambiguity resolution. The following two examples help illustrate this point:

Example 1. Temporarily ambiguous word sequences give rise to intermediate representations. For instance, the sentence fragment *the insect examined* ... is ambiguous between a past-participle and a main verb interpretation of the verb *examined.* Thus the fragment's representation in the metric space is intermediate between, for example, the representation of *the insect knew* ... and the representation of *the insect known* ... If, as seems likely in this case, nouns like *insect* more often function as the object of verbs like *examined* in a corpus used to derive the representation, then the fragment *the insect examined* ... will be placed closer to the representation of *the insect known* ... than to the representation of *the insect knew* ... A noun with the opposite distributional tendency (e.g. *entomologist*) will have the opposite representational leaning.

Example 2. Grammatically unambiguous cases involving a mixture of signals can give rise to representational intermediacy. For example, *that person* ... will be placed in the metric space between *this person* ... and *that people* ... (as in *That people starve is unacceptable*) but closer to *this person* ... However, the possible continuations are consistent with only the Determiner + Singular Noun pattern (*this person* ...) and so the representational leaning in this direction is extremely strong, even though the presence of the word *that* in *that person* produces a bias in the direction of the sentential subject interpretation. This bias will influence the representation in a small way after the disambiguating word *person* has been encountered.

We can use the attractor mechanism to achieve an appropriate balance between structural and lexical influences in a variety of syntactic contexts. We hypothesise that in contexts in which lexical influences are robust, the processor lands in a range of intermediate positions between attractors, and thus takes different amounts of time to reach certainty, depending on which lexical items are involved. In such cases, lexical manipulations alone are expected to determine the state of the processor. Thus the model has a way of handling the sensitivity to lexical differences which two-stage models have trouble with. Moreover, in contexts where lexical effects are more subtle, we expect the processor to land close to a single attractor every time the context is encountered. In implementations of the model, we use a connectionist learning network trained from a corpus to generate processing locations and an explicit gravitational algorithm to measure gravitation time to an attractor.

The dynamical framework leads to a uniform treatment of frequency effects in parsing that is similar in spirit to recent attractor-based accounts of frequency and consistency effects in word recognition (e.g. Plaut, McClelland, Seidenberg, & Patterson, 1996), and of syntactic category shifts during language change (Tabor, 1994, 1995). Superficially contradictory effects of linguistic generalisations at different levels of traditional linguistic structure or *grains* (Mitchell et al., 1995) emerge as natural properties of the model. Moreover, many local processing difficulties that are typically attributed to syntactic misanalysis receive an alternative interpretation as *competition among attractors*, even when the processing system adopts the correct analysis. This competition account is consistent with claims made by many constraint-based models (e.g. Bates & MacWhinney, 1989; Hanna, Spivey-Knowlton, & Tanenhaus, 1996; MacDonald et al., 1994; Spivey-Knowlton, Trueswell & Tanenhaus, 1993; Spivey-Knowlton & Sedivy, 1995; Spivey-Knowlton & Tanenhaus, submitted; Tanenhaus & Trueswell, 1995).

CONTINGENT FREQUENCIES AND *THAT*

To evaluate the hypotheses introduced in the previous section, we explored a linguistic domain which seemed promising for observing emergent category effects and lexical-category interactions. The word *that* has several properties, making it a useful test case. *That* is ambiguous among multiple syntactic categories. For example, *that* can be a demonstrative determiner as in (3a), a complementiser as in (3b), a relative pronoun as in (3c), and a pronoun as in (3d). These category ambiguities can give rise to phrasal ambiguities, including the ambiguities in several structures that have figured prominently in the psycholinguistics literature.

3a. That experienced diplomat would be helpful to the lawyer.
3b. That experienced diplomats would be helpful made the lawyer confident.
3c. The experienced diplomat that the lawyer admired was helpful.
3d. The lawyer didn't believe the experienced diplomat said that.

We will focus exclusively on the ambiguity between *that* as a complementiser and *that* as a demonstrative determiner, an instance of a lexical category ambiguity that leads to phrasal ambiguity. When used as a demonstrative determiner, *that* introduces a noun phrase; when used as a complementiser, *that* introduces a sentence complement. This is illustrated in examples (3a) and (3b). In sentence (3a), *that experienced diplomat* is the subject noun phrase of a main clause, whereas in (3b), *that experienced diplomats* is the beginning of an extraposed sentence complement. The number of the noun disambiguates *that* as either a complementiser or a determiner. With a plural noun, *that* must be a complementiser because *that* is singular and demonstrative determiners have to agree in number with the noun they specify. With a singular noun, *that* must be a demonstrative because the head noun in a bare noun phrase (i.e. a noun phrase without a specifier) must be plural.

The relative frequency with which *that* is used as a complementiser and a determiner varies with syntactic environment. According to the Francis and Kučera (1982) counts based on the Brown corpus, *that* is used more frequently as a complementiser (70%) than as a demonstrative determiner (15%). However our analysis of the Brown corpus revealed that, at the beginning of a sentence, *that* is more often used as a determiner (35%) than as a complementiser (11%), whereas after a verb, *that* is more often used as a complementiser (93%) than as a determiner (6%). Note that the statistics associated with *that* run counter to the more general bias for a determiner that follows a verb to introduce an NP-object complement. In addition, when *that* follows a verb, an environment in which it is typically a complementiser, the subcategorisation properties of the verb determine whether a complementiser analysis is grammatical. *That* can only be used as a complementiser when it follows a verb permitting a sentence complement. This is illustrated by the examples in (4) using the verb *insisted*, which permits a sentence complement, and *visited*, which does not:

4a. Bill insisted that experienced lawyer would be helpful.
4b. Bill insisted that experienced lawyers would be helpful.
4c. Bill visited that experienced lawyer.
4d. *Bill visited that experienced lawyers.

Predictions from the Attractor Framework

In our dynamical systems model, different syntactic environments correspond to different regions of the representation space, and the local attractor configuration in each region reflects the context-dependent frequencies of occurrence of the different categorisations. Therefore, a reader's bias to interpret *that* as a complementiser versus a determiner should be influenced by contingent frequencies rather than just by simple lexical frequencies. In particular, when *that* is encountered at the beginning of a sentence, it will be affected by two attractors corresponding to the complementiser and determiner classifications. *That* will be placed closer to the *that*-(Det)-N attractor because "determiner" is the most common category at the beginning of a sentence, and *that* occurs more often as a determiner in this position. This should be reflected in a strong bias to process *that* as a determiner, a prediction that was tested in Experiment 1. *That* at the beginning of a sentence, where the determiner reading is more common, was compared with *that* after a verb, where the complementiser reading is more common.

A second prediction follows from the observation that the word *that* is nearly always a complementiser when it follows a verb—processing should be influenced by a strong *that-as-complementiser* attractor in this environment. This attractor should be strong enough to influence processing even when *that* follows a verb that does not permit a sentence complement. Experiment 2 tested this prediction by contrasting verbs like *insisted*, which strongly prefer to take a sentence complement (SC-bias verbs), with verbs like *visited*, which do not permit a sentence complement and typically occur with an NP complement (NP-bias verbs).

Attractor effects that are analogous to those seen for lexical category ambiguities should also be observed for phrasal ambiguities. *The*, and other determiners, typically introduce an NP-object complement when they follow a verb. This should result in a strong *NP-Det-object* attractor. Verbs that typically take sentence complements should form an *Sbar-complement* attractor. However, the NP-object attractor should still influence the processing of *the* when it follows an SC-bias verb. This prediction was tested in Experiment 3.

Experiment 1: Contingent Frequency Versus Simple Lexical Frequency

This experiment examined the ambiguity between *that* as a complementiser (e.g. The lawyer said *that* cheap hotels would be safe) and *that* as a demonstrative determiner (e.g. The lawyer said *that* cheap hotel would be safe). Reading times to *that*-adjective-noun sequences when they occurred at the beginning of a sentence were compared to when they followed an SC-bias verb. The number on the noun disambiguated *that* as a complementiser or a determiner. A plural noun disambiguates *that* as a complementiser because demonstrative determiners must agree in number with the noun they specify, and *that* is a singular demonstrative. A singular noun disambiguates *that* as a demonstrative because the head noun in a noun phrase without a specifier (i.e. a bare noun phrase) must be plural. Sample materials are presented in (5):

5a. The lawyer insisted that cheap hotel was clean and comfortable.
5b. The lawyer insisted that cheap hotels were clean and comfortable.
5c. That cheap hotel was clean and comfortable to our surprise.
5d. That cheap hotels were clean and comfortable surprised us.

Reading times to the noun and the words immediately following should be shorter when the number of the noun is congruent with the syntactic category that the reader has assigned to *that*. When *that* is interpreted as a complementiser, reading times should be shorter after a plural noun compared to after a singular noun. The opposite pattern should be observed when *that* is interpreted as a demonstrative. Crucially, the preferred resolution of *that* should interact with syntactic environment. In sentence-initial position, where *that* is more typically used as a determiner, reading times should be shorter after a singular noun compared to a plural noun. After a verb, where *that* is more typically used as a complementiser, reading times should be shorter following a plural noun compared to a singular noun.

Method

Participants. Thirty-six students from the University of Rochester participated for course credit. All were native speakers of English.

Materials. Four sentences were constructed for each of 20 *that* + adjective + noun sequences, by varying two properties of the sentences: (1) the noun was either singular or plural, disambiguating *that* as a demonstrative or as a complementiser, respectively, and (2) the *that*-phrase either came at the beginning of the sentence or it followed a verb. In this experiment, the test sentences used only verbs that typically occur with sentence complements, and rarely, if ever, permit a noun phrase complement. Verb-type is varied in subsequent experiments.

Each trial consisted of two sentences, with the second sentence being a natural continuation of the first. On critical trials, the target sentence was always the first sentence in the trial. Four lists were constructed by assigning each of the four sentences created from a particular *that* + adjective + noun sequence to a different list. The target sentences were pseudo-randomly combined with 42 distractor trials, for a total of 62 trials in each list. At least one filler trial appeared before each experimental trial, and conditions were balanced across the two halves of the stimulus lists.

Procedure. Stimuli were presented one word at a time using a moving window presentation format (Just, Carpenter, & Woolley, 1982) on a PC computer equipped with a Digitry CTS timing board and response box. Each trial began when the subject pressed the START button on the response box, causing the entire text to be displayed with each alpha-numeric character replaced by a dash(–), with normal spacing and punctuation. The participants controlled the word-by-word presentation of the stimuli by pressing the SCROLL button on the response box. Each button press caused the next word of the text to appear and the previous word to be replaced by dashes. Comprehension questions followed the sentences on approximately one-quarter of the trials. Participants responded by pressing YES or NO on the response box and then received feedback as to whether the answer was correct. Participants were instructed to read at a normal pace and carefully enough to answer the questions correctly. The experiment began with seven practice trials and lasted approximately 35 min.

Results and Discussion

Data from two participants who answered fewer than 80% of the questions correctly were replaced with data from additional participants. Mean reading times beginning with *that* and continuing through the auxiliary verb (e.g. *that cheap hotels is/are*) are presented in Table 1. Figure 1 plots the difference in reading times when the singular noun condition is subtracted from the plural noun condition. A positive difference indicates that readers were predominantly influenced by the *that*(Det)-N hypothesis, and a negative difference indicates that readers were predominantly influenced by the *that-as-complementiser* possibility. The word after the noun clearly shows the interaction predicted by the contingent frequency hypothesis: For sentences with an initial *that*, reading times were longer following a plural noun compared to a singular noun, whereas the opposite pattern held when *that* followed a verb.

We performed separate analyses of variance on participant and item reading time means. The factors were list (four lists) or item group (four groups), sentence type (verb followed by *that* or initial-*that*), noun type (singular or plural) and word position (*that*, adjective, noun and auxiliary verb).

The analysis revealed a three-way interaction among sentence type, noun type and word position [$F_1(4,128) = 6.02$, $P < 0.01$; $F_2(4,64) = 9.08$, $P < 0.01$]. The triple interaction is largely due to reading times to the word after the disambiguating noun (the auxiliary verb). At this position, there was an interaction between the number of the noun (noun type) and sentence type [$F_1(1,32) = 18.06$, $P < 0.01$; $F_2(1,16) = 5.86$, $P < 0.05$]. When *that* followed a verb, reading times at the auxiliary verb were longer in the singular noun condition compared to the plural noun condition, though this effect was only reliable by participants [$F_1(1,32) = 6.24$, $P < 0.05$; $F_2(1,16) = 3.04$, $P = 0.10$], indicating that readers initially assumed *that* was a complementiser. The opposite pattern occurred for sentences beginning with *that*. Reading times following the singular noun were shorter than those

TABLE 1
Mean Reading Times (msec) at Specified Word Positions in Experiment 1

	Sentence Region			
Condition	*that*	*cheap*	*hotel(s)*	*is/are*
Post-verb-*that*				
Sg. noun	414	453	484	492
Pl. noun	409	470	479	433
Initial-*that*				
Sg. noun	399	456	454	438
Pl. noun	381	461	479	563

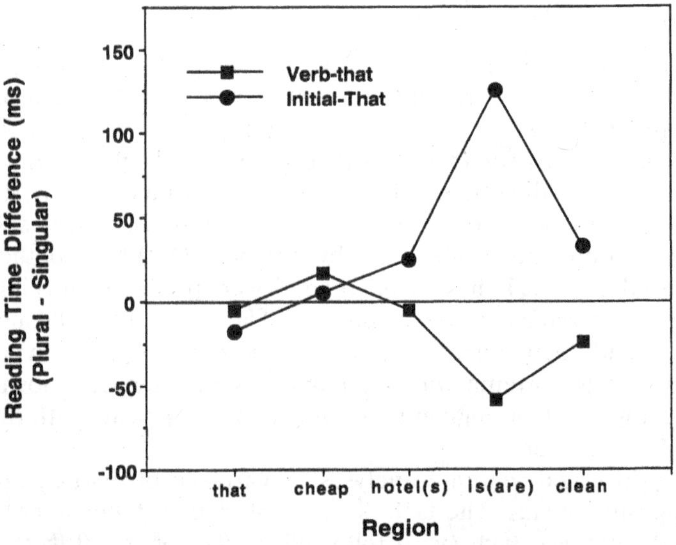

FIG. 1. Reading time differences between the plural and singular conditions in Experiment 1 for the region following the word *that* when it began a sentence (Initial-That) and when it followed the main verb (Verb-that).

after the plural noun [$F_1(1,32) = 22.28, P < 0.01$; $F_2(1,16) = 19.26, P < 0.01$], indicating that readers initially interpreted *that* as a demonstrative determiner.

These results document the importance of conditional frequency information in language processing. Whereas the absolute probabilities of syntactically ambiguous words are clearly not reliable predictors of processing difficulty across all syntactic environments, grammar-derived conditional probabilities may well be (Jurafsky, 1996). Two-stage models are capable of predicting this general situation because they hold that different sequences of syntactic categories give rise to different first-pass parsing strategies. These results indicate, however, that the choice of the default parse is predictable from statistical properties of the data people learn their language from, rather than from structural principles such as minimal attachment or late closure (Mitchell et al., 1995). Moreover, while a structural simplicity principle such as minimal attachment correctly predicts that a sentence-initial *that*–adjective sequence will be parsed as the beginning of an NP, rather than as a fronted *that* complement, it incorrectly makes the same prediction when a *that*–adjective sequence follows a verb. In the attractor model, statistical differences automatically give rise to different parsing preferences because, in every environment, the most common pattern is associated with the most powerful local attractor.

The statistically based attractor-model is also capable of predicting effects that look very much like structural complexity effects in cases where initial hypotheses need to be revised. Recall that the congruity effect (the difference in reading times when *that* was resolved in its preferred and unpreferred categories) in the initial-*that* condition was about twice the size of the congruity effect in the verb-*that* condition (140 *vs* 65 msec), even though the frequency asymmetry between the more frequent and less frequent reading was larger in the verb-*that* condition (93% complementiser *vs* 6% determiner) compared to the initial-*that* condition (35% determiner *vs* 11% complementiser).

In a symbolic parser, this asymmetry can be explained by taking into account the magnitude of the revision required in each condition. When an initial *that* which was originally taken to be a determiner has to be reanalysed as a complementiser, the noun phrase itself must be reanalysed as the subject of a subordinate clause. In contrast, reanalysis of *that* after a verb from a complementiser to a demonstrative does not affect the overall clause structure. In the attractor model, the asymmetry arises because a big structural revision requires the model to make a large jump across the representation space. This has the effect of it landing in an intermediate location that is relatively far from the nearest attractor, thereby increasing processing time. Later we show the details of how this result obtains in our implemented model.[3]

Experiment 2: Category-contingent Versus Verb-specific Contingent Frequencies

This experiment examined *that* when it followed a verb, comparing NP-bias verbs such as *visit* that do not permit a sentence complement with SC-bias verbs such as *insisted* that are typically used with a sentence complement and do not permit an NP complement. We predicted that the strong category-bias for *that* following a verb to be a complementiser would create a strong attractor that would make processing *that* as a determiner difficult, even when it followed an NP complement verb.

[3]It is possible that there is another reason for the difference in effect-size observed here: the sentential subject construction may be restricted to a relatively erudite speaking/writing style and thus may not occur as frequently in language samples from which typical speakers learn as it does in the Brown corpus, which we have used to estimate relative frequencies. If this is the case, our model will still make the appropriate effect-size prediction if trained on a more natural corpus. But the size difference would then be due simply to a difference in the relative strengths of the complementiser attractor and the determiner attractor, rather than to the revision-difficulty effect just described. It is our suspicion that whatever the natural frequency relationships are, the revision-difficulty effect contributes to the high latency, therefore we have felt it worthwhile to explain how our model captures such effects.

Method

Paricipants. Twenty-eight students from the University of Rochester participated for course credit. All were native speakers of English.

Materials. Four sentences were constructed for each of 20 adjective + noun sequences. Examples using *cheap hotel(s)* are presented in (6):

6a. The lawyer insisted that cheap hotel was clean and comfortable.
6b. The lawyer insisted that cheap hotels were clean and comfortable.
6c. The lawyer visited that cheap hotel to stay for the night.
6d. The lawyer visited those cheap hotels to stay for the night.

Each trial consisted of two sentences, with the second sentence being a natural continuation of the first. On critical trials, the target sentence was always the first sentence in the trial. For the sentence complement verbs, the verb was followed by *that*, an adjective, and then either a singular noun, which disambiguates *that* as a demonstrative in a *that*-less S-complement, or a plural noun, which disambiguates *that* as a complementiser. For the NP-bias verbs, the verb was either followed by *that*, an adjective and a singular noun, disambiguating *that* as a demonstrative, or by *those* followed by an adjective and a plural noun. *Those* was included as a referent-presupposing control. It could be argued that processing difficulty at *that* after an NP-bias verb reflects the fact that it is odd to use a definite determiner without first having introduced a referent. We used the plural *those* rather than the singular *this* as the control because in colloquial speech *this* is often used to introduce a referent despite its definiteness (e.g. *This guy walked in and ordered whiskey*).

Four lists were constructed by assigning each of the four sentences created from a particular adjective + noun sequence to a different list. The target sentences were pseudo-randomly combined with 42 distractor trials, for a total of 62 trials in each list. At least one filler trial appeared before each experimental trial, and conditions were balanced across the two halves of the stimulus lists.

Procedure. The procedure was the same as in Experiment 1.

Results and Discussion

Data from two participants who answered fewer than 80% of the questions correctly were replaced with data from additional participants. Mean reading times beginning with *that* and continuing through the two words that followed the noun (e.g. *that cheap hotels is/are clean*) are presented in Fig. 2.

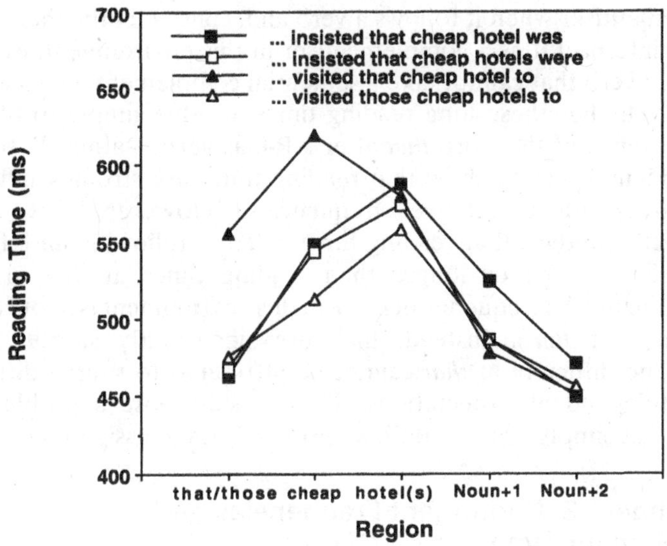

FIG. 2. Mean reading times following NP-bias and SC-bias verbs in Experiment 2.

The results can be understood most clearly by considering the NP-bias verbs and the SC-bias verbs separately. For the NP-bias verbs, reading times were considerably longer to *that* than to *those* at the determiner (*that* or *those*) [$F_1(1,24) = 5.31$, $P < 0.05$; $F_2(1,16) = 5.80$, $P < 0.05$] and at the following adjective [$F_1(1,24) = 23.59$, $P < 0.01$; $F_2(1,16) = 8.12$, $P < 0.05$]. Thus readers had difficulty processing *that* as a demonstrative, demonstrating effects of both the category-level bias and the subcategorisation properties of the specific verb (i.e. *that* after a verb is usually a complementiser and these verbs cannot take a complementiser). The results for the sentence complement verbs replicated those found in Experiment 1. Readers initially interpreted *that* as a complementiser rather than as a demonstrative determiner. Reading times after a singular noun (e.g. at *was*) were longer compared to reading times after a plural noun (e.g. at *were*) [$F_1(1,24) = 4.03$, $P = 0.056$; $F_2(1,16) = 5.16$, $P < 0.03$].

The prediction that reading times to *that* would be longer when it followed an NP-bias verb compared to when it followed an SC-bias verb was clearly confirmed. Reading times at *that* and at the following adjective were clearly longer after an NP-bias verb than after an SC-bias verb [$F_1(1,24) = 8.0$, $P = 0.01$; $F_2(1,16) = 6.15$, $P < 0.03$ at *that*; and $F_1(1,24) = 8.77$, $P < 0.01$; $F_2(1,16) = 2.98$, $P = 0.1$ at the adjective].

The results demonstrated a robust category contingent effect that was not eliminated by verb-specific subcategorisation information. *That* is typically a complementiser when it follows a verb and, consequently, there is a strong bias to interpret it as a complementiser in this environment, even when it follows a verb that cannot take a sentential complement. One could ask, of course, whether these long reading times are due simply to the low rate of occurrence of the word *that* after NP-bias verbs—after all, the point of Experiment 1 was to show that reading times are strongly influenced by context-dependent relative frequencies. However, this hypothesis incorrectly predicts that reading times at *those* following an NP-bias verb would be as long or longer than reading times at *that* in the same environment (the frequency of *those* in this environment is about 30% of the frequency of *that*). Instead, they are significantly shorter. Thus the processing difficulty at *that* cannot be attributed to simple differences in context-dependent expectations. These results pose a problem for any model that simply uses conditional probabilities to assign reading times.[4]

Experiment 3: Contingent Frequencies and Complement Type

The goal of this experiment was to determine whether contingent frequencies also influence phrasal ambiguity resolution. In addition to replicating the NP-bias verb followed by *that* and the SC-bias verb followed by *that* conditions from Experiment 2, we included conditions in which a noun phrase with the determiner *the* (*the*-adjective-noun) followed either an NP-bias or an SC-bias verb.

It is well-established that readers have a strong bias to parse a noun phrase after an NP-V sequence in a main clause as an NP object complement, as in (7a), rather than as the subject of a sentence complement, as in (7b). This bias is reflected in long reading times when the reader encounters the disambiguating verb phrase in a *that*-less sentence complement [e.g. *would cause* in (7b)], which disambiguates the preceding NP (*the angry man*) as the subject of the sentence complement rather than the object of the verb *warned*.

7a. John warned the man about the cheap hotel.
7b. John warned the angry man would cause trouble.
7c. John insisted the angry man would cause trouble.

Now, consider sentence (7c), in which a *that*-less sentence complement follows an SC-bias verb. A number of recent studies have found that readers have little or no processing difficulty at the verb phrase in the complement (Garnsey et al., 1995; Schmauder & Egan, 1995; Trueswell et al., 1993; but cf.

[4]N-gram models (e.g. Brown et al., 1992) and grammar-based conditional probability models (e.g. Jurafsky, 1996) are roughly of this sort.

Ferreira & Henderson, 1990). However, some of these studies have reported increased reading times at the noun phrase (e.g. *the angry man*) compared to noun phrase complements with a *that*, or noun phrases after NP-biased verbs. In a two-stage model, these effects at the NP would be interpreted as rapid revision effects in a system that initially ignores lexically specific structure. However, in an attractor-based system, this difficulty reflects the joint effect of two attractors: the Verb-NP-Det attractor and the Verb-S-Comp-*that* attractor. Thus it is another case of representational intermediacy, due to competing attractors.

Method

Participants. Twenty-eight students from the Univesity of Rochester participated for course credit. All were native speakers of English.

Materials and Procedure. Four sentences were constructed for each of 20 adjective + noun sequences. Examples are presented in (8):

8a. The lawyer insisted that cheap hotel was clean and comfortable.
8b. The lawyer insisted the cheap hotel was clean and comfortable.
8c. The lawyer visited that cheap hotel to stay for the night.
8d. The lawyer visited the cheap hotel to stay for the night.

The fillers, counterbalancing procedure and the experimental procedure were the same as those used in Experiment 2.

Results and Discussion

Data from four participants who answered fewer than 80% of the questions correctly were replaced with data from additional participants. Mean reading times beginning with *that* or *the* and continuing through the two words that followed the noun (e.g. *that cheap hotel is clean*) are presented in Fig. 3.

There was a three-way interaction between the type of verb (SC-bias or NP-bias), type of determiner (*that* or *the*) and the position of the word [$F_1(3,72) = 4.50$, $P < 0.01$; $F_2(5,80) = 4.32$, $P < 0.01$]. This result can be understood most clearly by considering several crucial comparisons. Reading times following *that* were again longer following NP-bias verbs than SC-bias verbs, replicating the pattern found in Experiment 2. In this experiment, however, the effect did not show up until the adjective [$F_1(1,24) = 9.84$, $P < 0.01$; $F_2(1,16) = 18.25$, $P < 0.01$].

Reading times were longer at the (singular) noun after an SC-bias verb with a *that* compared to an SC-bias verb with a *the* [$F_1(1,24) = 6.89$, $P < 0.02$; $F_2(1,16) = 4.10$, $P = 0.06$], and at the auxiliary verb [$F_1(1,24) = 6.55$, $P < 0.02$; $F_2(1,16) = 16.22$, $P < 0.01$]. This result indicates that readers had a

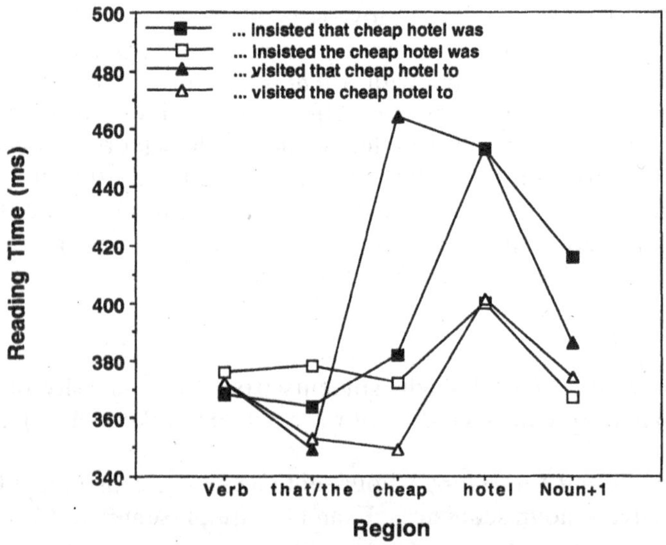

FIG. 3. Mean reading times following NP-bias and SC-bias verbs in Experiment 3.

bias to interpret *that* as a demonstrative until they encountered the singular noun, replicating the result found in Experiment 1. The full timecourse of the *that* effect following NP-bias verbs can be seen by comparing the NP-bias *that* and the NP-bias *the* conditions. Reading times in these conditions diverge at the adjective and converge after the noun.

Reading times were 25 msec longer at the determiner following SC-bias verbs than NP-bias verbs [$F_1(1,24) = 5.53$, $P < 0.05$; $F_2(1,16) = 2.23$, $P = 0.15$], and 20 msec longer at the adjective [$F_1(1,16) = 3.06$, $P < 0.10$; $F_2(1,16) = 2.23$, $P = 0.19$]. Although these results are only marginally reliable, a similar pattern was reported by Trueswell et al. (1993) and Garnsey et al. (1995). Furthermore, Experiment 4 replicates this effect with a larger sample of verbs, as will be seen later. The reason for the high variability across items will become clearer once we begin to explore the details of the attractors for this environment constructed by our simulations.

In sum, the results of this experiment further illustrate the interactions among attractors that we observed in Experiment 2. Reading times were again longer in the *that* condition following NP-bias verbs than SC-bias verbs, replicating the effect observed in Experiment 2. In addition, reading times were longer at *the* and the following adjective after SC-bias verbs compared to NP-bias verbs. While this effect was quite small, it was predicted to arise from competition between the NP-Det-object attractor and the Sbar-comp attractor at *the*. NP-bias verbs followed by *the* are easy to process because all the evidence favours placing the processor near the NP-object attractor. But in cases where an SC-bias verb is followed by *the*, the evidence from the verb favours the sentence complement attractor and the evidence from the word *the* favours the NP-object attractor. Again, the processor ends up in an intermediate position, far from both attractors, and thus gravitation time is high. In the next section, we diagram the attractors and show the relevant intermediate locations in our implemented model.

Summary of Contingent Frequency Effects

Four contingent (conditional) frequency results emerged from Experiments 1–3:

1. *That* at the beginning of a sentence was initially taken to be a demonstrative determiner, whereas *that* after a verb was taken to be a complementiser. These biases reflect the contingent frequencies in the language, as determined by corpus analyses, and were interpreted as being due to the relative strength of the *that*-complement and *that*-Det attractors in the two environments.
2. The difficulty of revising the interpretation of a sentence-initial *that* from a determiner to a complementiser was greater than revising the interpretation of a post-verbal *that* from a complementiser to a determiner. We hypothesised that this asymmetry arises because bigger structural revisions generally require the model to make large jumps across the representation space, resulting in it landing in an intermediate location that is relatively far from the nearest attractor.
3. Readers experienced processing difficulty when *that* followed a verb that did not permit a complementiser. Thus the category-based bias for *that* as a complementiser when it followed a verb still exerted large effects even when it ran counter to unambiguous verb-specific information. This was hypothesised to be a result of the strong effects of a *that*-complement attractor after a verb.
4. There was a bias to parse an NP beginning with the determiner *the* following a verb as an NP complement. This bias caused processing difficulty for NPs that followed even those verbs that nearly always occur with sentence complements. These effects were attributed to the strength of the NP-Det-object attractor.

It is important to note that the contingent frequency effects that are hypothesised to arise from the influences of attractors cut across different linguistic levels or grains. For example, results 1 and 3 show that in resolving a lexical category ambiguity, the processing system is sensitive to category-contingent frequencies. Result 4 shows that phrasal ambiguities are also sensitive to contingent frequencies.

IMPLEMENTING A DYNAMICAL SYSTEM

We earlier outlined how concepts from dynamical systems theory can be used to model the general correlation between ambiguity and increases in reading times. The central observation was that a dynamical system is dominated by the properties of a single attractor when it is sufficiently near to it, but it can show the simultaneous influences of several attractors when it is in a more intermediate location. This motivated letting attractors correspond to syntactic categorisations and letting different cases of lexical items in context vary according to whether they put a dynamical processing system close to one attractor or intermediate between several. We now describe an explicit model implementing these ideas and show how the model generates the pattern of the reading time results presented in Experiments 1–3.

Implementation

Implementing the model requires: (1) creating a similarity-based representational space with appropriate attractors that places the input somewhere in the representational space, and (2) implementing an algorithm that maps the attractor dynamics onto reading time.

The representational foundation of our dynamical model is its similarity-based representation space. We define a *visitation set* to be a set of points in the representation space visited by the processor while it processes a large corpus approximating natural usage.

Network Architecture

To create empirically testable representation spaces and visitation sets, we used the augmented simple recurrent network shown in Fig. 4. This network has exactly the same relaxation dynamics as the architecture of Elman's (1990, 1991) syntactic structure experiments, in which there was only one copy of the hidden layer. But there is a slight difference with Elman's device in the learning: at each time step, error signals from all pairs of successive hidden layers are added to the error signal under backpropagation. This is the technique known as "backpropagation through time" described in Rumelhart, Hinton and Williams (1986) and Pearlmutter (1995), with the proviso that only three prior time steps of hidden unit activation were taken into account. Summing error signals over three pairs

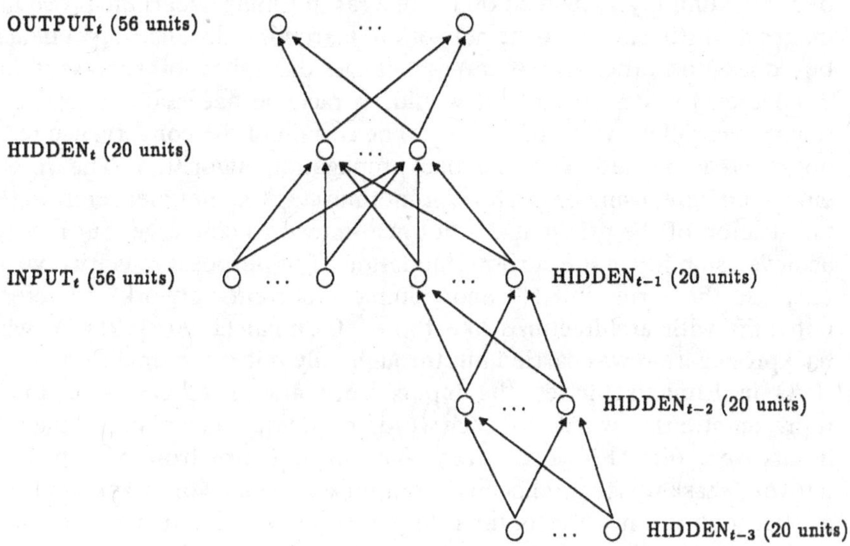

Activation functions:

Hidden layer t:

$$f(\text{net}_i) = \frac{1}{1 + e^{\text{net}_i}}$$

Hidden layers $t-1, t-2, t-3$:

The activation pattern on hidden layer $l-1$ is the same as the activation pattern that appeared on hidden layer l when the previous input was presented (for $l \in \{t, t-1, t-2\}$).

Output units:

$$f(\text{net}_i) = \frac{e^{\text{net}_i}}{\Sigma_k \, e^{\text{net}_k}}$$

where k ranges over output units and

$$\text{net}_i = b_i + \sum_j w_{ij} a_j$$

where b_i is the bias on unit i, a_j is the activation of unit j, and w_{ij} is the weight from unit j to unit i.

Cost function:

$$C = \sum_k t_k ln \, a_k$$

where k indexes output units, a_k is the activation of unit k, and t_k is the target for unit k. The weights were adjusted every time a new word was presented to the network.

FIG. 4. The recurrent connectionist network that forms the core of the attractor-based model.

of hidden unit layers instead of just one (as in Elman's learning procedure) makes it a little easier for the network to learn long-distance dependencies, but does not otherwise seem to change the types of representations discovered by the network. It would, in fact, be necessary to sum error signals over all previous time steps to be certain of the convergence results normally associated with the backpropagation algorithm. The method employed here, using only a few recent time steps, sometimes referred to as "truncation of the gradient", is not guaranteed to converge, but it always achieved stability in the current simulations. For purposes of clarity, we will only use the terms "SRN" and "simple recurrent network" to refer to networks with architectures like those of Elman (1990, 1991), in which backpropagation was carried out through only one prior time step.

As in Elman's model, the inputs were always taken to be localist representations of words: for each word, one unique bit was on, all the other inputs were off. The words were taken in sequence from a corpus. The network's task was to predict on the output layer what word was coming next at each point. Since the optimal target outputs under this set-up form a probability distribution, the output units employed the softmax activation function. The hidden units employed the fixed sigmoid activation function. The weights of the network were adjusted by backpropagation of the error signal through the network for the feedforward connections and through time for the recurrent connections (see Rumelhart et al., 1986). In the three simulations described below, we used the approximation of the error gradient that resulted from truncating the recurrent backpropagation after a fixed number of time steps (see Pearlmuter, 1995, for a discussion).

To generate training data for the models described in this section, we used probabilistic finite-state grammars which approximated those properties of English that were relevant in each experiment. We trained the network model on the output of the grammar until it seemed qualitatively to have learned all the distinctions encoded by the grammar and its average error had come near an asymptote.

The Dynamical Processor

We used the network to define a dynamical system for sentence processing. First, we created a visitation set by using the training grammar to generate a sample corpus of n words, feeding this corpus to the network with learning turned off, and recording the set of n hidden unit locations visited during the presentation of the sample. We interpreted this set of n points as a set of fixed bodies, all of equal mass, at locations $\vec{x}_1 \ldots \vec{x}_n$, and defined the following dynamical behaviour for a movable test body at any point, $\vec{x}$, in the space:

$$\frac{d\vec{x}}{dt} = m \sum_{i=1}^{n} \frac{(\vec{x}_i - \vec{x})}{r_i^p}$$

where r is the length of $(\vec{x}_i - \vec{x})$ and m is the mass of each fixed body.

The position of the movable test body at any time corresponds to the state of the processor. Each time the system gets a new word, the test body is placed in a new starting position in the representation space and it must gravitate to an attractor before the next word can be processed. When $p = 2$, this system is like a Newtonian gravitational system with a test body of mass 1 and velocity equal to 0 at infinite distance from the origin. The value of m determines how quickly the system travels along its trajectories, but varying it over the positive real numbers does not qualitatively affect the behaviour of the system. The value of n does affect the behaviour of the system in the sense that if one samples the space too sparsely, then the cluster structure does not reflect the structure of the grammar. It seemed to be necessary to set n to a higher value in the simulation of Experiment 1 than in the simulation of Experiments 2 and 3. We do not know why this is at present. The value of p determines the number of attractors in the system: if $p = 0$, then the system has only one attractor located at the centre of mass of all the fixed bodies; if p is greater than 0, there are multiple attractors, one at each fixed body, and there is a complex network of saddle points located at the centres of masses of dense clusters.[5] The implemented system (see below) is sensitive to the value of p in an important way and so we had to tune this parameter carefully.

To implement this dynamical system in a practical fashion, we made several simplifications. The attractors defined by equation (1) are singular points—the velocity of the test body goes to infinity at them and gets very large near them. To smooth out these singularities, we replaced r with r_{min} whenever r was less than r_{min}.[6] This put a cap on the influence that any one fixed body could have on the test body. It also had the effect of transforming the saddle points at cluster means into attractors. Thus attractors corresponded to behaviours that were classified as similar by the SRN. Note, however, that "cluster" and "classified as similar" are not precise terms. Indeed, the configuration of attractors in this implemented system varied as the value of p was changed. Crudely speaking, a smaller value of p implies fewer attractors and a larger value of p implies more attractors. We should note the relationship between p and the number of attractors is non-linear and there are ranges in which changing the value of p has no effect on the

[5]Saddle points are fixed points which attract trajectories from some regions of the space and repel them into others.

[6]This is roughly like assuming that the test body can never get any closer to a fixed body than r_{min}, although it does not treat the complex interactions at close range of bodies composed of real matter.

topology of the system. In other words, this variation is typical of bifurcation profiles in complex dynamical systems (see Strogatz, 1994, for an introduction).

The exponent p can thus be viewed as a "grain size" parameter, related to the grain size discussed by Mitchell et al. (1995). We adjusted this parameter in each simulation to make the set of attractors line up nearly perfectly with the set of states distinguished by the grammar. This important flexibility reveals a certain stipulativeness of the model, but it is significant that the correspondence was near perfect in the two simulations in which the states distinguished by the grammar were easily identified [the simulations of Experiments 1 and (2 and 3)], since there are many computation systems which the network + gravitation model cannot emulate no matter what value of p is used. With p set to achieve this near perfect line-up, we nevertheless saw influences of constraints at different traditional grains (lexical and phrasal), so the model achieved the desirable result of letting these levels interact without losing predictive power.

We used the simplest integration technique (i.e. Euler's method) to find approximations of the system's trajectories: take the change in the system's state at x to be $\Delta t(d\vec{x}/dt)$ for Δt, a small positive constant.[7] For simplicity, we fold the two proportionality constants, m and Δt, into one, $\mu = m\Delta t$ in the remaining discussion. The revised system is shown in equation (2):

$$\Delta\vec{x} = \mu \sum_{i=1}^{n} \frac{(\vec{x}_i - \vec{x})}{r_i^p}$$

Since the attractors of this system can be either complex cycles or stable fixed points, we detected them by looking for places where either the trajectory changed direction by more than 90° in one time step or where the velocity slowed to below a small value.[8] To model reading times for a sentence S consisting of words $w_i, w_2, \ldots, w_k$, we presented S one word at a time to the RCN and recorded the hidden unit locations $\vec{h}_1, \vec{h}_2, \ldots, \vec{h}_k$ associated with each word presentation. The predicted reading time at word w_k was then taken to be the number of time steps it took the system described in equation (2) to gravitate from $\vec{h}_k$ to an attractor.

Simulation of Experiment 1

We now describe a simulation of the central results of Experiment 1.

[7]We chose not to use a more exact integration technique like 4th order Runge-Kutta because such a method was, computationally, extremely costly and seemed to make little difference in the outcomes that concern us here.

[8]It turned out to work well to use r_{min} as this small value.

TABLE 2
Corpus-generating Grammar for Experiment 1 Simulation

0.90	S : Det[sg] N[sg] VP[sg] p
0.10	S : that N[pl] V[0][pl] V[AdjP][sg] AdjP p
0.60	VP[sg] : V[0][sg]
0.30	VP[sg] : V[S′][sg] that N[pl] V[0][pl]
0.10	VP[sg] : V[S′][sg] Det[sg] N[sg] V[0][sg]
[Zipf]	V[0][sg] : 0.44 sings, 0.22 stops, 0.14 talks, 0.11 whistles, 0.09 leaps
[Zipf]	V[0][pl] : 0.44 sing, 0.22 stop, 0.14 talk, 0.11 whistle, 0.09 leap
[Zipf]	V[S′][sg] : 0.34 thinks, 0.17 agrees, 0.11 insists, 0.09 wishes, 0.07 hopes, 0.06 remarks, 0.05 pleads, 0.04 speculates, 0.04 doubts, 0.03 hints
[Zipf]	V[AdjP][sg] : 0.44 is, 0.22 seems, 0.14 looks, 0.11 sounds, 0.09 becomes
[Zipf]	AdjP : 0.44 funny, 0.22 strange, 0.14 good, 0.11 tolerable, 0.09 surprising
[Zipf]	Det[sg] : 0.44 the, 0.22 that, 0.14 a, 0.11 this, 0.09 one
[Zipf]	N[sg] : 0.34 woman, 0.17 man, 0.11 dog, 0.09 cat, 0.07 marmot, 0.06 girl, 0.05 boy, 0.04 artist, 0.04 journalist, 0.03 sailor
[Zipf]	N[pl] : 0.34 women, 0.17 men, 0.11 dogs, 0.09 cats, 0.07 marmots, 0.06 girls, 0.05 boys, 0.04 artists, 0.04 journalists, 0.03 sailors

Training the Network

The grammar used in the simulation of Experiment 1 is shown in Table 2. The grammar generated the word *that* in the four different kinds of environments that were the focus of Experiment 1: determiner versus complementiser in sentence-initial position and determiner versus complementiser in post-verbal position. The relative frequencies within these environments did not correspond directly to estimates of frequencies in natural usage, but they were biased in the same direction relative to 50% (see Table 3). We chose simulation values that were less extreme than the corpus values to facilitate training the network. Later, we explore a network trained from an actual natural language corpus with more representative frequencies.

The relative frequencies of different lexical items within classes were set according to "Zipf's Law", which holds that a rank versus frequency plot of

TABLE 3
Comparison of Relative Frequencies in the Brown Corpus and Simulation 1 Grammar (Brown Corpus Statistics from the Penn Treebank)

Type of that	*Brown Corpus*	*Simulation Grammar*
Sentence-initial compl. *vs* det.	25%	34%
Post-verbal compl. *vs* det.	96%	93%

the vocabulary elements drawn from any large natural language corpus forms the cusp of a hyperbola (Zipf, 1949).[9] The law has been confirmed by Zipf and his successors as a fair approximation for numerous corpora in a wide range of languages. We have also observed that it gives a reasonable approximation within several of the main lexical categories in the Brown corpus (e.g. noun, verb, adjective, adverb, determiner) and therefore used it to assign frequencies to lexical items in the grammar.[10]

In the grammar used for simulating Experiment 1, there was a perfect correlation between whether *that* was used as a complementiser or determiner and whether it was followed by a plural noun or a singular noun. Thus the grammar generated sentences like *That dogs bark is undeniable* and *Josiah knows that dogs bark*, and sentences like *That dog barks* and *Josiah knows that dog barks*. However, it never generated sentences of the form *That a dog barks is undeniable* or *Josiah knows that a dog barks*. We decided not to include the latter types of sentences because recurrent networks have difficulty learning long-distance dependencies, without special training procedures (e.g. Elman, 1993). Creating a categorical relationship between the syntactic category of *that* and the number of the subsequent noun made it easier for the network to learn the long-distance dependency between the way *that* is used locally and the type of environment its clause occurs in. These unrealistic assumptions about the corpus may introduce some biases in the simulation which distort its correlation with the reading time data (i.e. the network gets unequivocal evidence that sentence initial *that* is a complementiser when it encounters a plural noun, whereas people do not). However, this distortion should not interfere with the expected effect of frequency contrasts on reading times.

Reading Time Predictions

To train the network for Experiment 1, we generated sentences at random using the Experiment 1 grammar and fed them to the network one word at a time. Thus there was not a finite training set but an open-ended sequence, and it was not useful to evaluate the total error over all training examples to determine the network's performance. For the simulations of Experiments

---

[9]In other words, if one orders (ranks) the vocabulary elements by their frequencies and then numbers them sequentially with the integers 1, 2, 3, and so forth, a plot of these integers versus the corresponding frequencies forms a hyperbola. This implies that if one plots the log of rank versus the log of frequency, the result should be a straight line.

[10]The Brown corpus rank-frequency plots of lexical classes seem, in fact, to be slightly biased in favour of lower frequency elements (i.e. the highest frequency elements seem to be missing from the tabulation), so a log-log plot is not linear but bowed slightly upward in the middle. We have found that distortions of this sort and even more radical divergence make little difference in the qualitative outcome of the simulation.

1, 2 and 3, the training grammar was a finite-state grammar with only a few states. Therefore, we were able to determine when the network was making all the right distinctions simply by inspecting its outputs in all the relevant conditions. We also measured error quantitatively as a weighted sum over current and preceding pattern errors [Error(t) = 0.99*Error(t − 1) + 0.01*$|C|$, where t indexes the time step and C is the error on the current pattern (see Fig. 4)] and made sure that this error asymptoted before we stopped training.

We used a learning rate of 0.03. For four out of four initial weight configurations, the Experiment 1 network learned all the distinctions in the training grammar by the time at least 400,000 words had been presented. In fact, it typically learned the distinctions in less than 100,000 presentations, but we ran the training longer to allow the hidden unit clusters to become a bit more distinct. We studied the representations for all four training episodes and found them to be essentially similar. The results reported here are based on one typical episode.

After a small amount of experimentation with parameter values, we set $n = 6000$, $p = 3.5$, $r_{\text{min}} = 0.01$ and $\mu = 0.00005$ for the simulation of Experiment 1. Figures 5 and 6 compare the human reading time data in Experiment 1 to the simulation results. The pattern of reading times generated by the model is similar to that observed in Experiment 1. The main difference is that the bulk of the processing difficulty occurs about a word later in the human data than in the simulation results. This may be because effects are often delayed by a word or two in self-paced reading. It also may be that the unrealistic simplicity of the training grammar contributes to the effect. For example, the fact that the number marking on a noun following the word *that* gives a categorical signal in the grammar as to the relation of the noun to the word *that*, means that the model encounters clear, unexpected information earlier than humans do (after all "That marmots ..." might turn out to be "That marmots' den ..." in English but not in the simulation grammar). These effects may weaken the synchrony of human and model results, but the source of the reading time contrasts is still plausibly the same in humans and in the model.

Why does the model make the appropriate predictions? The gravitational dynamical system for this simulation has three main attractive regions, corresponding to the three major types of categories represented in the grammar: verb, determiner and noun. Each of these regions contains several distinct attractors, which correspond to the different syntactic roles the words in each category can play. Since the effect of interest shows up on the nouns in this simulation, it is revealing to take a close-up look at the noun region.

Figure 7 shows (as black dots) the fixed bodies in the noun region in two dimensions. These dimensions are the first and second principal

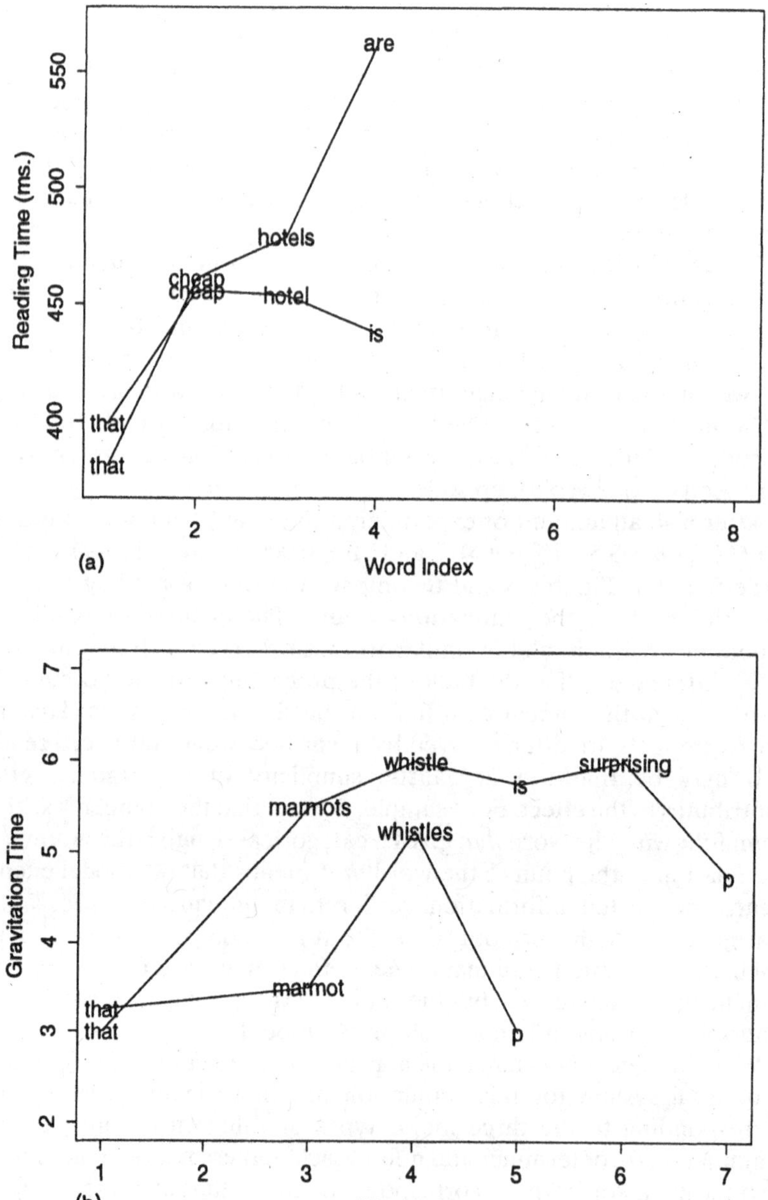

FIG. 5. Comparison of human participant results (a) and simulation results (b) for Experiment 1, initial *that* condition.

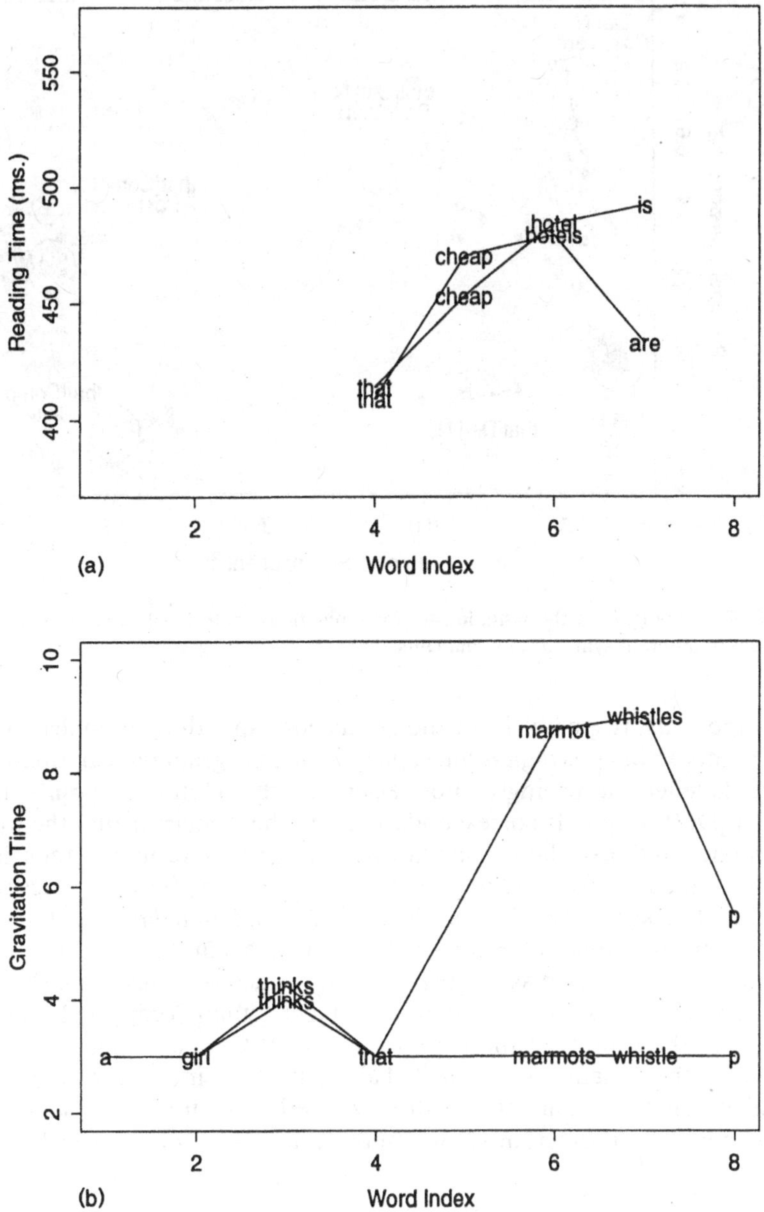

FIG. 6. Comparison of human participant results (a) and simulation results (b) for Experiment 1, post-verbal *that* condition.

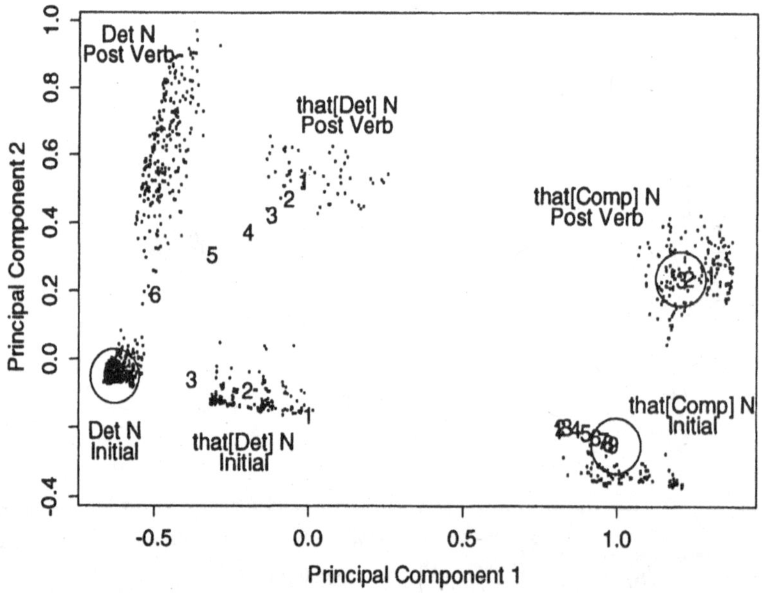

FIG. 7. A portion of the visitation set for simulation 1 with labelled clusters representing nouns in different syntactic environments.

components, respectively, of the points corresponding to nouns.[11] Clusters of points within this region correspond to distinct grammatical situations and are labelled accordingly. For example, the cloud of points labelled "that[Det] N, Initial" corresponds to nouns that occurred after the word *that* sentence-initially, where *that* was functioning as a determiner (thus the noun was singular). The cloud of points labelled "Det N, Initial" corresponds to nouns that occurred after some determiner other than *that* in sentence-initial position. The circles identify the three attractors in the noun region, which may be characterised as subject of an embedded sentence ("that[Comp] N, Post Verb"), subject of a sentential subject ("that[Comp] N, Initial"), and head of the subject of the matrix sentence ("Det N, Initial").[12] If the test body of the dynamical system is placed anywhere in the depicted region, it will gravitate to one of the three circled attractors. The sequences of numbers in the diagram show sample trajectories of the test body: each

[11]The first two components account for 80 and 15% of the variance in the noun subportion of the visitation set, respectively, so Fig. 7 shows nearly all of the structure of this subset.

[12]Note that the generating grammar contains only subject nouns, no object nouns or nouns in other syntactic positions.

trajectory starts at the point labelled "1" and proceeds in order of the sequence, ending finally at the attractor towards which it is heading.[13]

The three attractors in Fig. 7 correspond to the important syntactic distinctions that the grammar makes between nouns: there can be statistical differences between the behaviours of nouns within the same attractor basin, but these tend towards zero as larger and larger samples of the language are examined. In this sense, the dynamical model makes explicit the "emergent" organisation of the neural network representation which gives rise to syntactic constraints on processing. Moreover, although the syntactic distinctions between nouns made here are not the same ones that a linguist would choose for parsing the real language, English, if a linguist were studying the output of the training grammar, then the distinctions formed by the dynamical model would probably be the distinctions of choice.

The cluster arrangement in this region is robust under repeated training episodes with different random starting weights in the RCN. In four successive simulations, the same pattern appeared. In fact, the locations of the clusters are easy to predict based on the principle that locally ambiguous constructions receive intermediate representations: there are three clusters corresponding to the three distinct noun-states determined by the grammar—these are the clusters corresponding to the three attractors just mentioned. The remaining clusters correspond to non-distinct states which share features with other states: the "that[Det] N, Initial" cluster is near the subject determiner attractor but is displaced in the direction of the sentential subject region; the "Det N, Post Verb" cluster is near the subject determiner attractor but is displaced in the direction of other post-verbal structures; the "that[Det] N, Post Verb" cluster is near the subject determiner attractor but is displaced simultaneously in the direction of other post-verbal structures and in the direction of the embedded sentence structure (also introduced by the word *that*).

We can see from the trajectories shown in Fig. 7 how the model makes appropriate predictions. A singular noun following sentence-initial *that* ("that[Det] N, Initial") is processed quickly because it starts from a cluster right next to the powerful matrix subject attractor, which rapidly pulls it in. The matrix subject attractor is powerful because of the high frequency of matrix subjects. A plural noun following sentence-initial *that* ("that[Comp] N, Initial") takes longer to process because it lands near the much weaker sentential subject attractor. The sentential subject attractor is weaker because of the comparatively low frequency of sentential subjects. This contrast gives rise to the gravitation time difference at the noun shown in Fig. 5.

[13]The parts of the trajectory which are nearly at the attractor are not labelled so as to avoid confusing overlaps of labels.

On the other hand, a plural noun following post-verbal *that* ("that[Comp] N, Post Verb") is processed reasonably quickly because its trajectory starts very near the embedded subject attractor. By contrast, a singular noun following post-verbal *that* ("that[Det] N, Post Verb") takes somewhat longer to process, even though it is drawn in by the powerful subject attractor, because it starts quite far away from this attractor.

Two features of the dynamical system contribute to the correct predictions: (1) A strong attractor pulls the test body more quickly than a weak attractor—this predicts the general correlation between the frequency of a construction and its processing ease. (2) Gravitation takes longer if the starting point of a trajectory is close to an attractor rather than far away—this gives rise to the inverse correlation between the ambiguity of a construction and its processing ease. Thus the attractors both play the role of traditional categorical sentence fragment parses, and also interact to make appropriate predictions about the roles of frequency and similarity which constraint-based models have emphasised. Since the attractors develop through the learning process of the RCN, they are appropriately thought of as the "emergent properties" which constraint-based researchers have hypothesised to account for syntactic effects within a lexicalist framework (e.g. Juliano & Tanenhaus, 1994). It is important to note that attractors corresponding to higher level phrasal categories emerge even though the system is lexicalist in nature. This is important given that critics of both lexicalist and constraint-based models have often appealed to category-level biases that precede lexical heads as evidence against these approaches. Our results show that this type of argument is misleading.

The fact that the emergent properties are related to the learning process of the RCN raises the question of why we did not simply choose to work with the dynamical properties of the RCN. The RCN itself is a dynamical system in two senses: the recurrent connections in the hidden layer give rise to dynamical structures (cf. Rodriguez, 1995; Wiles and Elman, 1995) and the learning process is dynamical. We have chosen to adopt a separate dynamical system to interpret the representation adopted by the RCN because it seemed like the best way to capture the key conceptual generalisations we observe in processing. We chose not to work with the dynamical structures associated with the recurrent connections of the RCN because we did not find these useful for our purposes (a more detailed discussion of this point follows later). We also chose not to work directly with the dynamics of learning. We believe, however, that there may be an interpretation of the dynamics of learning which corresponds closely to the interpretation we create using the gravitational model: there are locations in the representation space associated with important categorical distinctions, and the representations assigned to specific items migrate towards these locations during the course of training. However, it is difficult to analyse these properties of the learning dynamics because the locations of the attractors are constantly changing. Further analysis of learning in this light may ultimately be helpful and we see this project as laying a foundation for such work.

Simulations of Experiments 2 and 3

Since the important grammatical environments in Experiments 2 and 3 did not require learning of the long-distance dependencies involved in Experiment 1, we used a more repesentative grammar, presented in Table 4. The network had 36 inputs, 5 hidden units and 36 outputs, and 3 time steps were unfolded in time during learning (Pearlmutter, 1995; Rumelhart et al., 1986).

The grammar for simulations 2 and 3 encodes the relevant overall bias in favour of assigning a complementiser interpretation in V + *that* sequences (Table 5, Line 1). The grammar assumes that the complementiser is present (i.e. not deleted) after about 70% of verbs introducing a sentence complement. This corresponds to the pattern found in the Treebank corpus once one eliminates sentence complements with nominative pronouns, which typically occur without complementisers (Table 5, Line 3). This gives

TABLE 4
Corpus-generating Grammar for Experiments 2 and 3 Simulation

1.00	Sroot : S p
1.00	S : NP VP
0.67 0.33	VP : VP[NP] VP : VP[S′]
0.67 0.33	VP[NP] : V[NP] NP VP[NP] : V[NP]
1.00	VP[S′] : V[S′] S′
0.67 0.33	S′ : that S S′ : S
1.00	NP : Det N
[Zipf]	Det : 0.44 the, 0.22 a, 0.14 which, 0.10 that, 0.10 those
[Zipf]	V[NP] : 0.34 called, 0.17 followed, 0.11 pulled, 0.09 caught, 0.07 pushed, 0.06 loved, 0.05 visited, 0.04 studied, 0.04 tossed, 0.03 grabbed
[Zipf]	V[S′] : 0.34 thought, 0.17 agreed, 0.11 insisted, 0.09 wished, 0.07 hoped, 0.06 remarked, 0.05 pleaded, 0.04 speculated, 0.04 doubted, 0.03 hinted
[Zipf]	N : 0.34 woman, 0.17 man, 0.11 dog, 0.09 cat, 0.07 blouse, 0.06 hat, 0.05 cake, 0.04 ball, 0.04 watch, 0.03 cypress

TABLE 5
Comparison of Relative Frequencies in the Brown Corpus and the Training Grammar for Simulations 2 and 3 (Brown Corpus Statistics from the Penn Treebank)

	Brown Corpus	*Simulation Grammar*
1. Complementiser interpretation of V + *that*	93%	80%
2. Relative frequency of NP complements *vs* sentential complements	79%	67%
3. Relative frequency of *that*-deletion in sentential complements (not counting cases in which the embedded subject is a nominative pronoun)	<50%	33%

rise to a strong complementiser attractor, which plays an important role in Experiment 2. The grammar also makes the realistic assumption that there is a high frequency of noun phrase complements in comparison to sentence complements (Table 5, Line 2). This gives rise to a strong direct object attractor, which plays a central role in Experiment 3. The grammar includes an option of using an NP-verb intransitively. This is not unrealistic, but in this case, the main point of including this feature was to facilitate learning the distinction between subjects and objects.

To train the network for simulations 2 and 3, we generated sentences at random using the Experiment 2/3 grammar and fed them to the network one word at a time. Again, the training grammar is a finite-state grammar with only a few states, so we were able to determine when the network had achieved satisfactory performance by inspection. We also checked to make sure the error measure described on p. 237 had asymptoted.

We used a learning rate of 0.03. For four out of five initial weight configurations, the network learned all the distinctions in the training grammar by the time at least 100,000 words had been presented. This grammar was a little harder to learn than the Experiment 1 grammar because of the dependency involved in making the subject/object distinction, and when the network failed, it was always because the network failed to clearly distinguish subjects and objects. We trained several of the successful networks up to the 400,000th word presentation to achieve tighter clustering of the hidden unit representations. In every such case we examined, a similar representation pattern emerged. The results reported here are based on one typical case.

For these experiments, we set $n = 2000$, $p = 2.4$, $r_{min} = 0.01$ and $\mu = 0.0002$ in the gravitational model. In this case, the parameter p needed to be fine-tuned to make a crucial distinction, which we will discuss shortly.

Figure 8 provides a comparison between the reading time data and the simulation results for the contrast between *those* and *that* and following an NP-complement verb (Experiment 2). Figure 9 compares the human and

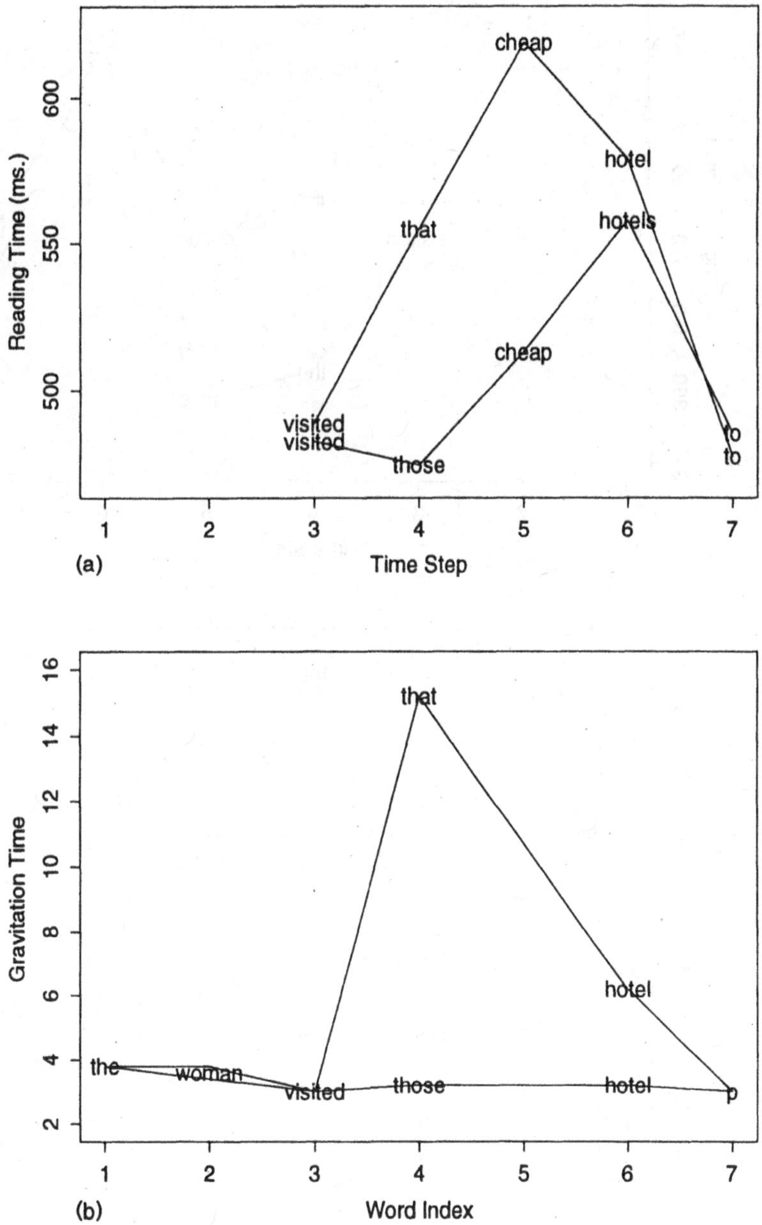

FIG. 8. Reading time at *that* compared with reading time at *those* following an NP-only verb. Comparison of human participant results (a) and simulation results (b) for Experiment 2.

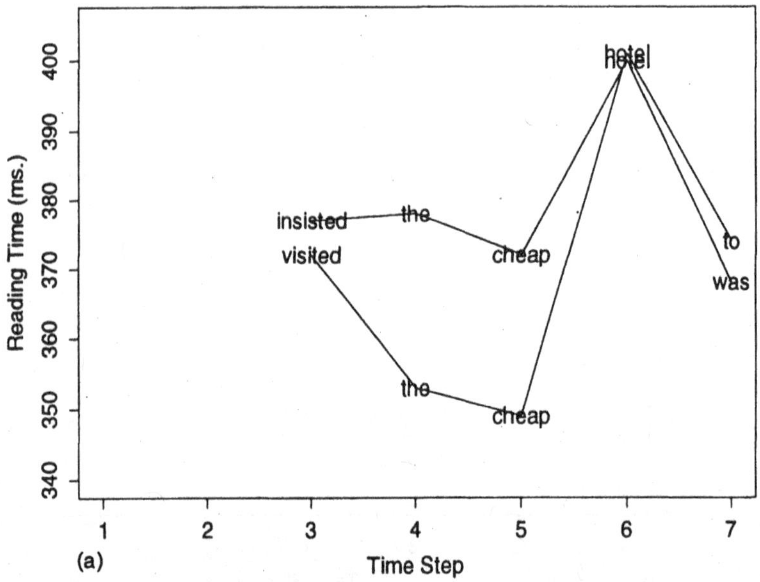

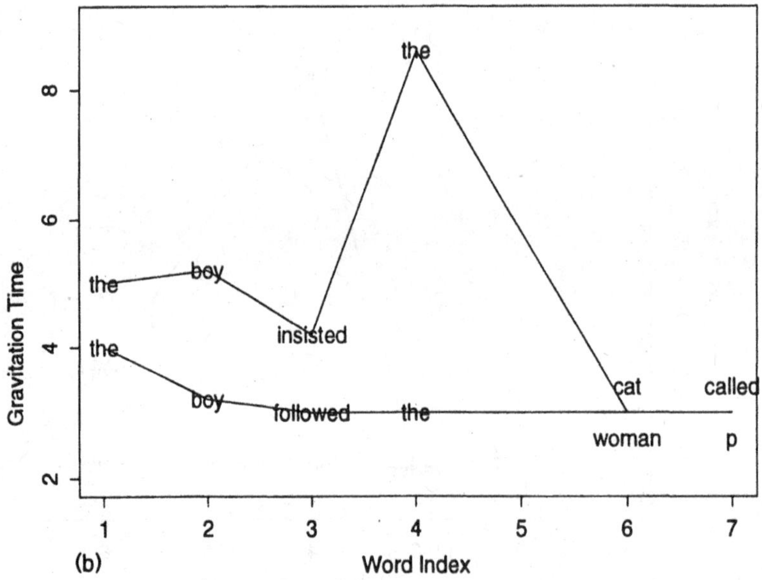

FIG. 9. Reading time at *the* following the verb: pure NP complement verbs versus (nearly) pure sentence complement verbs. Comparison of human participant results (a) and simulation results (b) for Experiment 3.

simulation results near the word *the* following SC-bias and NP-bias verbs (Experiment 3). Again, the human and model results are consistent. This time, both the model and the humans show increased processing time on the first disambiguating word, although, as we noted earlier, in a replication of Experiment 2, the anomaly did not show up until the next word after the disambiguating word (the adjective). The better alignment between the people and the model in these cases may be due to the presence of a stronger signal in the language in each case: the word *that* is very likely to be a complementiser; several of the SC-bias verbs of the experiment cannot occur with direct objects.

The dynamical system for these simulations also has three main attractive regions corresponding to the three major lexical categories: verb, determiner and noun. Again, each region contains several distinct attractors corresponding to the different syntactic uses of words in these classes. Here, the effect of interest shows up on the determiners so we concentrate on the determiner (+ complementiser *that*) subregion to interpret the results.

Figure 10 shows (black dots) the fixed bodies in the determiner (+ *that*) subregion in two dimensions, the first and second principal components of the determiner (+ *that*) sample.[14] In this region, there are three attractors, indicated by the three circles. The attractors correspond to the three grammatically distinct behaviours associated with determiners (and the word *that*) in the training grammar: in the middle right region of the figure, there is an attractor corresponding to subject determiners; in the lower right, one corresponding to object determiners; in the upper left, one corresponding to the complementiser use of *that*. Two distinct clusters lie in the basin of the object determiner attractor: there is a very dense cluster corresponding to unambiguous determiners like *the*, *a*, *one*, etc. ("V[NP]-Det"); there is a more sparsely populated cluster corresponding to the word *that* when it is used as an object determiner ("V[NP]-that"). There are also several clusters which lie in the basin of the subject determiner attractor: there is a dense cluster corresponding to unambiguous subject determiners that occur at the beginning of a sentence ("p-Det"); there are a couple of separate litte clusters corresponding to the word *that* when it is used at the beginning of a sentence ("p-that")—in this grammar, it can only be a subject determiner in this position. There are also two other small clusters in the subject determiner basin, corresponding to determiners following the word *that* and the word *that* following the word *that*—to keep the diagram uncluttered, these are not labelled in Fig. 10. The complementiser basin has only one distinctive cluster in it.

[14]The first three components account for 96% of the variance in the determiner subportion of the visitation set and the first two account for 72 and 20% of the variance, respectively.

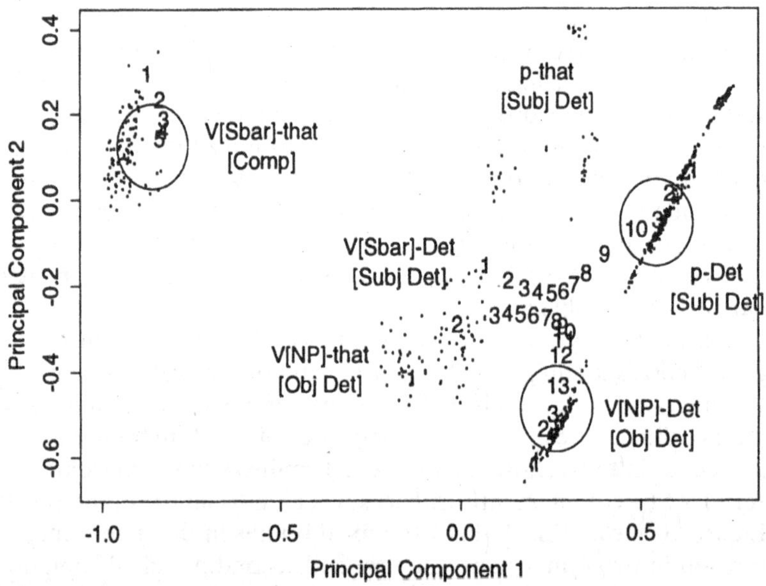

FIG. 10. A portion of the visitation set for simulations 2 and 3 with labelled clusters representing determiners following NP complement and sentential complement verbs.

In all cases, the peripheral clusters in each basin are displaced away from the attractors in a direction that reflects their formal ambiguity: the uses of *that* as a determiner are in the determiner basins, but are displaced in the direction of the complementiser attractor; the uses of unambiguous determiners immediately following SC-bias verbs are (mostly) in the subject determiner basin, but they are displaced simultaneously in the direction of the complementiser attractor and the object determiner attractor, reflecting, respectively, the facts that SC-bias verbs usually take complementisers in this grammar and determiners following verbs usually introduce direct objects.

Note that the clusters "V[Sbar]-Det" and "V[NP]-that" are not very separate from each other in the figure. This is partly a result of the fact that we are only displaying two principal components—these two clusters achieve much better separation on the third component. However, some of the instances of "V[Sbar]-Det" actually lie in the basin of attraction of the object determiner attractor. It took careful tuning of the parameter p to make the basin boundary between subject determiner and object determiner land roughly between these two clusters. Note that "misclassification" of some of the "V[Sbar]-Det" instances is not unreasonable—people may sometimes try to parse "the raccoon" in a sentence like "She insists the raccoon ..." as a direct object. However, this situation may also reflect a technical weakness of the current implementation. It is likely that a revision of the neural network model can make the attractor basins line up perfectly with the grammatically distinct classes (we return to this point in the General Discussion). More generally, however, this result demonstrates that a mix of two behaviours (correct and incorrect "initial" syntactic categorisation) that are distinctly different according to traditional parsers naturally arises out of our system.

Figure 10 makes it apparent how the model makes appropriate reading time predictions in Experiments 2 and 3. An unambiguous determiner like *those* following a transitive verb is processed relatively quickly because the processor starts in the dense cluster near the object determiner attractor and thus has only a small distance to travel to reach the attractor. A trajectory labelled "1 2 3" in the lower right of the figure provides an example of this case. By contrast, the ambiguous word *that* following a transitive verb takes quite a while to process because the processor starts in the "V[NP]-that" cluster, far from the attractor locus (trajectory "1 2 ... 1 3"). The processing of such a phrase is slowed down both by the influence of the complementiser attractor and by the influence of the subject determiner attractor. This is how the model predicts the major contrast observed in Experiment 2. Likewise, the ambiguous determiner *the* following a transitive verb is processed quickly, just as *those* is (again the trajectory "1 2 3" in the lower right is illustrative). The determiner *the* following an SC-bias verb takes longer to process because it starts far from the subject determiner attractor and is influenced significantly by both the complementiser attractor and the object determiner attractor (trajectory "1 2 ... 1 0"). In this way, the model predicts the contrast we focused on in Experiment 3. Figure 10 also shows illustrative trajectories for sentence-initial unambiguous determiners ("1 2 3" in the upper right) and for the word *that* following an SC-bias verb ("1 2 3 4 5" in the upper left). These two cases are about equally easy to process, but the "V[Sbar]-that" case has slower trajectories because it is a lower-frequency type but it is isolated enough that it forms its own attractor locus.

Thus these simulations illustrate how competition among attractors provides a natural way of modelling the processing difficulty associated with ambiguous elements. Also, the expected effects of category frequency are observed. Moreover, these simulations make it especially clear how formal similarities can give rise to increased processing time even in circumstances where the system is not making mistakes. We have, in the notion of an attractor basin properly containing an attractor, the tools to encode both major categorical distinctions (by distinguishing basins) and minor, similarity-based influences (by distinguishing elements within a basin in terms of their travel-time to the local attractor).

USING CORPORA TO TRAIN A RECURRENT NETWORK

The models presented in the section headed "Contingent frequencies and *that*", simulated processing of an entire *language*, using samples generated by a finite-state grammar in accordance with frequency patterns modelled on a natural language corpus. These simple global models have advantages over larger-scale models that incorporate a larger number of items. One advantage is that their representations can be analysed more easily. A second advantage is that global models can shed light on how experimental results based on different parts of a language are related to one another. However, there is no guarantee that the properties of these models will generalise to a larger-scale model trained from a real language corpus. Moreover, as we saw in the small-scale model of Experiment 1, there is an important question about which features of natural language to encode in a simulation grammar. Thus using a "toy" grammar to generate a corpus always raises questions about whether the behaviour of the system that depends upon the corpus input is actually due to distortions in the sample corpus. It was therefore important to see whether a model trained from a more realistic subset of a natural language corpus would exhibit the same properties as the models trained from small grammars. This modelling study also provided us with an opportunity to see whether a network trained from a natural corpus could simulate item-specific differences in reading times. This is an important test of the claim that the system is simultaneously sensitive to category-level and to item-specific generalisations.

Following Juliano and Tanenhaus (1994), we trained a recurrent network to predict the complement types that followed past-tense verbs, focusing on those verbs that permit sentence complements to varying degrees. The general architecture of the model is the same as the one used in the previous section (see Fig. 11). However, the simulation presented here differed from that in the previous section along three dimensions: the training set, the input representation and the predictive task the model was given.

The input layer contained 122 units, 72 of which represented verbs; the remaining 50 represented words, word categories and punctuation that could immediately follow the verb. Of the 72 units devoted to each of the verbs, the first 5 units were *similarity* units. Similarity units were assigned values determined from a principal components analysis performed on semantic similarity judgements. The similarity units let the model take advantage of the fact that verbs with similar complement structures typically have related semantics (Fisher, Gleitman, & Gleitman, 1991). While, in principle, a model might learn these similarities from co-occurrence information in a large training corpus, we chose to incorporate similarity into the representation because our training set was sparse and limited in

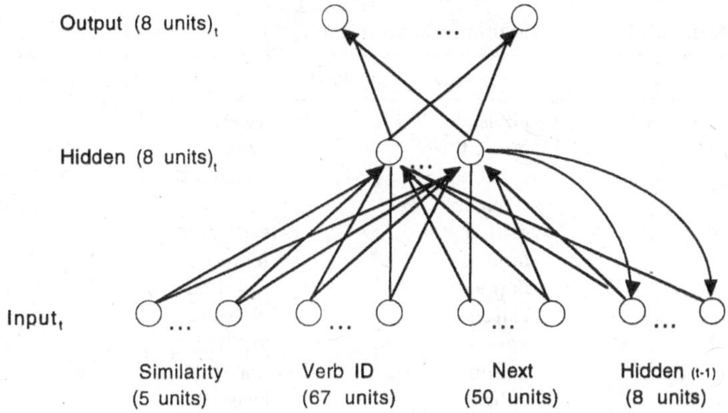

FIG. 11. (Simple) recurrent network from simulation 4. The activation pattern on hidden layer $t-1$ is set to the activation pattern of hidden layer t from the previous time step (as in Elman, 1990, 1991), indicated by the curved arrow from hidden layer t to hidden layer $t-1$.

syntactic variability. Models in which we eliminated similarity units showed the same pattern as the model presented here; however, they did not learn as well, and they accounted for less of the variance in human reading times.

The similarity data were generated in a study conducted in collaboration with Joshua Richardson. Three student participants were instructed to judge a set of 70 verbs on how similar in meaning they were to each other on a 9-point scale. Each verb in the set was paired with all of the other verbs, creating 4900 verb comparisons. These were randomly presented to the participants. We averaged the judgements of all three participants and performed a principal components analysis on the 70×70 matrix that resulted. The principal components analysis was used to reduce the 70 dimensions to the first five principal components, which together accounted for 60% of the variance. These five components were normalised to create a 5-unit vector for each verb.

The 67 units directly following the similarity units each identified a particular verb. Thus presenting a verb entailed setting the appropriate input values for the five similarity units for that verb and setting its identity unit to 1. The remaining 50 units at the input provided a localist representation for an item that could follow the verb in the corpus. These items could be one of 33 words (frequent articles, pronouns and prepositions), 6 types of punctuation, 10 category types, or "other", a general category that included the 6% of the items that did not fall into any of the other categories. The full set of verbs and "next" items is presented in Table 6.

The hidden layer and output layer each contained eight units. Each hidden unit was connected to itself and to all of the other hidden units. These

TABLE 6
Verbs and the Words that Followed Them ("Next" Items) from Simulation 4

Verbs			
accepted	advised	asserted	remembered
attempted	bought	bribed	shifted
claimed	conceded	conspired	speculated
crept	crouched	declared	stayed
disputed	drifted	estimated	visited
faded	fared	feared	wrote
felt	flopped	followed	reported
gave	glared	glowed	snarled
grabbed	grew	guessed	sprang
helped	hinted	hoped	tasted
implied	indicated	insisted	vowed
intended	invited	knew	revealed
left	looked	maintained	sounded
mentioned	needed	peered	staggered
pleaded	pledged	predicted	tended
pretended	proposed	protested	wept
realised	recalled	refused	

Words that followed verbs				
!	for	me	RB	those
,	he	my	she	to
.	her	NN	T	up
:	him	NNP	that	us
;	his	NNS	the	VBG
?	in	no	their	VBN
a	it	of	them	we
an	its	on	these	with
at	JJ	other	they	WRB
CD	JJR	our	this	your

recurrent connections among the hidden units are represented in Fig. 11 as $Hidden_{(t-1)}$. In the output layer, each unit represented one of the following complement types: adjectival (ADJ), adverbial (ADV), noun (NP), prepositional (PP), infinitival (INF), sentential (SC), verb (VP) and no complement (NC). The NC category signified end of clause or end of sentence punctuation.

Both the output and hidden units in this model had fixed sigmoid activation functions of the form shown in equation (3):

$$f(\text{net}_i) = \frac{1}{1 + e^{-\text{net}_i}} \tag{3}$$

where $\text{net}_i = b_i + \sum w_{ij}a_{ij}$, b_i is the bias on unit i, a_i is the activation of unit i, and w_{ij} is the weight from unit j to unit i. The cost function was taken to be the sum of the squared errors at each output unit over all patterns and is shown in equation (4):

$$C = \sum_{p}\sum_{i}(a_i - t_i)^2 \tag{4}$$

where i indexes the output units, p indexes the training patterns and t_i is the target value. The error signal was backpropagated through the layers and through one time step to adjust the weights on connections involving hidden units (e.g. Pearlmutter, 1995; Rumelhart et al., 1986).

The training set was taken from the combined Brown corpus and the Wall Street Journal corpus, both tagged and parsed by the Treebank Project (Marcus, Santorini, & Marcinkiewicz, 1993). The training set consisted of all the sentences in the corpus that contained any of our set of 67 past-tense verbs. Thirty of these verbs were targets for our modelling efforts; the other 37 verbs were chosen to create a sample preserving the relative frequency with which different complement types followed past-tense verbs in the full corpus. Table 7 compares the percentage of each of the eight major phrase types found in the Treebank corpus and in the training set. In general, the match is quite good, though sentence complements are somewhat over-represented because all the target verbs permitted sentence complements. Also, verb phrase complements were somewhat under-represented because, in the vast majority of these complements, the past-tense verb was followed by an auxiliary verb. Since individual auxiliary verbs have such high frequencies, the inclusion of even a single auxiliary in the training set would have badly over-represented the frequency of the VP complement category. We decided to overlook this discrepancy between the sample and the corpus because the auxiliary + past-participle pattern did not play a foreseeable role in the phenomena we were studying.

A training instance consisted of a past-tense verb, the word that followed the verb and a complement type. The word pairs and complement types were automatically extracted from the sentences in which they occurred in the corpus. An example is presented in (12).

TABLE 7
Comparison of the Percentage of Major Complement Types Following Past-tense Verbs in the Treebank Corpora (Brown and Wall Street Journal) and Experiment 4 Training Set

	Complement Type							
Source	*ADJ*	*ADV*	*NP*	*PP*	*INF*	*SC*	*VP*	*NC*
Treebank	5.5	5.8	38.7	11.4	5.1	3.4	15.8	7.6
Training set	4.8	4.9	43.1	12.1	6.6	6.3	2.4	6.7

12a. (S (NP (DT The) (NN lawyer)) (VP (VBD insisted) (SBAR (IN that) (S (NP (PRP$ his) (NN client)) (VP (VBD was) (NP (NN innocent)))))

12b. insisted that SBAR

A sentence from the corpus such as the sentence in (12a) would be transformed into (12b). Training the model with an instance from the corpus was carried out in two steps. First, for a verb like *insisted* in (12b), its semantic representation units and its identification unit were activated, then the model was trained to produce the complement type that followed the verb (SBAR in 12b) using backpropagation. Next, the verb input was set to zero and the unit corresponding to the item that followed the verb (*the* in 12b) was activated. The model was again trained to produce the complement. If the specific item that succeeded the verb was not one recognised by the model, then the category of the word was activated. Note also that the interconnections among the hidden units give a sequential component to the model's behaviour. After the first item of a two-item training pair was presented, the hidden unit activation from the current time step was recirculated to the hidden layer in the subsequent time step. Thus in the example above, *insisted* would influence the prediction the model makes when *the* is presented.

The complete training set consisted of patterns from 4798 sentences. The model was initialised with different starting weights for each of three training sessions and trained until the model's overall error (RMS) no longer seemed to decrease. On average, the model made seven passes through the training set.

To generate reading times from the hidden space of this large-scale model, we focused on the behaviour of the model when the word following the verb had been presented (hence including all the cases where a determiner occurred). We used the 4798 sentences of the training set to create a visitation set, which meant that n, the number of fixed bodies in the gravitational model, was 4798. After a little bit of probing, we set $p = 3.0$, $r_{\min} = 0.001$ and $\mu = 0.000005$.

Analysis of the Model

We began with some preliminary analyses of the model to see how the RCN was performing the prediction task. First, we determined that the RCN developed argument structure preferences by examining its predictions for the 10 verbs that most typically occurred with NP complements in the training set, and the 10 verbs that most typically occurred with sentence complements (we later used these same verbs in more detailed comparisons of the model's predictions and human reading time data). After presentation of the verb alone, the RCN correctly assigned the highest likelihood to the complement type that had the highest likelihood in the training set for each of these 20 verbs.

To examine the representations constructed by the RCN, we presented the trained RCN with just the verbs from the training set. We then collected the network's predictions for upcoming complements and performed a principal components analysis on the resulting output activation. Figure 12 shows all the verb types in the space defined by the first two principal components, the latter accounting for 66% of the variance. For purposes of discussion, we will classify verbs according to which complement was assigned the highest probability of the RCN. Different groups of verbs are clearly mapped to specific regions in space, as in the models described earlier. This reflects the fact that items group according to the environment they occur in and the phrase types that they predict. A second observation is that the different groups of verbs vary in how tightly they cluster. In the upper right, there is a tightly knit cluster consisting of verbs that are reliably followed by infinitive complements. Somewhat less tightly knit are verbs that strongly prefer an NP complement. These verbs are for the most part strung out in one dimension along the horizontal axis. Verbs that prefer a

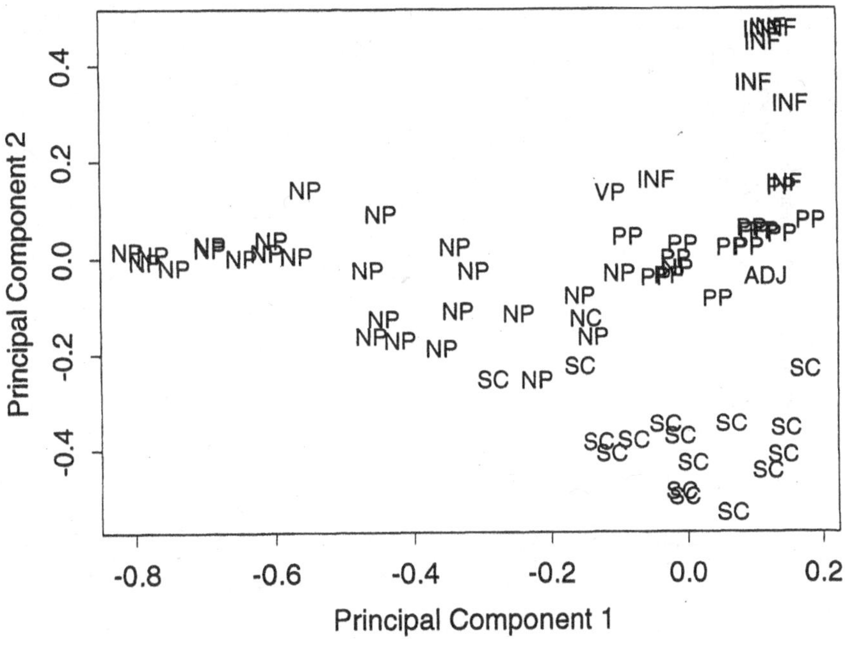

FIG. 12. Analysis (PCA) of predictions from simulation 4 when just the verbs are presented. Each verb is presented by the complement type it predicts in the simulation.

sentence complement form a somewhat loose association, spread along both dimensions. This results from the fact that SC-bias verbs take a variety of complement types. Also note that verbs are not assigned to discrete classes. Rather, they are located on a continuum. Verbs that regularly take both noun phrase complements and sentential complements (as determined by corpus analyses of the Treebank corpus) fill the space between NP-bias and SC-bias verbs, appearing closest to the class that they are most similar to in behaviour.

We also explored whether verb frequency itself had effects above and beyond argument structure preferences. Specifically, to determine whether effects of verb frequency were represented in the model's representational space, we compared the predictions that the model made when presented with each of our experimental verbs with the corpus probabilities of each verb. A plot of both predictions and probabilities in principal components space is shown in Fig. 13. Each arrow represents a verb: the butt of the arrow is its location in corpus probability space, and the head of the arrow represents its position in the model's prediction space. The arrows are longer for lower-frequency verbs compared to higher-frequency verbs [$t(18) = 3.11$, $P < 0.006$], indicating that lower-frequency items are pulled

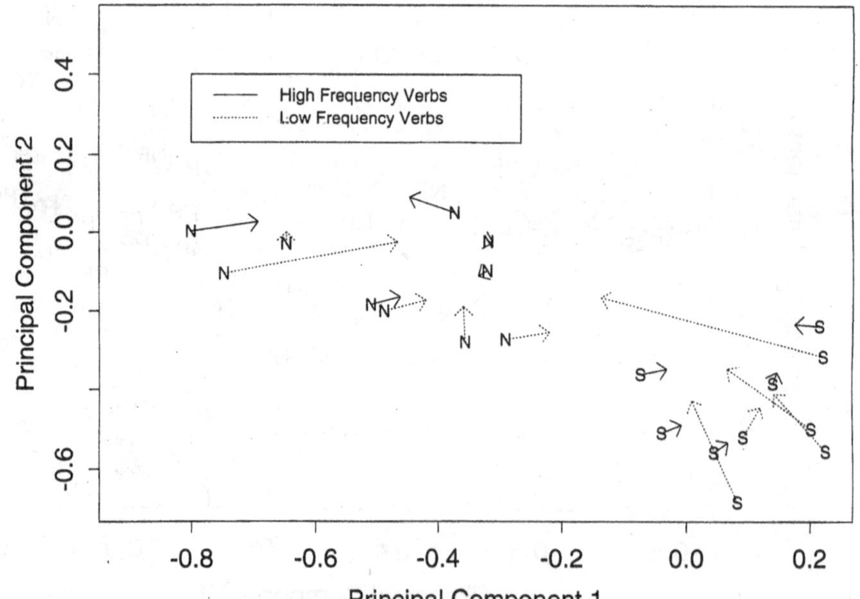

FIG. 13. Attractor effects on items mediated by frequency. N = NP-bias verbs, S = sentential complement verbs.

further from their locations in probability space towards locations associated with other classes.

In the previous section, we presented evidence that dynamical models based on simple grammars with a small number of prototypical lexical items in each class can predict a range of significant qualitative distinctions observable in human reading time data. It is also important to evaluate whether a model based on a more accurate corpus can predict item-specific variation in reading times. To this end, we conducted an experiment using many of the *that* and *that*-less complements that were presented to the large RCN trained on the Wall Street Journal data. We then correlated reading time predictions generated by the gravitational model based on the RCN with the human reading time data.

Experiment 4: Reading Times to NPs in Sentence Complements

Experiment 4 compared reading times to *that* and *that*-less sentential complements when they followed three broad classes of verbs: verbs that are typically followed by a sentential complement (SC-bias verbs); verbs that are typically followed by a noun phrase complement (NP-bias); and verbs that occurred approximately equally with both sentential and noun phrase complements (EQUI-bias). We tried to select verbs in which there was at least an approximate match between the corpus statistics and sentence completion data collected in our lab. It was important to take into account the completion data for two reasons. First, the sample in the Treebank corpus is relatively small and thus subject to errors, especially for lower-frequency verbs. Second, the verbs in the corpus appeared in a variety of syntactic constructions, many of which were quite different from the types of sentences presented in the experiment. The completions provided data for complement preferences in environments similar to those tested in the experiment. We were able to find verbs where the corpus statistics and the completions were in good agreement for the SC-bias and NP-bias verbs, but not for the EQUI-bias verbs, a point we will return to later.

The task we used was the "stop making sense" variant of self-paced reading introduced by Boland, Tanenhaus and Garnsey (1990). We chose this task because it is extremely sensitive to local syntactic and semantic anomalies and the results are more closely time-locked to the input than normal self-paced reading.

Method

Participants. Forty undergraduates from the University of Rochester participated in the experiment for course credit. All were native speakers of English.

Materials. We selected 48 verbs that permitted sentence complements: 16 strongly S-complement biased verbs, 16 strongly NP-complement biased verbs and 16 EQUI-biased verbs. While these classes are useful for grouping the data, the verbs were actually on a continuum with verbs within a class varying in the degree to which they occurred with S-complements. For instance, some of the SC-bias verbs are followed by sentence complements virtually all the time (e.g. *implied*), whereas some are not (e.g. *claimed*). This variability made it especially difficult to select EQUI-bias verbs. Some of the EQUI-bias verbs were closer to verbs in the SC-bias class with regard to the complement types they predicted, while others were more similar to verbs in the NP-bias class. Overall, selection of items for the EQUI-bias class was a compromise—the corpus and sentence completion data were in agreement for only about five of these verbs.

The base frequencies of the verbs were matched within verb class, with each class having similar frequency ranges and distributions. The verbs were embedded in 48 target sentences, each beginning with a determiner-noun NP followed by the main verb, which in turn was followed by either a *that* or a *that*-less sentence complement. The experimental items were combined with 144 filler sentences for a total of 192 trials. The critical sentences were counterbalanced across two lists, such that a verb that appeared with a *that*-less sentence complement in one list appeared with a *that* complement in the other list. Each critical sentence was followed by at least two filler sentences. Roughly 20% of the filler sentences did not make sense at some point for either syntactic or semantic reasons. None of the fillers contained experimental verbs or sentence complement constructions. Overall, 25% of the sentences in each list had a main verb followed by a sentence complement. The target sentences in each list were then pseudo-randomised to create four different orders. This ensured that each item would be rotated through different sections of the list to avoid position effects.

Procedure. Stimuli were presented on a colour monitor attached to an IBM PC with a Digitry CTS timing card. The monitor was set to display 80 characters per line, and all of the critical sentences fit on a single line, with the last word in each sentence accompanied by punctuation. Participants pressed a key on a response box to control the presentation of the sentences. Words accumulated one by one with each key press. Participants were instructed to press the same key as long as the sentence made sense. If the sentence stopped making sense, they were to press a NO button, which terminated the trial. Before the regular experiment began, participants were shown samples of nonsense sentences and received an explanation for each. They then completed 10 practice trials. The entire session lasted about 30 min.

Results

Responses were collected for eight word positions in each sentence beginning with the second word, which was the head noun of the subject. We collected both "stop making sense" judgements (*no*-judgements) and the time between button presses. We will briefly discuss the judgement data followed by the reading time data.

Judgement data. The sum of all the *no*-judgements at each word in the sentence was calculated and then averaged across three regions of the sentence: the verb, the noun phrase that follows the verb, and the succeeding auxiliary phrase. These averages were then converted into percentages. Figure 14 summarises the cumulative percentages of *no* responses for each region. Note that participants rarely judged a sentence to stop making sense until they reached the verb phrase in the complement clause.

The percentage of *no* responses was greater at the disambiguating auxiliary phrase in the complement for *that*-less complements compared to complements with a *that*. However, the degree to which participants rejected the sentences varied markedly with verb class. Participants responded *no* to approximately 20% of the trials in the NP-bias condition, 10% of the EQUI-bias trials and only 5% of the SC-bias trials. At the auxiliary phrase,

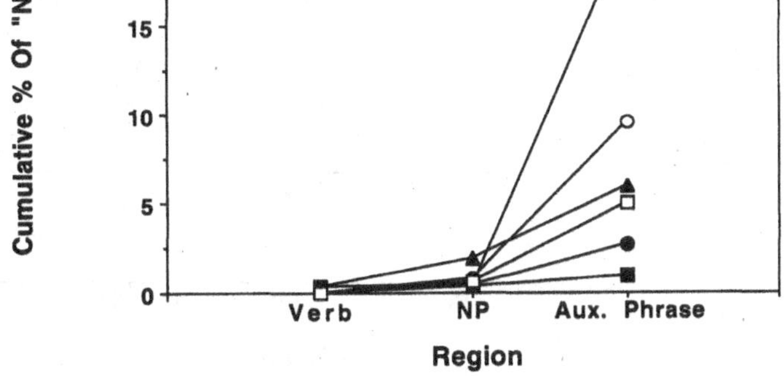

FIG. 14. Cumulative percentage of *no* responses following the different verb types in Experiment 4.

there was a main effect of complementiser on the percentage of *no*-judgements [$F_1(1,38) = 23.66$, $P < 0.001$; $F_2(1,6) = 13.16$, $P < 0.02$] and an interaction between complementiser presence and verb-bias [$F_1(1,72) = 3.70$, $P < 0.05$; $F_2(1,6) = 8.99$, $P < 0.03$]. Simple effects tests showed that the difference between the complementiser present and absent conditions was reliable for the NP-bias verbs [$F_1(1,38) = 39.62$, $P < 0.001$; $F_2(1,6) = 5.34$, $P = 0.06$] and the EQUI-bias verbs [$F_1(1,38) = 6.61$, $P < 0.01$; $F_2(1,6) = 8.99$, $P < 0.03$], but not for the SC-bias verbs.

Reading time data. Recall that reading times to the NP after a *that*-less SC-bias verb should be affected by the strong NP-as-object attractor. Figure 15 presents the difference in reading times at the NP in the *that* and *that*-less conditions. A positive difference reflects longer reading time in the *that*-less condition. The graph shows a large reading time difference for SC-bias verbs, a small difference for the EQUI-bias verbs and no difference for the NP-bias verbs. This was reflected in a verb-type × complementiser interaction [$F_1(2,76) = 4.94$, $P < 0.01$; $F_2(2,12) = 4.56$, $P < 0.05$]. Simple effects showed that the complementiser effect was significant only for the SC-bias verbs [$F_1(1,38) = 35.19$, $P < 0.001$; $F_2(1,6) = 10.05$, $P < 0.02$].

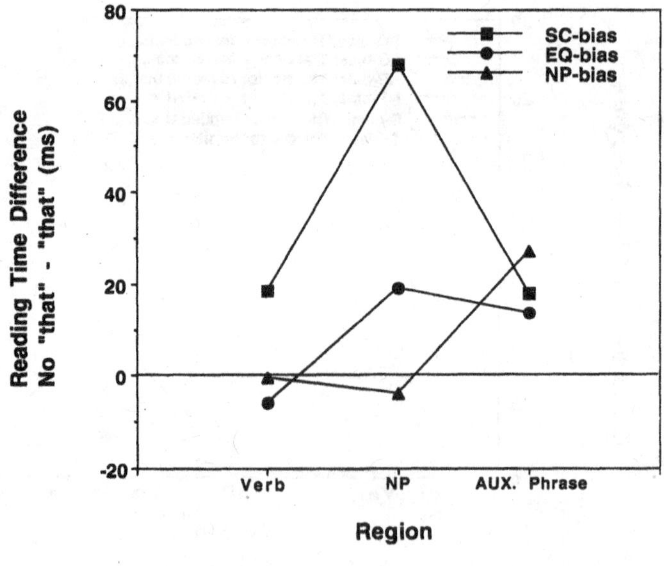

FIG. 15. Reading time differences between the *that* absent and *that* present conditions following different verb types in Experiment 4.

Comparison of the Model's Predicted Reading Times with the Human Data

We measured reading times as the number of time steps to reach an attractor according to equation (2).[15] We then computed a regression in which the model's gravitation time at the word *the* for each target verb was used to predict the difference between human reading times at *the* following a verb and human reading times at *the* following the complementiser *that* which followed the verb. It was important to use the differences to factor out spillover effects because of the frequency difference between "that" and the preceding verb.[16]

The simple regression displayed in Fig. 16 reveals a good positive correlation between the strength of the corpus model's predictions and human reading times at the region following the verb ($r^2 = 0.45$, $P < 0.00005$). It turns out that *the* is treated by the RCN of this simulation as

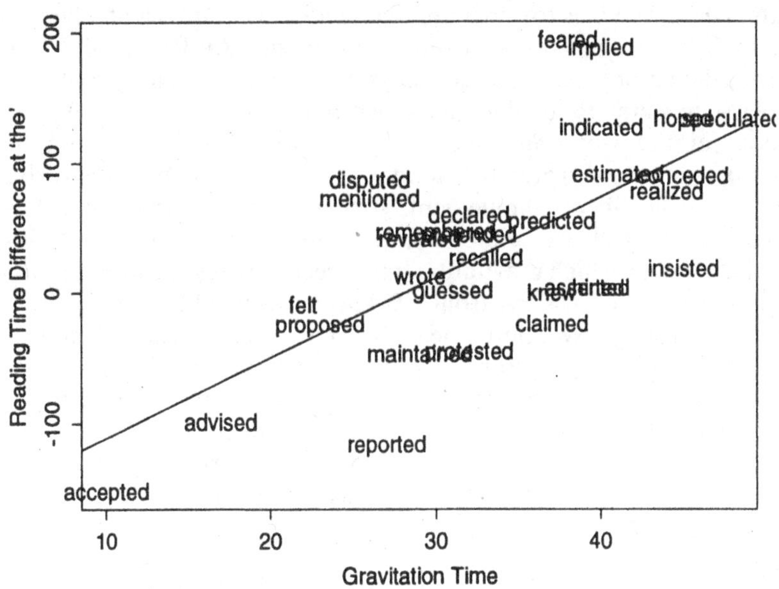

FIG. 16. Regression showing the predicted reading time from simulation 4 as a predictor of human reading difficulty in Experiment 4. $r^2 = 0.45$, $P < 0.00005$.

---

[15]We selected one of the three simulations at random for this analysis because it is meaningless to average over the hidden unit values of different simulations.

[16]In the model, spillover effects seem to be weaker, so we were able to get away without baselining. Since we did not train the model on sequences of the form "V that the", we had no way to baseline the model in the same way we did the humans.

a very strong indicator of a following NP complement. When any one of these 30 verbs is followed by *the* in the model, the model assigns the highest probability to NP complement. This is, of course, a significant error with respect to the target probabilities for all the SC-bias verbs and about half of the EQUI-bias verbs.[17] Correspondingly, in the gravitational model, all 30 of these cases of verb followed by *the* are in the same attractor basin. The attractor that they are all drawn to corresponds to a prototypical NP-bias verb. The verbs are arranged roughly on a cline according to how frequently they take NP complements versus Sbar complements: NP-bias verbs are closest to the attractor, EQUI-bias verbs are at an intermediate distance, and SC-bias verbs are the farthest away. This cline is correlated with the cline of reading times, so there is a good correlation between gravitation times and reading times.

The Experiment 4 simulations thus provide some indication of the potential of this framework to provide a close quantitative fit to reading time data. Moreover, an interesting further prediction is suggested by the framework. The bias towards predicting an NP complement when a verb is followed by *the* may be too strong in this model. An RCN trained to fit the corpus data more accurately (perhaps by training it longer) would probably give rise to a gravitational model with separate attractors for the SC and NP classes at the word *the*. Such a model would show a non-monotonic relationship between gravitation time and the propensity of the verb to take an NP (*vs* an Sbar) complement: strong NP-bias verbs would have low gravitation times because they are near the NP-attractor; EQUI-bias verbs would have fairly high gravitation times because they are in an intermediate region; while certain very strong SC-bias verbs would have low gravitation times because they would be near the Sbar complement attractor. Several likely instances of very strong SC-bias verbs in this sense (e.g. *said*, *thought*) were not included in the model because their high absolute frequencies would skew the corpus statistics. Nevertheless, the gravitational model leads us to expect that such high-frequency SC-bias verbs will show little reading time difficulty at the word *the*, so we leave this as a prediction to be tested in future research.

GENERAL DISCUSSION

Summary

We proposed a dynamical systems approach to parsing in which syntactic hypotheses are associated with attractors in a metric space and reading times correspond to the time it takes the processing system to gravitate to an

[17]When the verb alone is presented, as we noted above, the model appropriately distinguishes between complement types in most cases.

attractor from where it was initially placed in the space. This system predicts increased reading times when a sequence of words shows mixed evidence as to its proper classification, because mixed evidence results in an intermediate initial placement and hence a relatively long gravitation trajectory. These effects occur even when the word sequence is parsed correctly (i.e. when the processor is initially placed in the basin of attraction corresponding to the correct parse). Thus although the current model treats processing as a process of following a trajectory through a representation space, it is *not* equivalent to serial garden-path models, which assume that slowed reading times following an ambiguous region of a sentence typically reflect an incorrect first parse commitment followed by a time-consuming revision. Rather long reading times often reflect a competition process in the spirit of most constraint-based models. In addition, reading time differences can be associated with differences in the strength of attractors due to lexical frequency effects and the frequency with which higher-order grammatical categories occur in different environments.

Support for the approach came from a series of empirical effects which were predicted by the attractor framework. Experiment 1 showed that syntactic preferences across the same phrase types vary in ways that are predictable based on corpus-derived likelihoods. However, Experiment 2 showed that syntactic preferences are not completely predictable from the grammatical statistics of a corpus—sometimes even ungrammatical possibilities appear to exert an influence (for example, the possibility of treating *that* as a complementiser when it follows a verb that does not permit a sentence complement). Experiments 3 and 4 provided a related example—when reading an NP immediately following a sentence complement verb, readers seemed to be influenced by the hypothesis that the NP was a direct object.

Each of these effects was hypothesised to arise from either attractor competition associated with intermediate representations, or differences in the strengths of attractors associated with frequency differences, or a combination of these. These hypotheses were tested in simulations of Experiments 1–4. The simulations used a recurrent network trained on a word prediction task to (a) construct a similarity-based metric space from a training set generated by a corpus and (b) place the system at a point in that representational space as successive words in an input sentence were presented to the system. We then used an algorithm implementing a gravitational dynamical system to model reading times. More precisely, junctures between words in a corpus were assigned to locations in a representation space according to the similarity of preceding and following word sequences; a sample of such locations was interpreted as a set of point masses; processing involved putting a test body in the space and letting it gravitate towards the mass concentration that drew it most strongly. The model successfully categorised the linguistic input and simulated the reading time effects observed in the experiments. An analysis of the trajectories followed by the dynamical system showed how the reading time contrasts stemmed from the specified principles of dynamical processing.

The Role of the Dynamical Component

Given these initially promising results, it is important to evaluate both the potential contributions of this work and its limitations. The first question that arises is exactly what insights are being contributed by the dynamical component of the model. This question is particularly important because our implementation includes an RCN which performs the essential task of organising instances in the metric space, and one might well wonder what additional information the gravitational component is contributing.

In effect, the dynamical system provides a way of elucidating the organisational system adopted by the RCN and showing how it might plausibly be part of a processing system that generates observed reading time contrasts. In particular, the dynamical system permits us to providc explicit accounts of a number of well-known processing phenomena:

1. The time it takes the system to reach an attractor provides an explicit analog of human reading time.
2. The strength of an attractor corresponds to the enhancing effect of the frequency of a grammatical class on processing time.
3. The possibility of placing elements at contrasting distances from an attractor allows us to conceptually unify two sources of reading time contrasts:
   (a) Word strings containing ambiguous signals are mapped to intermediate clusters which do not form their own attractors and hence take a relatively long time to process.
   (b) Low-frequency elements within a grammatical class are mapped to a large cloud of positions around an attractor and hence take longer to process than the corresponding high-frequency elements, which are mapped to a smaller cloud around the same attractor.[18]

Although we have not emphasised property (b) here, we think it is an important advantage of the dynamical treatment that it allows us to unify increased processing time due to category-based ambiguity and increased processing time due to low frequency, by treating them both as stemming

[18]We have not focused on property (b) here, but it seems generally to be consistent with our implementation, and it is consistent with a number of results relating absolute word frequencies to reading time contrasts (Juliano & Tanenhaus, 1994; Trueswell et al., 1993).

from representational intermediacy. This is well-motivated on information-theoretic grounds: the processor should hedge its bets on categorically ambiguous items because they show a mixture of behaviours; it should also hedge its bets on low-frequency items because it has less experience with them and cannot be as sure of their behaviours.

4. The possibility of having aberrations in the phase space which do not correspond to differences in its topology[19] provides an appealing new approach (though not a full-fledged solution—see below) to the "grain size problem". In essence, it provides a way of thinking about "grain size" in a neural-network compatible medium.
5. The attractors correspond to the behaviourally important syntactic distinctions, and thus embody the "emergent properties" that have sometimes been hypothesised to account for syntactic effects in constraint-based models.

The role of the RCN in the model is to assign the instances of between-word junctures in the test corpus to positions in the representation space according to the statistical similarities among the surrounding-word contexts. In fact, it is fairly apparent in the cases of the simple grammars examined here why the RCN places each element where it does: there are clusters corresponding to junctures between words that are statistically distinct under the training grammar and these are spatially organised according to similarity; the density of elements within a cluster is roughly inversely related to distance from the cluster's centre of mass; junctures that contain locally ambiguous cues show residual effects of the stage when the network was primarily sensitive to immediate context effects—they are on the peripheries of the dense clusters for this reason. These principles are consequences of the well-known sensitivity of neural networks to frequency contrasts and the well-known diffusion of the error signal across layers in backpropagation. With an understanding of these principles, one can, in the case of the simple grammars of Experiments 1, 2 and 3, design a phase space by hand which looks very much like the neural network solutions (which reliably emerge over and over again on repeated training trials with different starting weights) and makes all the desired reading time predictions when the dynamics are applied. Certainly, in more complex grammars, the representational system adopted by an RCN may be harder to intuitively predict. We believe that the type of dynamical analysis proposed here may help identify the important features of the representation in such complex cases.

[19]For example, in the gravitational implementation, there are clusters which do not form their own attractors.

Potential Alternative Approaches

One natural alternative approach to the data we examine here would be to directly associate reading times with some property of the RCN. For example, one might try to use output error itself to predict reading times. While this approach is appealing in some respects, it also has some shortcomings. A model which predicted reading times from output error values would not be explicit about what computation was taking more time in some cases, less time in others. In other words, it would be a merely correlative model. Moreover, such an account would not be very revealing of the representational principles underlying its success: there would be nothing corresponding to a parse hypothesis in the model; there would be nothing revealed about the distinctions between different sources of reading time contrast (e.g. frequency of a class *vs* frequency of an element within a class *vs* multiple class membership of a word). Finally, in several of our models, the network learns "too well" for this approach to work well: certain hidden-layer distinctions which give rise to the appropriate reading time predictions are made very minimal on the output layer because they do not correspond to important behavioural differences in the training environment (e.g. the contrast in reading times between "that" and "those" in "The woman visited that hotel" *vs* "The woman visited those hotels"). Thus it would probably be hard to predict the important contrasts by examining output error alone.

Alternatively, one could model grammatically distinct processing states using a recurrent network by associating them with different points along transient trajectories (as in Rodriguez, 1995; Wiles & Elman, 1995), rather than with fixed points (e.g. attractors). This approach would make direct use of the attractor dynamics of RCNs themselves, rather than creating an additional dynamical overlay as we have done, and such simplicity is certainly desirable. However, it is not obvious to us what features of such models might be likely to correspond to reading times. Nor is it clear to us how to implement even finite-state grammars of any complexity using the transient-based computation principles, which seem to require perceiving certain special kinds of symmetry in the data. Thus while we believe that this approach represents a very interesting direction which may eventually help solve some of the most important problems in dynamical grammar representation, it does not seem useful at the present time for handling the processing data we observe.

Limitations of the Current Account

The current dynamical model, of course, has some serious limitations. Newtonian gravitation is not particularly realistic as a model of neural encoding. Nor is the mixture of RCN mechanisms and gravitational mechanisms particularly elegant. But there are at least two reasons to be interested in such a model anyway: (1) it predicts a range of data in a domain where very few implemented models have been put forth, and (2) Newtonian gravitation of the sort we describe is similar to the settling processes in a variety of neural networks which are somewhat better approximations of brain processing. We see it as an important challenge for future research to develop a neural network implementation that handles a similar range of phenomena. Meanwhile, our account provides a nice stepping stone in this direction because we show not only that a range of data can be implemented in a dynamical model with these kinds of properties, but also why the dynamical model makes the right predictions, and why other models fall short. In this way, we articulate a framework in which to develop a more neurally plausible dynamical model.

One possible implementation, closely related to our current proposal, is to combine a standard RCN hidden layer with a clean-up cycle (e.g. Hinton & Shallice, 1991; Hinton, Plaut, & Shallice, 1993) on the output layer. Such a model would be very similar to the gravitational model we discuss here, with the clean-up cycle doing the work of the gravitation mechanism. A potential technical challenge for this approach stems from the fact that clean-up unit layers tend to form attractors at the corners of the unit hypercube, but in the word prediction task, which we have chosen for its usefulness in studying phrase structure in a statistical setting, the output units need to converge on probability distributions, which are generally far from those corners.

Another possibility is to implement continuous activation settling in the recurrent hidden unit layer, for example by using Pineda's (1995) recurrent backpropagation (RBP) algorithm. RBP forms attractors corresponding to distinct classes defined by the training task, and locates them relative to one another according to principles of formal similarity. One might hope that competition between nearby attractors in this framework would lead to similar results to the ones we have observed here. A challenge for this approach is to handle the long-distance dependencies which are typical in natural language.

The current project is also limited in the range of processing phenomena it addresses. We have focused on reading time contrasts that are specifically related to syntactic class ambiguities. One may wonder if the framework is general enough to handle purely structural ambiguities, for example attachment ambiguities. In fact, structural ambiguities, including attachment ambiguities, are quite generally tied to differences in lexical felicity [e.g. "She watched the policeman with the **binoculars**" (ambiguous) *vs* "She watched the policeman with the **moustache**" (unambiguous)]. These differences are associated with different classes of words and thus give rise, in our model, to distinct attractors associated with distinct structural parses. Thus we expect the model to be able to make appropriate predictions about these kinds of cases as well, and are pursuing this hypothesis in ongoing research.

A Useful Reformulation

Finally, we mentioned above that the current model suggests a new approach to the "grain size" problem. In essence, the introduction of attractors and attractor basins into the metric space representational framework of statistical and neural network language research allows us to specify a "grain" above which behavioural distinctions are grammatically significant and below which they are not. This "grain" is indexed by the parameter p in the gravitational model, which determines which clusters of points will form their own basins of attraction and which will be grouped with other clusters. Thus p is a free parameter.

Nonetheless, the current proposal is an improvement over the processing models based on standard, discrete category grammars discussed by Mitchell et al. (1995), for those models appear to face a "grain paradox" in attempting to model the current data. For example, to treat the reading time slow-down at the word *that* after a transitive verb (Experiment 2) as stemming from a conflation of transitive and SC-bias verbs, such models presumably need to claim that on its first pass, the processor just looks at very broad lexical categories of words, treating all verbs as one type. At the word *that* itself, the principle of minimal attachment chooses the determiner option, since it is compatible with the minimal transitive structure and receives no negative signal, even when lexical details are taken into account, for the verb is transitive and *that* is a legitimate determiner. Choosing a smaller initial grain size that, say, distinguishes transitive from SC-bias verbs, will not help because the verb will select the appropriate structure immediately in this case.[20] In other words, no grain size choice is effective under standard representational assumptions. As researchers begin to document a wider range of statistical effects on parsing, we expect that numerous grain size paradoxes like these will emerge.

In the dynamical model, by contrast, we are able to choose a "grain size" independently of reading time considerations, thus allowing us to make the attractors line up almost perfectly with the behavioural distinctions. With attractors of this grain size, we get the appropriate signal-competition effects in reading times. It cannot be said that the current dynamical treatment solves the grain size problem because we have not explained how the right

[20]Nor would it help to adopt a different principle from minimal attachment, which causes the model to parse the "that N" after a transitive verb as the subject of an embedded sentence. Such a model would incorrectly fail to predict reading time difficulty at the embedded subject noun phrase in sentences of the form "NP V[Sbar] [NP VP_{Sbar}]".

grain size can be selected on the basis of behavioural considerations alone (i.e. independently of the training grammar which language learners clearly have no direct information about). Perhaps it can be said, though, that it transforms what was a grain size paradox into a theoretical question about why a certain grain size might emerge as optimal for learning, representational and processing considerations.

REFERENCES

Abraham, R.H., & Shaw, C.D. (1984). *Dynamics—the geometry of behavior*, Vol. 1. Santa Cruz, CA: Aerial Press.

Bates, E., & MacWhinney, B. (1989). Functionalism and the competition model. In B. MacWhinney & E. Bates (Eds), *The cross-linguistic study of sentence processing*. Cambridge: Cambridge University Press.

Bever, T.G. (1970). The cognitive basis for linguistic structures. In J.R. Hayes (Ed.), *Cognition and the development of language*. New York: John Wiley.

Boland, J.E., Tanenhaus, M.K., & Garnsey, S.M. (1990). Evidence for the immediate use of verb control information in sentence processing. *Journal of Memory and Language*, *29*, 413–432.

Brown, P.F., Pietra, V.J.D., DeSouza, P.V., Lai, J.C., & Mercer, R.L. (1992). Class-based n-gram models of natural language. *Computational Linguistics*, *18*, 467–479.

Charniak, E. (1993). *Statistical language learning*. Cambridge, MA: MIT Press.

Elman, J.L. (1990). Finding structure in time. *Cognitive Science*, *14*, 179–211.

Elman, J.L. (1991). Distributed representations, simple recurrent networks, and grammatical structure. *Machine Learning*, *7*, 195–225.

Elman, J.L. (1993). Learning and development in neural networks: The importance of starting small. *Cognition*, *48*, 71–99.

Ferreira, F., & Henderson, J.M. (1990). The use of verb information in syntactic parsing: A comparison of evidence from eye movements and segment-by-segment self-paced reading. *Journal of Experimental Psychology: Learning, Memory and Cognition*, *16*, 555–568.

Fisher, C., Gleitman, H., & Gleitman, L.R. (1991). On the semantic content of subcategorization frames. *Cognitive Psychology*, *23*, 331–392.

Francis, W.N., & Kučera, H. (1982). *Frequency analysis of English usage: Lexicon and grammar*. Boston, MA: Houghton Mifflin.

Frazier, L. (1987). Theories of syntactic processing. In J. Garfield (Ed.), *Modularity in knowledge representation and natural language understanding*. Cambridge, MA: MIT Press.

Frazier, L. (1989). Against lexical generation of syntax. In W.D. Marslen-Wilson (Ed.), *Lexical representation and process*, pp. 505–528. Cambridge, MA: MIT Press.

Frazier, L., & Rayner, K. (1982). Making and correcting errors during sentence comprehension: Eye movements in the analysis of structurally ambiguous sentences. *Cognitive Psychology*, *14*, 178–210.

Garnsey, S.M., Pearlmutter, N.J., Meyers, E., MacDonald, M.C., & McConkie, G.W. (1995). The relative contributions of structural biases and plausibility to sentence comprehension. Poster presented at the *36th Annual Meeting of the Psychonomics Society*, Los Angeles, CA, November.

Hanna, J.E., Spivey-Knowlton, M.J., & Tanenhaus, M.K. (1996). Integrating discourse and local constraints in resolving lexical thematic ambiguities. In *Proceedings of the 18th Annual Cognitive Science Conference*, San Diego, CA, July.

Hinton, G.E., & Shallice, T. (1991). Lesioning an attractor network: Investigations of acquired dyslexia. *Psychological Review*, *98*, 74–95.

Hinton, G.E., Plaut, D.C., & Shallice, T. (1993). Simulating brain damage. *Scientific American*, *269*, 76–82.

Juliano, C., & Tanenhaus, M.K. (1994). A constraint-based lexicalist account of the subject–object attachment preference. *Journal of Psycholinguistic Research*, *23*, 459–471.

Jurafsky, D. (1996). A probabilistic model of lexical and syntactic access and disambiguation. *Cognitive Science*, *20*, 137–194.

Just, M.A., Carpenter, P.A., & Woolley, J. (1982). Paradigms and processes in reading comprehension. *Journal of Experimental Psychology: General*, *111*, 228–238.

Kawamoto, A.H. (1993). Nonlinear dynamics in the resolution of lexical ambiguity: A parallel distributed processing account. *Journal of Memory and Language*, *32*, 474–516.

MacDonald, M.C., Pearlmutter, N.J., & Seidenberg, M.S. (1994). The lexical nature of syntactic ambiguity resolution. *Psychological Review*, *101*, 676–703.

Marcus, M.P., Santorini, B., & Marcinkiewicz, M.A. (1993). Building a large annotated corpus of English: The Penn treebank. *Computational Linguistics*, *19*, 313–330.

Mitchell, D.C. (1989). Verb guidance and other lexical effects in parsing. *Language and Cognitive Processes*, *4*, 123–154.

Mitchell, D.C., Cuetos, F., Corley, M.M.B., & Brysbaert, M. (1995). The linguistic tuning hypothesis: Further corpus and experimental evidence. *Journal of Psycholinguistic Research*, *24*, 469–488.

Pearlmutter, B.A. (1995). Gradient calculations for dynamic recurrent networks: A survey. *IEEE Transactions on Neural Networks*, *6*, 1212–1228.

Perko, L. (1991). *Differential equations and dynamical systems*. New York: Springer-Verlag.

Pineda, F.J. (1995). Recurrent backpropagation networks. In Y. Chauvin & D.E. Rumelhart (Eds), *Backpropagation: Theory, architectures, and applications*. Hillsdale, NJ: Lawrence Erlbaum Associates Inc.

Plaut, D.C., McClelland, J.L., Seidenberg, M.S., & Patterson, K. (1996). Understanding normal and impaired word reading: Computational principles in quasi-regular domains. *Psychological Review*, *103*, 56–115.

Pritchett, B.L. (1992). *Grammatical competence and parsing performance*. Chicago, IL: University of Chicago Press.

Rodriguez, P. (1995). *Representing the structure of a simple context-free language in a recurrent neural network: A dynamical systems approach*. Technical Report, University of California, San Diego, CA.

Rumelhart, D.E., Hinton, G.E., & Williams, R.J. (1986). Learning internal representations by error propagation. In D.E. Rumelhart, J.L. McClelland, & the PDP Research Group (Eds), *Parallel distributed processing*, Vol. 1, pp. 318–362. Cambridge, MA: MIT Press.

Schmauder, A.R., & Egan, M.C. (1995). Verb subcategorization information, argument fit, and on-line sentence processing. Poster presented at the *36th Annual Meeting of the Psychonomics Society*, Los Angeles, CA, November.

Spivey-Knowlton, M., & Sedivy, J.C. (1995). Resolving attachment ambiguities with multiple constraints. *Cognition*, *55*, 227–267.

Spivey-Knowlton, M., & Tanenhaus, M.K. (submitted). Syntactic ambiguity resolution in context: Modeling the effects of referential context and lexical frequency within an integration-competition framework.

Spivey-Knowlton, M., Trueswell, J.C., & Tanenhaus, M.K. (1993). Context effects in syntactic ambiguity resolution. *Canadian Journal of Experimental Psychology*, *47*, 276–309.

Strogatz, S. (1994). *Nonlinear dynamics and chaos*. Reading, MA: Addison-Wesley.

Tabor, W. (1994). The gradual development of degree modifier "sort of" and "kind of": A corpus proximity model. In *Proceedings of the 29th Annual Meeting of the Chicago Linguistics Society*, Chicago, IL, April.

Tabor, W. (1995). Lexical change as nonlinear interpolation. In *Proceedings of the 17th Annual Cognitive Science Conference*, Pittsburgh, PA, July.

Tanenhaus, M.K., & Trueswell, J.C. (1995). Sentence comprehension. In J. Miller & P. Eimas (Eds), *Speech, language, and communication*, Vol. 11, pp. 217–262. San Diego, CA: Academic Press.

Trueswell, J.C. (1996). The role of lexical frequency in syntactic ambiguity resolution. *Journal of Memory and Language, 35*, 566–585.

Trueswell, J.C., Tanenhaus, M.K., & Kello, C. (1993). Verb-specific constraints on sentence processing: Separating effects of lexical preference from garden-paths. *Journal of Experimental Psychology: Learning, Memory and Cognition, 19*, 528–553.

Trueswell, J.C., Tanenhaus, M.K., & Garnsey, S.M. (1994). Semantic influences on parsing: Use of thematic role information in syntactic disambiguation. *Journal of Memory and Language, 33*, 285–318.

Wiles, J., & Elman, J.L. (1995). Landscapes in recurrent networks. In *Proceedings of the 17th Annual Cognitive Science Conference*, Pittsburgh, PA, July.

Zipf, G.K. (1949). *Human behavior and the principle of least effort: An introduction to human ecology*. Reading, MA: Addison-Wesley.

LANGUAGE AND COGNITIVE PROCESSES, 1997, *12* (2/3), 273–306

Parsing of Garden-path Sentences with Reciprocal Verbs

Fernanda Ferreira and Karen K. McClure
Michigan State University, East Lansing, MI, USA

The question addressed in this study is how lexical information stored with verbs is used during the earliest stages of syntactic analysis. The properties of a novel type of verb we term "reciprocal verbs" were examined in three experiments. Reciprocal verbs include *hug* and *kiss*—verbs that alternate between a transitive (e.g. *Bill hugged Mary*) and an intransitive form (*Bill and Mary hugged*), but whose intransitive form requires a conjoined subject. In three experiments, readers were presented with garden-path sentences containing reciprocal verbs, and their eye movements were monitored. The experiments demonstrate that information from the reciprocal verb influenced the earliest stages of syntactic parsing. Implications for models of parsing are discussed, focusing in particular on the argument structure of reciprocal verbs as well as the role of argument-structure frequency in parsing.

INTRODUCTION

For a sentence to be assigned a syntactic structure, the language comprehension system must have access to a grammar, which states the general syntactic principles and constraints of the language, and a parser, which accesses this database of syntactic information and applies it to the incoming lexical string in real time. Typically, the basic operations of the parser are largely opaque. However, ambiguity, which is common in human languages (Frazier, 1987; MacDonald, Pearlmutter, & Seidenberg, 1994), allows some aspects of the parser's functioning to be uncovered. For example, the noun phrase (NP) *Rosa* in the sequence *John knew Rosa* . . . is ambiguous: it could serve as either the object of the verb *knew* or as the

Requests for reprints should be addressed to Fernanda Ferreira, Psychology Research Building, Department of Psychology, Michigan State University, East Lansing, MI 48824-1117, USA. E-mail: fernanda@pilot.msu.edu

This work was supported in part by NSF Grant SBR-9319272. We would like to thank two anonymous reviewers for their thoughtful comments on an earlier draft of this paper. All materials used in these experiments are available by anonymous ftp to eyelab.msu.edu subject of a complement clause (*John knew Rosa would be waiting for him when he got home*). The parser could resolve this temporary syntactic ambiguity in one of two general ways. The first is for the parser to use one or more decision rules for selecting only one of the possible analyses; the second is for the parser to compute any and all analyses for which evidence exists.

The most influential model of the type incorporating decision rules is the garden-path model proposed by Frazier and colleagues (Frazier, 1978, 1987; Frazier & Rayner, 1982). Construction of a syntactic analysis is based on two principles: minimal attachment and late closure. The minimal attachment principle states that the parser does not construct any potentially unnecessary nodes. The parser is inherently conservative, and would rather end up having to create new structure than having to delete already existing structure. Thus the parser prefers the direct object analysis of *John knew Rosa* ... because that analysis requires fewer nodes than does the sentence complement analysis. The late closure principle states that the parser prefers to attach new material (a word, phrase or clause) into the constituent that is currently available, rather than postulating a new constituent or going back to an older one. Thus, given a string such as *After Mary left Tom* ... , the parser takes *Tom* to be the object of *left* rather than the subject of a new clause. This preference arises because the verb phrase (VP) of which the verb *left* serves as head is the phrase that is most available.

These general parsing principles may typically lead to a correct syntactic parse. An analysis of a large corpus of sentences has shown that sequences of the form NP-V-NP frequently map onto the grammatical roles subject-verb-object (Juliano & Tanenhaus, 1994). However, some sentences will require reanalysis. For example, in *After Mary left Tom cried*, the initial analysis on which the NP *Tom* serves as direct object must be relinquished in favour of one in which the phrase is the subject of *cried*. According to the garden-path model, the reanalysis of the sentence is assisted by a specialised device termed a *thematic processor*, which contains information about the various assignments of thematic roles to syntactic constituents, including the plausibility and frequency of the different analyses (Rayner, Carlson, & Frazier, 1983). On this view, sentences are processed in two stages. In the first stage, the parser constructs the analysis dictated by the minimal attachment and late closure principles. In the second stage, the parser evaluates that structure with respect to information contained in the thematic processor. Should syntactic reanalysis be required, this evaluation from the thematic processor may aid in the construction of a new syntactic structure.

The garden-path model is often referred to as a "serial" model, but this terminology may be misleading. The garden-path model is often considered serial because the parser initially entertains only one syntactic structure, the one conforming to minimal attachment and late closure. However, the model is not serial in the sense of postulating large delays in the use of syntactic versus non-syntactic information sources. Thus the reanalysis of an ambiguous string may begin immediately upon detection of incongruence between the initial syntactic analysis and thematic information. For instance, given the string *After the vase broke the boy* . . . , the NP *the boy* will initially be assigned as object of *broke*, but reanalysis may begin immediately, aided by the thematic processor's knowledge that the verb *broke* is often used intransitively when the subject (in this case, *the vase*) is a plausible theme (the so-called ergative structure; Clifton, 1993; Haegeman, 1991). Furthermore, the thematic processor (but, crucially, not the parser) is presumed to have access to all possible analyses and to consider the various alternatives in parallel.

The garden-path model has been most directly contrasted with a class of models known as *constraint-based* models (Juliano & Tanenhaus, 1994; MacDonald et al., 1994; Trueswell, Tanenhaus, & Kello, 1993). These models differ in some of their details, but they share a number of fundamental features. First, the parser is presumed not to require any special-purpose decision principles. Instead, any grammatically licensed analysis may be activated, and the strength of an analysis depends on the evidence for it. Consider again the string *After the vase broke the boy*... Both the analysis on which *the boy* is an object and the analysis on which it is a subject would be activated. However, the former analysis would be weaker than the latter, because *the vase* makes an implausible agent but does make a plausible theme. Thus the intransitive analysis gains strength at the expense of the alternative. An analysis with little support—for example, an infrequent structure or a structure lacking any contextual support—might receive no activation at all. The constraint-based model can account for the vast literature demonstrating garden-path effects, as follows: If a variety of sources of information (lexical, syntactic, contextual) bias a string towards one reading but a competitor analysis ultimately turns out to be correct, the parser will be garden-pathed. The garden path occurs not because the parser has any inherent bias towards one structure or another, but because an analysis for which little evidence was available early in the parse turned out to be the one ultimately required (e.g. *Bill saw the apple wasn't ripe*).

A specific point of comparison between the garden-path and the constraint-based models is often thought to be in the use of lexical information during parsing—more specifically, the use of information stored with individual verbs about the types of phrases with which they co-occur. Consider the string *After Mary left Tom* ... As mentioned earlier, the NP *Tom* could function as either the object of *left* or the subject of a new clause; the late closure principle leads to a preference for the former structure. However, although the verb *leave* permits both structures, the transitive use is more frequent (Connine et al., 1984). Following other researchers (e.g. MacDonald et al., 1994; Tanenhaus, Carlson, & Trueswell, 1989), we will refer to this type of information as *argument-structure information.* An argument structure for a given verb indicates the type of syntactic constituents with which it co-occurs, the grammatical roles (subject, object, and so on) and thematic roles (e.g. agent, patient) of those constituents, and the relative frequency of the structure. One verb may have more than one argument structure, as *leave* does, for example.

According to the garden-path model, the fact that the transitive structure for *leave* is more frequent than the intransitive structure is not relevant to the initial parse of the string. The sequence *After Mary verbed Tom* would be misanalysed regardless of whether a verb with a transitive bias were used or a verb with an intransitive bias (e.g. *walk*). The verb information is used after the initial parse has been constructed to renalyse the incorrect syntactic structure. In contrast, for the constraint-based model, the bias of the verb is one source of information that is used right from the beginning to influence the strength of the alternative parses of the ambiguous string. If a verb were biased strongly enough and other sources of information were not in conflict, it is possible that no garden-path effect would be observed at all with putatively garden-pathing structures. In practice, the empirical differences between the two models can be difficult to observe—the garden-path model can accommodate a null finding of syntactic structure with the assumption that the reanalysis took place quickly, and the constraint-based model can accommodate a null finding of some non-syntactic cue with the assumption that the cue was not sufficiently strong. Nevertheless, the following general prediction can be stated: The garden-path model predicts that garden-path effects will be observed even with verbs strongly biased towards the syntactically less-preferred structure (less preferred according to minimal attachment and late closure); the constraint-based model predicts that they will not.

Unfortunately, even if only those studies that used a sufficiently sensitive task for measuring processing load across a sentence are considered (typically, the moving window technique or eye-movement monitoring), the existing evidence on this question is mixed. Consistent with the garden-path model is work showing garden-path effects even with verbs strongly biased against the preferred interpretation given by minimal attachment and late closure (Anes & Ferreira, 1993; Clifton, 1993; Ferreira & Henderson, 1990; Kennedy, Murray, Jennings, & Reid, 1989; McElree, 1993). Consistent with the constraint-based model are studies demonstrating null effects of structure with appropriately biased verbs (Osterhout, Holcomb, & Swinney, 1994; Trueswell et al., 1993). However, one structure appears to be particularly resilient to verb effects, and that is the structure illustrated in the example *After Mary left Tom cried.* To the best of our knowledge, no-one has shown that this structure is as easy to process as an appropriate control sentence (what constitutes an appropriate control will be discussed later in this paper), no matter what type of verb is placed in the position of *left*. For example, Adams, Clifton and Mitchell (1992) used intransitive verbs such as *sneeze* and still found evidence for garden-pathing; Anes and Ferreira (1993) reported a similar finding. The robustness of this garden-path effect constitutes some of the strongest evidence for the garden-path model and, in particular, for the division of labour between the processes that assign an initial analysis and those that perform reanalysis. However, constraint-based models can accommodate this finding by noting two important facts about the structure *After Mary left Tom cried*: First, as mentioned earlier, sequences of the form NP-V-NP are often resolved towards a subject-verb-object structure. Thus any particular verb information must outweigh this strong general bias in the language. Second, in its written form, this sentence would often have a comma after *left*. Researchers operating within the constraint-based approach point out that the absence of a comma may itself be a cue—in this case, a cue that the first clause should be kept open (Juliano & Tanenhaus, 1994).

As the above exposition should make clear, researchers in the field of parsing often seem to assume the existence of just these two major positions with respect to the use of lexical information during initial parsing: one is that verb information will influence the initial parse, the position associated with constraint-based models; the other is that verb information will not influence the initial parse, the position associated with the garden-path model. However, we believe that at least three coherent positions can be distinguished. First, verb information may influence initial parsing decisions because the frequency of various argument structures stored with a verb contributes towards the activation levels of candidate structures. A second possibility is that verb information may influence initial parsing decisions by licensing or permitting a given argument structure. On this view, only structures permitted by a verb are created, but all permitted structures are equally viable. For example, given a string such as *After Mary arrived Bill*..., the direct object analysis would not be created because *arrive* does not include an argument structure allowing a direct object. But for a string such as *Because Mary walked the meeting* ..., the direct object analysis would be constructed both because of the late closure principle and because the transitive structure is allowed by the verb—crucially, even though the transitive structure is less frequent than other alternatives (and despite the anomalous nature of the phrase *walked the meeting*). The third position is that verb information would have no influence at all, because the initial parse entirely ignores lexically specific information. We will argue in the General Discussion that much of the existing literature on verb effects in parsing (including the present work) supports the second position—that is, the initial parse must be an interpretation licensed by a verb (contrary to the garden-path model), but the frequency with which that interpretation occurs has little effect (contrary to the constraint-based model).

We chose to examine these issues with a class of verbs we term *reciprocal verbs* (Gleitman, Gleitman, Miller, & Ostrin, 1996). These verbs have unique properties that may allow for a deeper understanding of how verb information is used during parsing. Consider the following two sentences:

1a. Bruce dated Demi at one time.
1b. Bruce and Demi dated at one time.

Sentence (1a) is straightforward: *date* is used as a regular agent–patient verb, expressing the proposition that the agent Bruce dated the patient Demi. However, sentence (1b) is distinctive. With a plural subject and no object, this structure can mean that Bruce dated Demi and that also, at the same time, Demi dated Bruce (Gleitman et al., 1996). In other words, this latter syntactic form induces a reciprocal reading (one that could be paraphrased as *Bruce and Demi dated each other at one time*). Thus the verb *date*, like many other verbs, alternates between a transitive and intransitive use. However, most optionally transitive verbs when used in their intransitive form leave an argument of the verb unspecified. For example, *Bill ate last night* is a grammatical sentence, but the theme of the action of eating is left unstated. Thus, in some sense, this sentence is semantically incomplete. What is interesting about the structure shown in (1b) is that the intransitive form with a plural subject does not omit an optional argument; the argument-structure of the verb is "saturated" by the sentence's constituents, meaning that all thematic roles are assigned to syntactic positions.[1]

Because the intransitive form of sentences with reciprocal verbs has the important property that no thematic roles are left unassigned, this structure would seem to be crucial for addressing the question of whether verb information can influence the initial interpretation of a sentence. Thus the goal of our first experiment was to determine whether early closure sentences containing a reciprocal verb and a conjoined subject would be any more difficult than late closure sentences with a singular subject and object. To preview our findings, they were not. In the second experiment, we directly compared early and late closure versions of sentences containing reciprocal verbs with early and late closure versions containing non-

[1]What precisely is the thematic structure of these verbs? This question is complex. In the sentence *Bruce and Demi dated*, Bruce and Demi are both the agents and patients of the dating action. What is peculiar here is that one NP is playing more than one thematic role. This type of structure would thus seem to pose problems for the theta-criterion (Chomsky, 1981), which states that the assignment of thematic roles to syntactic constituents is one-to-one. However, Jackendoff (1987) has provided other linguistic evidence to show that the theta-criterion does not provide an adequate description of how thematic roles are assigned to phrases.

reciprocal optionally transitive verbs. We found that the pattern of results with the two types of verbs was quite different: garden-path effects were observed with optionally transitive verbs but not with the reciprocal verbs. In the third and final experiment, we compared reciprocal and non-reciprocal optionally transitive verbs in early closure sentences that either did or did not contain a comma. The purpose was to investigate whether reanalysis was completed before the disambiguating region of the sentence was read. We found evidence for garden-path effects with the non-reciprocal optionally transitive verbs but not with the reciprocal verbs. Together, these experiments suggest that lexical information from verbs can influence the initial parse of a sentence. However, we will argue in the General Discussion that while the results show an influence of lexical information, they do not support frequency-based approaches (MacDonald et al., 1994; Trueswell et al., 1993) to syntactic parsing.

EXPERIMENT 1

The aim of Experiment 1 was to determine whether garden-path effects would be observed with reciprocal verbs. Participants read sentences while their eye movements were monitored. The sentences they read ultimately conformed either to an early or a late closure structure, and the subject of the sentence was either singular or conjoined. If verb information can be used to avoid a garden path, then we should find that the early closure structure with a reciprocal verb and a conjoined subject is no more difficult to process than a late closure structure with a singular subject and a direct object. Accordingly, we set up the following conditions:

2a. After Demi and Bruce dated the agent announced the wedding. (Early closure, conjoined subject)
2b. After Demi dated the agent the columnist announced the wedding. (Late closure, singular subject)
2c. After Demi dated the agent announced the wedding. (Early closure, singular subject)
2d. After Demi and Bruce dated the agent the columnist announced the wedding. (Late closure, conjoined subject)

Sentences (2a) and (2b) differ in closure but are similar in that both contain the appropriate number of arguments for the verb *dated*. Thus we will refer to these versions as the "good arguments" conditions. If verb information can be used to prevent a garden path, the early closure sentence illustrated in (2a) should be no more difficult than the late closure sentence given in (2b). If the verb information is unavailable to the parser during the construction of its initial syntactic analysis, then sentence (2a) should be more difficult than (2b), because (2a) is inconsistent with late closure. The next two conditions are predicted to be difficult by both theories: (2c) should be difficult both because the structure is early closure and because the verb *date* is missing an important (although perhaps not an obligatory) argument (Gleitman et al., 1996); (2d) should be difficult because the sentence contains an unexpected argument (i.e. the object is unexpected if participants take a reciprocal reading of the conjoined-subject + verb combination), and because the sentence describes a somewhat unusual state of affairs (that two people of different sexes would be dating a third person). Thus we will refer to these versions as the "bad arguments" conditions.

Method

Participants. The participants were 24 undergraduates from Michigan State University, who participated in the experiment in exchange for partial credit in their introductory psychology courses. All participants were native speakers of English and were naive with respect to the hypotheses of the experiment.

Materials. We selected 18 different verbs to be used in this experiment, all of which had a reciprocal form, according to our intuitions.[2] Each of the 18 verbs was placed in two different sentence frames, where by frame we mean a basic sentence type which was varied to create the four experimental conditions. For example, the verb *dated* occurred in two frames, one of which is shown in sentences (2a)–(2d), and the other of which is shown below:

3a. After Richard and Cindy dated the writer rewrote the story.
3b. After Richard dated the writer the editor rewrote the story.
3c. After Richard dated the writer rewrote the story.
3d. After Richard and Cindy dated the writer the editor rewrote the story.

The result was 36 different experimental sentences. We also constructed 63 filler sentences which had a variety of different sentence forms, about half of which were made up of two clauses.

In an attempt to make the experimental materials somewhat more interesting to our undergraduate participants, we created sentences using names of famous poeple (e.g. Demi and Bruce refer to two film actors) or

[2]Generally, intuition is not the best basis on which to select experimental materials. However, as will be seen in the rest of this paper, norms collected for the second experiment verify our intuitions. In addition, the results of this experiment will show that the reciprocal verbs eliminated the garden-path effect. Use of intuition would have been much more problematic had the experiment turned out so that the reciprocal verbs did not override the preference for late closure structures.

famous entities (e.g. well-known sports teams). As examination of (2) and (3) suggests, this property of our stimulus materials might have affected the likelihood that participants obtained a reciprocal reading of the sentences. For example, sentence (3d) might be especially difficult because the names Richard and Cindy induce a reciprocal reading (much more so than would names of non-famous people or of famous people not known to have been a couple at some time), which must then be overridden to make sense of the object *the writer*. We acknowledge that this may be an issue, but any concerns should be alleviated by the second experiment, in which famous names were not used.

Each sentence was followed by a "yes/no" comprehension question. For half of the sentences the correct answer was "yes", and for the other half the correct answer was "no". The sentences, together with their associated questions, were organised into a master list. Each subject saw a single item in only one of the four experimental conditions, but across items, received all conditions of the experiment. Each subject received a different random order of the experimental and filler sentences.

Apparatus. The sentences were presented on a Zenith flat-screen VGA monitor and eye movements were monitored with an ISCAN RK-416 high-speed eyetracker. The eyetracker and monitor were interfaced with a 486-33 microcomputer, which permitted automatic presentation of the stimuli and collection of the eye movement data.

Procedure. Upon arriving for a session, each subject was seated comfortably with his or her head placed in a chin and forehead rest to minimise head movements. The subjects participated in one practice block of 10 trials and then participated in the experimental session. A trial consisted of the following events. First, the experimenter checked the calibration accuracy of the eye movement system. Next, the subject was asked to fixate on a cross on the left edge of the computer screen. The experimenter then pressed a button, and an entire sentence was displayed. None of the sentences exceeded one line on the computer monitor. Participants were instructed to read through each sentence silently and to press a button when they understood the sentence. The experimenter then pressed a button to reveal a comprehension question about the previous sentence. Participants were to respond "yes" or "no" to the questions by pressing prespecified buttons. A short break was given midway through the trials, and participants were also told that they could take a break at any other point between trials if they wished to do so.

Design and Analysis. The experiment was analysed as a 2 × 2 factorial. The first variable was whether the sentence had an optimal or non-optimal number of arguments (good *vs* bad arguments). The second variable was closure (early *vs* late). The dependent measures included first-pass reading times (the sum of all fixations in a region of the sentence prior to exiting that region), total reading time (the sum of all fixations in a region) and regressive eye movements into a region (the percentage of trials on which a regression into a given sentence region from an earlier region of the sentence occurred). First-pass reading times are conventionally viewed as reflecting initial parsing decisions; total reading time and regression pattern are viewed as reflecting the parser's attempts to reanalyse any incorrect syntactic decisions and semantically integrate the information in the sentence.

For the purposes of data analysis, the sentences were divided into regions. The regions will be described using the stimuli in (2) and (3) as examples. The first region included just the reciprocal verb (for the sentences in (2) and (3), the word *dated*). The following region is the ambiguous NP, which includes only the immediately post-verbal NP (*the agent* for (2) and *the writer* for (3)). The next region we term the "disambiguating region"—the part of the sentence indicating how the ambiguous NP must be analysed—and consists of the second verb (*announced* for (2) and *rewrote* for (3)). The phrase "disambiguating region" is a bit misleading for the late closure sentences, because the second post-verbal NP (*the columnist* for (2) and *the editor* for (3)) may also sometimes serve as the disambiguating part of these sentences. We report the results of this second post-verbal region at the end of the Results section. The last region of the sentences covers whatever comes after the disambiguating region (*the wedding* for (2) and *the story* for (3)). The data were analysed with both participants (F_1) and items (F_2) as random effects.

Results

Comprehension questions were answered correctly on over 90% of trials; no differences in accuracy across conditions were observed. Data for the eye movement measures include all trials. (The pattern of results found with just correct trials included did not differ from the pattern including all trials.)

Reciprocal Verb Region. First-pass reading times across all regions of the sentences in the four conditions are shown in Table 1. For the region consisting of the reciprocal verb (e.g. *dated*), there was no effect of closure (both $F < 1$), no effect of the arguments variable (all $P > 0.05$), and no interaction between the two variables (both $P > 0.05$). These results are to be expected, as the closure of the sentences and the goodness of the arguments are not yet decided at this early point in the sentences.

TABLE 1
First-pass and Total Reading Times (msec): Experiment 1

	Region							
	First Verb		*Ambiguous NP*		*Disambiguating Word*		*Rest of Sentence*	
Measure	*FP*	*TT*	*FP*	*TT*	*FP*	*TT*	*FP*	*TT*
Good arg./EC	249	424	391	688	252	429	207	355
Good arg./LC	303	559	387	751	263	423	257	366
Bad arg./EC	274	680	430	913	285	541	306	465
Bad arg./LC	265	540	356	839	223	508	326	557

Abbreviations: NP, noun phrase; FP, first-pass reading time; TT, total reading time; EC, early closure; LC, late closure.

Total reading time across the regions in the four experimental conditions is also shown in Table 1. As can be seen from this table, total reading time on the reciprocal verb was shorter in the good arguments condition than in the bad arguments condition (610 *vs* 492 msec) [$F_1(1,23) = 20.71$, MSe = 16248, $P < 0.05$; $F_2(1,35) = 18.36$, MSe = 31629, $P < 0.05$]. Total reading time was unaffected by closure (both $F < 1$). The interaction between these two variables was reliable [$F_1(1,23) = 12.96$, MSe = 455954, $P < 0.05$; $F_2(1,35) = 34.05$, MSe = 16614, $P < 0.05$]. The early closure/good arguments condition was shorter than the two late closure conditions ($P < 0.05$); the two late closure conditions did not differ from each other ($P > 0.65$); and the early closure/bad arguments condition was reliably slower than the two late closure conditions ($P < 0.05$). Regressions to this region were more common in the bad arguments than in the good arguments condition (32.7 *vs* 19.5%) [$F_1(1,23) = 18.11$, MSe = 230, $P < 0.05$; $F_2(1,35) = 10.97$, MSe = 480, $P < 0.05$].

Ambiguous Region. For first-pass reading times on this region (e.g. *the agent*), there was a suggestion of an effect of closure [$F_1(1,23) = 3.84$, MSe = 9325, $0.05 < P < 0.10$; $F_2(1,35) = 1.89$, MSe = 15629, $P > 0.15$]. This tendency is probably spurious, because the closure of the sentences is not yet decided at this point. The arguments variable had no effect (both $F < 1$) and there was no reliable interaction (both $P > 0.10$).

Total reading time was shorter in the good arguments than the bad arguments condition (720 *vs* 876 msec) [$F_1(1,23) = 13.32$, MSe = 44059, $P < 0.05$; $F_2(1,35) = 24.33$, MSe = 34598, $P < 0.05$]. There was no effect of closure (both $F < 1$). The interaction between these two variables was marginal by participants and significant by items [$F_1(1,23) = 2.77$, MSe = 41027, $0.05 < P < 0.10$; $F_2(1,35) = 4.61$, MSe = 32589, $P < 0.05$]. Reading times were similar in the early closure/good arguments and late closure/good arguments conditions (688 and 751 msec respectively), but were significantly longer in the late closure/bad arguments condition (839 msec; $P < 0.05$). Reading times were longest in the early closure/bad arguments condition (913 msec; $P < 0.05$).

Regressions to this region were affected by the arguments variable [$F_1(1,23) = 8.42$, MSe = 179, $P < 0.05$; $F_2(1,35) = 4.48$, MSe = 471, $P < 0.05$]. Regressions occurred on 27.7% of trials in the bad arguments condition and 19.8% of trials in the good arguments condition.

Disambiguating Region. First-pass reading times on this region (e.g. *rewrote*) are given in Table 1. Reading times did not show a main effect of either experimental variable (all $P > 0.15$). However, the two variables interacted [$F_1(1,23) = 4.75$, MSe = 666, $P < 0.05$; $F_2(1,35) = 3.01$, MSe = 8123, $0.05 < P < 0.10$]. The late closure/good arguments and the early closure/good arguments conditions did not differ reliably (263 and 252 msec; $P > 0.05$). The early closure/bad condition was significantly slower (285 msec) than these two conditions ($P < 0.05$), and, oddly, the late closure/bad condition was significantly shorter (223 msec) than those same two conditions ($P < 0.05$).

Total reading time on the disambiguating region was not significantly affected by either variable (all $P > 0.10$) and regressions from this region did not show any systematic pattern.

End-of-sentence Region. First-pass reading times (see Table 1) on the end-of-sentence region (*the story*) were unaffected by closure (both $F < 1$), but were affected by the arguments variable: Reading times were longer in the bad arguments condition than in the good arguments condition (316 *vs* 232 msec) [$F_1(1,23) = 4.07$, MSe = 41580, $P < 0.05$; $F_2(1,35) = 2.71$, MSe = 44924, $0.05 < P < 0.10$]. The two variables did not interact (both $P > 0.20$). Total reading times were longer in the bad arguments than in the good arguments condition (511 *vs* 361 msec), but the effect was marginal by participants and items [$F_1(1,23) = 4.07$, MSe = 41580, $0.05 < P < 0.10$; $F_2(1,35) = 2.71$, MSe = 44924, $0.05 < P < 0.10$]. No other effects were significant (all $P > 0.20$). Regressions from this region showed no systematic pattern.

Second Post-verbal NP. This region exists only for the two late closure sentences. First-pass and total reading times did not differ in this region. First-pass reading times were 305 and 287 msec in the good and bad arguments conditions respectively, and total reading times were 472 and 424 msec respectively (all $F < 1$).

Discussion

The critical finding from this experiment is that first-pass reading times on the disambiguating word of the sentences were equivalent in the late closure and early closure "good arguments" conditions—that is, in the two conditions in which the argument structure of the verb was properly satisfied. This result suggests that the garden-path effect typically associated with early closure structures can be overridden when the critical verb is a reciprocal verb and occurs with the appropriate number of arguments. The evidence from the total time data reinforce this conclusion. For each region, the early closure/good arguments condition was either the fastest overall, or was no slower than the late closure/good arguments condition.

The one anomalous finding was that first-pass reading times on the disambiguating region were remarkably short in the late closure/bad arguments condition. To understand why this effect might have occurred, consider what the participant has read up to the point just before the disambiguating word is encountered in an example such as *After Richard and Cindy dated the writer the editor* ... The reader at this point has four entities to maintain in memory. It is possible that some participants on some trials become confused and simply give up on the sentence, deciding to start over in the hope of discovering a sensible interpretation. (Note from Table 1 that first-pass reading times on the ambiguous NP were also shortest in this condition.) This would lead one to expect that first-pass reading times on the disambiguating word (and preceding NP) would be short in this condition and that total reading times throughout the sentence would be long, just the pattern that was obtained in Experiment 1.

We also found that reading times on the second post-verbal NP in the two late closure conditions were the same regardless of whether the first verb occurred with the appropriate number of arguments. This result could be taken to indicate that comprehenders reading that second NP have not yet come up with a satisfactory interpretation of these sentences, and indeed do not compute one until they reach the end of the sentence. One reason for this delay in obtaining an interpretation may have to do with the presence of ambiguities in these sentences in addition to the ones we identified and experimentally manipulated. For example, the sequence *After Richard (and Cindy) dated the writer the editor* could continue *fired the press had a field day*. On this interpretation, the comprehender constructs a reduced relative interpretation of the NP *the writer the editor*. Indeed, this reduced relative interpretation of the post-verbal NP is possible even when the second post-verbal NP is not present—that is, in the early closure conditions (e.g. *After Richard and Cindy dated the writer fired by the editor* ...). Our point here is not to try to provide a coherent account of the patterns of reading times by invoking this additional ambiguity; rather, we wish to draw attention to the presence of multiple ambiguities in these sentences, because the presence of these ambiguities may account for some of the less central patterns of data in this experiment. These other ambiguities should perhaps be identified and manipulated more systematically in future work—for example, by varying whether verbs ambiguous between a past-tense and past-participle reading are used.

The results of Experiment 1, then, suggest that information from reciprocal verbs can prevent a garden path from occurring. To test this possibility further, we conducted a second experiment. For this experiment, we included both reciprocal verbs and non-reciprocal (but optionally transitive) verbs in the same study, so that we could compare their properties directly. We also decided not to include the late closure, conjoined subject condition in this experiment, for two reasons. The first and most important reason is that we needed to keep the number of conditions in the experiment to a manageable size (especially given the limited number of verbs with the appropriate properties available for rotating through the conditions). The other reason we eliminated the late closure, conjoined subject condition is that it appears to be so confusing to subjects (based on the results of Experiment 1) that we doubt it can provide any useful information about garden-path effects and how they are influenced by the argument-taking properties of verbs.

EXPERIMENT 2

The purpose of this experiment was to compare the processing of garden-path sentences containing reciprocal verbs with those containing optionally transitive verbs. Within each verb type, three sentence forms were used. Examples are shown below.

Reciprocal verb

4a. After Jose and the bride kissed the party began in earnest.
4b. After Jose kissed the bride the party began in earnest.
4c. After Jose kissed the party began in earnest.

Optionally transitive verb

5a. After Jose and the bride signalled the party began in earnest.
5b. After Jose signalled the bride the party began in earnest.
5c. After Jose signalled the party began in earnest.

Version (a) is the early closure sentence form with a conjoined subject (and no object). If reciprocal verbs can block garden-pathing, then reading times on the disambiguating word (*began*) should be fast in (4a) but slow in (5a). Version (b) is the late closure sentence form with a singular subject and object. This version should be equivalently easy to process in both (4b) and (5b) (that is, regardless of verb type). Version (c) is the early closure sentence form with a singular subject (and no object). This sentence type should be difficult for both verb types, but the difficulty should be exaggerated in the reciprocal verb condition (4c). This prediction follows because reciprocal verbs can be used intransitively only if the subject is plural; other optionally transitive verbs do not have this restriction. Thus sentence (4c) is somewhat anomalous, and so should be difficult for participants to comprehend.

Method

Participants. Thirty-six participants were recruited from the same subject pool as in Experiment 1.

Materials. To identify reciprocal and optionally transitive verbs, we conducted a norming study in which 24 participants from our subject pool were asked to construct sentences using a specified verb. Each participant constructed a single sentence for each of 80 different verbs. Responses were then classified as follows. Each sentential subject was identified as singular or plural. The material following the verb was categorised as either a direct object or a non-object (e.g. a prepositional phrase, an adverbial phrase, or no following material). The object continuations constituted the transitive uses and the non-object continuations constituted the intransitive uses. Reciprocal verbs were identified as those verbs that were used both transitively and intransitively, but whose intransitive use always coincided with a plural subject. For the optionally transitive verbs, we selected verbs with the same degree of transitivity as the reciprocal verbs (approximately 65% transitive uses; all other uses classified as intransitive), but for which intransitive uses occurred with singular and not plural subjects. Cases in which participants provided a reciprocal anaphor (e.g. *each other*) after the verb were discarded, because this form induces a reciprocal reading in verbs that are otherwise not reciprocal. (Many non-reciprocal verbs used with a plural subject and a reciprocal anaphor as object can be interpreted reciprocally, as in *Mary and Susan saw each other* but **Mary and Susan saw* vs *Mary and Susan kissed each other* and *Mary and Susan kissed*.)

It should be noted that we will refer to the two classes of verbs as "reciprocal verbs" and "optionally transitive verbs". However, reciprocal verbs are also obviously optionally transitive; indeed, the two verb types were matched on degree of transitivity for this experiment (all were verbs used transitively approximately 65% of the time, as assessed in our norming study). Thus the term "optionally transitive" should be interpreted as shorthand for "optionally transitive but not reciprocal".

From these norms, we identified 18 reciprocal verbs and 18 optionally transitive verbs. We used these to construct 36 different experimental sentences, each of which occurred in one of six different conditions, as exemplified in (4) and (5). We also constructed 63 filler sentences for the experiment. A "yes/no" comprehension question was created for each experimental and filler sentence. For half of the sentences the correct answer was "yes", and for the other half the correct answer was "no". The sentences, together with their associated questions, were organised into a master list. Each participant saw a single experimental item in only one of the six conditions, but across items, received all conditions of the experiment. Each participant received a different random order of the experimental and filler sentences.

Apparatus and Procedure. The apparatus and procedure were the same as in Experiment 1.

Design and Analysis. The experiment was analysed as a 2 × 3 factorial. The first variable was verb type: reciprocal *vs* optionally transitive. The second variable was sentence type: early closure with a conjoined subject, early closure with a singular subject, and late closure with a singular subject. These conditions will be referred to as the early-conjoined, early-singular and late closure conditions, respectively. The dependent measures were first-pass reading time and total reading time. Regressions into a region were also analysed, but showed no statistically reliable patterns and so will not be discussed further.

Sentences were divided into scoring regions as follows: the first verb (*kissed vs signalled* in examples (4) and (5)); the ambiguous NP, which was always the NP immediately following the first verb (*the party* in (a) and (c) and *the bride* in (b)); the disambiguating region (*began*); the rest of the sentence (*in earnest*); and the second post-verbal NP, which occurred only in the two late closure (b) conditions (*the party*).

Results

Comprehension questions were answered correctly on 88.3% of trials. Accuracy was similar across experimental conditions (ranging from 86 to 90%), and the pattern of data including only correct trials did not differ from the pattern with all trials included. Analyses of eye movement data reported below are based on all experimental trials.

First Verb. First-pass reading times across all regions of the sentences in the six conditions are shown in Table 2. Recall that the first verb of the sentence could be either reciprocal (e.g. *kissed*) or optionally transitive (e.g.

TABLE 2
First-pass and Total Reading Times (msec): Experiment 2

	Region							
	First Verb		*Ambiguous NP*		*Disambiguating Word*		*Rest of Sentence*	
Measure	*FP*	*TT*	*FP*	*TT*	*FP*	*TT*	*FP*	*TT*
Op. Tran./LC	205	423	341	670	178	321	328	530
Op. Tran./EC	218	437	379	780	243	433	370	619
Op. Tran./EC	194	395	304	765	219	411	352	620
Recip./LC	187	351	333	557	233	391	330	550
Recip./EC	191	347	368	645	192	312	328	538
Recip./EC	205	333	286	684	215	382	318	542

Abbreviations: NP, noun phrase; FP, first-pass reading time; TT, total reading time; EC, early closure; LC, late closure; Op. Tran., optionally transitive; Recip., reciprocal.

signalled). First-pass reading times on the verb were affected by this verb type variable: reading times were longer in the optionally transitive condition (206 msec) than in the reciprocal condition (179 msec). The effect was significant by subjects [$F_1(1,35) = 4.59$, MSe = 8633, $P < 0.05$], but marginal by items [$F_2(1,35) = 2.77$, MSe = 15778, $P > 0.10$]. This difference is largely uninterpretable, however, because the two types of verbs were not controlled for frequency or character length. Sentence type had no effect (both $P > 0.20$) and there was no interaction between the two variables (both $F < 1$).

Total reading times across the regions in the six experimental conditions are also shown in Table 2. Total reading times on this region were more robustly affected by the verb type variable [$F_1(1,35) = 11.55$, MSe = 25938, $P < 0.05$; $F_2(1,35) = 10.83$, MSe = 27461, $P < 0.05$]. Reading times were 344 msec in the reciprocal verb condition and 418 msec in the optionally transitive condition. As stated above, the cause of this difference is unclear, because the two verb types were not equated on standard lexical variables such as length and frequency. However, given the somewhat marked status of reciprocal verbs (i.e. reciprocal verbs permit their thematic patients or themes to occur in subject position), it is reassuring that in this experiment they appear to be easier to process than the optionally transitive verbs. No other effects were reliable (all $F < 1$).

Ambiguous Noun Phrase. First-pass reading times (see Table 2) on the next region, the ambiguous noun phrase (*the party* in our example), were not affected by verb type (both $P > 0.25$). However, there was an effect of sentence type [$F_1(1,35) = 5.55$, MSe = 19811, $P < 0.05$; $F_2(1,35) = 3.98$,

MSe = 19401, $P < 0.05$]. Regardless of verb type, reading times were shortest in the early-singular condition (295 msec), intermediate in the late closure condition (337 msec), and longest in the early-conjoined condition (373 msec).

The total reading time data also showed a main effect of sentence type [$F_1(1,35) = 3.59$, MSe = 73595, $P < 0.05$; $F_2(1,35) = 3.93$, MSe = 68977, $P <$ 0.05]. Total time spent on the ambiguous noun phrase did not differ for the two early closure conditions (712 and 724 msec for the conjoined and singular conditions respectively; $P > 0.05$), and reading times were longer in these conditions than in the late closure condition (614 msec; $P < 0.05$). Verb type also had a reliable effect on total reading time [$F_1(1,35) = 9.15$, MSe = 71490, $P < 0.05$; $F_2(1,35) = 10.94$, MSe = 71626, $P < 0.05$]. Reading times were shorter for reciprocal verbs (628 msec) than for optionally transitive verbs (738 msec), an apparent spillover effect from the previous region. There was no interaction between these two variables (both $P > 0.35$).

Disambiguating Region. For the first-pass reading times on the critical disambiguating region of the sentence (*began*), a significant interaction occurred between the verb and sentence type factors [$F_1(2,70) = 5.30$, MSe = 9467, $P < 0.05$; $F_2(2,70) = 7.30$, MSe = 11809, $P < 0.05$]. The means are given in Table 2. The reciprocal and optionally transitive verbs differed reliably in the late closure condition (233 and 178 msec respectively; $P <$ 0.05) and the early-conjoined condition (192 and 243 msec; $P < 0.05$), but did not differ in the early-singular condition (215 and 219 msec; $P > 0.05$). The crucial finding for the hypothesis that verb information can influence early parsing decisions is that the early-conjoined condition was shorter when a reciprocal verb had occurred earlier compared with an optionally transitive verb; indeed, the early-conjoined condition was fastest overall for the reciprocal verbs, but slowest for the optionally transitive verbs. There were no main effects (all $F < 1$).

The total reading time data show the same pattern as the first-pass data (Table 2). The interaction between verb and sentence type was reliable [$F_1(2,70) = 8.83$, MSe = 18625, $P < 0.05$; $F_2(2,70) = 7.14$, MSe = 44259, $P <$ 0.05]. Total reading time for the late closure sentence type was reduced in the optionally transitive verb condition compared to the reciprocal verb condition (321 *vs* 391 msec; $P < 0.05$). For the early-conjoined sentences, reading times were longer in the optionally transitive condition than in the reciprocal condition (433 *vs* 312 msec; $P < 0.05$). Total reading time was similar for the two types in the early-singular condition (382 msec for reciprocal verbs and 411 msec for optionally transitive verbs; $P > 0.05$). The effect of sentence type was reliable by items [$F_2(1,35) = 3.95$, MSe = 29983, $P < 0.05$], but not by subjects [$F_1(1,35) = 1.73$, MSe = 17352, $P > 0.15$]. There was no reliable effect of verb type (both $P > 0.15$).

Rest of Sentence. First-pass reading times for the material in the sentence remaining after the disambiguating region were unaffected by either variable (all $P > 0.25$), and there was no interaction (both $F < 1$). Total reading time was also unaffected by the experimental variables (all $P > 0.20$).

Second Post-verbal NP. First-pass reading times on the second post-verbal NP (which occurred only in the two late closure conditions) were 336 msec in the reciprocal verb condition and 345 msec in the optionally transitive condition (both $F < 1$). Total reading times were shorter when the sentence occurred with a reciprocal verb (572 *vs* 685 msec; both $P < 0.05$). We reported similar findings above: Reading times are often shorter for sentences containing a reciprocal verb. This result seems to suggest that reciprocal verbs are easier to process than similar optionally transitive verbs, and that material in a sentence is easier to incorporate with such verbs.

Discussion

The goal of this experiment was to compare the processing of garden-path sentences containing reciprocal verbs and optionally transitive verbs. The crucial finding was that for reciprocal verbs, first-pass reading times on the disambiguating word were shorter in the early closure/conjoined condition, while for optionally transitive verbs, first-pass reading times were slowest in this same condition. Indeed, the pattern of data for the two verb types was virtually complementary. A similar pattern was evident in the total reading time data. However, other results from this experiment were unexpected. We predicted that reading times for the early closure/singular subject condition would be longer for reciprocal verbs than for optionally transitive verbs, because sentences with a singular subject and a reciprocal verb are somewhat anomalous (e.g. *After Jose kissed the party began in earnest*). Instead, we found that the two conditions were equivalent. We further predicted that reading times in the late closure condition would be equivalent for the two verb types, because in both conditions the syntactic and semantic demands of the verb appear to be properly met. Instead, we found that reading times were longer for reciprocal verbs than for optionally transitive verbs. These same unexpected results were found in both the first-pass and total reading time data. We suspect that any attempt to explain these findings should be deferred until these results are successfully replicated.

Even if we focus exclusively on the finding that the early closure/conjoined condition was shortest for reciprocal verbs but slowest for optionally transitive verbs, it is still possible to view the results as consistent with garden-path models of parsing. It is possible that the region we considered crucial for deciding between the predictions of the two models in Experiments 1 and 2 is actually located beyond the point in the sentences at which the garden path is resolved. That is, it is possible that when participants encounter *When Jose and the bride kissed the party* . . . , they attempt to attach *the party* as an object of *kissed*, as the garden-path model would predict. That syntactic decision may then be revised quickly, before the next word (which we have categorised as the "disambiguating region") has been encountered. Thus reading time differences would not be observed on the disambiguating region, because the initial misanalysis and reanalysis occurred just immediately before in the sentence, in the ambiguous region. Indeed, recall from our earlier description of the thematic processor that reanalysis should operate in just this way. The parser constructs a direct object analysis for *When Jose and the bride kissed the party*, but the thematic processor immediately detects that a better analysis (given the properties of the verb) is available. Reanalysis would then occur before the (putatively) disambiguating region of the sentence was read.

To examine this possibility, stimuli must be constructed that allow processing on the ambiguous region (*the party*) to be examined. One way to accomplish this goal is to compare the processing of early closure sentences with and without commas in the appropriate locations. For example, consider sentence (6):

6a. After Jose and the bride kissed / signalled the party began in earnest.
6b. After Jose and the bride kissed, / signalled, the party began in earnest.

In the (b) conditions, the two clauses are separated by a comma, and so the parser should not be tempted to take *the party* to be an object of the first verb. The (a) conditions should permit the tempting misanalysis to occur. Thus reading times on *the party* can be compared. From the results of the previous two experiments, we predicted that reading times on *the party* would be longer when the comma did not occur, but only in the optionally transitive verb condition. This prediction follows because if participants use the information from the conjoined subject and the reciprocal verb to avoid a garden path, then there should be little temptation to take *the party* to be an object, and so there should be little difference between the condition in which a comma is present versus one in which the comma is absent.

EXPERIMENT 3

For this experiment, we examined the processing of sentences such as (6), in which the verb was either reciprocal or optionally transitive, and either contained a disambiguating comma or not. The purpose of the experiment was to determine whether garden-path effects would be observed on the ambiguous noun phrase of the sentence, as the garden-path model of parsing might predict.

Method

We recruited 36 participants from the same subject pool as in the previous experiments. The apparatus and procedure were the same as in the previous studies. The materials were adapted from the ones used in Experiment 2. We used only the conjoined subject conditions from the 36 experimental sentences used in that experiment, leaving us with two versions, one in which the verb was reciprocal, and the other in which the verb was optionally transitive. This verb type factor was crossed with comma present versus absent, resulting in the four conditions shown in (6). There were 64 filler sentences constructed for the experiment. Eleven had two commas, 21 had one comma and 32 had no commas. Again, a "yes/no" comprehension question was asked after each sentence.

The design of this study was 2 (verb type) × 2 (comma present *vs* absent), and data analysis procedures were the same as those described for the previous experiments. Sentences were divided into scoring regions as in Experiment 2. However, we make a crucial prediction about first-pass reading times on the ambiguous region which can be tested in two planned comparisons: The prediction is that, for reciprocal verbs, there will be no difference between the comma-present and comma-absent conditions; for optionally transitive verbs, the comma-absent condition should be reliably longer. Thus, rather than testing for the interaction in this region, we will report the results of these planned comparisons. Other differences between this experiment and the previous ones are that now the region consisting of the first verb also includes a comma in the comma-present conditions, and that the critical region is the ambiguous noun phrase of the sentence.

Results

Comprehension questions were answered correctly on 89.9% of trials. Accuracy was similar across experimental conditions (ranging only from 89 to 90%), and the pattern of data including only correct trials did not differ from the pattern with all trials included. Analyses of eye movements data reported below are based on all experimental trials.

First Verb. First-pass reading times across all regions of the sentences in the four conditions are shown in Table 3. First-pass reading times on the first verb were not affected by verb type (both $F < 1$), but were affected by the presence of a comma [$F_1(1,35) = 5.02$, MSe = 6735, $P < 0.05$; $F_2(1,35) = 3.72$, MSe = 6154, $0.05 < P < 0.10$]. Reading times were 265 msec with a comma and 296 msec without. There was no reliable interaction (all $P > 0.25$).

TABLE 3
First-pass and Total Reading Times (msec): Experiment 3

	Region							
	First Verb		*Ambiguous NP*		*Disambiguating Word*		*Rest of Sentence*	
Measure	*FP*	*TT*	*FP*	*TT*	*FP*	*TT*	*FP*	*TT*
Recip. verb/ no comma	300	484	440	738	270	382	407	565
Recip. verb/ comma	255	369	421	612	274	389	372	576
Op. Tran. verb/ no comma	291	596	447	927	287	499	409	619
Op. Tran. verb/ comma	275	494	399	657	260	421	429	635

Abbreviations: NP, noun phrase; FP, first-pass reading time; TT, total reading time; Op. Tran., optionally transitive; Recip., reciprocal.

Total reading times across the regions in the four experimental conditions are also shown in Table 3. Total reading times were longer for optionally transitive verbs than for reciprocal verbs (545 *vs* 427 msec) [$F_1(1,35) = 33.22$, MSe = 15074, $P < 0.05$; $F_2(1,35) = 16.87$, MSe = 30858, $P < 0.05$]. This effect was seen in Experiment 2 as well: Even though reciprocal verbs have somewhat marked syntactic properties, they apparently take less time to read in these experiments than do the optionally transitive verbs. However, as was noted previously, this result could be due to lexical factors that were not controlled in this experiment. Reading times were longer in the comma-absent condition than the comma-present condition (540 *vs* 431 msec) [$F_1(1,35) = 18.07$, MSe = 23406, $P < 0.05$; $F_2(1,35) = 28.72$, MSe = 15500, $P < 0.05$]. Not surprisingly, participants spend more time on this portion of the sentence when it is more ambiguous—that is, when it does not include a comma.

Ambiguous Noun Phrase. As was described above, the ambiguous noun phrase is the crucial region for distinguishing the predictions of the garden-path model and a model that allows verb information to guide the initial parse of a sentence. For the garden-path model, there should be a reliable difference in first-pass reading times between the comma-absent and comma-present conditions for both verb types. For the alternative model, the difference should be found only for optionally transitive verbs, not for reciprocal verbs. Planned comparisons supported this alternative model. For reciprocal verbs, reading times were 440 msec in the comma-absent condition and 421 msec in the comma-present condition, a non-reliable 19 msec difference (standard error of the mean = 17.5 msec). For optionally transitive verbs, reading times were 447 and 399 msec in the comma-absent and comma-present conditions respectively, a reliable 48 msec difference (standard error of the mean = 16.6 msec).

Total reading time showed a similar but not identical pattern. For reciprocal verbs, total reading time was 738 msec in the comma-absent condition and 612 msec in the comma-present condition, a reliable 125 msec difference (standard error = 27.5 msec). For optionally transitive verbs, reading times were 927 and 657 msec in the same two conditions, a robust 270 msec difference (standard error = 30.1 msec). Thus, in total reading time, we see a cost associated with the absence of the comma for both reciprocal and optionally transitive verbs. However, the cost is much greater for the latter verb type.

Regressions from this region were affected by absence of the comma: regressions occurred on 34.5% of trials in the comma-absent condition and 24.1% of trials in the comma-present condition [$F_1(1,35) = 27.66$, MSe = 141, $P < 0.05$; $F_2(1,35) = 16.60$, MSe = 268, $P < 0.05$]. No other effects were reliable (all $P > 0.05$). Thus it appears that readers made more regressions in the more ambiguous condition, the one in which a comma did not separate the two clauses.

Disambiguating Word. First-pass reading times on this region were not affected by any variable (all $F < 1$). For reciprocal verbs, reading times were 270 and 274 msec in the comma-absent and comma-present conditions respectively, a non-reliable difference of 4 msec in the wrong direction (standard error = 17.4 msec). For optionally transitive verbs, reading times were 287 and 260 msec in the same two conditions, a non-reliable difference of 27 msec (standard error = 17.4 msec).

The total reading time data showed a similar pattern. For reciprocal verbs, total reading time was 382 and 389 msec in the comma-absent and comma-present conditions respectively, a non-reliable 7 msec difference in the wrong direction (standard error = 36.2 msec). For optionally transitive verbs, total reading time was 499 and 421 msec in the same two conditions, a reliable 78 msec difference (standard error = 36.2 msec). Thus, with reciprocal verbs, there is no cost associated with the absence of the comma; for optionally transitive verbs, the absence of the comma makes the sentence more difficult to comprehend.

Rest of Sentence. First-pass reading times on the rest of the sentence were not affected by the experimental variables (all $P > 0.25$). Total reading time was somewhat longer for the sentences containing optionally transitive verbs than for the sentences containing reciprocal verbs (627 *vs* 570 msec), but this difference was not reliable [$F_1(1,35) = 1.78$, MSe = 65351, $P > 0.15$; $F_2(1,35) = 3.23$, MSe = 63918, $0.05 < P < 0.10$].

Discussion

The crucial prediction in this experiment concerned first-pass reading times on the ambiguous noun phrase of the sentences. We found that for optionally transitive verbs, reading times on this noun phrase were longer in the condition in which the comma was absent compared with the condition in which the comma was present. This result may be taken to indicate that, without the informative cue provided by the comma, the parser took the ambiguous noun phrase to be the object of the optionally transitive verb. This misanalysis was corrected while the parser was still attending to this phrase, so that reading times on the subsequent region did not show a penalty due to the absence of the comma. In contrast, we found that for reciprocal verbs, reading times on the ambiguous noun phrase did not differ depending on the presence or absence of the comma. This result may be taken to indicate that the parser is likely to correctly analyse the noun phrase as the subject of the second clause whether or not a disambiguous comma is present. Thus when participants encounter *the party* in *After Jose and the bride kissed the party*, the information about the reciprocity of the verb *kissed*, together with the plurality of the subject, allows *the party* to be correctly parsed.

GENERAL DISCUSSION

We conducted three experiments to investigate the processing of garden-path sentences containing reciprocal verbs to determine whether information from verb argument structure can influence the initial parse of a sentence. One particular model that predicts no influence is the garden-path model; an example of a model predicting an influence is the constraint-based model. In Experiment 1, we found that early closure sentences containing a reciprocal verb and a conjoined subject were no more difficult than late closure sentences with a singular subject and object. This result suggests that garden-path effects typically found with early closure sentences can be overridden when the sentence contains a reciprocal verb along with the appropriate number of arguments. These results are consistent with a model allowing verb effects to occur during initial syntactic processing.

The second experiment was conducted to compare reciprocal and non-reciprocal verbs in the same study. We again found that the critical information contained in the reciprocal verb influenced the initial parse of the sentence—the early closure/conjoined condition was read faster when the sentence contained a reciprocal verb compared with the same type of sentence with an optionally transitive verb. Again, these results are consistent with a model permitting influence from the verb during the earliest stages of parsing.

However, the results of the first two experiments could still be accommodated by the garden-path model. It is possible that reanalysis occurred before the disambiguating region of the sentence was encountered—that is, on the ambiguous NP. The third experiment was conducted to investigate this possibility. We manipulated whether the experimental sentences included a reciprocal or an optionally transitive verb, and whether they contained a disambiguating comma. We found that the first-pass reading times for the ambiguous regions of the sentences with optionally transitive verbs were longer in the condition in which the comma was absent compared with the condition in which the comma was present. In contrast, when these same sentences contained reciprocal verbs, first-pass reading time on the ambiguous region did not differ depending on the presence or absence of the comma. This result suggests that with reciprocal verbs, the parser correctly analysed the noun phrase as the subject of the second clause whether or not the disambiguating comma was present.

The critical conclusion from our experiments, then, is that under at least the circumstances examined in our experiments, information from specific verbs can be used during the earliest stages of syntactic analysis. This result is incompatible with the strictest version of the garden-path model, and consistent with the broad class of constraint-based models. However, recall from the Introduction that at least three different positions with respect to the use of verb information during parsing can be distinguished. One position predicts no effect of verb information at all, and this is the position associated with the most extreme version of the garden-path model. Another predicts that the most frequent analysis associated with a verb will be the one initially constructed, and this is the position associated with most constraint-based models. And an intermediate position predicts that verb information will be used so that no lexically forbidden analysis can be entertained, but if a structure is created due to minimal attachment and late closure and if that structure is lexically licensed, then it will be constructed initially, regardless of its frequency. The results from the three experiments described here rule out the first model but are consistent with the latter two. However, we will argue that when evidence from a wider range of studies investigating argument structure effects is considered, the intermediate model receives the most empirical support.

To construct this argument, we will proceed through the various critical results we believe any model of parsing must account for. We will begin with the following:

(a) If the parser is faced with an ambiguity in which it could make an NP the object of a main verb or the subject of a complement clause (an ambiguity that can be eliminated with the complementiser *that*, as in *Bill claimed (that) Mary was tall*), and if the verb permits the latter structure almost exclusively, the parser does not consider the direct object analysis (Trueswell et al., 1993; but see Kennison, submitted). Thus it appears that the parser is reluctant to consider an infrequent analysis, even when that analysis is the one favoured by the minimal attachment principle.

(b) If the parser is presented with the choice of making an NP the object of a main verb or the subject of a new independent clause (an ambiguity that can be eliminated with a comma), the parser prefers the direct object analysis, even when the verb rarely if ever occurs with direct objects (Adams et al., 1992; Anes & Ferreira, 1993; Juliano & Tanenhaus, 1994; Mitchell, 1987). The parser appears to construct a generally preferred analysis—the one consistent with late closure—even when the verb hardly permits the analysis. (Note that Juliano and Tanenhaus give a different, constraint-based explanation of the same tendency.)

These two apparently contradictory results can be accommodated in two possible ways. One is to state that the late closure strategy is more powerful than the minimal attachment strategy—the latter is more easily overridden by lexically specific information. The second possibility is to state that a comma is a more powerful cue than a complementiser, and so the absence of a comma virtually compels the parser to construct a direct object analysis.

Fortunately, the results of our experiments rule out both of these possible explanations. For all three experiments, the ambiguity (at least according to the garden-path model) invoked the late closure strategy, and could be disambiguated with a comma. Yet, we saw that garden-path effects were eliminated—the parser favoured an analysis in which the NP served as the subject of a new independent clause rather than the object of the verb in the previous clause. Thus a model of parsing must be developed which can account for the above two findings along with the main result from our experiments:

(c) If the parser is presented with the choice of making an NP the object of a verb or the subject of a new independent clause (an ambiguity that can be eliminated with a comma), and if the first verb is reciprocal and the subject is conjoined, the parser prefers the analysis where the NP serves as the subject of a new clause. This analysis is inconsistent with the late closure strategy, and also requires the parser to override any tendency it has to consider the absence of a post-verbal comma a cue for the direct object analysis. In addition, it is crucial to note that a structure including a reciprocal verb with a conjoined subject does permit a direct object analysis. That is, there is nothing ungrammatical about a sequence such as *Bruce and Demi dated the agent*.

It appears to us, then, that the set of findings any model must account for is quite complicated. In particular, the model must provide some type of answer to two crucial questions. First, why is the direct object analysis not considered when the parser encounters a conjoined subject and reciprocal verb (as in *After Bruce and Demi dated the agent*), given that the analysis is indeed grammatical? Second, why would the parser not consider this grammatical analysis but yet attempt what appears to be an ungrammatical analysis in sequences such as *After Bill sweated the boy left the room*? Note that the pragmatic difficulty of *Bruce and Demi dated the agent* cannot be appealed to given that *Bill sweated the boy* is presumably both syntactically and pragmatically unfavoured.

First, we will consider the question why the direct object analysis is not constructed for a sequence consisting of a conjoined subject and a reciprocal verb (e.g. *After Bruce and Demi dated the agent*). Our explanation of this result requires that we be explicit about the information contained in the argument structures of reciprocal verbs, a category of verbs that has received next to no linguistic analysis (but see Gleitman et al., 1996). The notion of an argument structure relies on the distinction between arguments and adjuncts. Arguments are constituents lexically licensed by a verb; adjuncts are modifier phrases not specifically licensed by a verb (e.g. Jackendoff, 1990). For example, in the sentence *Mary saw Tom on Friday*, the verb *saw* specifies two arguments: the agent *Mary* and the theme *Tom*. These two NPs are arguments because the meaning of the verb *see* requires that there be a see-er and a thing that is seen. Note that arguments do not have to be explicitly expressed; the sentence *Tom was seen on Friday* is perfectly acceptable. However, the argument that is missing is implicitly represented, and recently Mauner, Tanenhaus and Carlson (1995) have shown that these implicit arguments are mentally filled in during sentence comprehension. In contrast, the phrase *on Friday* is an adjunct—it is a modifier that can be tacked onto virtually any sentence, and is not specified by the lexical meaning of the main verb (or any other argument-taking lexical item).

According to theories of sentence comprehension in which verb information is used during parsing (and this includes both the garden-path model and constraint-based models), the information from verbs that is useful to the parser is information about argument structure. So let us consider what the argument structure of a reciprocal verb such as *kiss* might be. One argument structure is clear. It looks like the following:

7. kiss: ⟨*agent*, patient⟩

This argument structure states that the verb *kiss* can occur with a subject and object, the former serving as agent, and the latter as patient (the italicised role is the subject, or, more precisely, the external argument of the verb).

The use of this argument structure can be seen in the sentence *Jose kissed the bride*.

What is the argument structure for the alternative structure, the one that played such a crucial role in our experiments? We contend that it must look something like the following:

8. kiss: ⟨*agent/patient* plural, 0⟩

This argument structure includes information that is somewhat unusual. First, it includes the information that the subject is plural. (We have obtained evidence in ongoing work that plurality is actually not sufficient to induce the reciprocal reading and that the phrase must actually be conjoined; however, because discussion of this work is beyond the scope of this paper, we will specify just that the NP must be plural.) Second, the argument structure states that this plural NP is both the agent and the patient of the kissing action. Third, the argument structure states that no object should occur in this structure. In other words, we are assuming that the absence of an object is explicitly represented. This assumption is required, because once an object is inserted into the structure, the reciprocal reading of the conjoined subject NP disappears (*Jose and the bride kissed the caterer* means that Jose and the bride together kissed the caterer but not each other).

Now, consider what happens when the parser attempts to structure the sequence *After Jose and the bride kissed*. At the point where the verb *kiss* is encountered, its argument structures become activated. The sequence partially matches the first argument structure, but it provides an even better match to the second, because of the combination of the plural subject and the reciprocal verb. As a result, the second argument structure would rapidly become more activated at the expense of the first. Now, when the parser encounters the next constituent in the sequence, *the party*, the information from that second argument structure exerts its influence. The argument structure explicitly rejects a direct object, and so the NP is not entertained in that syntactic position. Instead, another possible analysis is constructed, namely the one on which it serves as the subject of a new clause.

At this point, it might seem unlikely that the activation level of the first argument structure would have decreased all the way down to zero. Therefore, why would the parser not consider the direct object analysis, at least to some extent, for the sequence *After Jose and the bride kissed the party*? Our response to this question relies crucially on the distinction between arguments and adjuncts, and especially on the suggestion that arguments are stored with lexical items, while adjuncts are constructed on the fly, so to speak, as needed. When the phrase *on Tuesday* is encountered for a sentence such as *Mary saw Tom on Tuesday*, no prestored structure containing the adjunct phrase is accessed; instead, the phrase is attached and then processed semantically, and this yields an adjunct interpretation.

Consider what the parser would have to do to make *the party* a direct object in the above sequence—it would have to relinquish an argument interpretation in favour of an adjunct interpretation for part of the subject NP, the part incorporating just the conjoined phrase (*and the bride*). To see that this is so, recall our analysis up to this point: The parser encounters *After Jose and the bride kissed*, the two argument structures for *kiss* become activated, and the second gains at the expense of the first (because the subject NP is plural and the second argument structure specifies a plural subject). Crucially, the second argument structure requires that the two conjuncts of the conjoined subject be interpreted in an argument-like way—both the NP *Jose* and the NP *the bride* are required for the reciprocal reading. To obtain the late closure analysis of this same sequence instead, the conjoined portion of the plural subject would have to be interpreted like any other conjoined phrase as a prototypical example of adjunction.[3] In other words, the entire subject (*Jose and the bride*) would still be interpreted as an argument of the verb, but the conjoined portion of that subject (*and the bride*) would not figure in a lexically licensed interpretation (exactly as in any other non-reciprocal case, such as *Jose and the bride smiled*). Thus we would argue that for a model of parsing to accommodate our data, it must assume that lexically licensed analyses—that is, argument analyses—are favoured (during initial parsing) over adjunct analyses (as in Abney, 1989).

Thus the answer to the first question—why the parser does not consider a direct object analysis for the sequence *After Jose and the bride kissed the party*—is that doing so would require giving up an analysis in which constituents have been identified as arguments in favour of one in which the

---

[3]Munn (1993), for example, argues that the syntactic structure of a phrase such as Jose and the bride is as follows:

```
              NP
            /    \
    NP              BP
    |              /  \
   Jose           B      NP
                  |      |
                 and   the bride
```

In such a structure, the conjunction *and* is the head of an endocentric structure, which he terms a Boolean phrase (BP). The BP is then adjoined to the first conjunct, so that the BP is an adjunct, while the entire NP of which it is a part can serve as the argument of some phrase. The structure of the NP *Jose and the bride* must be different from this one when the reciprocal reading is intended, because (crucially) the two conjuncts are required by the verb, so that the BP is not an adjunct. Determining the correct structure in this case is a project for future work.

constituents are to serve as adjuncts, and the parser prefers to consider argument-based over adjunct-based analyses (Abney, 1989).[4]

The second question we set up earlier in this General Discussion was the following: Why does the parser attempt what appears to be an ungrammatical analysis for sequences such as *After Bill sweated the boy left the room*? In other words, why would the lexical information that *sweat* is an intransitive verb be ignored by the parser? To explain this tendency, it is necessary to examine more closely the alleged intransitivity of this class of verbs. It is now common practice in psycholinguistics to obtain evidence for the argument structures of various verbs by conducting normative studies. These studies (including the present one) follow a common script (e.g. Anes & Ferreira, 1993; MacDonald, 1994; Trueswell et al., 1993): Participants are given a list of verbs and asked to generate a sentence for each verb. The participants' responses are then scored. This procedure has shown verbs such as *sweat* to be intransitive—that is, few if any participants produce sentences in which an NP-like phrase occurs in the immediately post-verbal position. However, we have also informally observed that if we probed a participant during the experimental debriefing sessions by asking a question such as, "Is it possible to sweat anything", the participant would often give a reply such as, "Of course, I was really sweating an exam I took this morning, but it turned out to be easy". The problem, then, appears to be that the more colloquial uses of these verbs are not spontaneously offered by our participants in the normative studies (e.g. *sweat the exam*, *talk a good game*). To address this problem, we recently conducted a normative study in which we introduced two changes to the typical procedure: We asked participants to use colloquial language and we requested at least three different sentences for each verb. With this procedure, we have found that the preferred use of verbs such as *sweat* is intransitive, but a small number of transitive uses are provided as well. Thus a major step in addressing our second question is to debunk the myth that these verbs are indeed

[4]This claim might seem to be at odds with the work of Clifton, Speer and Abney (1991). Their experiments were designed to pit any tendency to make phrases adjuncts against the tendency to minimally attach phrases. They argued from their results that the minimal attachment preference was stronger. However, this interpretation of their results depends on assumptions regarding phrase structure that are not entirely uncontroversial—for example, that nodes intermediate between heads and maximal projections (X-single-bar nodes) are not created unless required. In addition, the stimuli used in their two experiments were not normed for plausibility, and so it is possible that the non-minimal attachment versions were associated with longer reading times because they were less plausible than the sentences in the other conditions.

intransitive, in the sense of having no argument structure permitting a direct object.[5]

If many of the allegedly intransitive verbs such as *sweat* do indeed have an argument structure permitting a direct object slot (and the verbs used in any psycholinguistic experiment will include a large set of these items), then we no longer have the problem of explaining why the parser attempts a syntactic structure that cannot be accommodated by any argument structure. However, a different question must be addressed: Even if a transitive argument structure exists for *sweat*-type verbs, it is much less frequent than the intransitive argument structure. Why does the parser attempt the less frequent analysis first?

To answer this question, let us consider in more detail what the two argument structures at issue here—the transitive and intransitive structures—look like. Let us continue with the verb *sweat*:

9. sweat: ⟨*experiencer*, theme⟩
   sweat: ⟨*experiencer*⟩

Thus the transitive structure follows an NP-V-NP template; the intransitive structure has only the NP-V components of this same template. Now let us consider the bottom-up input the parser receives in a sequence such as *After Bill sweated the boy left the room*. Note that the transitive argument structure matches this input better than does the intransitive structure; more precisely, the transitive structure allows more of the input to be syntactically analysed than does the intransitive structure. To explain the tendency to misanalyse *After Bill sweated the boy left the room*, then, we would argue that it is necessary to appeal to a principle similar to what Pritchett (1988) termed the principle of theta-attachment: The parser prefers to construct the analysis that allows as many constituents as possible to be analysed as arguments of the argument-assigner (a verb in all of our examples). We will call this the maximal-arguments principle. The transitive structure for *sweat* is less frequent than the intransitive structure, but it allows more syntactic phrases to be analysed as arguments than does the intransitive structure. Therefore, it is attempted first during syntactic processing.

Why does the maximal-arguments principle not lead to consideration of the direct object analysis in the case of sentences with reciprocal verbs? Here, the distinction between arguments and adjuncts is essential, as we argued earlier. Constructing the direct object analysis for sequences such as

---

[5]A handful of verbs such as *arrive* seem to forbid a direct object under virtually all circumstances. However, such verbs are so rare that they cannot be used exclusively in standard psycholinguistic experiments in which at least a dozen or so different tokens of the same verb type are required. Thus the behaviour of verbs such as *arrive* is contaminated by the behaviour of the more common *sweat*-type "intransitive" verbs.

After Jose and the bride kissed the party began in earnest requires relinquishing an analysis on which the material prior to the post-verbal NP is categorised as arguments in favour of one in which that material is re-categorised as adjuncts. The parser is loathe to do this—indeed, the maximal-arguments principle actually predicts this. In general, then, the parser attempts to analyse sequences of constituents so that, as much as possible, phrases are interpreted as arguments of the relevant argument-assigner.

At the beginning of this section, we described three critical results for which any model of parsing must provide an account. The first was the following: when the parser is faced with an NP that can be categorised as the direct object of the preceding verb or the subject of a complement clause (the complement serving as an argument of the same verb), the parser chooses the more frequent analysis. Can this result be accommodated by the maximal-arguments principle we have formulated to account for the second and third critical results? The answer, we believe, is yes. Consider a verb such as *know*, which permits both a direct object and a complement clause:

10. know: ⟨*experiencer*, theme⟩
    know: ⟨*experiencer*, proposition⟩

Note that the maximal-arguments principle cannot choose between these two argument-structure alternatives: both allow the post-verbal NP to be analysed as an argument of the verb. Thus, because the principle cannot adjudicate between these alternatives, frequency plays a role instead, so that the more frequent of the two structures is the one selected by the parser.

In summary, we have argued that the results of our experiments, as well as the results of several other recent studies, can be accommodated if we assume something like the maximal-arguments principle. An implication of this principle for our model concerns the way in which syntactic structures are created during comprehension. Consider that syntactic structures can be "built from" lexical items in one of two possible ways: one is to project phrases upward from lexical heads (e.g. create an NP based on the presence of a noun) and then assign roles to those phrases (e.g. adjunct *vs* argument, agent *vs* patient); the other is to project phrases downward from lexical items based on the content of argument structures (e.g. predict the existence of an NP when the verb *see* is encountered). The model we have proposed takes phrases that have already been independently created and then assigns them to various roles; the most crucial for the purpose of this paper is the role of argument versus adjunct. Thus the model only allows syntactic structure to be created in a bottom-up fashion, upward from lexical items. In contrast, constraint-based models allow syntactic structure to be created both bottom-up (from lexical items) and top-down (from argument structures). When a verb such as *see* is encountered, the node for its corresponding object is predicted (based on argument structure frequencies) and so the NP node is created by the parser (MacDonald et al., 1994).

This difference between the two approaches leads to contrasting empirical predictions. Our model predicts that the parser will only be "surprised" when it encounters a sequence which does not conform to the maximal-arguments principle (e.g. *After Bill sweated the boy left the room*); it will not be surprised to encounter a particular constituent as long as it is licensed by some argument structure. In contrast, according to the constraint-based model, the comprehender should actually encounter difficulties if a particular type of syntactic constituent predicted to occur based on the relevant argument-assigner's most frequent argument structure failed to materialise. Thus the model we have outlined here not only allows us to account for the results of our experiments as well as some other recent work in parsing, it also allows us to generate some predictions for distinguishing among competing models of the language comprehension system.

REFERENCES

Abney, S. (1989). A computational model of human parsing. *Journal of Psycholinguistic Research*, *18*, 129–144.

Adams, B.C., Clifton, C.E., & Mitchell, D.C. (1992). Syntactic guidance in sentence processing. Poster presented at the *33rd Annual Meeting of the Psychonomic Society*, St. Louis, MO, November.

Anes, M.D., & Ferreira, F. (1993). Verb transitivity and parsing preferences. Poster presented at the *6th Annual CUNY Sentence Processing Conference*, Amherst, MA, March.

Chomsky, N. (1981). *Lectures on government and binding*. Dordrecht: Foris.

Clifton, C.E. (1993). Thematic roles in sentence parsing. *Canadian Journal of Psychology: Special Issue on Reading and Language Processing*, *47*, 222–246.

Clifton, C.E., Speer, S., & Abney, S.P. (1991) Parsing arguments: Phrase structure and argument structure as determinants of initial parsing decisions. *Journal of Memory and Language*, *30*, 251–271.

Connine, C.M., Ferreira, F., Jones, C., Clifton, C.E., & Frazier, L. (1984). Verb frame preferences. *Journal of Psycholinguistic Research*, *13*, 307–319.

Ferreira, F., & Henderson, J.M. (1990). The use of verb information in syntactic parsing: A comparison of evidence from eye movements and word-by-word self-paced reading. *Journal of Experimental Psychology: Learning, Memory and Cognition*, *16*, 555–568.

Frazier, L. (1978). *On comprehending sentences: Syntactic parsing strategies*. Unpublished doctoral dissertation, University of Connecticut, Storrs, CT.

Frazier, L. (1987). Sentence processing. In M. Coltheart (Ed.), *Attention and performance XII*, pp. 559–586. Hillsdale, NJ: Lawrence Erlbaum Associates Inc.

Frazier, L., & Rayner, K. (1982). Making and correcting errors during sentence comprehension: Eye movements in the analysis of structurally ambiguous sentences. *Cognitive Psychology*, *14*, 178–210.

Gleitman, L.R., Gleitman, H., Miller, C., & Ostrin, R. (1996). Similar, and similar concepts. *Cognition*, *58*, 321–376.

Haegeman, L.M.V. (1991). *Introduction to government and binding theory*. Oxford: Blackwell.

Jackendoff, R.S. (1987). The status of thematic relations in linguistic theory. *Linguistic Inquiry, 18*, 369–412.

Jackendoff, R.S. (1990). *Semantic structures.* Cambridge, MA: MIT Press.

Juliano, C., & Tanenhaus, M.K. (1994). A constraint-based lexicalist account of the subject/object attachment preference. *Journal of Psycholingistic Research, 23*, 459–471.

Kennedy, A., Murray, W.S., Jennings, F., & Reid, C. (1989). Parsing complements: Comments on the generality of the principle of minimal attachment. *Language and Cognitive Processes, 4*, S151–S176.

Kennison, S. (submitted). The role of verb information in syntactic ambiguity resolution.

MacDonald, M.C. (1994). Probabilistic constraints and syntactic ambiguity resolution. *Language and Cognitive Processes, 9*, 157–201.

MacDonald, M.C., Pearlmutter, N.J., & Seidenberg, M.S. (1994). The lexical nature of syntactic ambiguity resolution. *Psychological Review, 101*, 676–703.

Mauner, G., Tanenhaus, M.K., & Carlson, G.N. (1995). Implicit arguments in sentence processing. *Journal of Memory and Language, 34*, 357–382.

McElree, B. (1993). The locus of lexical preference effects in sentence comprehension: A time-course analysis. *Journal of Memory and Language, 32*, 536–571.

Mitchell, D.C. (1987). Lexical guidance in human parsing: Locus and processing. In M. Coltheart (Ed.), *Attention and performance XII*, pp. 601–633. Hillsdale, NJ: Lawrence Erlbaum Associates Inc.

Munn, A. (1993). *Topics in the syntax and semantics of coordinate structures.* Doctoral dissertation, University of Maryland.

Osterhout, L., Holcomb, P.J., & Swinney, D.A. (1994). Brain potentials elicited by garden-path sentences: Evidence of the application of verb information during parsing. *Journal of Experimental Psychology: Learning, Memory and Cognition, 20*, 786–803.

Pritchett, B.L. (1988). Garden path phenomena and the grammatical basis of language processing. *Language, 64*, 451–484.

Rayner, K., Carlson, M., & Frazier, L. (1983). The interaction of syntax and semantics during sentence processing: Eye movements in the analysis of semantically ambiguous sentences. *Journal of Verbal Learning and Verbal Behavior, 22*, 358–374.

Tanenhaus, M.K., Carlson, G., & Trueswell, J.C. (1989). The role of thematic structures in interpretation and parsing. *Language and Cognitive Processes, 4*, SI211–SI234.

Trueswell, J.C., Tanenhaus, M.K., & Kello, C. (1993). Verb-specific constraints in sentence processing: Separating effects of lexical preference from garden-paths. *Journal of Experimental Psychology: Learning, Memory and Cognition, 19*, 528–553.

LANGUAGE AND COGNITIVE PROCESSES, 1997, *12* (2/3), 307–348

The Role of Lexical Heads in Parsing: Evidence from German

Lars Konieczny

University of the Saarland, Saarbrücken, Germany

Barbara Hemforth, Christoph Scheepers and Gerhard Strube

University of Freiburg, Freiburg, Germany

Theories of sentence processing can be classified by the role that lexical heads play in first-pass parsing. In some theories, syntactic structure cannot even be built before it is licensed by a head (Abney, 1989; Prichett, 1992), whereas in other models, at the opposite extreme, only major category information in lexical items is used during the rule-based initial structure building process (Ferreira & Henderson, 1990; Mitchell, 1987). In this paper, we will introduce a fully incremental model that accounts for attachment preferences by the linear order of lexical heads in the surface structure and their thematic properties. The principle of "parameterised head attachment" and a serial variant, the SOUL mechanism, will be discussed on the basis of three on-line experiments on NP- and PP-attachment in German verb-second and verb-final sentences.

INTRODUCTION

While no-one would deny that lexical information influences parsing, there is nevertheless still some debate about when it is used, or, more specifically, whether it has an *immediate* influence on parsing decisions, or whether it is only used to *select* suggested structures which have been generated by purely

Requests for reprints should be addressed to Lars Konieczny, Computation Linguistics, Universität des Saarlandes, Gebäude 17.3, Im Stadtwald, D-66041 Saarbrücken, Germany. E-mail: lkon@coli.uni-sb.de

The work presented in this paper was supported by a grant from the German Research Foundation (Deutsche Forschungsgemeinschaft, DFG, Grant No. Str. 4-1/3). By the time the experiments were run, the first author was working at the University of Freiburg. We wish to thank our students Thomas Mulack, Thilo Weigel, Christoph Hoelscher and Nick Ketley for running the experiments and for their helpful comments on earlier versions of the manuscript. We would also like to thank Don Mitchell and two anonymous reviewers for their valuable comments.

syntactic principles. Within the lexical filter hypothesis (Mitchell, 1987), lexical information is only considered to determine the basic syntactic categories of the words in a sentence during the first analysis. Other lexical information (e.g. about probable complements of a head) is proposed "to reject or to confirm whatever analysis has been constructed on purely syntactic information" (Frazier, 1987a, p. 524; cf. Mitchell, 1987, 1989).

There are two major features of German that make it particularly interesting for the investigation of lexical processes. First, many syntactic constraints are expressed in the morphology of lexical items such that there is a higher degree of variability in constituent ordering. Second, and consequently, the variability in ordering heads and their complements permits us to vary the availability of prominent lexical information during the timecourse of on-line sentence processing. In German main clauses, for instance, the verb has to appear as the second constituent in the sentence (1, 2), whereas in subclauses it usually follows its arguments and modifiers (3, 4):[1]

1. Susanne verzierte den Kuchen mit dem frischen Obst.
   Susan decorated the cake with the fresh fruit.
2. Gestern gab der Freund der Tochter einen Kuß.
   Yesterday gave the friend (to) the daughter a kiss.
   Yesterday the friend gave the daughter a kiss.
3. Daß Susanne den Kuchen mit dem frischen Obst verzierte,...
   That Susan the cake with the fresh fruit decorated,...
   That Susan decorated the cake with the fresh fruit,...
4. Daß der Freund der Tochter einen Kuß gab,...
   That the friend (to) the daughter a kiss gave,...
   That the friend gave a kiss to the daughter...

Models of human sentence processing can be classified along many lines, two of which will be discussed in this paper: the amount of lexical information used for initial attachment decisions and whether or not the structural alternatives are pursued in parallel. We will argue that initial attachment decisions in parsing are influenced by the availability of lexical

---

[1]Exceptions to this rule are structures with extrapositions like (i) and (ii), where it is more common to extrapose the infinitival complement:

i. Weil der Mann zu kommen gebeten wurde,...
   Because the man to come asked was,...
   Because the man was asked to come,...
ii. Weil der Mann gebeten wurde zu kommen,...
   Because the man asked was to come,...
   Because the man was asked to come,...

heads which provide an attachment site for an argument or a modifier. We will present evidence from three eyetracking experiments on PP- and NP-attachment which support this hypothesis. A serial account of the principle of parameterised head attachment that predicts the observed parsing preferences will be discussed.

In the following sections, we will try to relate current approaches to the classification given above and, in particular, to position parameterised head attachment within this classification in relation to comparable accounts on human language processing. We will only consider models that postulate more or less universal parsing principles (for a discussion of linguistic tuning, see Hemforth, Konieczny, & Scheepers, 1994, in press).

THE GARDEN-PATH MODEL

The garden-path model (Frazier & Rayner, 1982; Frazier & Fodor, 1978; Frazier, 1979, 1987a, 1987b, 1990) is one of the most prominent accounts of human language processing. The syntax processor is proposed to work autonomously during the first analysis—that is, initial parsing decisions cannot be influenced directly by higher-level processes at the semantic or pragmatic level. The status of lexical information is not entirely clear. On the one hand, it is assumed that structures which are rendered ungrammatical by lexical information are never built. According to the *lexical filter hypothesis* (Mitchell, 1987, 1989), on the other hand, lexical information is not (necessarily) fully exploited during initial analysis. Whereas major category information is considered necessary for syntactic structure building, subcategorisation information may come in only at a later stage (Frazier, 1987a,b; Frazier, Clifton, & Randall, 1983; but see Clifton, Frazier, & Connine, 1984, for evidence of the early use of verb-frame information). Since parsing is rule-driven, structure can be built even if lexical heads licensing the integration of current items are not yet available. Attachment does not have to be delayed until phrasal structure can be projected from the respective lexical heads. The parser works incrementally word-by-word in a serial depth-first manner, such that in cases of structural ambiguity, only one analysis will be pursued (first analysis constraint). Two main conflict resolution principles guide the parser's selections in the first analysis (Frazier, 1987a):

5. *Minimal attachment*
   Do not postulate any potentially unnecessary nodes.

6. *Late closure*
   If grammatically permissible, attach new items into the clause or phrase currently being processed (i.e. the clause or phrase postulated most recently).

Minimal attachment ensures that in cases of structural ambiguity, the parser builds the simplest possible structure during the first analysis. Late closure guarantees that new constituents are immediately attached to prior material, minimising the chance of exceeding the working memory limitations. If the first analysis later proves to be unacceptable according to syntactic, semantic or discourse-pragmatic reasons, a time-consuming reanalysis is induced which is measurable by higher processing cost. There is a great deal of empirical evidence which apparently supports these assumptions. Well-known examples are sentences such as (7), in which the [$_{PP}$ with binoculars] is preferably attached to the VP (Frazier & Rayner, 1982), as predicted by minimal attachment:

7. The spy saw the cop with binoculars.
   a. The spy [$_{VP}$ saw [$_{NP}$ the cop] [$_{PP}$ with binoculars]]
   b. The spy [$_{VP}$ saw [$_{NP}$ [$_{NP}$ the cop] [$_{PP}$ with binoculars]]]

When read from left to right, an attachment-conflict occurs on reading the article of the object-NP because it is possible either to attach the object-NP directly to the VP (7a) or to postulate a complex NP with an extra NP node (7b). However, because this extra NP node will possibly turn out to be unnecessary in later processing, minimal attachment will hinder its construction in favour of a direct integration into the VP. Now, when at a later stage the prepositional phrase is read, only the integration of the PP into the VP (7a) can take place without reanalysis.

Based on their current approach, *construal theory*, Frazier and Clifton (1996) have restricted the application domain of the garden-path model. Only if at least one of the structural alternatives constitutes a "primary relation" is the attachment ambiguity resolved by structural principles, namely, minimal attachment and late closure. *Primary relations* are roughly the relations that hold between a predicate and its dependents (i.e. the arguments, as well as the dependents of these arguments). For other relations—for example, clear modifying relations, as in relative clause attachment—the theory assumes that the parser makes no initial commitment to a particular syntactic alternative. In these cases, structural biases or preferences are induced by thematic or pragmatic principles, respectively.

With respect to the materials used here, however, predictions do not change: the PPs and NPs used in the studies presented can stand in a primary relation to their functors in at least one of the structural alternatives. Hence, the ambiguity should still be resolved by minimal attachment and late closure, respectively. We will therefore not discuss construal theory any further here.

The Use of Lexical Information

In several empirical studies, it has been demonstrated that attachment preferences like those observed for sentences like (7) can be biased by lexical information, in particular by the complement or argument structure of the verb (e.g. Ford, Bresnan, & Kaplan, 1982; Konieczny, 1989; Konieczny, Scheepers, Hemforth, & Strube, 1994; Tanenhaus, Boland, Mauner, & Carlson, 1993). For example, in a self-paced reading study, Konieczny (1989) showed that for comparable sentences in German there was a preference for integrating the ambiguous PP into a complex object-NP when the verb did not prefer a prepositional complement.

Multiple-constraint Satisfaction Models

Numerous multiple-constraint satisfaction models have been proposed recently (e.g. Juliano & Tanenhaus, 1994). MacDonald, Pearlmutter and Seidenberg (1994) proposed a detailed lexicalist model in which the same kind of constraint satisfaction process is assumed to work for lexical access as well as for sentence processing. They postulate enriched lexical entries with minimal phrase structure information which are activated in parallel during sentence processing. Activation is a function of the frequency of a particular lexical form. By the process of "linking", lexical projections are integrated in the sentential context with a strong preference for the most frequent lexical alternative. Sentential and supra-sentential contexts interact with the activation of lexical entities. No purely structure-based principles like minimal attachment or late closure are assumed.

The interactive multiple-constraint approach is supported by evidence from studies (e.g. MacDonald, 1994) which have demonstrated that frequency biased verb frames influence parsing decisions in a variety of attachment ambiguities, such as main verb/reduced relative ambiguities (8) and PP-attachment ambiguities.

8. The rancher knew that the nervous cattle {a. pushed b. moved} into the crowded pen was afraid of the cowboys. (MacDonald, 1994)

The relative frequency of simple past versus past-participle readings of the respective form as well as the relative frequency of their transitive versus intransitive readings is assumed to predict garden-path effects in sentences like (8).[2]

In a related, though modular, class of models (cf. Crain & Steedman, 1985), all syntactic alternatives are built in parallel. Higher-order infor-

[2]In (8), the verb "pushed" is supposed to be preferably transitive, so reduced or no garden-path effects are predicted because a reduced relative reading is strongly biased by the succeeding preposition "into".

mation selects the best alternative grounded on lexical, semantic or pragmatic principles. In this account, as well as in the strongly lexicalist ones, no structural principles are assumed, and parsing preferences may be rephrased as interpretational preferences.

Parameterised Head Attachment

Konieczny et al. (1994; see also Hemforth, Konieczny, Scheepers, & Strube, 1992; Konieczny, Hemforth, & Strube, 1991) proposed the *parameterised head attachment* principle to account for a variety of initial analysis phenomena. Parameterised head attachment is the guiding principle in a serial *first analysis* model (i.e. a garden-path type of model) pursuing only one analysis in the case of a structural ambiguity. Parameterised head attachment predicts that the first syntactic analysis is determined by a hierarchy of three sub-principles (p1-3) recurring to the linear ordering of lexical heads and their lexical properties, including thematic preferences. In these respects, parameterised head attachment is a serial garden-path variant of lexicalist models.

9. *Parameterised head attachment*

   p1. *Head attachment* (Konieczny et al., 1991)
   If possible, attach a constituent to a phrase whose lexical head has already been encountered.
   If further attachment possibilities exist for the critical constituent, then

   p2. *Preferred role attachment*
   Attach constitutent *i* to a phrase (within the current clause) whose head highlights a theta-role for *i*.
   If further attachment possibilities exist for the constituent, then

   p3. *Recent head attachment*
   Attach the constituent to the phrase whose head was encountered most recently.

The basic idea of parameterised head attachment is that the parser initially builds syntactic structures which can be evaluated semantically as soon as possible. In this sense, processing is assumed to be "semantics-oriented", meaning that the parser is forced to attach an ambiguous constituent preferably to the phrase whose semantically most relevant constituent, the lexical head, has already been encountered (p1), such that the discourse entity introduced by the ambiguous phrase can be related to other entities in the discourse model.

The NP *the sock* in (10a), for instance, is initially attached to the VP of the "while" clause, although it could also have been attached as the subject of the matrix clause, as in (10b). In the first case, the head "mending" has already been encountered, while the matrix verb is yet to come in the latter.[3]

10a. [[While Paul was $[_{VP}$ $[_{V}$ mending] $[_{NP}$ the sock]]]...
10b. [[While Paul was $[_{VP}$ $[_{V}$ mending]]] $[_{S}$ $[_{NP}$ the sock]...

If the attachment ambiguity cannot be resolved by (p1)—that is, if more than one potential head is available—the parser will be guided by the role-taking (and highlighting) properties of the heads involved (p2). In (11), for example (cf. Abney, 1989), the PP *in the Volvo* is predicted to be interpreted as the argument of the noun *interest* in (11a), but as the argument of the verb *interest* in (11b):[4]

11a. Peter discussed his interest in the Volvo.
11b. Peter could interest the man in the Volvo.

If further attachment ambiguities remain, as in the case of the ambiguous PP *on the balcony* in (12), the constituent will be attached to the phrase whose head has been processed most recently (p3), namely, the NP *the actress*, instead of the NP *the servant* in (12):

12. Somebody shot the servant of the actress on the balcony.

A Strictly Serial Variant of Parameterised Head Attachment

As it stands, parameterised head attachment entails both serial and parallel operations. Principle application, on the one hand, is serial: only if a principle earlier in the hierarchy cannot resolve an ambiguity will the next principle be applied. But for this very reason, there is also parallelism: only the detection of an ambiguity (i.e. the computation of multiple attachment hypotheses) determines whether or not the next principle in the hierarchy must be applied. Furthermore, if the principles of parameterised

---

[3] Verbs are assumed to be the lexical heads of clauses here.

[4] These predictions have been questioned by Clifton, Speer and Abney (1991), who found a minimal attachment preference irrespective of thematic preferences. However, their interpretation of the results obtained in their eyetracking study has been criticised (Konieczny, 1996): Clifton et al. ground their interpretation only on measures that excluded regressions to earlier regions. On the other hand, the regression probabilities they provided suggest that readers might have been garden-pathed more strongly in cases where reanalysis into a non-argument position was required. Furthermore, in a more recent and more thoroughly set up study, Schütze and Gibson (1996) established an argument preference contradicting minimal attachment.

head attachment were interpreted as heuristics (rather than as more general principles reflecting the outcome of a yet-to-be-specified algorithm), all potential attachment sites would have to be consulted to establish the linear order of their heads and the ambiguous phrase itself, as well as their role-highlighting properties. In this sense, parameterised head attachment seems to involve a fair amount of (local) parallelism.

Konieczny (1996; Konieczny & Strube, 1995), on the other hand, provides a strictly serial (algorithmic) approach – the Semantics-Oriented Unification-based Language (SOUL) processing mechanism – the predictions of which meet those of parameterised head attachment. The system can roughly be sketched as follows. Proceeding in a word-by-word, left-to-right manner, each new item attempts to attach itself to the currently visible node in the current partial phrase marker. If attachment to that site fails, another node becomes visible, and attachment is attempted again. Which node becomes visible, then, is partly determined by the relative position of a potential attachment site within the right edge of the current phrase marker (the lower the node, the earlier or more likely it will become visible). However, if a node is highlighted by the thematic properties of a head encountered previously in the current clause (i.e. if its lexical highlighting exceeds a certain threshold), it will pop to the foreground and become visible, even if it is located higher in the current phrase marker.[5]

The mechanism is inherently serial: since only one attachment site is visible at a time, attachment alternatives do not have to be hypothesised in parallel or compete with each other. Foregrounding is also competition-free: whether or not an attachment site pops out in the first place is independent of potential competitors, since it is solely determined by the lexical highlighting properties of the heads involved and the linear order in which they occur. Nevertheless, the predictions of SOUL can be shown to meet those of parameterised head attachment (see Konieczny, 1996, for a detailed description of the SOUL mechanism).

Throughout the remainder of this paper, we will consider the SOUL mechanism to be an algorithmic specification of the principle of parameterised head attachment, which specifies the behaviour of the human sentence processing mechanism in a more general way. When speaking of the predictions of parameterised head attachment and its sub-principles later, we assume that the predicted behaviour emerges from the SOUL machinery, rather than from a heuristic application of the principle itself.

[5]Highlighted nodes are put onto a stack, which is consulted by the incoming item before (the right edge of) the current phrase marker itself. Therefore, foregounding of highlighted nodes persists even after further nodes are added lower in the current phrase marker. Only if another node is highlighted by a head encountered more recently will it be pushed to the background.

MOTIVATION

Parameterised head attachment, and thus SOUL, have gained empirical support from a series of self-paced reading studies on PP- and NP-attachment ambiguities, using a design logic and materials similar to those in Experiment 1, presented below (Konieczny et al., 1994). In brief, in these experiments, attachment preferences in sentences like (1–4) were demonstrated to depend on the availability and internal structure of lexical heads (Strube, Hemforth, & Wrobel, 1990b). In verb-final constructions, there was a consistent preference to attach a structurally ambiguous constituent to the preceding NP, whereas attachment preferences in verb-second sentences depended on the particular properties of the respective preceding heads.

A major problem of the self-paced reading technique, however, is that reading is slowed down substantially, so that "semantics-oriented" processing in those experiments may have resulted from the reduced processing speed and thus not reflect normal reading. Therefore, we conducted a series of eyetracking studies on PP- and NP-attachment ambiguities which will be presented in the next three sections.

In the first experiment, the influence of the availability of lexical information as well as the properties of lexical heads (thematic preferences) on PP-attachment preferences in isolated sentences was investigated. In Experiment 2, we present data on PP-attachment in verb-second and verb-final sentences in neutral contexts, thus only varying the availability of the thematic frame information. The evidence on attachment preferences in verb-final sentences will be extended to NP-attachment preferences in Experiment 3.

EXPERIMENT 1

In the first experiment, we used two sets of verbs, which differed with respect to their bias towards taking a PP as an argument. One set of verbs, like "to watch" and "to hit", showed a strong preference for a with-PP (mostly instrumentals), whereas the others, like "noticed" and "to catch sight of", did not (see Spivey-Knowlton & Sedivy, 1995, for a similar verb manipulation), which had been checked in pre-tests described below (Strube et al., 1990b).[6]

Second, the PP was varied so that its content forced or strongly biased either an attachment to the VP (13, 15) or to the NP (14, 16). Material was carefully selected according to pre-tests such that verb arguments were as

[6]Unfortunately, the pre-tests did not give us enough material to construct minimally contrasting sentences for the two lexical preference conditions, so different sentences had to be constructed for each condition of the factor "lexical preference".

plausible for verbs as noun modifiers were for nouns, whereas the respective alternative attachment was highly implausible.

Additionally, we took advantage of the variability of verb-placement in German sentences, as it shows up in subclauses, as in (17) to (20), in comparison to main clauses, as in (13) to (16). The important thing to note here is that the main verb appears at the clause-final position in the subclauses, so that the ambiguous PP is read before the verb of which it could be a complement. Note that the linear ordering of the direct object NP and the PP (NP < PP) is canonical in both verb-second and verb-final constructions; that is, placing the PP before the NP would be marked in both cases.

Norming the Materials

Lexical Preferences. Three hundred transitive verbs were chosen from a lexicon of German verbs. After excluding very low-frequency verbs, ambiguous verbs and verbs with separable prefixes (e.g. *ansehen*, to look at), 196 verbs remained in the pool for our first pre-study (Strube, Hemforth, & Wrobel, 1989, 1990a, 1990b).

Pre-study 1. The first pre-study was a sentence completion task. Half the 28 subjects were asked to complete sentence fragments like "He watched..." with an NP and a verb-modifying PP; the remaining subjects were asked to complete the fragment with a complex NP consisting of an NP and a PP (the task was described without using linguistic categories and examples were given so that we could be sure that subjects understood the instructions). The sentence fragments were presented on a computer monitor. As soon as the subjects had decided on a completion for the sentence fragment, they pressed a button and the respective completion was recorded. The time between the presentation of the sentence fragment and the button press was used for a first classification of the verbs. Only unambiguous and correct sentence completions were analysed. A verb was classified as preferentially taking a verb-modifying PP when the time for finding a complex-NP completion was at least marginally reliably longer than the time for finding an NP plus verb-modifying PP completion. Verbs were classified as preferentially not taking a verb-modifying PP if the time for finding an NP plus verb-modifying PP completion was at least marginally reliably longer than the time for finding a complex NP completion. Nineteen verbs were not classifiable by this procedure.

Pre-study 2. In pre-study 2, subjects were presented with 177 sentence fragments consisting of a pronominal subject, a verb and an object (e.g. "He watched the man..."). Only NPs were used as objects, which were produced

TABLE 1
PP-Attachment: Experimental Design of Experiment 1

Verb-second		
3-place verb		
VP-biased	13.	Marion beobachtete das Pferd mit dem neuen Fernglas. Marion watched the horse with the new binoculars.
NP-biased	14.	Marion beobachtete das Pferd mit dem weißen Fleck. Marion watched the horse with the white patch.
2-place verb		
VP-biased	15.	Marion erblickte die Schlange mit dem starken Teleobjektiv. Marion caught sight of the snake with the strong telephoto lens.
NP-biased	16.	Marion erblickte die Schlange mit dem spitzen Giftzahn. Marion caught sight of the snake with the sharp poisonous fang.
Verb-final		"Ich habe gehört, daß..." (I have heard that...)
3-place verb		
VP-biased	17.	Marion das Pferd mit dem neuen Fernglas beobachtete. Marion the horse with the new binoculars watched. Marion watched the horse with the new binoculars.
NP-biased	18.	Marion das Pferd mit dem weißen Fleck beobachtete. Marion the horse with the white patch watched. Marion watched the horse with the white patch.
2-place verb		
VP-biased	19.	Marion die Schlange mit dem starken Teleobjektiv erblickte. Marion the snake with the strong telephoto lens caught sight of. Marion caught sight of the snake with the strong telephoto lens.
NP-biased	20.	Marion die Schlange mit dem spitzen Giftzahn erblickte. Marion the snake with the sharp poisonous fang caught sight of. Marion caught sight of the snake with the sharp poisonous fang.

under both instructions in pre-study 1. The sentence fragments were presented as a paper-and-pencil questionnaire. Subjects were asked to complete the fragments with a PP. After making all completions, subjects were asked to indicate whether they meant to modify the verb or the object-NP by their completions. Verbs were classified as preferentially taking a PP if reliably more verb-modifying completions were produced. In contrast, verbs were classified as preferentially not taking a PP if reliably more object-NP completions were produced. Only verbs which were classified in the same category by both pre-studies were used for constructing the test items.

Pre-study 3: Semantic bias. For each of the 71 verbs remaining in the pool after pre-studies 1 and 2, three sentences were constructed. In one version, the PP was supposed to be strongly biased as verb-modifying; in a second version, it was supposed to be strongly biased as object-modifying.

Additionally, we constructed a third fully ambiguous version of each sentence. The semantic bias was tested using a paper-and-pencil questionnaire. For each version of the materials, two structurally unambiguous versions were constructed: an unambiguously verb-modifying version (21a) and an unambiguously object-modifying version (21b).

21a. The man was watched with the binoculars.
21b. The man with the binoculars was watched.

Seventy-seven subjects were asked to judge whether the situation described by the respective sentence was possible (yes, no) and, if so, whether it was easy to imagine (rating from 1 = not at all to 5 = very well). Six questionnaires were constructed so that the presentation of the six disambiguated versions for each verb was roughly balanced across subjects. Only materials for which the semantically biased versions were judged possible and very imaginable in the matching construction and impossible in the non-matching construction were used in the main experiment.

Definiteness of the Direct Object NP. It has been argued (Crain & Steedman, 1985) that definite direct object NPs in isolated verb-NP-PP constructions induce a bias towards an attachment to the VP, because an unmodified definite NP presupposes a less complex discourse model (including only one antecedent) than a modified definite NP (at least two antecedents). Spivey-Knowlton and Sedivy (1995) provided data that support this prediction for English verb-NP-PP constructions. Strube et al. (1989) also ran a study to investigate the definiteness effect in German verb-NP-PP constructions. Among various other structures, semantically ambiguous sentences were presented for which the definiteness of both the object-NP and the PP-object was varied. The object-NP and the PP-object were either both definite (22a), both indefinite (22b), or varied in definiteness (22c, d).

22a. Susan decorated the cake with the chocolate heart.
22b. Susan decorated a cake with a chocolate heart.
22c. Susan decorated the cake with a chocolate heart.
22d. Susan decorated a cake with the chocolate heart.

In this study, subjects had to indicate whether they interpreted the PP as verb-modifying or as object-modifying. For indefinite/indefinite, indefinite/definite and definite/indefinite constructions, a much more pronounced bias for a verb-modifying PP could be established than for definite/definite constructions (percentage of verb-modifying interpretations: indef/indef = 71.7; def/indef = 78.8; indef/def = 72.7; def/def = 58.6; main effect of definiteness, likelihood ratio chi-square change: 10.479, $df = 3$, $P < 0.02$). Since most of the PP-internal NPs in Spivey-Knowlton and Sedivy's experiment 5 are indefinite (at least 25 of 32), the particularly strong VP-bias in definite/indefinite constructions is highly compatible with their findings. We will not account for this particular result here. To minimise the potentially biasing influence of definiteness in the following experiments, however, we only used definite/definite constructions.[7]

Method

Subjects. Twenty undergraduates (native speakers of German) from the University of Freiburg were paid to participate in the study. All of them had normal, uncorrected vision and they were naive to the purpose of the study. During an experimental session of about 40 min duration, each of the subjects had to read 45 isolated sentences and "yes/no" questions while their eye movements were monitored by a Dual Purkinje Image Eyetracker. The results of two subjects had to be excluded because of too many track losses.

Materials and Design. The experimental sentences were maniuplated according to a 2×2×2 within-subjects design with the factors verb placement (final *vs* second), lexical preference (3-place verb *vs* 2-place verb) and semantic bias (VP- *vs* NP-attachment biased). The order of the sentences was randomised. For each experimental condition, three sentences were presented, resulting in 24 target sentences per subject. The materials were rotated such that every sentence from every set was presented to an equal number of subjects. However, the exclusion of two subjects led to an imbalance. Excluding two more subjects, quasi-randomly chosen to obtain a balanced distribution of the materials, did not change any of the effects described in the following sections. One sentence had to be excluded because of too many missing data points. Additionally, there were 29 filler sentences.

Procedure. Prior to the experiment, each subject was fitted to a headrest to prevent head movements during reading. This was followed by a brief calibration procedure and a warm-up block of five successive filler sentences. The experiment was then made up of four blocks. Each block was initiated by a brief calibration procedure and contained 10 sentences, two filler sentences followed by eight randomly mixed target and filler sentences. Before a sentence was presented, the subject had to fixate a cross on the screen that indicated the start-position of the sentence-string. When the subject had finished reading the sentence, he or she pressed a button that erased the sentence from the screen. Each sentence in the experiment was

[7]Since these are off-line preferences, and since we have not run an on-line experiment investigating definiteness effects yet, it is unclear whether these effects are relevant for first analyses.

then followed by a simple "yes/no" question which the subject was to answer by pressing one of two buttons (left-hand button = "yes"; right-hand button = "no"). The subjects were asked to read normally. They answered with a high degree of accuracy (93%), which did not vary across conditions.

Apparatus. The subjects' eye movements were monitored by a Generation 5.5 Dual Purkinje Image Eyetracker. Viewing was binocular, but eye movements were recorded only from the right eye. The eyetracker was connected to an AT 386 computer, which controlled stimulus-presentation and stored the output from the eyetracker. The sampling rate for data collection was 1 kHz. The sentences were presented on a 20-inch colour monitor, beginning at the sixth column of the character matrix. The subject was seated 83 cm from the screen, so that three letters equalled 1° of visual angle. External distractions and light reflections were screened off by a black tube and the room was darkened slightly.

Dependent Variables and Data Analyses. The data were summarised for each single-word region, resulting in four dependent variables, namely first-pass reading times (also called gaze durations for single-word regions), total reading time and regression-path durations (RPDs). First-pass reading time is the sum of all fixations on a region starting with the first fixation on the region until there is a saccade to another region. However, if a subsequent region has been read before, first-pass reading time is set to zero. The total amount of time spent on a word including the time for re-reading was taken as the total reading time. Regression-path durations are the sum of all durations of fixations in the regression path; that is, in the stream of fixations starting with the first fixation on a region and including all fixations up to the point where there is a forward saccade past the region under consideration. Regression-path durations have been demonstrated to be more sensitive to garden-pathing than first-pass reading times (see Konieczny, 1996). However, at clause boundaries, and especially at the end of a sentence, RPDs become contaminated by various unspecific re-reading events. To reduce the noise at clause boundaries, only the *first* regression path was therefore taken as an indicator of garden-pathing, in which all but the first re-readings of previous regions before passing on to the next region (or pressing a button) were excluded. This measure is referred to as the *first RPD* measure. In the presentation of the data, we will focus on the first RPDs whenever clause boundaries are involved and on total RPDs otherwise. That means, in cases where reading times on the PP in verb-second sentences are part of the statistical analyses, we always report first RPDs.

In some cases, the reader does not fixate a certain word at all, as is frequently observed for short words or highly predictable words (e.g. Just

& Carpenter, 1980; Rayner & Pollatsek, 1989). These cases were excluded from the data analyses. Consequently, the data reported in the following section represent "conditionalised" scores (see Rayner & Pollatsek, 1989).

Since we are primarily interested in the influence of sentential (syntactic and semantic) context on the processing of words, we have to check for effects that reflect only processes at the word level. An important factor in word processing is word length, defined by the number of character spaces of the word (Just & Carpenter, 1980). To account for word length, one can either treat it as a covariate in the analysis of variance, or eliminate its effect in the score taken as a dependent variable. It is a common procedure to divide the reading time score by the number of characters in the region. However, this procedure has been demonstrated to yield a non-linear function of word length on reading time, thus potentially leading to substantial distortions, especially in short regions (Trueswell, Tanenhaus, & Garnsey, 1994). Furthermore, there are a number of other lexical factors like word frequency, concreteness of a word, etc. (see Just & Carpenter, 1980), that contribute to the reading time score of a word. Therefore, we used z-scored lexical decision times for each word as a covariate in our statistical analyses of this experiment, which resulted in a more accurate estimate of word-level processing effects than word length alone. Lexical decision times were taken from a pre-study conducted with a different group of subjects. In this pre-study (see Hemforth, 1993), all words from the materials of several experiments were listed. Two word lists were constructed. For each of the word lists, every second word was exchanged for a pronounceable nonword consisting of the same letters. Each list was presented to 24 subjects (all students from the University of Bochum). Lexical decision times for each correctly recognised word were individually z-standardised for each subject. The mean standardised lexical decision times were used as covariates in the following experiments. These mean lexical decision times correlate highly with length ($r = 0.70$) and gaze durations on the respective words (varying between $r = 0.55$ and $r = 0.70$ in different experiments). Length alone usually correlates reliably with gaze durations too (between $r = 0.40$ and $r = 0.50$ in different experiments), but not as highly as lexical decision times.

Hypotheses. Parameterised head attachment predicts different PP-attachment preferences, depending on the position of the verb and, for verb-second sentences, depending on the lexical preferences of the verb. The critical constituent, where an attachment preference can at first be detected, is the PP itself, and especially the noun within the PP, because at this point sufficient semantic bias information becomes available for the thematic processor to determine the plausibility of the first analysis of the parser.

When a verb-final sentence is read from left to right, the head of the VP is still not available on the first reading of the PP. However, the head of the object-NP has already been read. Thus, rather than delaying the attachment until the end of the sentence, the PP should initially be attached to the object-NP (*head attachment*). If the thematic processor regards this preferred attachment as implausible, as in the case of a PP-object biased for VP-attachment, reanalysis is begun, during which the alternative VP-modifying reading is generated. The reanalysis should require some additional time on the part of the processor. For that reason, the reading time on the noun of a VP-attachment biased PP should be reliably longer than on an NP-attachment biased PP-object.

In verb-second sentences, the lexical heads of both potential attachment sites, the VP and the object-NP, have already been processed when the PP is encountered. Consequently, preferred role attachment should cause the PP to be attached initially to the VP if the verb highlights the thematic role potentially taken by the PP. If it comes to a clash between the preferred role attachment of the PP and semantic bias, as is the case when the PP-object is an implausible verb argument, longer reading time scores should be observable, which result from the initiation of a reanalysis. If the verb does not highlight a role that can be taken by the PP, the PP is initially attached to the most recent head (i.e. the object noun). This causes the processor to initiate reanalysis when a VP-attachment biased PP-object is read. Seen as a whole, parameterised head attachment predicts an interaction of lexical preference and semantic bias for verb-second sentences, such that the reading scores on the PP-object should be longer if semantic bias contradicts either of the verb-dependent PP-attachment preferences.

Furthermore, an overall interaction of the factors verb placement, lexical preference and semantic bias can be predicted which results from the differing PP-attachment preferences in the different conditions of verb placement.

The garden-path model (or construal theory) does not predict different attachment preferences for different verb positions or verb-frame information. Depending on the structure of German VPs assumed, either the structurally less complex (presumably VP-) attachment is assumed, or, if the attachment alternatives do not differ in complexity, late closure predicts attachment to the most recently postulated phrase (i.e. the object-NP).

Predictions from lexicalist constraint satisfaction approaches, if set up appropriately, may be similar to those from parameterised head attachment. Since structure building occurs mainly on the basis of lexical projections, only the object-NP is available as an attachment site for the PP in verb-final sentences. Assuming a phrase is preferably attached rather than left dangling, predictions are comparable to parameterised head attachment. A "head attachment" preference thus emerges as a consequence of the head-drivenness of lexicalist models, in combination with a preference for attaching items as opposed to leaving them unattached. In verb-second sentences, the particular lexical properties of the verb as well as the object-NP can influence attachment preferences.

Although the experiments reported here were not designed to distinguish between the two classes of models, it is important to point out two major differences between multiple-constraint models, or restricted parallel models (Gibson, 1991), and SOUL. First, since SOUL is a serial approach, no penalty for maintaining multiple analyses should be observable in the ambiguous region. On the other hand, in models permitting multiple analyses to be maintained in parallel, or multiple constraints competing with each other, an increased processing load on ambiguous regions can be predicted at least under certain circumstances, namely, if the constraints or analyses locally competing with each other are almost equi-biased (MacDonald et al., 1994).

The second major difference between the two approaches is that parameterised head attachment is embedded in a model where the phrase structure is fully assembled incrementally, even if the licensing heads are not yet available. The constraint satisfaction model put forward by MacDonald et al. (1994), on the other hand, can be understood as a head projection approach, where no structure building is possible without the respective lexical heads. Since the attachment ambiguity at the PP is semantically disambiguated at the PP itself, we will not be able to discriminate between the predictions of these two accounts on the basis of the data of the first two experiments, as we will not be able to tell whether any observed penalty results from a two-staged serial model or an interactive constraint competition mechanism. We will return to this issue later.

Results

All reading time measures were submitted to a full factorial $2 \times 2 \times 2$ analysis of variance for repeated measures, including the factors verb placement, lexical preference and semantic bias. Since lexical preference was varied between items, this factor had to be realised as a between-items factor in the F_2-analyses. For word-by-word analyses, the z-scored lexical decision times per word were included as a covariate. Table 2 shows the first-pass reading times, first (and total) RPDs and total reading times for the prepositional object noun by levels of verb placement, semantic bias and lexical preference.

No significant interaction between verb placement and semantic bias was established in any of the measures. The interaction only showed up marginally in the subject analyses for total reading times, with total reading times being longer for VP-biased PPs than for NP-biased PPs in verb-final sentences (655 *vs* 528 msec), whereas total reading times for VP-biased PPs were slightly shorter than total reading times for NP-biased PPs in verb-second sentences (694 *vs* 711 msec) [$F_1(1,16) = 3.55$, $P < 0.08$; $F_2(1,22) = 2.77$, $P < 0.12$].

The linear contrasts in first-pass reading times for the two conditions of verb placement resulted in a simple effect of semantic bias in verb-final sentences: VP-attachment biased PP-objects showed reliably longer first-pass reading times than the NP-attachment biased condition (380 *vs* 323 msec) [$F_1(1,16) = 6.31$, $P < 0.03$; $F_2(1,21) = 3.39$, $P < 0.08$]. In verb-second sentences, however, no reliable effect of semantic bias was found in first-pass reading times.

The same pattern of results was obtained for total RPDs, which were increased in verb-final sentences with a VP-attachment bias compared to sentences with an NP-attachment bias (472 *vs* 389 msec) [$F_1(1,16) = 6.03$, $P < 0.03$; $F_2(1,21) = 5.03$, $P < 0.04$], whereas RPDs for NP- and VP-attachment biased PP-objects did not differ reliably in verb-second sentences.

Total reading times were also increased if the semantic bias opted for a verb-argument reading in verb-final sentences (655 *vs* 528 msec for NP-biased PPs) [$F_1(1,16) = 3.97$, $P < 0.07$; $F_2(1,21) = 5.45$, $P < 0.04$]. Though no statistically reliable interaction of lexical preference and semantic bias showed up for total reading times in verb-final sentences (all $F < 1.5$), the facilitation of NP-attachment seems to be mainly due to sentences with 2-place verbs according to *post-hoc* analyses.

TABLE 2
First-pass Reading Times, First (and Total) Regression-path Durations, and Total Reading Times (msec) for the Noun of the PP in Experiment 1 by Levels of Verb Placement (Final *vs* Second), Semantic Bias (VP-biased *vs* NP-biased) and Lexical Preference

	VP-biased		*NP-biased*	
	3-place	*2-place*	*3-place*	*2-place*
First-pass reading times				
verb-final	367	393	331	297
verb-second	460	549	492	464
First regression-path durations (total RPDs in parentheses)				
verb-final	441 (445)	473 (499)	411 (411)	359 (367)
verb-second	1168 (1422)	1537 (1789)	1591 (1819)	1257 (1497)
Total reading times				
verb-final	585	725	578	478
verb-second	685	720	738	605

A three-way interaction of verb placement, lexical preference and semantic bias in first RPDs was found, but only in the subject analyses [FRPDs: $F_1(1,16) = 6.32$, $P < 0.03$]. This three-way interaction is due to a two-way interaction of lexical preference and semantic bias in verb-second sentences, such that for 2-place verbs, first RPDs were longer for VP-biased PPs than for NP-biased PPs, whereas the opposite effect was obtained for 3-place verbs [FRPDs: $F_1(1,16) = 6.12$, $P < 0.03$; $F_2(1,22) = 2.85$, $P < 0.10$]. The interaction of lexical preference and semantic bias was far from being statistically reliable in verb-final sentences (all $F < 1$).

No reliable effects of semantic biases or lexical preferences showed up at the verb for any of our dependent variables, either for verb-second or for verb-final sentences.

Discussion

The general pattern of results is consistent with the predictions of parameterised head attachment and replicates the pattern found in the self-paced reading studies of Konieczny et al. (1994), although not quite as clearly. The most important measures to be considered here are the first-pass reading times and the first regression-path durations on the noun of the PP. For regression-path durations on the PP-object, a reliable overall interaction of the factors verb placement, lexical preference and semantic bias was found, which had been predicted by different preference principles in different verb placement conditions. For verb-second sentences, an interaction of lexical preference and semantic bias was found in first regression-path durations, as was predicted by preferred role attachment: If the verb highlighted the argument role for the PP, the first regression-path duration was longer for an NP-attachment biased PP-object than for a VP-attachment biased PP-object, as predicted by preferred role attachment. In verb-final sentences, the first-pass reading time on the PP-object, as well as the total RPD, was shorter in the semantically NP-attachment biased condition than in the VP-attachment biased condition, as was predicted by head attachment.

EXPERIMENT 2

One of the reasons why the effects in the preceding experiment might have been obscured by noise in the data is that in the materials used, the critical region of the sentences differed between the experimental conditions. This is true for lexical preference as well as the semantic bias conditions. Since eye movements are particularly sensitive to superficial differences between strings, it could be argued that the differences we found may at least partially be due to these non-minimal contrasts. Therefore, we conducted a further experiment in which the critical region was held constant in all conditions.

TABLE 3
PP-Attachment in Neutral Contexts: Experimental Design of Experiment 2

Pre-target context	Sarah hatte vergeblich versucht, einen wirklich schönen Liebesbrief zu verfassen. Sarah had tried in vain to write a really beautiful love letter.
Verb-second	
VP-biased	23. Sarah / entzündete / das Papier / mit / der Gasflamme, / bevor sie / den Brief in den Kamin legte, was ihr selbst etwas kitschig vorkam. Sarah lit the paper with the gas flame before she put the letter in the chimney, which seemed kitschy even to herself.
NP-biased	24. Sarah / löschte / die Lampe / mit / der Gasflamme, / bevor sie / ... Sarah put out the lamp with the gas flame before she...
Verb-final	
VP-biased	25. Daß Sarah / das Papier / mit / der Gasflamme / entzündete, / bevor sie / den Brief in den Kamin legte, kam ihr selbst etwas kitschig vor. That Sarah lit the paper with the gas flame before she put the letter in the chimney seemed kitschy even to herself.
NP-biased	26. Daß Sarah / die Lampe / mit / der Gasflamme / löschte, / bevor sie / ... That Sarah put out the lamp with the gas flame before she...
Final sentence	Sie gab sich gern einer melancholischen Stimmung hin. She liked to surrender herself to a melancholic mood.

Different biases were induced by the words in the sentential context preceding the critical region (examples 23–26 in Table 3), including the verb and the direct object NP. Lexical preferences were not varied in this experiment, as we were mainly interested in the verb-position effect, and including lexical preferences turned out to be technically almost intractable.[8] The majority of the verbs we used were biased to take an instrumental-PP.

Another concern with Experiment 1 is the fact that we presented the sentences in isolation without any context. Reading strategies for isolated sentences might differ from normal reading of coherent text. Reading can be slowed down, for example. Since parsing preferences are very sensitive to the timecourse of incoming information, it might be the case that different effects show up if more time is spent on a region. To address this problem, we presented two neutral context sentences with the experimental sentences, one preceding and one following the experimental sentence.

[8]This is because verbs and direct object NPs were chosen so that the PP could plausibly be understood as *either* an instrument *or* an NP-attributive. Including lexical preferences in the design would have required that each of the two verbs needed for each sentence type was coupled by a semantically similar 2-placed verb. Such verbs turned out to be almost impossible to find in most cases.

Method

Materials and Design. The experimental sentences were manipulated according to a 2 × 2 within-subjects design with the factors verb placement (second *vs* final) and semantic bias (VP- *vs* NP-attachment biased). Semantic bias was checked in a pre-study fully equivalent to pre-study 3 described for Experiment 1. All sentences were presented in neutral contexts with one sentence preceding and one sentence following the target sentence. The order of the sentences was randomised. For each experimental condition, four sentences were presented, resulting in 16 target sentences per subject. These 16 sentences were taken from a pool of 16 sets of sentences differing in content. The materials were rotated such that every sentence from every set was presented to an equal number of subjects. Additionally, there were 32 filler texts.

Subjects. Sixteen undergraduates (native speakers of German) from the University of Freiburg were paid to participate in the study. All of them had normal, uncorrected vision and they were unfamiliar with the purpose of the study. During an experimental session of 45 min duration, each subject had to read 50 texts while their eye movements were monitored by a Dual Purkinje Image Eyetracker.

Procedure. The experiment was made up of six blocks plus a warm-up block of two training texts. Each block was initiated by a brief calibration procedure and contained eight texts—one filler text followed by seven randomly mixed target or filler texts.

The reading time scores were summarised for each region of a sentence as indicated by the slashes in Table 3, and were submitted to a full factorial 2 × 2 analysis of variance for repeated measures including the factors attachment-bias (VP *vs* NP) and verb position (ambiguous *vs* unambiguous).

Since we did not have access to lexical decision times for the words used in this experiment, we had to eliminate the word-length effect in the reading time scores: the slope of the regression of word length on first-pass reading times was calculated on a non-critical region (the NP preceding the structurally ambiguous PP) and the product of slope and number of characters was subtracted from all reading time measures. All of the scores reported in the next sections were thus adjusted for word-length. We will concentrate on first-pass reading times and the regression-path durations at the critical sentence-positions—that is, the PP-Object (det + noun), and the main verb.

TABLE 4
First-pass Reading Times, First (and Total) Regression-path Durations and Total Reading Times (msec) for the PP-object in Experiment 2 by Levels of Verb Placement (Final *vs* Second) and Semantic Bias (VP-biased *vs* NP-biased)

	VP-biased		*NP-biased*	
	Verb-final	*Verb-second*	*Verb-final*	*Verb-second*
First-pass reading times	192	282	162	243
First regression-path durations (total RPDs in parentheses)	337 (417)	493 (504)	260 (271)	757 (899)
Total reading times	572	542	600	827

Results

A reliable interaction of verb placement and semantic bias was established for first regression-path durations at the PP-object [FRPDs: $F_1(1,15) = 10.55$, $P < 0.01$; $F_2(1,15) = 10.69$, $P < 0.01$], as well as an interaction in the item analyses for total reading times [$F_1(1,15) = 1.94$, NS; $F_2(1,15) = 5.78$, $P < 0.05$]. For both measures, reading times were reliably increased if NP-attachment was semantically biased in verb-second sentences [FRPD: $F_1(1,15) = 12.49$, $P < 0.01$; $F_2(1,15) = 10.87$, $P < 0.01$; TRT: $F_1(1,15) = 11.51$, $P < 0.01$; $F_2(1,15) = 10.41$, $P < 0.01$]. For verb-final sentences, on the other hand, total regression-path durations were marginally increased if VP-attachment was biased [TRPD: $F_1(1,15) = 4.26$, $P < 0.06$; $F_2(1,15) = 2.89$, $P < 0.11$].

At the verb of verb-final sentences, first regression-path durations as well as total reading times were numerically longer if the PP was semantically biased towards NP-attachment, but the effect was significant only for TRTs in the subject analysis [FRPDs: $F_1(1,15) = 2.93$, $P < 0.11$; $F_2(1,15) < 1$, NS; TRT: $F_1(1,15) = 4.96$, $P < 0.05$; $F_2(1,15) = 3.73$, $P < 0.08$].

TABLE 5
First-pass Reading Times, First (and Total) Regression-path Durations and Total Reading Times (msec) at the Verb in Experiment 2 in Verb-second and Verb-final Sentences by Levels of Semantic Bias (VP-biased *vs* NP-biased)

	VP-biased		*NP-biased*	
	Verb-final	*Verb-second*	*Verb-final*	*Verb-second*
First-pass reading times	200	273	185	279
First regression-path durations (total RPDs in parentheses)	365 (411)	273 (293)	460 (588)	292 (311)
Total reading times	319	415	459	567

Discussion

Though not completely reliably so, the data from Experiment 2 support the evidence on the influence of verb placement found in Expriment 1. Even if we place the material in fairly neutral contexts, the interaction between attachment preferences in verb-second and verb-final sentences shows up at the PP-object. In this experiment, this cannot be due to superficial differences in the critical regions, because they were identical across all conditions.

The shorter reading times on the clause-final verb in VP-attachment biased conditions can be explained, since the pre-verbal PP to be interpreted in these cases as a verbal argument already constrains the interpretation of the verb to come more than a pre-verbal complex NP does. However, only a very cautious interpretation of reading times at the verb is possible because the verbs differed for the two semantic bias conditions.

EXPERIMENT 3

The validity of a parsing principle like parameterised head attachment cannot only be substantiated by experiments on a single structural phenomenon like PP-attachment. Parameterised head attachment is supposed to be valid for the whole range of structural ambiguities it can be applied to. In this section, we focus on processing local NP-attachment ambiguities in German verb-final constructions.[9] As illustrated in (29) and (30) (see Table 6), these constructions can induce a local conflict associated with a morphological case-marking ambiguity.

Locally, the [NP *der Sängerin*] can either be interpreted as an indirect object (i.e. a dative-marked argument) of the verb (as in 29), or as a genitive-marked modifier of the subject NP *der Arzt* (as in 30), since it is morphologically ambiguous with respect to case marking. The structural ambiguity is resolved when the verbal participle at the end of the VP is encountered: *Geben* (to give) in (29) requires an indirect object in the dative case, and thus demands the critical NP to be part of the VP (27).

27. $[_{S'}$ $[_{C^0}$ Daß]
    $[_{S}$ $[_{NP}$ der Arzt]
    $[_{VP}$ $[_{NP}$ der Sängerin] $[_{NP}$ ein Medikament] $[_{V}$ gegeben]
    $[_{aux}$ hat]]]...]

Entdecken (to discover), on the other hand, is a simple transitive verb. Therefore, the final structure of (30) is given in (28), in which the critical NP is part of a complex subject-NP:

[9] Some of the materials in the Appendix are modified versions of Bader's (1990) materials.

TABLE 6
NP-Attachment: Experimental Design of Experiment 3

NP2: Case-ambiguous		
VP-biased	29.	Daß der Arzt der Sängerin ein Medikament gegeben hat, wußte niemand. That the doctor [the singer[fem, {gen/dat}]] a remedy given has, knew nobody. Nobody knew that the doctor has given a remedy to the singer.
NP-biased	30.	Daß der Arzt der Sängerin ein Medikament entdeckt hat, wußte niemand. That the doctor [the singer[fem, {gen/dat}]] a remedy discovered has, knew nobody. Nobody knew that the doctor of the singer has discovered a remedy.
NP2: Case-unambiguous		
VP-biased	31.	Daß der Arzt dem Sänger ein Medikament gegeben hat, wußte niemand. That the doctor [the singer[masc, dat]] a remedy given has, knew nobody. Nobody knew that the doctor has given a remedy to the singer.
NP-biased	32.	Daß der Arzt des Sängers ein Medikament entdeckt hat, wußte niemand. That the doctor [the singer[masc, gen]] a remedy discovered has, knew nobody. Nobody knew that the doctor of the singer has discovered a remedy.

28. [$_{S'}$ [$_{C^0}$ Daß]
    [$_{S}$ [$_{NP}$ der Arzt] [$_{NP}$ der Sängerin]]
    [$_{VP}$ [$_{NP}$ ein Medikament] [$_{V}$ entdeckt] [$_{aux}$ hat]]]...]

The same structures apply for sentences like (31) and (32), where the critical NP is unambiguously case-marked as *dative* (31) or *genitive* (32), respectively. Note that the ambiguity is not resolved by plausibility in this experiment: all ambiguous NPs were plausible modifiers of the preceding NP. Disambiguation is forced by the subcategorisation requirements of the verb or by the case marking of the NP itself.

Predictions

As will be shown, the three classes of models discussed above differ with respect to the positions in the sentences where processing difficulties are to be expected, as well as in the prediction of the particular conditions under which these difficulties should appear. At first, we will sketch the different predictions regarding the influence of morphological case marking, and then we will turn to effects to be predicted at the VP-participle.

Case Marking of the Second NP

Predictions of Parameterised Head Attachment. According to parameterised head attachment, the parser initially tries to attach the structurally ambiguous NP to the preceding NP, as a result of the head attachment principle: Since the head of the subject NP, but not the head of the VP, is already available when the ambiguous phrase is read, the integration of the PP into a complex subject-NP is attempted. Only after the case marking of the second NP is checked and found to be incompatible with the preferred NP-modifying reading should the attachment to the VP be attempted. This is the case if the second NP is unambiguously dative-marked, since dative NPs cannot modify NPs in German. The earliest point in the sentence where a case-matching conflict can occur is thus at the determiner of the critical NP.

Predictions of the Garden-path Model. When the parser processes the determiner of the subject-NP, it can either directly attach the subject-NP to the S-node, or it can generate an additional NP-node for a complex NP (27, 28). According to minimal attachment, the parser should avoid the latter in the first analysis, because a potentially unnecessary node would have to be postulated. Hence, the parser initially generates a simple subject-NP. When the critical second NP *der Sängerin* is perceived, it can easily be integrated into a VP (27), whereas interpreting it as a modifier of a complex subject-NP would require revision of the simple NP analysis.[10] Consequently, the morphologically ambiguous NP *der Sängerin* will be preferably attached to the VP as a complement. With respect to the morphological case marking of the second NP, no early effects can be predicted within the garden-path model. Note that there are several verbs in German (e.g. *gedenken*, ≅ to remember) which require a genitive-case complement, as in (33):[11]

[10] It has been pointed out by a reviewer that this prediction only holds if the VP node has been predicted top-down before the ambiguous NP is encountered. Otherwise, the VP node would have to be predicted bottom-up from the NP, rendering the VP attachment locally no more complex than the adjoining to the subject-NP. Then, however, late closure—not minimal attachment—applies, resulting in an NP-to-NP attachment preference. It is not clear to the authors how the top-down prediction of a VP can be avoided within garden-path theory, since the integration of the sentence-initial subject to the S-phrase marker requires the application of a grammar rule, such as S → NP VP. Note that the application of grammar rules, not the postulation of nodes *per se*, is considered responsible for parsing complexity in the garden-path model (Frazier, 1989).

[11] The fact that such verbs are rather rare is irrelevant, since the principle-based approach of the garden path does not consider the relative frequency of a given lexical form or the probability of a certain syntactic structure during the first analysis. During reanalysis, however, the thematic processor may suggest alternatives on the basis of any kind of evidence available. Therefore, it could be argued that as soon as the thematic processor comes up with a preference different from the one based on the application of minimal attachment or late closure, a reanalysis can be instantiated, such that case marking can also be predicted to have an early effect in the constructions under consideration. However, this raises a conceptual problem: How can the thematic processor come up with the alternatives that are discarded or simply not encountered by the parser?

33. Als der Arzt des Sängers gedachte,...
    When the doctor [the singer $_{[masc,\ gen]}$ remembered],...
    When the doctor remembered the singer,...

Thus even if the parser takes the case marking of the critical NP into account as soon as possible (i.e. when the determiner of the critical NP is read), an unambiguous genitive case marking cannot explicitly hinder VP-attachment. Consequently, effects due to the case marking of the second NP are unlikely to appear before the verb becomes available.

Predictions of Multiple-constraint Models. In contrast to the PP-attachment experiments presented in Experiments 1 and 2, predictions from paramaterised head attachment and at least some variants of multiple-constraint models differ for NP-attachment ambiguities. The bias to attach an ambiguous NP in these constructions to the preceding NP or to the VP respectively, does not appear to be particularly strong; intuitively, no bias at all can be perceived by most informants and no conscious garden path results from either diambiguation. If structural alternatives are considered in parallel, an ambiguity effect should show up at the ambiguous feminine NP (*der Sängerin*); that is, it should take longer to process ambiguous NPs in comparison to the unambiguous masculine NPs (*des Sängers* or *dem Sänger* respectively). In head-driven (lexicalised multiple-constraint) models (e.g. Lewis, 1993; Stevenson, 1993), however, attachments can only take place if they are licensed by a lexical head, hence only attachment to the preceding NP is possible at this point in time. Then, the predictions meet those of parameterised head attachment.

The Argument Structure of the VP-participle

Predictions of Parameterised Head Attachment. No conflict will occur at the VP-participle when the preceding critical NP has already been disambiguated by its morphological case marking, provided that no genitive-complement verbs are used. Therefore, a delay in processing resulting from reanalysis at the participle is only to be expected in sentences with ambiguous case marking of the critical NP. The structurally ambiguous NP is initially attached to the subject NP, according to head attachment. Thus there should be no conflict with a simple transitive participle which requires only a direct object in addition to the subject. However, when a ditransitive (or preferably ditransitive) VP-participle is read, the preferred analysis has to be revised because the indirect object position remains empty. Hence, a time-consuming reanalysis should be detectable at a ditransitive participle.

Predictions of the Garden-path Model. The VP-participle determines the final decision of the parser. If the argument structure of the VP-participle is compatible with the initial parse, no reanalysis is required. Since minimal attachment forces the parser to postulate an indirect object in the dative or genitive case, only a subcategoriser which provides such an argument position will be easily processed. Otherwise, there should be measurable processing cost due to reanalysis. In any case, a simple transitive verb (or the region immediately following it) should therefore take longer to read.

Multiple-constraint Models. If the ambiguity at the NP has been resolved by a competition process involving almost equi-biased alternatives, reading times on the participle should be increased after ambiguous second NPs, because reanalysis will be necessary in a substantial portion of sentences read (see Frazier, in press; Mitchell, 1994). If only attachment to the subject-NP was possible, according to a strong head projection approach, participles that force VP-attachment should be more difficult. In the cases where attachment to the subject-NP was ruled out by the dative case marking of the second NP, integrating the dangling NP may increase reading times.

Methods

Subjects. Twenty-four undergraduates (native speakers of German) from the University of Freiburg were paid to participate in the study. All of them had normal, uncorrected vision and they were unfamiliar with the purpose of the study. During an experimental session of 45 min duration, each of the subjects had to read 64 isolated sentences while their eye movements were monitored by a Dual Purkinje Image Eyetracker.

Materials. The experimental sentences in this study were manipulated according to a 2 × 2 within-subjects design with the factors attachment-bias (VP-attachment *vs* NP-attachment, related to the argument-taking properties of the respective VP-participle) and case marking of NP2 (ambiguous *vs* unambiguous). For each experimental condition, 6 sentences were presented, resulting in 24 sentences per subject. Each subject was presented with a different set of materials. Additionally, there were 40 filler sentences, structurally different from the target sentences. The order of the sentences was randomised. The target sentences were presented on two lines on the screen, separated by two empty lines after the comma. Consequently, all of the critical regions were presented on the same line.

Procedure. The experiment was made up of seven blocks plus a warm-up block of five successive filler sentences. Each block was initiated by a brief calibration procedure and contained nine sentences—one filler sentence followed by eight randomly mixed target sentences or filler sentences, respectively. An exception was the last experimental block, which was made up of one filler sentence and four test/filler sentences.

The fixation duration measures were summarised for each word of a sentence,[12] and were submitted to a full factorial 2 × 2 analysis of variance for repeated measures including the factors attachment-bias (VP *vs* NP) and case marking of NP2 (ambiguous *vs* unambiguous). To check word-length effects, the number of characters per word was considered as a covariate in the statistical analyses.[13] All of the reported effects in the next sections are thus adjusted with respect to word length. We will concentrate on the first-pass reading times and the regression-path durations at the critical sentence-positions (i.e. determiner of the second NP, and the VP-participle) because, as we noted earlier, these measures are assumed to be the most sensitive ones in detecting the points of the first analysis where a syntactic reanalysis is induced. However, regression-path durations have to be handled with some care in clause-final positions, because they may reflect sentence wrap-up or rechecking processes in these positions.

Results

Determiner of the Second NP. At the determiner of the second NP, neither first-pass reading times, nor regression-path durations, showed reliable differences across the experimental conditions (all $F < 1.6$). However, since determiners are always difficult positions to look at, it seemed reasonable to inspect the data more carefully.

It is known from several eyetracking studies that particularly short words are frequently skipped during reading (e.g. Just & Carpenter, 1987; Rayner & Pollatsek, 1989). This also became apparent in our experiment: The critical determiner, which has a string length of only three character spaces, was skipped in nearly 55% of the cases. This may have resulted in too few fixations for a valid data analysis. However, the fact that short words are often not fixated does not necessarily mean that they are not processed at all. During a fixation, in addition to the actual word being processed, sometimes

[12] Fixation durations greater than the 97th percentile at a given word were treated as extreme values, and were therefore excluded from data analysis. This was done for each experimental condition separately, thus keeping the design balanced. Zero-length reading time scores were also treated as missing, so that the data are expressed as "conditionalised" scores (see Rayner & Pollatsek, 1989). Additionally, 16 cases had to be excluded because of too many track-losses.

[13] We did not use the same technique as in the previous experiment for length adjustment, because there was no viable pre-critical region to provide us with a reliable estimate of length effects without being contaminated by experimental effects. Since an adjustment based on the slope of the critical region itself is almost equivalent to including length as a covariate, we chose this technically less demanding option.

a succeeding word is also processed if it falls into the identification span of eight character spaces to the right of the fixation (see Rayner & Pollatsek, 1989). We can predict not only why the determiner of the second NP is skipped, but also where the effects of the second determiner are to be found. It may well be that subjects have parafoveally recognised the determiner of the second NP while they were fixating the immediately preceding subject noun. Especially if the subject noun is fixated more than once during the first analysis, the determiner very likely falls completely within the identification span of these fixations, since it is a very short word. Therefore, it is plausible to assume that in cases where the determiner of the second NP is skipped, it has been processed (at least partially) during fixations on the preceding subject noun.

To account for this, we carried out additional data analyses with first-pass reading times summed over the region containing the subject noun and the determiner of the second NP (see Table 7). This means that the first-pass reading times (including zero first-pass reading times) of the particular words of that region were simply added up. All cases in which the summed first-pass reading time measure revealed a zero score were treated as missing in the following analyses.

A marginal two-way interaction of the factors attachment-bias and case marking of NP2 was found on the region containing the subject noun and the second determiner [$F_1(1,22) = 3.24, P < 0.09$; $F_2(1,23) = 3.09, P < 0.09$]. This interaction is reducible to a marginal difference between the two attachment-bias conditions in the case of unambiguous case marking of NP2: if case marking demands an attachment to the VP (dative case), the first-pass reading times tend to be longer than in the NP-attachment condition

TABLE 7
First-pass Reading Times (msec) Summed Over the Region Containing the Subject Noun and the Second Determiner, First-pass Reading Times on the Participle and First Regression-path Durations on the Participle in Experiment 3 by Levels of Attachment-bias (VP-biased *vs* NP-biased) and Case Marking of NP2 (Ambiguous *vs* Unambiguous)

	VP-biased		*NP-biased*	
	NP2-ambiguous	*NP2-unambiguous*	*NP2-ambiguous*	*NP2-unambiguous*
First-pass reading times, summed over subject noun and second determiner	376	401	370	363
First-pass reading times for the participle	472	383	380	382
First regression-path durations for the participle	669	609	643	603

(genitive case) [$F_1(1,22) = 3.47$, $P < 0.08$; $F_2(1,23) = 3.90$, $P < 0.06$]. Not surprisingly, there was no difference (F_1, $F_2 < 0.5$) between both ambiguously case-marked NPs (both NPs were identical in both conditions). Testing the relative influence of the case marking of NP2 in each of the attachment-bias conditions revealed no reliable effect (all $F < 1.5$).

VP-participle. The average first-pass reading times on the VP-participle in the respective conditions of attachment-bias and case marking of NP2 are shown in Table 7. A significant (at least in analyses across subjects) two-way interaction of the factors was found [$F(1,22) = 5.81$, $P < 0.03$; $F_2(1,22) = 3.98$, $P < 0.06$]. If the case marking of the second NP is ambiguous, longer first-pass reading times result for a participle which requires a dative-case complement (VP-attachment) than for a simple transitive participle (NP-attachment) [$F_1(1,22) = 5.29$, $P < 0.05$; $F_2(1,22) = 4.48$, $P < 0.05$]. If the second NP is unambiguously case marked, the first-pass reading times on the participle do not differ across the attachment-bias conditions. Additional analyses revealed a reliable difference between the two case marking conditions if the participle forces VP-attachment: the first-pass reading times are longer in the ambiguous than in the unambiguous case marking condition [$F_1(1,22) = 7.07$, $P < 0.02$; $F_2(1,23) = 2.06$, $P = 0.16$]. In the NP-attachment condition, however, the case marking of the second NP shows no effect on the first-pass reading times at the participle (F_1, $F_2 < 0.5$).

The mean first regression-path durations for the VP-participle are listed in Table 7. Descriptively, the overall pattern of FRPDs is comparable to the first-pass reading times pattern, since the highest regression-path durations are observable for a dative-complement participle (VP-attachment) in the case of ambiguous case marking of NP2. However, the two-way interaction of the factors attachment-bias and case marking of NP2 did not reach significance [$F_1(1,22) = 1.27, P = 0.26$; $F_2(1,22) = 1.75, P = 0.20$]. Instead, the case marking of the second NP showed a reliable main effect (but only in the subject analysis): the FRPDs on the participle were prolonged in the ambiguous case marking condition (656 msec) compared with the unambiguous case marking condition (606 msec) [$F_1(1,22) = 4.49$, $P < 0.05$; $F_2(1,23) = 1.19$, $P = 0.29$].

Discussion

The experiment revealed evidence of the construction of a complex subject-NP during the first structural analysis of the sentences considered: the summed first-pass reading times of the region containing the first noun and the (presumably parafoveally processed) second determiner tended to be longer when an unambiguous dative case marking of the second NP hindered its attachment to the preceding subject-NP. Thus there is support for an immediate influence of case marking in the direction predicted by parameterised head attachment, especially by head attachment. At the participle, the first-pass reading times were reliably prolonged when a ditransitive verb required the critical NP to be attached to the VP, provided that no early disambiguation had already taken place. There is thus evidence for an NP-to-NP over NP-to-VP attachment preference in both early and late disambiguation. This result contradicts the prediction of minimal attachment, whereas it is fully consistent with head attachment.

It must be noted, however, that the NP-attachment bias obtained in Experiment 3 can at least partially be explained by the fact that the NP in some of the sentences tested stand in an argument relation to the preceding NP if read as a genitive. Indeed, there are several instances of relational expressions in the materials, such as *father* and *admirer*. The preferences found can thus be accounted for without reference to head attachment, since preferred role attachment would predict a thematic expectation, and thus an NP-to-NP attachment preference in these cases as well. We can see no way of countering this argument but to point out that although this might have happened in the ambiguities looked at in Experiment 3, thematic expectation can definitely be ruled out as an account of the PP-attachment preferences in the verb-final constructions used in Experiments 1 and 2. For the general pattern, then, head attachment is still required. It would be interesting to see, however, whether the results obtained can be replicated using less relational nouns, such as *dog* in (34). Such studies are currently underway (Friederici & Steinhauer, pers. comm.; Konieczny, Hemforth, & Scheepers, work in progress).

34. Peter wußte, daß der Hund *der Bibliothekarin* eine Wurst gestohlen hat.
    Peter knew, that the dog the librarian$_{[gen,\ dat]}$ a sausage stolen has.
    a. "Peter knew that the dog has stolen a sausage *from the librarian*". Or:
    b. "Peter knew that the dog *of the librarian* has stolen a sausage".

One might also be tempted to argue that late closure applies to the constructions investigated here (see footnote 10). In fact, the data on processing German verb-final constructions, like those considered here and in Konieczny et al. (1994), can be correctly predicted by late closure. Note, however, that late closure wrongly predicts an initial NP-attachment preference for PPs in verb-second sentences like (13) or (14).

Serialism. The data provide evidence for a serial account of parsing ambiguities, such as outlined in the SOUL mechanism (Konieczny, 1996). In the region including the first noun and the determiner of the second noun, summed first-pass reading times for the ambiguous determiner *der* are no longer than the first-pass reading times for the "easier" unambiguous condition *des*. Comparably, first-pass reading times on the participle are no longer in the condition with ambiguous second NPs than in the "easier" transitive condition. An ambiguity effect only shows up in total regression-path durations, probably reflecting somewhat increased re-checking or wrap-up processes for cases in which the second NP was ambiguous (note that the participle is very close to the end of the clause).

GENERAL DISCUSSION

The data presented in the last three sections give a fairly consistent picture of attachment processes in verb-second and verb-final clauses. The verb-position effect is clearly the most important and compelling finding. Phrases which can either be attached to a preceding noun phrase or to the verb phrase tend to prefer attachment to the preceding noun, if the verb is not yet encountered. This particular pattern of results meets the predictions of head attachment. Alternatively, however, the results so far might also be due to the property of head-drivenness of lexicalised parsing accounts. Following a head projection strategy, syntactic structures can only be constructed on the basis of available lexical heads from which they are projected or licensed, respectively (cf. Abney, 1989; Pritchett, 1992). When the ambiguous phrase in verb-final sentences is read, there would be no VP-node to which it can be attached, since the respective VP-licensing head would still be missing. Consequently, the only way to integrate the NP or PP into the currently built sentence structure is to attach it as a modifier to the preceding subject or object NP, respectively.

Problems with a Strict Head Projection Approach

There are indicators in the results presented here that this is not what happened. Consider the sentences with unambiguous case marking of the second NP: we found an immediate penalty when the dative determiner hindered the construction of a complex subject-NP, indicating that the mismatch was actually detected. If the parser is forced to leave the phrase dangling until the verb is encountered, and provided the integration of each argument adds a certain cost to processing the head, verbs in unambiguous dative sentences (ditransitives) should take at least slightly longer to process than verbs in unambiguous genitive cases (transitives). However, subjects took no longer reading ditransitive VP-participles in early disambiguated cases than reading simple transitives (note that the regression-path durations for ditransitives with early disambiguation even tended to be shorter than in both ambiguous case marking conditions). This might be taken as an indicator that a morphologically unambiguous dative-case NP has been reanalysed as a VP-constituent *before* the verb was available.

But there is stronger evidence against the head projection assumption. In several other studies, the head projection assumption turned out to be incompatible with evidence from German verb-final constructions, showing that phrases are attached to partial phrase markers of the sentence even before the relevant lexical head (the verb) is read. Bader and Lasser (1994) investigated constructions like (35):

35a. ...., daß [sie$_{nom}$ ... [zu fragen] erlaubt hat].
...., that she ... to ask permitted has.
that she has given permission to ask...
35b. ..., daß [[sie$_{acc}$ ... zu fragen] erlaubt worden ist].
..., that her ... to ask permitted been is.
that permission has been given to ask her...

Note that there are two licensing verbs, to which the ambiguous pronoun *sie* can be attached. The "matrix"-verb of the subclause [... *erlaubt*...] succeeds the infinitival form of the verb *fragen* in the embedded complement. If—as it can be assumed—subjects read from left to right, according to licensing structure parsing, (35b) should be easier to process, since *fragen* precedes *erlaubt* as a possible licenser of *sie*. When the attachment of *sie* is delayed until a licenser is read, the first possible and therefore preferred attachment should be as in (35b). However, (35b) is one of the rare German constructions eliciting a conscious garden-path effect, whereas (35a) is not, which totally contradicts the predictions of the head projection hypothesis. If we assume instead that the pronoun is immediately interpreted as the subject of the matrix clause, the attachment to the infinitive *fragen* is not even considered during processing, such that the integration with the active-voiced verb complex *erlaubt hat* can immediately succeed. On the other hand, when *erlaubt worden ist* marks the sentence passive-voiced, the pronoun could only be integrated if it was dative, which it is not, resulting in a garden path.[14]

In two further studies on German verb-second sentences, Hemforth (1993), using a self-paced reading technique, and Konieczny (1996), using eyetracking, investigated whether dispreferred object-topicalisations are detected before the verb is encountered. Their results strongly suggest that subject- and object-NPs fronted to the *Vorfeld*-position in verb-second main clauses such as (36a, b) are attached to a phrase marker of the sentence even before the verb occurs: unambiguous non-subject case marking leads to

[14]Note that German passive constructions must occur without a nominative marked subject if the object in the corresponding active construction bears lexical case (i.e. dative or genitive).

longer processing times on the NP before the licensing head, the verb, is read, if the NP is fronted to the "usually subject"-Vorfeld-position.

36a. Der gute Schauspieler$_{nom}$ bewunderte die kluge Frau.
The good actor admired the smart woman.
36b. Den guten Schauspieler$_{acc}$ bewunderte die kluge Frau.
The smart woman admired the good actor.

In general, there is plenty of strong evidence that complements and (potential) subjects are in fact integrated into the sentence structure before licensing information is available. Hence, the verb-position effect observed in the studies presented here cannot emerge from head-projection. We assume that the human sentence processor incorporates a mechanism like head attachment: although it would be possible to attach a constituent to a phrase whose lexical head has not yet been encountered, the preference is to attach it to a phrase whose head is already available.

Head Attachment *vs* Immediate Interpretation

As pointed out by Konieczny et al. (1991), an ambiguity resolution behaviour comparable to that of head attachment can apparently also be predicted within a weakly interactive locally parallel approach which incorporates a principle such as *immediate semantic integration*. Suppose that all syntactic attachment alternatives are generated in parallel locally and that a certain alternative is then picked if it allows a relation between the new discourse entity and an old one to be established immediately (cf. Crocker, 1992). Clearly, a head attachment preference almost directly falls out of such an architecture. There are two aspects in the data that render this approach unlikely. First, there is absolutely no sign of local parallelism in the data. Second, the head attachment effect in Experiment 3 could be observed even at the *determiner* of the ambiguous phrase. Semantic integration, however, logically requires the semantic head (i.e. the noun) of the ambiguous phrase to be encountered. Therefore, we propose head attachment as a property of the (serial) parser, not as a by-product of a weakly interactive parallel architecture.

Lexical Guidance *vs* Filter Revisited

If the verb has already been encountered, attachment preferences depend on the theta-role preferences of the respective heads. This particular finding is in line with numerous findings on the early use of detailed lexical and thematic information (Clifton et al., 1984; Juliano & Tanenhaus, 1993; Konieczny, 1989; Strube et al., 1990b; Tanenhaus, Carlson, & Trueswell,

1989; Trueswell et al., 1994). Nevertheless, it has been argued (Mitchell, 1989) that the lexical effects obtained in studies like the one presented here are still compatible with a lexical filter approach (Mitchell, 1987, 1989), in which lexical information does not determine the first analysis but only later analyses. Since the ambiguous PP was encountered several words after the verb, a sufficient amount of time might have passed for lexical preferences to be imposed. Evidence for a filter approach comes from studies on sentences with a supposedly strictly intransitive verb followed by a noun phrase, such as (37):

37. After the child sneezed the doctor prescribed a course of injections.

Mitchell (1987) and Adams et al. (1991) reported evidence indicating that the NP *the doctor* is initially interpreted as the direct object of the verb *sneezed*, even though *sneezed* is strictly intransitive. However, Konieczny and Strube (1995) pointed out that a substantial proportion of the verbs used in their materials had a rare but still possible transitive form. Attachments might therefore have been made in some of the cases, before they were ruled out by means of plausibility, yielding a significant effect on average. There is therefore no need to assume that detailed lexical information is ignored during initial structure assembly. All that is needed to account for the data, then, is a model that *attempts* to attach the NP to the verb initially, regardless of its lexical preferences. This is exactly what parameterised head attachment (and SOUL) predicts, due to the highest priority of head attachment (or the eager attachment behaviour of incoming signs). Summing up, there is currently no convincing evidence for a two-staged lexical filter approach, while there is plenty of evidence for the immediate use of lexical information, including thematic preferences. Since detailed lexical information is used in both types of models at some point, it is more parsimonious to assume that it is accessed and used during the initial stage of structure assembly.

CONCLUSIONS

The general pattern of results fully meets the predictions of parameterised head attachment and in particular those of its serial, algorithmic variant SOUL, while other approaches appear to be questioned by the results discussed here. The predictions of the model were substantiated by a series of on-line experiments showing that the attachment ambiguity resolution behaviour of the human parser is determined by the linear ordering of the lexical heads involved and their detailed lexical properties. Lexical heads can have a guiding influence on parsing decisions; however, parsing can proceed without licensing lexical heads being available. The SOUL mechanism provides a parsing algorithm that strongly relies on lexical information without falling back on an empirically untenable head projection approach.

REFERENCES

Abney, S. (1989). A computational model of human parsing. *Journal of Psycholinguistic Research*, *18*, 129–144.

Adams, B.C., Clifton, C., Jr, & Mitchell, D.C. (1991). Lexical guidance in sentence parsing. Poster presented at the *Meeting of the Psychonomics Society*, San Francisco, CA, November.

Bader, M. (1990). *Syntaktische Prozesse beim Sprachverstehen: Theoretische Überlegungen und experimentelle Untersuchungen.* Magisterarbeit an der Albert-Ludwigs-Universität Freiburg.

Bader, M., & Lasser, I. (1994). German verb-final clauses and sentence processing: Evidence for immediate attachment. In C. Clifton, L. Frazier, & K. Rayner (Eds), *Perspectives in sentence processing*, pp. 225–242. Hillsdale, NJ: Lawrence Erlbaum Associates Inc.

Clifton, C., Frazier, L., & Connine, C. (1984). Lexical expectations in sentence comprehension. *Journal of Verbal Learning and Verbal Behavior*, *23*, 696–708.

Clifton, C., Jr, Speer, S., & Abney, S.P. (1991). Parsing arguments: Phrase structure and argument structure as determinants of initial parsing decisions. *Journal of Memory and Language*, *30*, 251–271.

Crain, S., & Steedman, M. (1985). On not being led up the garden path: The use of context by the psychological parser. In D.R. Dowty, L. Karttunen, & A. Zwicky (Eds), *Natural language parsing: Psychological, computational, and theoretical perspectives*, pp. 320–358. Cambridge: Cambridge University Press.

Crocker, M. (1992). *A logical model of competence and performance in the human sentence processor.* Unpublished PhD thesis, University of Edinburgh, Edinburgh.

Ferreira, F., & Henderson, J.M. (1990). Use of verb information in syntactic parsing. *Journal of Experimental Psychology: Learning, Memory and Cognition*, *16*, 555–568.

Ford, M., Bresnan, J., & Kaplan, R.M. (1982). A competence-based theory of syntactic closure. In J. Bresnan (Ed.), *The mental representation of grammatical relations*, pp. 727–796. Cambridge, MA: MIT Press.

Frazier, L. (1979). *On comprehending sentences: Syntactic parsing strategies.* Bloomington, IN: Indiana University Linguistics Club.

Frazier, L. (1987a). Sentence processing: A tutorial review. In M. Coltheart (Ed.), *The psychology of reading*, pp. 559–586. Hillsdale, NJ: Lawrence Erlbaum Associates Inc.

Frazier, L. (1987b). Syntactic processing: Evidence from Dutch. *Natural Language and Linguistic Theory*, *5*, 519–559.

Frazier, L. (1989). Against lexical generation of syntax. In W. Marslen-Wilson (Ed.), *Lexical representation in process*, pp. 505–528. Cambridge, MA: MIT Press.

Frazier, L. (1990). Parsing modifiers: Special purpose routines in the human processing mechanism. In D.A. Balota, G.B.F. D'Arcais, & K. Rayner (Eds), *Comprehension processes in reading*, pp. 303–331. Hillsdale, NJ: Lawrence Erlbaum Associates Inc.

Frazier, L. (in press). Constraint satisfaction as a theory of sentence processing. *Journal of Psycholinguistic Research.*

Frazier, L., & Clifton, C. (1996). *Construal.* Cambridge, MA: MIT Press.

Frazier, L., & Fodor, J.D. (1978). The sausage machine: A two stage parsing model. *Cognition*, *6*, 291–325.

Frazier, L., & Rayner, K. (1982). Making and correcting errors during sentence comprehension: Eye movements in the analysis of structurally ambiguous sentences. *Cognitive Psychology*, *14*, 178–210.

Frazier, L., Clifton, C., & Randall, J. (1983). Filling gaps: Decision principles and structure in sentence comprehension. *Cognition, 13*, 187–222.

Gibson, E. (1991). *A computational theory of human linguistic processing: Memory limitations and processing breakdown.* Unpublished PhD dissertation, Carnegie Mellon University, Pittsburgh, PA.

Gibson, E., Pearlmutter, N., Canseco-Gonzalez, E., & Hickok, G. (1996). Recency preference in the human sentence processing mechanism. *Cognition, 59*, 23–59.

Hemforth, B. (1993). *Kognitives Parsing: Repräsentation und Verarbeitung sprachlichen Wissens.* Sankt Augustin: Infix.

Hemforth, B., Konieczny, L., Scheepers, C., & Strube, G. (1992). SOUL-Processing: Semantikorientierte Prinzipien menschlicher Sprachverarbeitung. In G. Görz (Ed.), *KONVENS-92*, pp. 198–208. Berlin: Springer.

Hemforth, B., Konieczny, L., & Scheepers, L. (1994). Probabilistic or universal approaches to sentence processing: How universal is the human language processor? In H. Trost (Ed.), *KONVENS-94*, pp. 161–170. Berlin: Springer.

Hemforth, B., Konieczny, L., & Scheepers, C. (in press). Syntactic attachment and anaphor resolution: Two sides of relative clause attachment. In M. Crocker, M. Pickering, & C. Clifton (Eds), *Architectures and mechanisms for language processing.* Cambridge: Cambridge University Press.

Juliano, C., & Tanenhaus, M.K. (1993). Contingent frequency effects in syntactic ambiguity resolution. In *Proceedings of the 15th Annual Conference of the Cognitive Science Society*, pp. 593–598. Hillsdale, NJ: Lawrence Erlbaum Associates Inc.

Juliano, C., & Tanenhaus, M.K. (1994). A constraint-based lexicalist account of the subject/object attachment preference. *Journal of Psycholinguistic Research, 23*, 459–471.

Just, M.A., & Carpenter, P.A. (1980). A theory of reading: From eye fixations to comprehension. *Psychological Review, 87*, 329–354.

Just M.A., & Carpenter, P.A. (1987). *The psychology of reading and language comprehension.* Boston, MA: Allyn and Bacon.

Konieczny, L. (1989). *Zum Verstehen von strukturellen Ambiguitäten: Der Einfluß von Kontext, Weltwissen und lexikalischen Präferenzen.* Diplomarbeit an der Ruhr-Universität Bochum.

Konieczny, L. (1996). Human sentence processing: A semantics-oriented parsing approach. *IIG-Berichte 3/96.*

Konieczny, L., & Strube, G. (1995). SOUL: A cognitive parser. In *Proceedings of the 17th Annual Conference of the Cognitive Science Society*, pp. 631–636. Mahwah, NJ: Lawrence Erlbaum Associates Inc.

Konieczny, L., Hemforth, B., & Strube, G. (1991). Psychologisch fundierte Prinzipien der Satzverarbeitung jenseits von Minimal Attachment. *Kognitionswissenschaft, 2*, 58–70.

Konieczny, L., Scheepers, C., Hemforth, B., & Strube, G. (1994). Semantikorientierte Syntaxverarbeitung. In S. Felix, C. Habel, & G. Rickheit (Eds), *Kognitive Linguistik: Repräsentationen und Prozesse*, pp. 129–158. Opladen: Westdeutscher Verlag.

Lewis, R. (1993). *An architecturally-based theory of human sentence comprehension.* Unpublished PhD thesis, Carnegie Mellon University, Pittsburgh, PA.

MacDonald, M. (1994). Probabilistic constraints and syntactic ambiguity resolution. *Language and Cognitive Processes, 4*, 35–56.

MacDonald, M., Pearlmutter, N., & Seidenberg, M.S. (1994). The lexical nature of syntactic ambiguity resolution. *Psychological Review, 101*, 676–703.

Mitchell, D.C. (1987). Lexical guidance in human parsing: Locus and processing characteristics. In M. Coltheart (Ed.), *Attention and performance XII: The psychology of reading*, pp. 601–618. London: Lawrence Erlbaum Associates Ltd.

Mitchell, D.C. (1989). Verb-guidance and other lexical effects in parsing. *Language and Cognitive Processes, 4*, 123–155.

Mitchell, D.C. (1994). Sentence parsing. In M.A. Gernsbacher (Ed.), *Handbook of psycholinguistics*, pp. 375–410. San Diego, CA: Academic Press.

Prichett, B. (1992). *Grammatical competence and parsing performance.* Chicago, IL: University of Chicago Press.

Rayner, K., & Pollatsek, A. (1989). *The psychology of reading.* Englewood Cliffs, NJ: Prentice-Hall.

Schütze, C.T., & Gibson, E. (1996). The role of argument preference in English PP attachment. Paper presented at the *9th Annual CUNY Conference on Human Sentence Processing*, New York, March.

Spivey-Knowlton, M., & Sedivy, J. (1995). Resolving attachment ambiguities with multiple constraints. *Cognition, 55*, 227–267.

Stevenson, S. (1993). *A constrained active attachment model for resolving syntactic ambiguities in natural language parsing.* Doctoral dissertation, University of Maryland.

Strube, G., Hemforth, B., & Wrobel, H. (1989). *Kognitive Modellierung und empirische Analyse von Prozessen der Satzverarbeitung.* Second Technical Report, Ruhr Universität Bochum.

Strube, G., Hemforth, B., & Wrobel, H. (1990a). Auf dem Weg zu psychologisch fundierten Modellen der Sprachverarbeitung: Echtzeitanalysen des Satzverstehens. In S. Felix, S. Kanngießer, & G. Rickheit (Eds), *Sprache und Wissen. Beiträge des DFG-Forschungsschwerpunktes Kognitive Linguistik*, pp. 115–134. Opladen: Westdeutscher Verlag.

Strube, G., Hemforth, B., & Wrobel, H. (1990b). Resolution of structural ambiguities in sentence comprehension: On-line analysis of syntactic, lexical and semantic effects. In *Proceedings of the 12th Annual Conference of the Cognitive Science Society*, pp. 558–565. Hillsdale, NJ: Lawrence Erlbaum Associates Inc.

Tanenhaus, M., Carlson, G., & Trueswell, J.C. (1989). The role of thematic structures in interpretation and parsing. *Language and Cognitive Processes, 4*, 211–234.

Tanenhaus, M., Boland, J., Mauner, G., & Carlson, G. (1993). More on combinatory lexical information: Thematic structure in parsing and interpretation. In G. Altmann & R. Shillcock (Eds), *Cognitive models of speech processing: The second Sperlonga meeting*, pp. 297–319. Hove: Lawrence Erlbaum Associates Ltd.

Trueswell, J.C., Tanenhaus, M.K., & Garnsey, S.M. (1994). Semantic influences on parsing: Use of thematic role information in syntactic ambiguity resolution. *Journal of Memory and Language, 33*, 285–318.

APPENDIX A: MATERIALS FOR EXPERIMENT 1 (VERB-FINAL VERSIONS ONLY)

3-place verbs

1. Mir wurde erzählt, daß Ulla die Großmutter mit (VP dem liebevollen Kuß / NP der starken Gicht) beglückte.
2. Man sagte mir, daß Ingrid den Freund mit (VP dem überraschenden Anruf / NP dem starken Schnupfen) erfreute.
3. Gestern erfuhr ich, daß Iris die Rentnerin mit (VP der fetzigen Rockmusic / NP dem grauen Rock) störte.
4. Man sagte mir, daß Oliver die Wand mit (VP dem großen Schneeball / NP dem offenen Fenster) bewarf.
5. Man sagte mir, daß Anton das Publikum mit (VP der guten Vorstellung / NP der hohen Erwartung) belustigte.
6. Mir wurde erzählt, daß Hartmut das Mädchen mit (VP der hölzernen Daumenschraube / dem traurigen Gesicht) folterte.

7. Gestern erfuhr ich, daß Barbara das Reh mit (VP dem riesigen Fernglas / NP dem schwarzen Brandzeichen) beobachtete.
8. Neulich höte ich, daß Thomas den Bauernschrank mit (VP dem feinen Pinsel / NP der schiefen Tür) bemalte.
9. Man erzählte mir, daß Marion die Torte mit (VP der praktischen Spritztülle / NP dem starken Mokkageschmack) verzierte.
10 Gestern erfuhr ich, daß Karl das Heft mit (VP dem altmodischen Füllfederhalter / NP der ungewöhnlichen Papierstärke) beschriftete.
11. Mir wurde erzählt, daß Veronika die Tischdecke mit (VP der feinen Nadel / NP dem eingefaßten Rand) bestickte.
12. Neulich hörte ich, daß Herbert die Tür mit (VP dem schweren Schrank / NPdem häßlichen Abziehbild) versperrte.

2-place verbs

13. Gestern erfuhr ich, daß Franz den Dackel mit (VP der weißen Krücke / NP dem struppigen Fell) stieß.
14. Man sagte mir, daß Martin den Bankraub mit (VP der polizeilichen Einsatztruppe / NP dem großen Schaden) untersuchte.
15. Man sagte mir, daß Susanne das Kind mit (VP dem eingepackten Präsent / NP dem blonden Zopf) beschenkte.
16. Gestern erfuhr ich, daß Patrick den Strauch mit (VP dem neuen Schuh / NP der zarten Blüte) zerknickte.
17. Man sagte mir, daß Gabi den Pullover mit (VP der elektrischen Maschine / NP der schmalen Knopfleiste) strickte.
18. Man sagte mir, daß Norbert das Haus mit (VP dem gefährlichen Gewehr / NP dem spitzen Erker) bewachte.
19. Man sagte mir, daß Heike die Natter mit (VP dem starken Teleobjektiv / NP dem spitzen Giftzahn) erblickte.
20. Neulich hörte ich, daß Hannah das Kind mit (VP dem alten Schauermächen / NP der frechen Stupsnase) ängstigte.
21. Gestern erfuhr ich, daß Florian den Blumenstrauß mit (VP dem klapprigen Wagen / V) brachte.
22. Man erzählte mir, daß Helmut den Patienten mit (VP der heilenden Salbe / NP der klaffenden Wunde) verarztete.
23. Mir wurde erzählte, daß Sabine die Schatulle mit (VP dem ersten Weihnachtsgeld / NP dem sicheren Geheimfach) erwarb.
24. Gestern erfuhr ich, daß Nicole den Jungen mit (VP dem lustigen Lied / NP dem gebrochenen Bein) tröstete.

APPENDIX B: MATERIALS FOR EXPERIMENT 2

1. Eines Abends saß Familie Schmidt mit dem Nachbarssohn Peter gemeinsam im Wohnzimmer.
   Daß Peter (VP das Kind *mit dem Schauermärchen ängstigte* / NP *das Buch mit dem Schauermärchen* verstand), obwohl es erst sieben Jahre alt war, beunruhigte die Eltern.
   So endete es wieder damit, daß das Kind nicht schlafen konnte.
2. Bruno war für seine Brutalität berüchtigt. An einem nebligen Herbstnachmittag war er im Wald unterwegs.

Daß Bruno (VP den Hasen *mit dem Gewehr erschoß* / NP *den Jäger mit dem Gewehr* fesselte), als dieser auf einer Lichtung erschien, war der Anfang vom Ende seiner Verbrecherlaufbahn.
Kurz darauf wurde er gefaßt und eingesperrt.

3. In der ersten Einstellung des Krimis sah man den Hauptakteur Felix in einem Gasthaus.
Daß Felix (VP das Brot *mit dem Messer schnitt* / NP *den Koch mit dem Messer* knebelte), als er den Polizisten am Tresen entdeckte, wirkte etwas stilisiert.
The fact that Felix cut the bread with the knife as he discovered the policeman at the Von da an war der Film allerdings ziemlich realistisch.
4. Der Herbergsvater, der immer streng darauf achtete, daß Ruhe und Ordnung herrschten, hatte den frechen Paul besonders auf dem Kieker.
Weil Paul (VP die Deckte *mit der Zigarette versengte* / NP *den Schüler mit der Zigarette* verprügelte), als der Herbergsvater gerade einmal kurz kinausgegangen war, merkte dieser zunächst nichts von dem Vorfall.
Als der Herbergsvatger davon erfuhr, war Paul schon über alle Berge.
5. Martin und seine Freunde tauschten oft und gerne Geschenke aus.
Als Martin (VP den Rahmen *mit der Laubsäge bastelte* / NP *den Werkzeugkoffer mit der Laubsäge* verpackte), die er von seinem alten Freund Tim geschenkt bekommen hatte, fiel ihm etwas ein.
Er mußte Tim unbedingt wieder einmal schreiben.
6. Sarah hatte vergeblich versucht, einen wirklich schönen Liebesbrief zu verfassen.
Daß Sarah (VP das Papier *mit der Gasflamme entzündete* / NP *die Lampe mit der Gasflamme* löschte), bevor sie den Brief in den Kamin legte, kam ihr selbst etwas kitschig vor.
Sie gab sich gern einer melancholischen Stimmung hin.
7. Rita fuhr gerade rückwärts aus der Garage, als sie im Rückspiegel etwas vorbeihuschen sah.
Als Rita (VP die Katze *mit der Dreiklanghupe erschreckte* / NP *den Wagen mit der Drieklanghupe* zerkratzte), während sie versuchte auszuweichen, geriet sie beinahe in Panik.
Weil sie die Einfahrt gestreift hatte, mußte sie schließlich 900 DM für eine neue Lackierung bezahlen.
8. Bandleader Robbi war mit seiner Band bei seiner Plattenfirma, um aus einer Reihe alter Aufnahmen eine neue CD zusammenzustellen.
Weil Robbi (VP den Produzenten *mit dem Gitarrensolo beeindruckte* / NP *das Musikstück mit dem Gitarrensolo* bearbeitete), das er schon vor Jahren eingespielt hatte, kam ihm eine Idee.
Noch am gleichen Abend fing er an, ein neues Stück zu schreiben.
9. Claudia machte für eine Auto-Illustrierte Testfahrten.
Daß Claudia (VP den Scherbenhaufen *mit den Brietreifen überrollte* / NP *den Sportwagen mit den Breitreifen* untersuchte), bevor sie die Bremsen testete, war im Plan vorgesehen.
Claudia arbeitete immer sehr gewissenhaft.
10. Als Lärmforscher an einem psychologischen Institut machte Tim im Auftrag des Umweltministeriums eine Studie im ruhig gelegenen Südpark.
Daß Tim (VP den Spaziergänger *mit dem Motorgeräusch belästigte* / NP *das Tonband mit dem Motorgeräusch* zerstörte), indem er es immer wieder abspielte, war so nicht geplant.
Tim übertrieb gerne ein wenig.
11. Susanne war Kommissarin bei der Drogenfahndung. Gerade verfolgte sie zwei Schmuggler, die zu Fuß fliehen wollten.
Als Susanne (VP die Grenze *mit dem Hubschrauber erreichte* / NP *die Plattform mit dem Hubschrauber* sah), ohne die burschen zu entdecken, gab sie beinahe auf.
Damn verständigte sie jedoch die Kollegen von Interpol, die sofort Unterstützung Zusagten.

12. Der kleine Jochen hatte immer eine diebische Freude daran, die Putzfrau seiner Mutter zu ärgern.
    Da Jochen (VP das Fenster *mit dem Wischwasser bespritzte* / NP *den Eimer mit dem Wischwasser* (beklebte), als sie gerade nicht hinsah, bekam er später Ärger.
    Doch daran war Jochen gewöhnt, und er plante schon wieder neue Streiche.
13. Hans nutzte die Osterferien, um endlich einmal Ordnung in seinen Garten zu bringen.
    Während Hans (VP das Loch *mit der Steinplatte bedeckte* / NP *den Tisch mit der Steinplatte* säuberte), bevor er das Laub zusammenkehrte, freute er sich auf die erste Grillparty.
    Es mußte noch viel gemacht werden, vor allem das Unkraut sprießte überall.
14. In der Mittagspause ging Luise in ihr Lieblingsrestaurant.
    Daß Luise (VP das Essen *mit der Kreditkarte bezahlte* / NP *die Brieftasche mit der Kreditkarte* verdreckte), als der Kellner das Dessert brachte, erregte Aufmerksamkeit.
    Danach eilte sie in ihr Geschäft zurück.
15. Richard war in ein modernes Apartment umgezogen. Nun mußte er sich mit der modernen Technik erst einmal zurechtfinden.
    Während Richard (VP die Temperatur *mit der Fußbodenheizung reglete* / NP *die Wohnung mit der Fußbodenheizung* versicherte), wie es ihm der Makler erklärt hatte, ägerte er sich über die hohen Nebenkosten.
    Seine alte Wohnung war wesentlich günstiger gewesen.
16. Als Inhaberin eines exklusiven europaweiten Kurierdienstes, hatte Sabine viel zu tun.
    Als Sabine (VP das Paket *mit dem Privatjet flog* / NP *den Piloten mit dem Privatjet* überprüfte), da es sich um einen vertraulichen Auftrag handelte, kam ihr irgendetwas merkwürdig vor.
    Es war das erste mal, daß sie bei einem Auftrag ein ungutes Gefühl hatte.

APPENDIX C: MATERIALS FOR EXPERIMENT 3 (VERB-FINAL VERSIONS WITH AMBIGUOUS N2 ONLY)

1. Daß der Referent der Ministerin eine Geheimakte (VP überreicht hat / NP vernichtet hat), hatte der findige Redakteur seit kurzem vermutet.
2. Weil der Chef der Abteilungsleiterin einen Schnaps (VP gegönnt hat / NP getrunken hat), regten sich viele sehr auf.
3. Daß der Arzt der Sängerin ein Wundermittel (VP verabreicht hat / NP entwickelt hat), rettete letztendlich die Vorstellung.
4. Nachdem der Anwalt der Angeklagten einen Vergleich (VP empfohlen hatte / NP erwirkt hatte), wurde die Verhandlung zunächst ausgesetzt.
5. Ob der Wachdienst der Firma weiteren Ärger (VP erspart hätte / NP verhindert hätte), konnte die Konzernleitung nicht mit Gewißheit sagen.
6. Obwohl der Schulfreund der Tochter eine Ohrfeige (VP gegeben hat / NP bekommen hat), gingen die Eltern nicht in die Sprechstunde.
7. Daß der Gast der Schwester den Abwasch (VP überlassen hat / NP übernommen hat), war nicht anständig.
8. Daß der Diener der Gräfin einen Zinteller (VP geschenkt hat / NP erhalten hat), fand die Haushälterin sehr bemerkenswert.
   Weil der Gesandte der Königin die Taktik erklärt hatte, konnte ein Teilsieg errungen werden.
   Because the envoy explained his tactics to the queen, a small victory was won.
9. Weil der Gesandte dem König die Taktik (VP erklärt hatte / NP geändert hatte), konnte ein Teilsieg errungen werden.

10. Weil die Tante der Frau ein Haus (VP vermachte hatte / NP besessen hatte), war das Auskommen der Familie gesichert.
11. Daß der Trainer der Manschaft die Zigaretten (VP entzogen hat / NP versteckt hat), war leider wirkungslos geblieben.
12. Da ker Kurier der Füstin einen Brief (VP geschickt hatte / NP verloren hatte), kam es zum Eklat.
13. Da der Professor der Studentin eine Arbeit (VP übertragen hatte / NP beendet hatte), konnten noch Termine für den nächsten Tag vereinbart werden.
14. Daß der Manager der Künstlerin mehr Geld (VP versprochen hat / NP verlangt hat), wußte Anna als Erste.
15. Da der Detektiv der Rektorin den Dieb (VP gebracht hat / NP erwischt hat), konnte gleich die Polizei gerufen werden.
16. Weil der Kapitän der Fregatte den Ankerplatz (VP gezeigt hat / NP gekannt hat), konnte das Schiff problemlos anlegen.
17. Daß der Vorgesetzte der Gesellin eine Ferienreise (VP untersagt hatte / NP unternommen hatte), widersprach allen Vereinbarungen.
18. Da der Leiter der Forschergruppe den Erfolg (VP verübelt hat / NP bezweifelt hat), erfuhr die Öffentlichkeit erst sehr spät davon.
19. Weil der Berater der Inhaberin alle Gesetzeslücken (VP verraten hatte / NP verbreitet hat), geriet die Firma in die Medien.
20. Da die Verehrer der Filmdiva die Autogrammkarten (VP entrissen hatten / NP gesammelt hatten), erwarteten manche Kritiker einen großen Erfolg.
21. Da die Mutter der Prinzessin sämtliche Skandale (VP verziehen hatte / NP ertragen hatte), herrschte einigermaßen Friede im Schloß.
22. Daß der Vater der Braut den Hof (VP übereignet hatte / NP versteigert hatte), fanden die meisten Gäste äußerst merkwürdig.
23. Da der Dienstherr der Beamtin die Verantwortung (VP übergeben hatte / NP bestritten hatte), blieben die wahren Schuldigen lange Zeit im Dunkeln.
24. Da der Betreuer der Sprinterin ein Dopingmittel (VP gespritzt hatte / NP verwendet hatte), wurden die Wettkämpfe zunächst unterbrochen.

LANGUAGE AND COGNITIVE PROCESSES, 1997, *12* (2/3), 349–399

Lexical Structure and Parsing Complexity

Suzanne Stevenson
Rutgers University, New Brunswick, NJ, USA

Paolo Merlo
University of Geneva, Geneva, Switzerland

In recent work on sentence processing, lexical frequencies have been proposed as a primary mechanism for syntactic and lexical disambiguation. In this paper, we instead focus on the consequences that the structural configuration of lexical knowledge has for the timecourse of parsing. We concentrate on reduced relative clauses and propose a new lexical-structural analysis for those verbs that are difficult in this construction, manner of motion verbs.

The interaction between the proposed lexical structure and the competitive attachment parser (Stevenson, 1994b) explains the persistent difficulty of this construction with a manner of motion verb, even in disambiguating contexts (e.g. a reduced relative in object position) or with non-ambiguous past participle verb forms. Weighted influences on the activation competition are possible with other verbs, and the model can therefore also explain data that demonstrate contextual effects on reduced relatives with simple transitives.

Consequences for the frequency-based models, and all models which base the explanation of the difficulty on the ambiguity of the past participle form, are discussed.

INTRODUCTION

The last several decades of development in syntactic theory have seen a shift from large systems of complex rules to systems of simple interacting constraints (e.g. Chomsky, 1981; Grimshaw, in press). As rule systems have

Requests for reprints should be addressed to Suzanne Stevenson, Department of Computer Science, CoRE Building, Busch Campus, Rutgers University, New Brunswick, NJ 08903, USA. E-mail: suzanne@ruccs.rutgers.edu

We gratefully acknowledge the financial support of the Rutgers Center for Cognitive Science (RuCCS), the administrative support provided by Trish Anderson of RuCCS, and the time volunteered by our informants at RuCCS and at the University of Geneva. We thank Charles Clifton, Sven Dickinson, Uli Frauenfelder, Jane Grimshaw, Luigi Rizzi, Mike Tanenhaus, John Trueswell and three anonymous reviewers for helpful comments and discussion on earlier drafts of the manuscript.

become simpler, lexical representations correspondingly have become richer (cf. Bresnan, 1982), and it has become accepted terminology to speak of syntactic structure as being "projected from the lexicon". Recently, the line between the lexical and syntactic components of the grammar has become even more blurred. Hale and Keyser (1993) have put forward a proposal in which lexical entries consist of entire phrases, with potentially embedded complement structure. Their theory of lexical structure accounts for lexical regularities using the same constraints on structural configurations as those that apply in the syntax. Thus as the phrase structure rules governing syntactic structure have become de-emphasised, lexical information has become more and more articulated, until lexical entries have themselves become, in a very real sense, syntactic.

The same evolution of the relation between syntax and the lexicon has occurred within models of human sentence processing. Ford, Bresnan and Kaplan (1982) provided an early and influential investigation of the effect of individual lexical information on human parsing. Currently, the crucial idea of syntax being projected from the lexicon has developed to a point at which, at least in some central theories, the lexicon is the primary repository of syntactically relevant information. Current constraint-based approaches to modelling human sentence processing suggest that perhaps all of the relevant processing distinctions can be traced to distinctions in lexical information (e.g. MacDonald, Pearlmutter, & Seidenberg, 1994; Spivey-Knowlton & Sedivy, 1995; Spivey-Knowlton, Trueswell, & Tanenhaus, 1993; Trueswell, 1996). Furthermore, these approaches have recently focused on frequency as the key aspect of lexical information in determining preferred interpretations. For example, MacDonald et al. (1994) specifically propose that possible syntactic phrases are stored with an individual lexical item, and these phrases are activated in proportion to the frequency of the lexical item or its conjunction of features. Co-occurrence frequencies may come into play among features of a single lexical item, as well as among features across combinations of lexical structures.

We are in general agreement with syntactic and processing approaches that emphasise rich lexical representations as the source of structural analyses. It is also clear that lexical frequencies contribute to the ease or difficulty of processing particular sentences. However, we feel that the recent attention to frequency effects has been too narrowly focused, and has largely disregarded the critical role of structure in determining interpretation preferences. We note that the very richness of lexical representations makes it unlikely that frequency is the only aspect of lexical structure that is relevant to processing, and we propose that the structural configuration of the lexical knowledge itself has consequences for processing behaviour. Our claim is that the structural properties of an analysis are crucial, including the structural distinctions arising from individual lexical information. In particular, we examine the lexical structure of certain verb subclasses, and the effect that the various structures have on the processing of reduced relative clause constructions.

Sentences (1) and (2) each exhibit a main verb/reduced relative (MV/RR) ambiguity at the italicised verb, which can be either a main verb or a past participle:

1. The horse *raced* past the barn fell.
2. The butter *melted* in the microwave was lumpy.

The striking aspects of these examples is their sharp contrast in acceptability: although they exhibit the same structural ambiguity, the first is a classic garden path, while the second is readily understood. Pure structure-based accounts rely on the greater complexity of the reduced relative construction to explain its unacceptability in the first sentence (e.g. Ferreira & Clifton, 1986; Frazier, 1978; Frazier & Fodor, 1978), but are unable to account for the ease of the second sentence. Similarly, grammar-based accounts proposed by Pritchett (1992) and Gibson (1991) have claimed that the optional intransitivity of *raced* is the factor causing difficulty in sentence (1), but this also incorrectly predicts that *melted* too should cause a garden path in sentence (2). In contrast to these structural explanations, frequency-based accounts have proposed instead that the ease or difficulty of this construction depends in crucial ways on the frequencies of the ambiguous verb in its various relevant forms—main verb/past participle, active/passive, intransitive/transitive (MacDonald et al., 1994; Trueswell, 1996). In relying on continuously valued frequency information, the constraint-based accounts can potentially address the range of difficulty that has been observed in the processing of this ambiguity (e.g. MacDonald, 1994; Trueswell, Tanenhaus, & Garnsey, 1994).

However, there are two problems with accounts that rely primarily on frequency differentials as the explanation of the degree of difficulty of reduced relative clauses. First, the extremely difficult reduced relatives, such as in sentence (1), remain unacceptable even in unambiguous contexts (e.g. *The stablehand groomed the horse raced past the barn*). Since constraint-based models emphasise relative activation of structures, they do not explain why the reduced relative interpretation would be completely unavailable to the sentence processor, when it is the only possible alternative. Second, while frequency is proposed as a crucial factor in resolving ambiguity, the source of frequency differentials has heretofore been completely unaddressed. Our work is partially motivated by the importance of discovering possible underlying causes of frequency differences, rather than accepting them as primary influences in and of themselves.

Our claim is that the structure of reduced relative clauses has a critical effect on processing behaviour. In contrast to earlier structure-based theories, we contend that the relevant structural distinctions arise from differences in individual lexical structure, not solely from general syntactic information. Our proposal is that there is a structural distinction at the syntactic level between some well-known lexical semantic verb classes. This difference in structure correlates with whether a verb yields easy or difficult reduced relative constructions. We note that the relevant differences between verbs is finer-grained than the optional intransitivity proposed by Pritchett (1992) and Gibson (1991) mentioned above. Crucially, we observe that the prototypically difficult reduced relative sentences are those that contain a manner of motion verb (e.g. *raced* or *floated*), which are a subclass of *unergative* verbs. We extend the lexical semantic work of Hale and Keyser (1993) to account for the linguistic theoretic properties of this verb class. We argue that the transitive use of an unergative verb has a particularly complex syntactic structure that arises from its lexical properties.

We examine the consequences of this structural analysis within the framework of the competitive attachment parser (Stevenson, 1994a, 1994b), a computational model of the human sentence processing mechanism. The parser is a parallel network model in which the activation of structure is restricted by the properties of the competitive attachment mechanism. These specific restrictions lead to a severe garden-path effect in the processing of reduced relatives with unergative verbs. Other verbs yield reduced relatives that are interpretable within the model, and are therefore open to the weighted influences (such as lexical frequencies) that the parser encodes with activation. Thus we will show that the interaction of the proposed linguistic structure with the critical computational assumptions of the processing model yield a precise account of the range of observed difficulty in MV/RR ambiguities.

LEXICAL AND SYNTACTIC REPRESENTATIONS

We begin our account with the observation that the prototypically difficult reduced relatives, *The horse raced past the barn fell* and *The boat floated down the river sank* (Bever, 1970), both contain a manner of motion verb. We first describe the properties of verbs of this lexical semantic class (the unergatives) and a related class (the unaccusatives), and discuss their relative acceptability in the reduced relative (RR) construction. We then develop a linguistic analysis of the two verb classes, and show how linguistic factors motivate the assumption of a more complex syntactic structure for RRs with unergatives.

Verb Classes and Reduced Relative Clauses

On inspection of a set of manner of motion verbs, related to those in the classic garden-path RRs, we find that the following verbs all lead to a severe garden path in the RR construction: *advance*, *sail*, *march*, *rotate*, *walk* and *glide*, illustrated in the RRs in (3).

3a. The students advanced to the next grade had to study very hard.
3b. The clipper sailed to Portugal carried a crew of eight.
3c. The troops marched across the fields all day resented the general.
3d. The model planet rotated on the metal axis fell off the stand.
3e. The dog walked in the park was having a good time.
3f. The ship glided past the harbor guards was laden with treasure.

Surprisingly, manner of motion verbs are difficult in a RR even when they have an *unambiguous* past-participle form; for example, *run*, *withdraw* and *fly*, exemplified in the sentences in (4).

4a. The greyhound run around the track all day was tired.
4b. The children withdrawn from the religion class could study music instead.
4c. The albatross flown to Australia was very tired.

To confirm our intuitions, we asked a number of our non-linguist colleagues for informal acceptability judgements on these verbs. All of the sentences with an ambiguous main verb/past participle form, as well as the sentence with *run*, were judged completely unacceptable. The sentences with the unambiguous past participle forms (other than *run*), although eliciting less uniform responses, were mostly judged very degraded to completely unacceptable. Note that all of the examples were intended to be neutral or biased towards a RR interpretation. For instance, we anticipated that *The albatross flown to Australia was very tired* would be perceived as odd, if presented out of context. Informants were asked their judgements within a discussion of a children's movie in which they had just been told that two mice flew an albatross to Australia. In other words, in addition to the fact that the past participle *flown* is unambiguous, the discourse situation was biased towards a RR reading.

We also found that *ring*, another verb with an unambiguous past participle, was difficult in the RR construction, as in (5):

5. The bell rung only at Easter rusted from disuse.

Sound emission verbs such as *ring* are related to manner of motion verbs in having the relevant lexical and syntactic properties discussed here, and our results apply equally to them. To simplify the presentation, we will focus on manner of motion verbs, but the interested reader should bear in mind that our claims extend to the sound emission verbs as well.

In English, manner of motion verbs form a subclass of verbs that share critical syntactic properties (Levin, 1993; Levin & Rappaport Hovav, 1995). In the intransitive form, these verbs may be classified as unergative verbs, as we see from the application of some standard tests for unergativity in Table 1 (Levin & Rappaport Hovav, 1995). A subset of manner of motion verbs appear in an intransitive/transitive alternation, as shown in sentences (6) and (7); it is this subclass of verbs that interests us, since the RR construction requires the transitive use of a verb.

6a. The horse raced past the barn.
6b. The rider raced the horse past the barn.

7a. The lions jumped through the hoop.
7b. The trainer jumped the lions through the hoop.

We observe that the transitive form of unergative verbs is the causative counterpart of the intransitive form (see Brousseau & Ritter, 1991; Hale & Keyser, 1993; but also cf. Levin & Rappaport Hovav, 1995). That is, the subject of the intransitive form becomes the object of the transitive form, and the new subject is the causer of the same action as expressed in the intransitive. A first conjecture then might be that the causative nature of the transitive form is the critical component of unergative verbs that leads to processing difficulty in the RR construction.

To explore this hypothesis, we turned our investigation to unaccusative verbs (Levin, 1993), such as *melt* or *grow*, since they can also occur in an intransitive/transitive alternation related by causativisation, as shown in sentences (8) and (9):

8a. The butter melted in the pan.
8b. The cook melted the butter in the pan.

9a. Rice grows in Northern Italy.
9b. Farmers grow rice in Northern Italy.

In contrast to the unergative verbs, we found that the following unaccusative verbs, with either an ambiguous or unambiguous main verb/past participle

TABLE 1
Standard Tests for Unergativity with Some Manner of Motion Verbs

Test for Unergativity	*Example*
The "X's way" construction	*The horse raced its way to victory.*
The false object construction	*The athlete ran herself ragged.*
The use of a durative phrase	*The troops marched for three hours.*

form, were easily interpreted in a RR construction: ambiguous—*melt*, *mutate*, *pour*, *rotate*, as in (10); unambiguous—*begin*, *break*, *freeze*, *grow*, *fly*, as in (11).

10a. The witch melted in the Wizard of Oz was played by a famous actress.
10b. The genes mutated in the experiment were used in a vaccine.
10c. The oil poured across the road made driving treacherous.
10d. The picture rotated 90 degrees was easy to print.

11a. The lecture begun with a Robin Williams joke was very entertaining.
11b. The window broken in the soccer game was soon repaired.
11c. The chicken frozen to zero degrees lasted for 3 months.
11d. The rice grown in Northern Italy contains more starch than Indian rice.
11e. The kite flown over the water soon went out of sight.

Again, we informally surveyed our non-linguist colleagues and found that unaccusative RRs were overwhelmingly judged completely fine, with a few responses of them being slightly degraded.

Note that two of the verbs, *rotate* and *fly*, were also included in our list of unergative verbs. Following Levin and Rappaport Hovav (1995), we assume that the lexical semantics of a verb and its arguments *combine* to determine the classification as unergative or unaccusative. For example, Levin and Rappaport Hovav note that, for a manner of motion verb to be unergative, the agent of the action—namely, the agent of the action expressed by the verb in either the intransitive or transitive form—must have internally caused motion, such as with animals or engines. In *The mice flew an albatross to Australia*, *fly* is unergative because an albatross has internally caused motion. On the other hand, in *The girls flew a kite on the beach*, *fly* is unaccusative, as a kite does not have internally caused motion. The same is true for *rotate*, which distinguishes between *to rotate a model planet* (unergative) and *to rotate a picture* (unaccusative), where only the model planet can have internally caused motion by spinning on its axis. The classifications and acceptability judgements of these two verbs thus depend on the specific sentences used. Both ambiguous verbs, *rotate* and *fly*, were difficult in a RR in their unergative use, and easy in their unaccusative use. We can therefore account for differences in difficulty of the same verb in RR constructions when modifying different types of NPs in terms of the lexical semantic classification of the verb with that type of argument.

The clear patterning of difficulty with the verbs in question reveals two important facts about the unergative and unaccusative verb classes in the RR construction. First, the unergative RRs are all mostly or completely unacceptable, while the unaccusative RRs are all completely acceptable or only slightly degraded. Second, the ease or difficulty of the reduced relative construction appears to be relatively insensitive to the ambiguity of the past participle. Even unergative verbs whose past tense/past participle forms are not ambiguous cause difficulty in a reduced relative clause (e.g. *run* and *withdraw*). Given these observations, our basic conclusion is that RRs containing a manner of motion verb never appear to be easy.[1] Moreover, we must abandon our conjecture that causativisation alone is responsible for the difficulty of unergative RRs. We are left with a puzzle in which two similar verb classes—those having an intransitive/transitive alternation related by causativisation—behave very differently in the RR construction, largely along verb class lines. Next we delve below the surface similarity of these verb classes to determine the critical differences between the two.

The Lexical Structural Analysis

We propose that the crucial distinction lies in the difference in assignment of thematic, or theta, roles between unergative and unaccusative verbs. Theta roles are labels that identify the lexical semantic content of the argument of a verb. These labels depend on the type of verb, and are therefore said to be assigned from the verb to the arguments. Consider examples (6) and (8), repeated here as (12) and (13):

12a. The horse raced past the barn.
12b. The rider raced the horse past the barn.

13a. The butter melted in the pan.
13b. The cook melted the butter in the pan.

In an intransitive unergative, such as (12a), the subject NP *the horse* is an agent, which performs the core action. In a transitive unergative, for example (12b), the subject NP *the rider* is the causal agent—the agent of the causing action—but the object NP *the horse* is the agent or actor of the actual racing. These relationships are perhaps even more evident in the sentence

---

[1]It was pointed out to us that the ease of *The car driven on the long trip was in bad shape* presents an apparent counterexample to this statement, since *drive* expresses a manner of motion (R. Lewis, pers. comm.). However, *drive* does not have the same causative alternation as we have seen with *race* or *jump*. In *Sara drove the car to school*, note that Sara is causing the car to move, but she is not causing the car to *drive*. Note also that the intransitive alternant of *Sara drove the car to school* is *Sara drove to school*, not *The car drove to school* (cf. *The trainer jumped the lions through the hoop/The lions jumped through the hoop*). These observations lead us to conclude that the transitive use of *drive* should not be classified as a causative unergative. Thus the verb does not present the relevant unergative alternation that we analyse here, but rather belongs to the class of verbs that can occur with an implicit object, such as *eat* or *read*. Although we did not investigate these verbs in detail, we have no reason to expect them to cause processing difficulty in the RR construction, since they do not have the same lexical or syntactic structure as unergative verbs under our proposal.

The trainer jumped the lions through the hoop. By contrast, the subject of an intransitive unaccusative is clearly a theme or patient, the entity undergoing the action, as in sentence (13a). In the transitive form (13b), the NP subject *the cook* is again the causal agent, and the NP object is, as in the intransitive form, a theme.

While the peculiarly agentive nature of the object of manner of motion verbs has been remarked before (Cruse, 1972; Hale & Keyser, 1987), several accounts describe the object of the verb as a theme (Harley, 1995; Levin & Rappaport Hovav, 1995). We think that the latter approach is seriously flawed, as it voids the notion of theta role of any semantic sense, since the object has a clear agentive role in the action. The agentive nature of the object of transitive manner of motion verbs is confirmed by the fact that the causer argument can only be a true agent, never an instrument or a natural force (Cruse, 1972; Levin & Rappaport Hovav, 1995): cf. the unergatives in (14) (from Levin & Rappaport Hovav, 1995) with the unaccusatives in (15).

14a. *The downpour marched the soldiers to the tents.
14b. *The firecracker jumped the horse over the fence.

15a. The ice storm froze the pipes.
15b. The radiation mutated the genes.

This pattern suggests that the object of an unergative cannot be subordinated to a subject that receives a lesser role in the thematic hierarchy (Jackendoff, 1972). In fact, as (16) shows, the object is necessarily agentive for the causative unergative to be grammatical (Cruse, 1972):

16a. John flew the falcon.
16b. *John flew the sparks.

Building on this difference in thematic role assignments of the two verb classes, we develop an account based on Hale and Keyser's (1993) approach to lexical syntax, which, in turn, draws on Baker's (1988) incorporation theory and on the proposal of a uniform mapping between theta roles and syntactic structure (the Uniformity of Theta Assignment Hypothesis; Baker, 1988, p. 46) at the syntactic level. Hale and Keyser (1993) assume that thematic roles correspond to a given structural configuration within a lexical semantic structure. Thus the difference in thematic role assignment between the two classes of verbs under discussion is evidence of a difference in underlying lexical structure. Hale and Keyser argue that the lexical entry of a verb captures its lexical semantics in a syntactic structure *within* the lexicon. The syntactic nature of the lexical entry allows the application of syntactic processes at the level of lexical representation. Verb forms may be created through the combination of lexical items with abstract verbal morphemes, such as DO, BECOME and CAUSE (Dowty, 1979). The combination operation is one of syntactic head movement within the lexical structure (see Fig. 1). The verb incorporates into the morpheme (Baker, 1988), leaving behind a trace, which is subject to the head movement constraint. Consequently, the verb with the incorporated morpheme(s) enters the syntax as a single unit.

For example, continuing Hale and Keyser's (1993) analysis, an intransitive unaccusative such as *melt*, which is a change of state verb, consists of an adjectival head *melted* that incorporates into the abstract verbal head BECOME. On the other hand, an intransitive unergative such as *race*, which is an activity verb, is generated by the lexical incorporation of a noun *race* into the abstract verbal head DO.[2] Theta roles are assigned in these structures as follows. The specifier position (i.e. the sister to the X′ level) of the BECOME morpheme is designated in the lexical structure as the theme of the incorporated verb, by predication with the adjectival phrase in complement position (see Fig. 1). However, the specifier of the abstract verb DO is left empty because, according to Hale and Keyser, a specifier cannot be

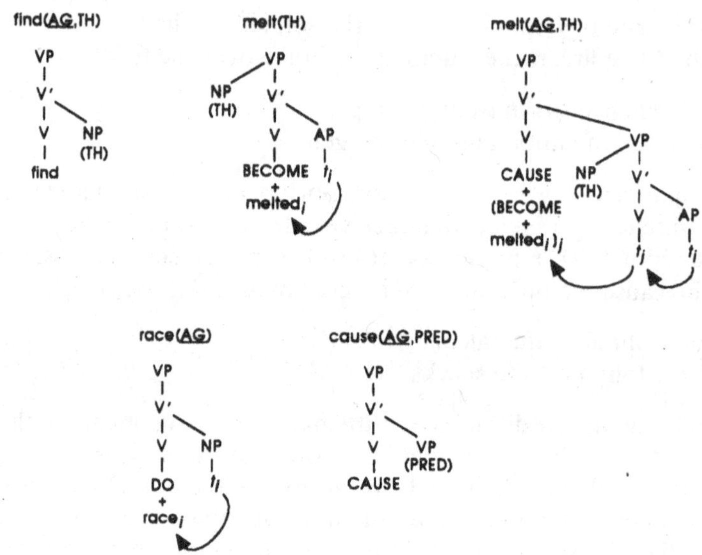

FIG. 1. Lexical entries, showing thematic grids and verb incorporation, for various verb types. Thematic role abbreviations: AG, agent; TH, theme; PRED, predicate. External arguments are underlined.

[2]Note that this analysis entails that ambiguous verbs such as *rotate* and *fly*, discussed earlier, have two lexical entries—one for the unergative use and one for the unaccusative use. But this is true for any account that recognises the thematic distinction between an object that has internally caused motion (an agent) and an object that does not (a theme). Ambiguous verbs such as these must, then, at a minimum, have multiple thematic assignment possibilities listed in the lexicon; for example (agent) and (theme) for the intransitive usages.

in a predication relation with an NP in complement position (such as the complement of DO), since the NP is not a predicate. The agent of the *race* activity must therefore be inserted at the syntactic level, at which point predication with the incorporated verb is possible. The agent is a true external argument in the sense that it is external to the lexical structure. Thus the agent theta role is not mapped from the lexicon, but is instead projected by a syntactic rule by virtue of the extended projection principle (Chomsky, 1981).

The causative counterpart for each of these types of verbs requires further incorporation with the abstract verbal morpheme, CAUSE. In the case of the unaccusative verb *melt*, the incorporation can occur directly in the lexical structure, because the argument structure of the verb is complete—that is, all of its theta roles have been assigned to positions within the lexical structure. Specifically, Hale and Keyser propose that because the theme argument of *melt* (i.e. BECOME + *melted*) is internal to the VP headed by BECOME in the lexical entry, the VP can be further embedded as the lexical complement of another verb. Figure 1 shows the lexical derivation of the causative form of *melt*. Note that, again, the agent of the action, in this case the causal agent, cannot be inserted in the lexical structure. An argument can only be inserted in the lexicon when it is in a predication relation with an AP or PP. The agent of CAUSE must be inserted in the syntax.[3]

Within this framework, an unergative verb like *race* cannot be causativised in the lexicon, because the predicate (DO + *race*) is not saturated—it has an agent theta role that can only be inserted in the syntax. Because the agent argument is missing from the lexical structure, the predicate cannot be further embedded as a complement to an additional verbal head within the lexicon. Hale and Keyser (1993) do not address the problem that, nevertheless, a causative form for a subset of these verbs does occur, as evidenced by the transitive alternations above in sentences (6) and (7). We extend their account by proposing that an operation of syntactic causativisation may apply in the case of an unergative verb. For the transitive use of *race*, for example, both the abstract morpheme CAUSE and the incorporated activity verb *race* (DO + *race*) must be projected into the syntax (see Fig. 2). There, the agent of the racing action can be inserted into the specifier position of the verb *race*. The abstract verb CAUSE takes the VP

[3]Belletti and Rizzi (1988) observe that the agent theta role seems to have a special status in the mapping of theta roles to syntax. They note that psych verbs can be argued to have all the mappings of the pair (experiencer, theme) onto syntactic configurations; that is, the theme can be the object or the subject, and the experiencer can be the object, the subject or the indirect object. But there is no verb that has a similar alternation between (agent, theme). If there is an agent, it seems to have to be the theta role that is mapped onto the external argument position (i.e. the subject). This supports Hale and Keyser's (1993) idea that theta roles have a functional relation to structure and that they are "invisible" as such in syntax, and it derives that agents are always the external argument.

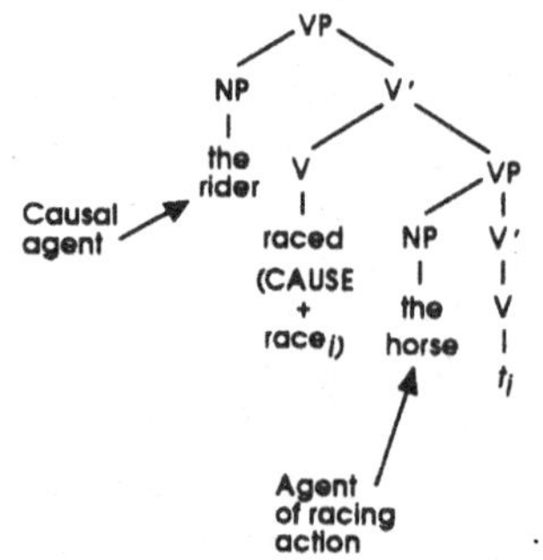

FIG. 2. An unergative verb is made transitive through an operation of causativisation (incorporation of the verb with the abstract causative morpheme, CAUSE), which applies in the syntactic structure, not in the lexicon.

headed by *race* as its complement, and an agent of causation is inserted into its specifier position.

The proposal of a different form of causativisation for unaccusative and unergative verbs is not without precedent. Romance languages show a clear asymmetry of these two types of verbs with respect to causativisation, as the unaccusative alternation is quite productive both in French and Italian, while unergative verbs cannot be transitive under any circumstances. As observed by Levin and Rappaport Hovav (1995), morphological processes also confirm the different nature of the causative alternation in these two classes of verbs, as in Hebrew, which allows causatives of both unaccusatives and unergative verbs. Unaccusatives show morphological marking of the intransitive member of the pair (like Italian and French), while unergative causatives show that the transitive form is morphologically derived from the intransitive. Thus Levin and Rappaport Hovav also conclude that unergative verbs are formed by a different causativisation process than the one that applies to unaccusatives.

At this point, it is worthwhile reporting why we did not just assume that the relevant difference between unaccusative and unergative verbs is that unaccusative verbs have an adjectival passive (Bresnan, 1982; Levin & Rappaport, 1986). The claim is that an adjectival passive entails a simpler RR structure, without an empty operator and a trace in object position, and therefore could account for the relative ease of unaccusative RRs. On applying the standard tests for adjectival passives, this distinction did not seem to correspond to verb classes. For instance, we found that while unaccusatives are easier in the adjectival *un-* affixation than manner of motion verbs (*unmelted*, *unpoured*, **unrun*, **unraced*), some sound emission verbs are acceptable as complements of a raising predicate (e.g. *The bell remains unrung*)—another test of the adjectival nature of the passive form. (Recall that sound emission verbs are the other subclass of unergative verbs that fall within our analysis.) Moreover, both kinds of verbs are hard in *wh*-fronting constructions (e.g. **How grown was the rice? *How flown was the kite? *How marched were the troops? *How flown is the albatross?*), thus showing that they are verbal passives. Neither of the two classes appears to be easily modified by adjectival adverbs (e.g. **The very grown rice*, **The very run greyhound*), while unaccusatives, if truly adjectival, should be acceptable. Finally, we observe that unaccusative past participles have a verbal nature in other languages, as is shown by clitic-affixation in languages like Italian which show this construction, exemplified in (17):

17a. Il burro sciolto nella pentola venne usato per ammorbidire la torta.
"The butter melted in the pan was used to moisten the cake"

17b. Scioltolo nella pentola, il burro venne usato per ammorbidire la torta.
"melted-it in the pan, the butter was used to moisten the cake"

17c. Scioltone un pezzo nella pentola, il burro venne usato per ammorbidire la torta.
"melted-of-it a piece in the pan, the butter was used to moisten the cake"

Therefore, we conclude that the verbal/adjectival distinction is unsatisfactory, as it fails to select the right subset of verbs with respect to processing difficulty.

Although we believe that semantic factors are important to the classification of verbs as unergative or unaccusative (cf. the discussion above regarding the ambiguous verbs *fly* and *rotate*), we think that the processing difficulty differential is better explained at the syntactic level, and that such an account is no more complex than a purely semantic one. Hale and Keyser's (1993) proposal accounts for distributional properties of lexical items in English (for example, why causativisation of unergatives is so limited), which would remain unexplained under a purely semantic account. The explanation is available at no extra theoretical cost, as a mapping between argument structure and syntactic structure is independently needed for the definition of the semantic–syntax interface. In other words, there has to be a set of linking rules between roles and grammatical functions which determines for a given lexical entry what argument becomes the subject, and which the object, for instance. The mapping adopted here (modifying Baker, 1988, and Hale & Keyser, 1993) is the simplest one, where the theme is always an object and the agent always a subject at the relevant level of representation, D-structure. Lastly, a syntactic account is supported by a vast body of studies showing that the lexical semantics of unaccusative and unergative verbs entails different syntactic behaviour, for instance in the distribution of partitive and reflexive clitics in Romance languages (Belletti & Rizzi, 1988; Burzio, 1981), in the alternation of auxiliary verbs (Burzio,

1981, 1986), and in the form of resultative constructions (Levin & Rappaport Hovav, 1995).

Syntactic Consequences of the Analysis

For verbs that have undergone incorporation within the lexicon, we propose that while the structure of a lexical entry is visible to lexical operations, these articulated lexical structures are not visible to the syntactic level of processing. Figure 3 shows the relation between the underlying (articulated) lexical structures, and the resulting syntactic structures for various verbs. As can be seen in the figure, a verb that results from lexical incorporation—a sequence of head movements within a nested lexical entry—appears in the syntax in a conflated form, within a simple VP. All arguments from the various levels of lexical structure appear as direct complements to the projected verb, except for the external argument (if there is one), which is inserted in the syntax into the specifier of the verb phrase (the [spec, VP] position), and moved into the [spec, IP] position to satisfy independent constraints of the grammar (Koopman & Sportiche, 1991).

We make the assumption that all internal arguments appear in the syntax as complements of the verb, regardless of the underlying lexical form, because of the dual nature of certain thematic roles in the lexical and syntactic structures. For example, as shown in Fig. 3, intransitive unaccusative verbs such as *melt* have their sole theme argument in the specifier position of the lexical structure headed by the incorporated verb, capturing the predication relation between the argument and the adjective. However, there is also clear cross-linguistic evidence that this same argument shares syntactic properties with objects in complement position (Burzio, 1981, 1986). If the lexical entries themselves are simplified, we lose the lexical structural relationships that give content to the thematic roles. But if the entire lexical structure is projected, then the crucial syntactic generalisations are lost. Furthermore, the thematic requirements encoded by the lexical structure are irrelevant to the syntactic level of processing. By partitioning the information into the relevant level of structure (lexical structure *vs* syntactic structure), with a well-defined mapping between the two, we capture the full set of regularities that apply at each level of representation (cf. the approach taken in lexical-functional grammar; Kaplan & Bresnan, 1982).

Recall that our central proposal is that transitive unergatives cannot be formed through lexical incorporation, and must therefore undergo causativisation in the syntax. A transitive unergative, such as *race*, requires that two verbal structures be projected into the syntax, the lexically incorporated *race* (DO + the NP *race*) and the abstract verbal morpheme CAUSE (see Fig. 3). Since both are projected into the syntax, the nested

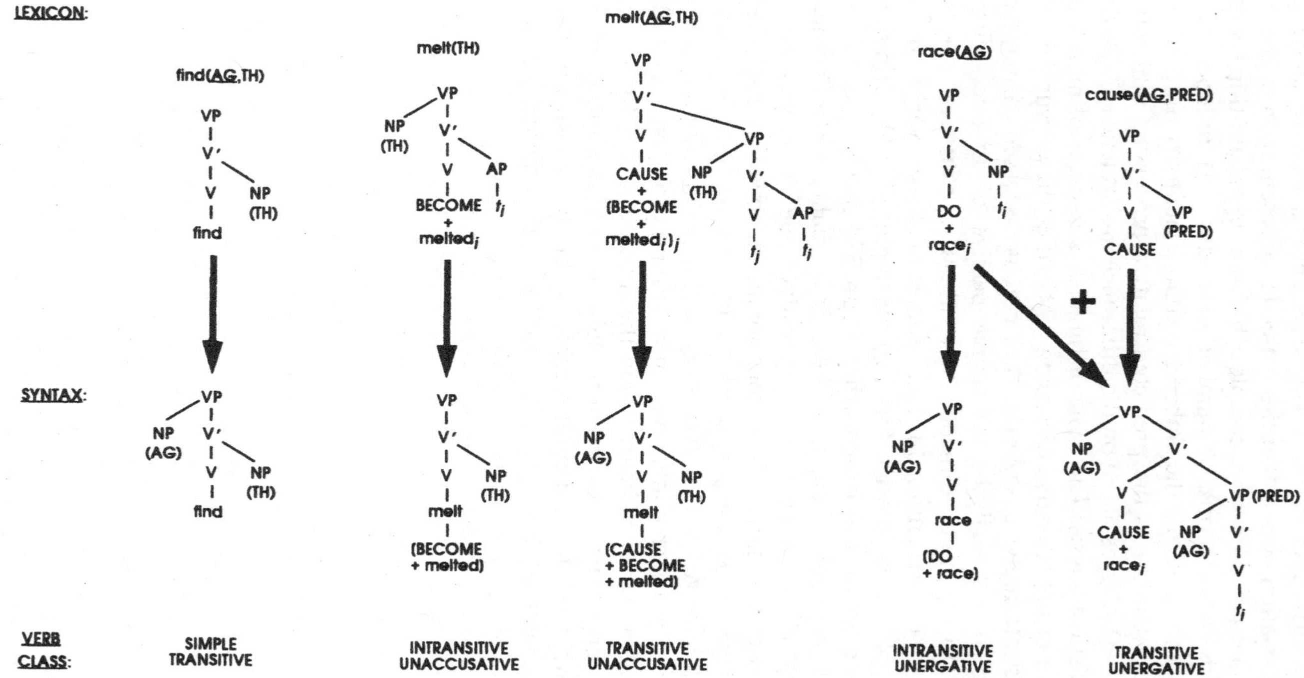

FIG. 3. Lexical entries and the corresponding syntactic structures for various verb types.

verbal structure cannot be conflated in the same way as described above for lexically incorporated verbs. As can be seen in Fig. 4, the syntactic operation of causativisation entails that the syntactic representation of the transitive form of unergatives is more complex than the representation for transitive unaccusatives—in terms of number of nodes and number of binding relations, and in having the embedded complement structure.

Table 2 summarises the predicted relative processing difficulty for the different verb classes based on the difference in syntactic complexity under this linguistic analysis. The table distinguishes manner of motion verbs as unergative or unaccusative according to whether they occur with an object which has internally caused motion or not, as discussed earlier. Note that, according to our analysis, the simple passive of an unergative is also expected to be more difficult than others, because of the increased complexity of structure. In fact, some of these verbs are actually unacceptable in the passive form, for example *glide* (J. Grimshaw, pers. comm.); we discuss this issue further on pp. 388–390.

We are claiming, then, that there is a qualitative difference in the processing of unaccusatives and unergatives due to the greater structural complexity of unergatives. This does not mean, however, that other factors such as lexical frequencies, semantic fit, context, etc., play no role in processing such verbs. However, those factors will be limited in helping an unergative RR, which is inherently more complex (or worse, as we discuss in the processing sections below) than the unaccusative RRs. Unaccusative RRs are more open to non-structural influences because those influences are not overwhelmed by structural complexity effects, as we will see shortly. Unaccusative RRs, therefore, will exhibit a range of difficulty depending on the specific lexical items and specific context.

Given these gradient effects, a natural question, then, is whether unaccusatives can be as difficult in a RR as unergatives, which would weaken our claim of a qualitative difference between the two. For instance, the

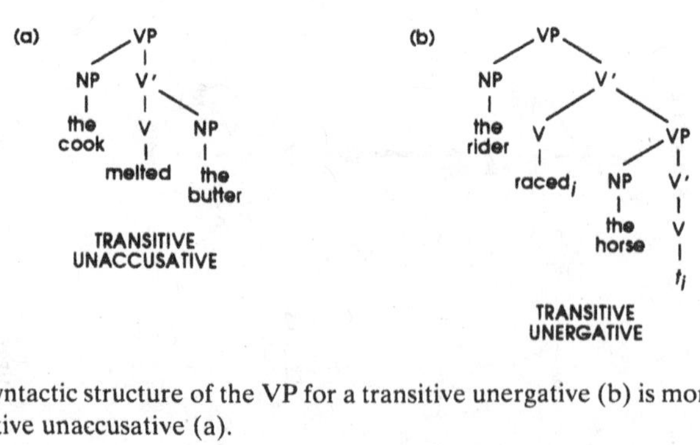

FIG. 4. The syntactic structure of the VP for a transitive unergative (b) is more complex than that of a transitive unaccusative (a).

TABLE 2
Predictions of Relative Difficulty for Different Verb Classes with Different Types of Objects

		Reduced Relative		
		Ambiguous	*Unambiguous*	*Passive*
Unaccusative	Change of state	easier	easier	easier
	MOM + external motion object	easier	easier	easier
Unergative	Sound emission	harder	harder	harder
	MOM + internal motion object	harder	harder	harder

Note: MOM = manner of motion verb; "internal motion object" is an object with internally caused motion, and "external motion object" is an object with externally caused motion; see text for discussion.

following sentences of questionable acceptability were brought to our attention by an anonymous reviewer:

18a. The candy caramelised in an hour burned.
18b. The wax solidified into abstract shapes melted.
18c. The paper yellowed in the sun shrank.

The RRs in (18) each contain a change of state verb, which we have classified as unaccusative, yet these sentences are more difficult than might be expected under our account. However, a structure-based description of their difficulty might also be available. It can be observed that the verbs in these examples belong to that subclass of change of state verbs that express an internally caused eventuality. Compare, for instance, the different acceptability of a sentence where the change of state is indirectly brought about by some natural force, but is not caused by a volitional agent, as in (19a), to a sentence where the subject can be volitional, as in (19b). Note, moreover, that although the subject of (19b) is volitional, an interpretation of the sentence in which the yellowing of the papers was done without intention is very strongly preferred.

19a. The sun yellowed the papers.
19b. ??The chain-smoker yellowed the papers.

The same observation appears to be true of the verb *solidify*, since the change of state is probably lexicalised as internal, making the expression of a volitional causal agent awkward, as in sentence (20a). The verb *harden*, on the other hand, expresses an externally caused eventuality, making (20b) perfectly acceptable.

20a. ??The sculptor solidified the wax.
20b. The sculptor hardened the wax.

The difference between these two sublcasses of verbs of change of state—internally caused and externally caused eventualities—has led Levin and Rappaport Hovav (1995) to claim that the correct characterisation of the lexical semantics of those verbs that map onto the unergative argument structure is "internally caused verbs", while externally caused verbs correspond, syntactically, to unaccusatives (see also our discussion of *fly* and *rotate* above). From this perspective, it is not surprising to find that the verbs in (18) are harder than other change of state verbs. Whether they have the same structure as unergative manner of motion verbs will be addressed in future research.

To briefly summarise, the linguistic analysis presented in this section posits lexical and syntactic differences between unergative and unaccusative verbs. Next we describe a processing model that is sensitive to these distinctions.

OVERVIEW OF THE PROCESSING MODEL

The competitive attachment model is a parallel spreading activation architecture, consisting of a network of simple processing nodes whose configuration directly represents partial parse trees. The model dynamically builds syntactic structures by incrementally activating processing nodes in response to a sentence, and determining the appropriate network connections among them. Parse tree attachments between individual syntactic phrases represented within the network are determined through distributed processing, involving both symbolic and numeric information. The propagation and checking of symbolic features determines the grammaticality of potential phrase structure attachments, based on Government and Binding Theory (Chomsky, 1981; Rizzi, 1990). Numeric activation captures the relative strengths of the valid alternatives, and accumulates within a stable configuration representing a partial parse tree for the input seen thus far. The competition for activation among the possible syntactic analyses is the central mechanism of the architecture, since it is responsible for resolving both lexical ambiguity and attachment ambiguity. The core aspects of the symbolic and numeric processing components of the model, including the competitive attachment mechanism, are implemented in a computer system. Detailed results of experiments with the implemented parser have previously been reported (Stevenson, 1993a, 1994b).

In what follows, we present the properties of the competitive attachment parser that are relevant to the analysis of reduced relative constructions. First, we describe the competitive processing within the model, which determines preferences among possible structural representations within the network. Then we turn to another essential aspect of the model, the limitations on the structures that can be represented. The parser is constrained by several computationally motivated restrictions arising from the requirements of the dynamic network creation and competitive activation processes of the model. These restrictions precisely define a narrow range of possible structural hypotheses. In particular, the constraints on the model generally limit the occurrence of processing nodes that represent empty structure. Because empty structure (empty operators and traces) plays an important role in the analysis of reduced relative clauses, these constraints are of central concern; we will see later that they are crucial to explaining the garden-path status of unergative RRs. We conclude the overview of the parser with an explanation of the processing of verbal projections and syntactic causatives under the linguistic analysis proposed above.

The Competitive Attachment Operation

The network of alternative parse tree structures is dynamically created in the model by activating two types of processing nodes. Phrasal nodes are activated from a pool of $\overline{X}$ templates, and their symbolic features and activation level are initialised based on an input token's lexical entry. Figure 5 shows a sample $\overline{X}$ template and its instantiation. A second type of processing node represents the potential attachments between phrasal nodes. Attachment nodes are established between two phrasal nodes that are potential *sisters* in the parse tree; Fig. 6 shows the resulting representation of basic $\overline{X}$ relations in the network. The symbolic features and activation level of an attachment node depend on the information it receives from the two phrasal nodes it connects to (the potential parse tree sisters). An attachment node that is highly activated (above an empirically determined threshold) represents an actual sisterhood relation within the current syntactic analysis. If an attachment node is not activated above threshold, its activation level goes to zero, and the attachment does not participate in the parse. Attachment nodes that are activated above threshold can take on a range of activation levels, but for simplicity attachment nodes are shown in all figures as black when fully activated, hatched when partially activated, and white when inactive.

FIG. 5. A sample $\overline{X}$ template and its instantiation as a verb phrase.

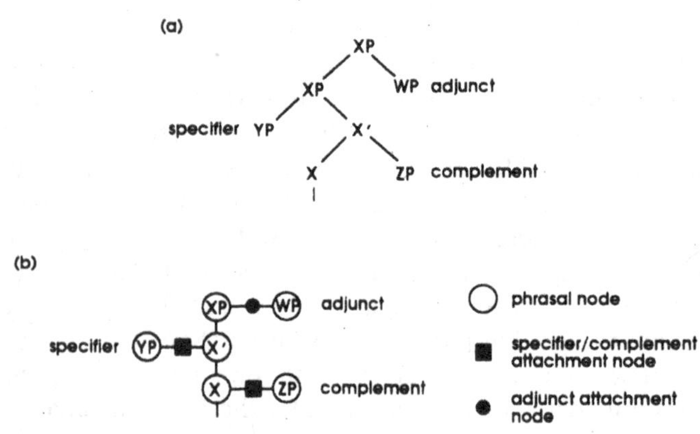

FIG. 6. (a) The basic structure of an $\overline{X}$ phrase and (b) its representation in the competitive attachment network.

When an input token is read, the parser activates the appropriate phrasal nodes. For an ambiguous input token (that is, one with more than one lexical entry), multiple syntactic phrases are activated, each in proportion to the frequency of the corresponding lexical entry. Since the current implementation of the model has no learning component, all frequency values must be estimated (e.g. from corpus data or norming studies). After activating the appropriate phrasal nodes, the parser allocates attachment nodes to represent the potential attachments between the new phrasal nodes and previously structured phrasal nodes. As shown in Fig. 7, attachment nodes are established between a new phrasal node and any potential sister node along the right edge of an existing parse tree structure. The network then enters its competitive attachment phase that determines which of these potential attachments will become highly activated. Each phrasal and

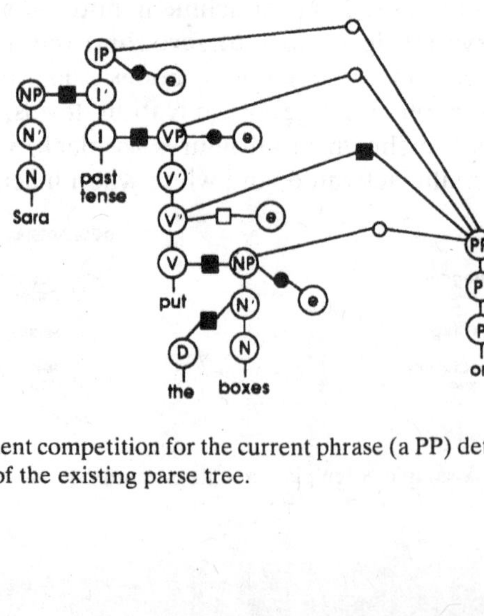

FIG. 7. The attachment competition for the current phrase (a PP) determining its attachment along the right edge of the existing parse tree.

attachment node iteratively updates and outputs its symbolic features and numeric activation, until the network settles into a stable state in which all attachment nodes either have a high activation level or have an activation level of zero. The highly activated attachment nodes represent the winning attachment decisions established during the current competitive attachment phase. Figure 8 shows the final network structure for a complete sentence, and the parse tree that it represents.

Two types of competitions occur during the network processing described above. An *attachment competition* is a competition at a single phrasal node for the best attachment node to activate. For example, in Fig. 7, the PP node must decide whether to activate the attachment to the NP node (as an adjunct of the NP) or the attachment to the V′ node (as the second complement of the verb), or an even higher adjunct attachment to the VP or IP. Since multiple attachments for a phrasal node may be grammatical, a competitive output function (Reggia, 1987) weighs the evidence for an attachment, and allocates activation from the phrasal node to its attachment nodes in proportion to the evidence for each potential attachment. The numeric evidence for an attachment includes frequency information, such as subcategorisation preferences, as well as the current activation level of the attachment node. Phrasal nodes thus "hedge their bets" by favouring attachments that are already more highly activated.

This type of interaction is important, since attachment competitions at a single phrasal node do not play out in isolation, but are influenced by the competitive activation decisions being made by other phrasal nodes. For example, referring once more to Fig. 7, the competition that takes place among the potential attachments to the PP node is crucially affected by the competitions at the NP, V′, VP and IP nodes, which in turn each have two attachment nodes to choose between. (The nodes labelled "e" in the figure

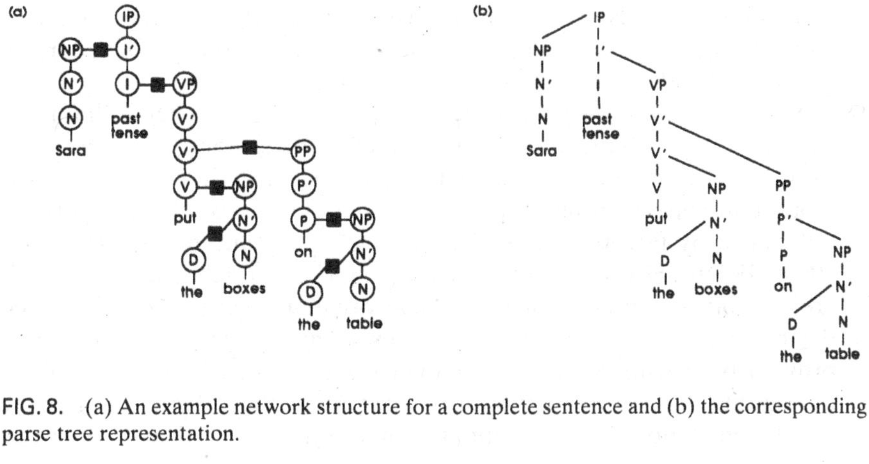

FIG. 8. (a) An example network structure for a complete sentence and (b) the corresponding parse tree representation.

are *empty nodes*, which are described in the following subsection.) Competitive effects thus propagate through the network over time. When all of the attachment competitions stabilise, the set of active attachment nodes for each syntactic phrase represents the current (sisterhood) attachments for that phrase, and inactive attachment nodes connected to that phrase are deleted. The behaviour of the implemented system is evaluated in terms of the attachments that are activated, the number of iterations of network processing (i.e. propagation of symbolic and numeric information) that are required, and the precise activation levels of active attachment nodes.

A *lexical competition* uses precisely the same competitive process to determine which of multiple syntactic phrases to activate in response to an ambiguous input token. For example, we mentioned that some verbs, like *rotate* and *fly*, are ambiguous between an unergative and unaccusative classification; such verbs have multiple lexical entries and activate a set of phrasal nodes corresponding to each. Of greater relevance to the results we report below, a verb that has a main verb/past participle ambiguity will activate two VPs, one with the features appropriate to the main verb usage, and one with the features of the past participle usage. Each input token uses a competitive function to output activation to its possible phrasal realisations and choose between them, analogous to the attachment competition process. Since multiple ambiguous input tokens can lead to a large fan-out of competing structures, the competitive activation function must focus activation quickly onto a single alternative. A phrase that makes successful attachments within the current parse tree structure increases in activation, and is thus more likely to be favoured with additional activation from the input token and to win the competition. This lexical competition has not been incorporated into the computer system. However, based on the prior extensive testing of the implemented attachment process, we can accurately predict the actions of the parser on the examples here, since the behaviour depends on the same critical properties of the competition mechanism. In the simulations described below, the predicted relative activation levels of the structures are reported.

Note that all attachment decisions are made through the parallel competition which involves the attachment nodes connecting a new phrase to the right edge of an existing partial parse tree, as shown in Fig. 7. When more than one analysis is possible, the outcome of the competition is influenced by factors such as recency, frequency and context (Stevenson, 1994a, 1994b). However, not all logically possible attachment configurations are possible within the network, since any reanalysis of structure is limited to the consistent reattachment of phrases along the right edge of a tree—previously structured phrases cannot be freely restructured to accommodate new input (cf. a similar restriction in Sturt & Crocker, 1996). This right edge restriction follows from computational limitations of the competitive attachment function (Stevenson, 1993a, 1994b). Only a precisely limited form of reanalysis can be accommodated within the normal attachment operation of the parser, and reanalyses which fall outside of the possible structural reconfigurations have been shown to correspond to a range of well-known garden-path effects (Stevenson, 1993a, 1994a, 1995). The model therefore exhibits a range of difficulty within the class of constructs parsable within its normal attachment operation, but may also exhibit qualitatively different behaviour due to constraints on the possible network configurations that can lead to sharp garden paths.

Restrictions on Empty Structure

The model has additional constraints on possible network configurations that arise due to computational limitations that affect the hypothesising of empty phrase structure. These restrictions are of particular relevance here, since the representation of a reduced relative clause requires the use of empty syntactic elements. In this section, we simply motivate and describe the constraints, and leave discussion of their ramifications to the next section, where we show how their interaction with the linguistic analysis of unergative verbs explains the difficulty of unergative RRs.

Empty Nodes. For a particular network configuration to represent a valid partial parse tree, each phrasal node must activate a certain number of attachment nodes to satisfy its grammatical properties. However, the competitive function, which determines the amount of activation to output to attachment nodes, cannot be successfully parameterised to activate a variable number of attachments. Specifically, the competitive output function *can* be tuned to effectively activate exactly one attachment—as needed for an obligatorily transitive verb. But it cannot be adjusted to allow the activation of zero or one attachment node—as needed for an optionally transitive verb, or even an obligatorily transitive verb whose complement has not been reached in the input. Since the competitive function can bring about activation of exactly one attachment node, but not zero or one, those phrasal nodes that license an attachment must have an attachment node to activate *at all times*. To accommodate this—and to maintain uniformity of numeric processing across all phrasal nodes—every phrasal node automatically posits an attachment to an *empty* node. The attachment to this "dummy" node provides an attachment node to activate even when no overt phrase is available to attach to.

Figure 9 shows the empty nodes that are activated with an $\overline{X}$ template; each attachment site connects to an attachment node that in turn connects to an empty node. (Empty nodes are labelled "e" in the figures, and are omitted in figures where they are irrelevant.) Because empty nodes occur at all

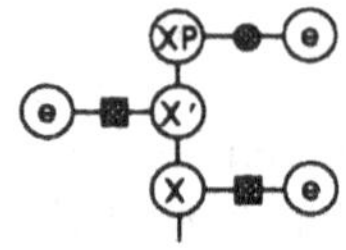

FIG. 9. Empty nodes are activated in conjunction with every phrase, at each attachment site.

possible attachment sites, they can be used to represent null elements required in a parse—that is, the empty categories or traces of Government and Binding Theory. Traces are phonetically null elements that appear in the position of a syntactically displaced element—for example, in the underlying position of the NP that moves from object to subject position in the passive construction. In the reduced relative construction, empty nodes are needed to represent both the trace of passive movement, and the empty operator in the specifier of the relative clause. The role of an empty node as an empty category is determined within the network by the attachment and binding relations in which the node participates.

Because they initially have no overt evidence, empty nodes at first have only minimal activation, and the attachment node they connect to is therefore only weakly activated. As the parse of the input progresses, empty nodes may participate in further processing in a number of different ways. First, as noted above, empty nodes are sometimes required in a syntactic analysis to represent empty categories. The co-indexation of an empty node with an overt phrase licenses the node as an empty category and instantiates its symbolic features, thereby increasing its activation level (see Stevenson, 1993b, 1994a, for the effects of the active co-indexation mechanism on filler–gap preferences and reanalysis). Second, if an empty node occurs in a position that requires an attachment and it is *not* co-indexed, it will remain only weakly activated. If an overt phrase competes with the empty node for attachment to the same site, the overt phrase—which is always more highly activated—will win the competition over the weakly activated empty node. Third, a default attachment to an empty node is often replaced in the attachment competition by an attachment to an overt phrase projected from the input. For example, in Fig. 7, the illustrated attachment competition replaces the default attachment of an empty node to the V′ node with the attachment of the new PP node to the V′ node. Finally, an empty node may occur in a structural location that does not require attachment of a phrase (e.g. as the complement to an intransitive verb). In this case, its grammatical constraints will be vacuously satisfied, and it will therefore immediately become fully activated.

Empty Phrases. Because the parse tree is dynamically allocated within a distributed processing environment, the hypothesising of structure without incontrovertible evidence in the input must be prohibited in general.

Although this limitation is necessary to curb the potential explosion of nested empty structure (which could quickly exhaust the available processing nodes in the parser), it must be relaxed in some highly restricted cases. For example, empty nodes are required to achieve consistent behaviour in the competitive output function, but an empty node is only a single, "dummy" phrasal node—the minimum required to provide an attachment site for each phrasal node to activate an attachment to. Allocating articulated empty structure (i.e. a full phrase) is also permitted in some circumstances to keep a connected parse tree at all times. Specifically, an *empty phrase*, X-X′-XP, is activated in a situation where an overt phrase requires it to make an attachment to the existing parse tree. For example, given a node that can occur as the specifier of a following phrase, the node can activate an attachment as sister to the X′ of an empty phrase to its right. (This is clearly specific to English; in a head-final language, a node may activate an empty projection to which it can attach as the complement.) Since an empty phrase is composed solely of empty phrasal nodes, it will initially be only weakly activated. Hence, an input phrase will only successfully activate an attachment as the specifier of an empty phrase if there is no other attachment node (to non-empty structure) that it can activate.

It should be emphasised that both forms of empty structure—empty nodes and empty phrases—are independently motivated, by the requirements of the competitive output function in the case of empty nodes, and by the requirement to maintain a connected structure in the case of empty phrases. Furthermore, they both take the minimal form necessary to support the aspect of processing that necessitates them. Their properties are therefore independently justified, and not just established to obtain some particular parsing behaviour.

Projecting Structure in the Parser

The computational principles of the competitive attachment model, in conjunction with the linguistic representations presented on pp. 362–364, lead to the following processing approach to projecting syntactic structure:

1. Structure is projected from a lexical item, where projection entails the activation of potential extended projections.
2. A verb activates extended projections based on its final (possibly incorporated) position in the lexical structure.
3. The internal structure of the VP of the extended projection encodes features from the predicate argument structure of the verb.

Following Grimshaw (1991), we assume that projections in the syntax consist of a single *lexical* phrase optionally dominated by some number of compatible *functional* phrases. Although our results are entirely compatible with an extended projection analysis of nouns (i.e. as either NPs or DPs), here we will only be concerned with the extended projection of verbs. For example, a verb may be projected into the syntax as a single verb phrase (VP), an inflection phrase (IP) with the VP as its complement, or a complementiser phrase (CP) with the IP and VP embedded (see Fig. 10). The VP of each potential extended projection has the specifier and complement requirements determined by the lexical features of the (possibly incorporated) verb. The three potential extended projections will compete for activation from the single verb that initiated their activation, and must also compete for attachments to the existing and developing partial parse tree structures. The winning extended projection is thereby determined by the syntactic requirements of the construction in which the verb participates. Here we assume that the subject of the clause must appear in the [spec, IP] position, and the tense features or auxiliary verbs in the head of the IP, so at least the IP level is required. For simplicity, then, we will not display the bare VP possibility in the figures. The CP projection is also required when an element of the analysis must occur in either the head of the CP (e.g. a complementiser such as *that*) or in the specifier of the CP (e.g. a WH-operator, such as an overt WH-question word, or an empty operator, as in the reduced relative).

Initially, the attachment sites of each of the $\overline{X}$ phrases of an extended verbal projection (VP, IP or CP) will have attachments to empty nodes, as described above. The lexical information associated with the verb will put constraints on the interpretation of the empty nodes at the specifier and complement attachment sites. If an attachment is not required at the site (e.g. as in the case of the complement position of an intransitive verb), then the category of the attachment site is set to NONE. This specification indicates that no phrase need be attached at that site; an empty node attached there will therefore be fully activated, representing a grammatical structure with

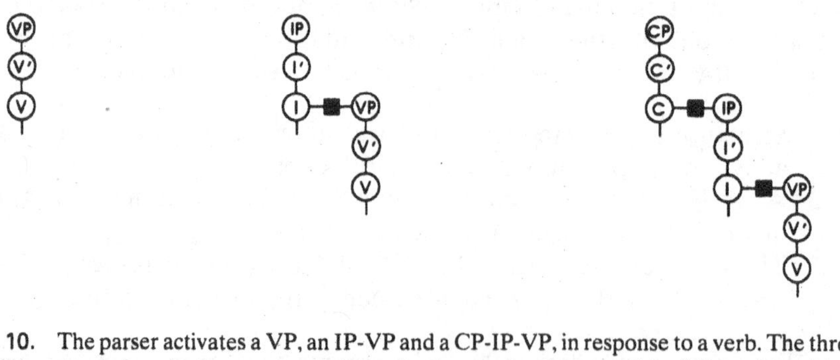

FIG. 10. The parser activates a VP, an IP-VP and a CP-IP-VP, in response to a verb. The three possible extended projections compete for activation, and only one will be fully activated in a stable network.

no attachment at that site in the parse tree. If an attachment *is* required at the site (e.g. as in the case of the complement position of an obligatorily transitive verb), then the category of the attachment site is set to an actual grammatical category. This specification indicates that the attachment site requires an attachment to a phrasal node of that category. There are two grammatical possibilities in this case. Either the empty node at that site must participate in a valid binding relationship to license it as a trace, or the attachment to the empty node must be replaced by an attachment to an overt phrase. The latter situation is illustrated in Fig. 7, in which the overt PP replaces the empty node as the second complement of the verb.

Figure 11 shows the VP of the extended projections that are initially activated in response to several different types of verb. A simple transitive verb, such as *find*, activates extended verbal projections in which the VP directly reflects the lexical structure of the verb. The empty node attached to the V has its category feature set to NP, for the internal argument. The empty node in [spec, VP], attached to the V′, has its category feature set to NP, for the external argument. (Recall that the external argument is inserted into the specifier position of the VP, and then moves to the specifier position of the IP.) An incorporated verb, such as *melt*, activates extended verbal projections based on its position following incorporation within the lexical structure. The form of *melt* created from incorporation of BECOME and

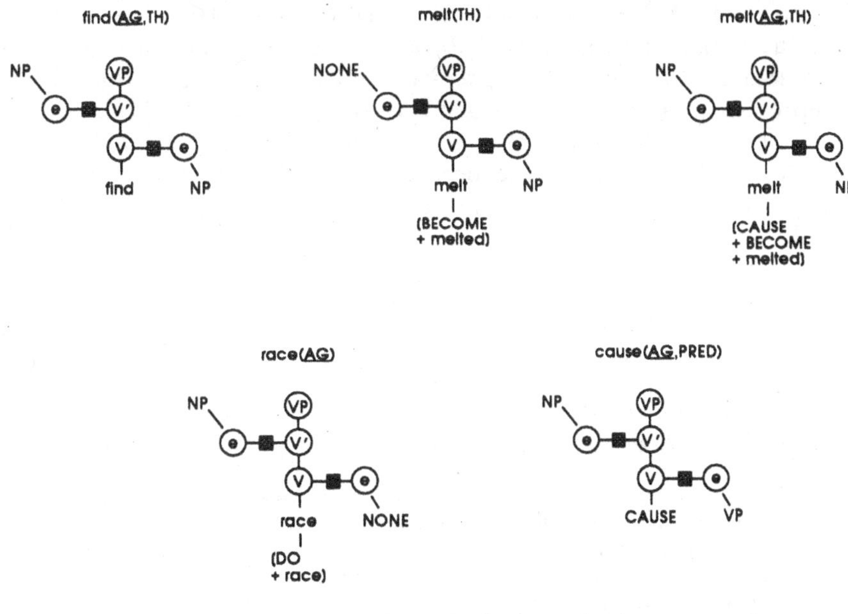

FIG. 11. The VP structures initially activated by the parser in response to various types of verbs.

melted is realised as an extended projection of V, in which the VP has a single internal argument and no external argument. The NP that occurs in the [spec, VP] of the abstract element BECOME (the theme) is realised in the syntax as a direct object of the incorporated verb. Thus this form of *melt* will have an empty node in the complement attachment position whose category is set to NP by the V node. Since it has no external argument, the empty node attached to the V′ has its category set to NONE. The form of *melt* created from incorporation of CAUSE, BECOME and *melted* is also realised as an extended projection of V with a single internal argument. Again the internal NP argument is realised in the syntax as a direct object of the incorporated verb. The difference between this form of *melt* and the intransitive form is that this form also has an external argument to assign (the causal agent). Here the empty node attached to the V′ has its category set to NP.

Unergative verbs are distinguished from unaccusative verbs in that the lexical rule of causativisation cannot apply, as described on pp. 358–360. The only lexical entry available for a verb such as *race* is the intransitive form (see Fig. 3). In the extended projections of an unergative verb, the core VP is therefore one in which the specifier position must be filled by an NP subject, but the complement position is required to be empty. Thus, as shown in Fig. 11, the category of the empty node attached to the V node is NONE. For an unergative verb to be used in the transitive alternation, it must be combined *in the syntax* with the abstract causative morpheme, CAUSE. For example, Fig. 12 shows the network structure for the VP *race the horse*. Only in the syntax can the [spec, VP] of *race* be filled, since it is an external argument. In contrast to a causative unaccusative, the syntactic representation here must include a verbal projection for both CAUSE and *race*, and the two phrases must be explicitly attached (using an attachment node) in the network.[4] The processing of an unergative in a causative construction in the competitive attachment parser is described in the following section.

[4]A precise account of which unergatives can undergo causativisation remains elusive, both under our proposal and those of others (e.g. Hale & Keyser, 1993; Levin & Rappaport Hovav, 1995). One possibility is that causativisation of unergatives is a productive process, as proposed by Levin and Rappaport Hovav (1995), but that the added syntactic complexity we propose discourages its use. For now we simply assume that CAUSE is linked in the lexicon to the unergative verbs with which it can so combine. However, although there may be an explicit link indicating those unergatives which can act as complements to CAUSE, this is distinct from the process of *lexical* causativisation of the unaccusatives. In the unergative case, the two verbal structures cannot be incorporated because of the lack of an argument in the [spec, VP] position of the lexical structure of the unergative (e.g. as shown for *race* in Fig. 3).

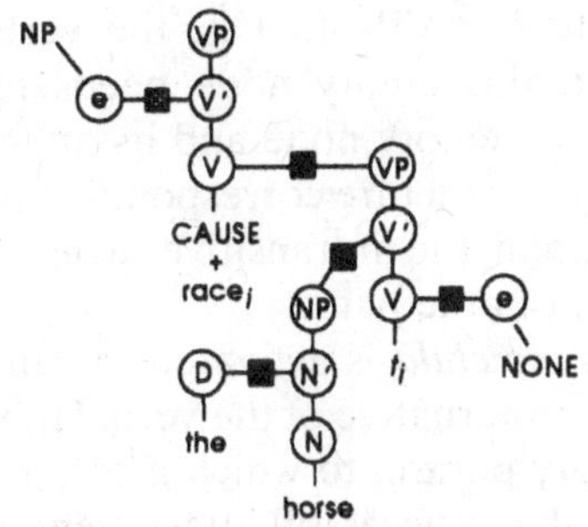

FIG. 12. The network structure for the VP of the syntactic causativisation of an unergative verb, in which the verb is incorporated with the abstract causative morpheme, CAUSE.

Processing a Syntactic Causative

Consider the sentence *The parents withdrew the child from the class.* When the unergative verb *withdrew* is processed, two interpretations are possible: either the lexical form of the verb is used directly, or the verb is syntactically incorporated with the abstract causative morpheme CAUSE. The parser activates the possible extended projections IP-VP and CP-IP-VP for each of the two alternatives, all four of which compete for activation. The CP portion of each CP-IP-VP projection is an empty structure with no overt evidence, and so neither of them can become fully activated (cf. Grimshaw, in press, and Baković, in press, concerning the projection of minimal structure). At this point, then, the highly activated competitors are the two IP-VP forms, one corresponding to the intransitive form of the verb and one to the causative form, as shown in Fig. 13. In each case, the core VP has an empty node attached as sister to the V. In the intransitive alternative, the argument requirements of *withdraw* dictate that the empty node has category NONE—that is, the verb licenses no attachment, and so the empty node becomes fully activated. Since all the phrasal and attachment nodes are fully activated, the complete structure is fully activated. By contrast, in the causative alternative, the argument requirements of CAUSE dictate that the

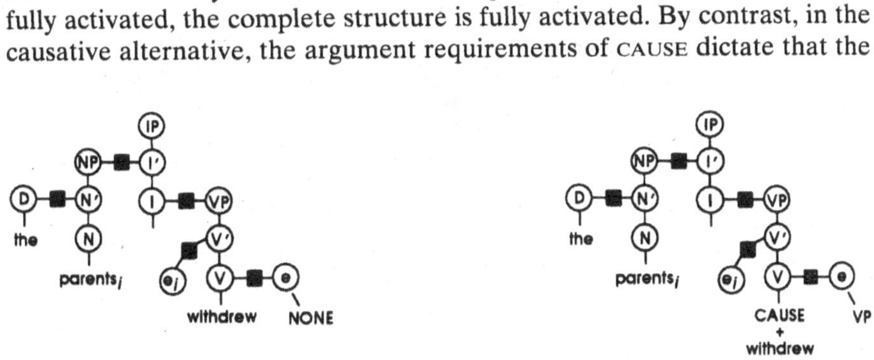

FIG. 13. The two best competitors activated in response to the input *the parents withdrew.*

empty node has category VP—that is, the verb takes an obligatory VP complement, and so this empty node needs to be bound to have full activation. Because the empty node and its attachment node are not fully activated, the complete structure corresponding to the causative alternative has less activation than the intransitive structure, and is therefore less preferred at this point in the parse.

When the NP for *the child* is activated, it cannot attach directly as the complement of either alternative of the verb. However, the NP also triggers activation of an empty phrase, to which it can attach as the specifier. This empty phrase *can* make a successful attachment, as the verbal complement of the incorporated causative verb. At this point, *withdrew* can also bind the empty head of the hypothesised verbal projection, forming a valid syntactic structure, as shown in Fig. 14.

THE PROCESSING OF REDUCED RELATIVE CONSTRUCTIONS

This section presents the central results of the paper: the consequences of our linguistic analysis and processing model for the interpretation of reduced relative clauses. We show that inherent restrictions on the parsing mechanism interact with the proposed syntactic analysis to account precisely for the difficulty of unergative reduced relatives in contrast to other verb types. We begin with the processing of verbs that have a main verb/past participle ambiguity. We assume that such a verb has three lexical entries that are homophonous: an active main verb, an active past participle and a passive past participle. We also assume that a reduced relative clause is a CP-IP-VP projection with an empty operator in [spec, CP]. The empty operator in the competitive attachment parser is realised as an empty node

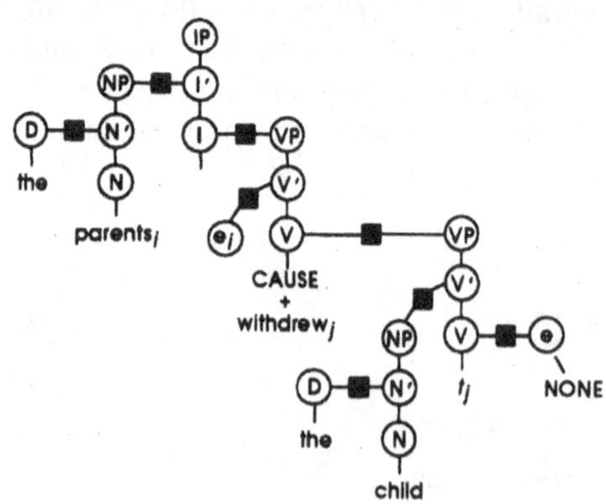

FIG. 14. The network encoding the syntactic structure for *The parents withdrew the child*, containing the transitive alternation of the unergative verb *withdrew*.

in [spec, CP] which binds an empty node in [spec, IP], which in turn binds an empty node complement of the VP. [Note that other linguistic analyses are possible (e.g. Siloni, 1994), but whether the RR is assumed to be a CP or DP is irrelevant for the results here.]

Obligatorily Transitive Verbs

First, consider a reduced relative construction with an obligatorily transitive verb, as in *The bird found in the room died* (Pritchett, 1988), whose syntactic structure is shown in Fig. 15. At the point that *found* is processed, the main verb alternative will yield the two competing extended projections shown in Fig. 16. Because the empty node in [spec, CP] cannot be interpreted as an empty operator, the CP has no evidence (neither a head nor a specifier), and the CP-IP-VP projection becomes less active. Thus the IP-VP is the most activated projection for the main verb reading. The past participle reading will similarly activate two extended projections, as shown in Fig. 17. We will only consider the attachment between the past participle projection and the NP *the bird* in which the verbal projection is a modifier of the NP, since the NP cannot grammatically attach to the specifier position in any of the extended projections. The IP-VP of the past participle form will have an empty node in [spec, IP] which can bind the empty node that is complement to the V node, but the empty node in [spec, IP] is left unbound, and the projection cannot support the predication relation with the noun modified by the reduced relative. The CP-IP-VP has the same binding relation between the empty nodes attached to the [spec, IP] and complement of V positions. But here the empty node in [spec, CP] is able to bind the node in

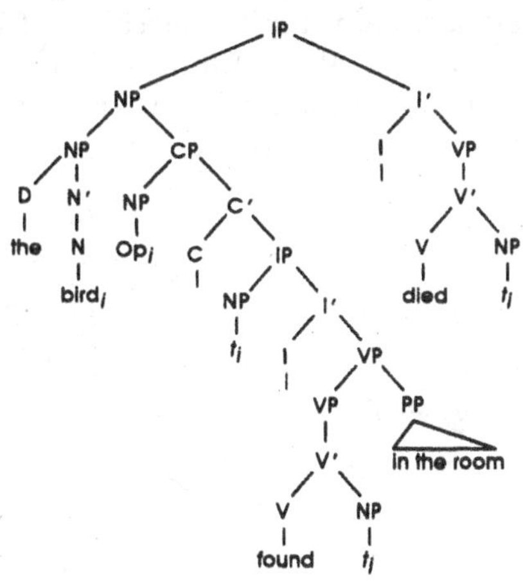

FIG. 15. The syntactic structure for a reduced relative construction, in *The bird found in the room died.*

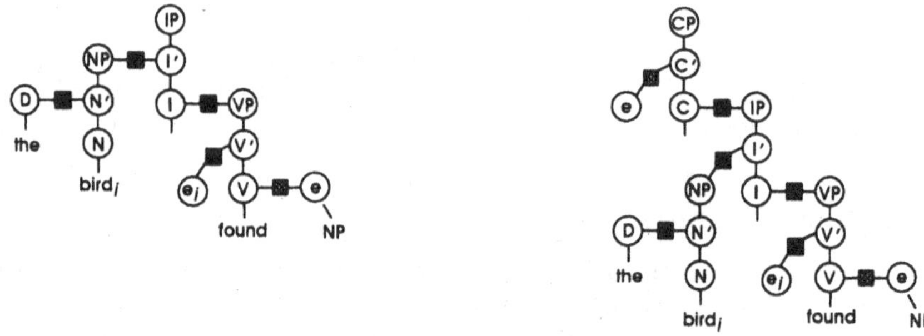

FIG. 16. The extended projections within the network corresponding to the main verb reading of *found*.

[spec, IP] and participate in the predication relation with the noun *bird*. This establishes the empty node in [spec, CP] as an empty operator, leading to a grammatical reduced relative construction. Because the empty nodes in the CP-IP-VP projection are all interpreted, this extended projection has more activation than the IP-VP alternative.

This leaves two competing alternative interpretations: (1) the IP-VP projection corresponding to the main verb lexical entry of *found*, which has the NP *the bird* attached as its subject, and has an empty node as the complement of the VP; and (2) the CP-IP-VP projection corresponding to the past participle lexical entry of *found*, which modifies the NP *the bird*. Neither alternative emerges as a clear winner, since the first is waiting on a required complement, and the second is waiting on a (presumably required) predicate. When the PP *in the room* is processed, it can attach to either structure, and does not settle the competition, although the activation of the main verb reading is decreasing for lack of a binder for the empty object. The closeness of the competition allows for the effects of context and theta role compatibility to influence preferences at this stage (MacDonald, 1994; Trueswell et al., 1994). Given the compatibility of the NP *the bird* with either

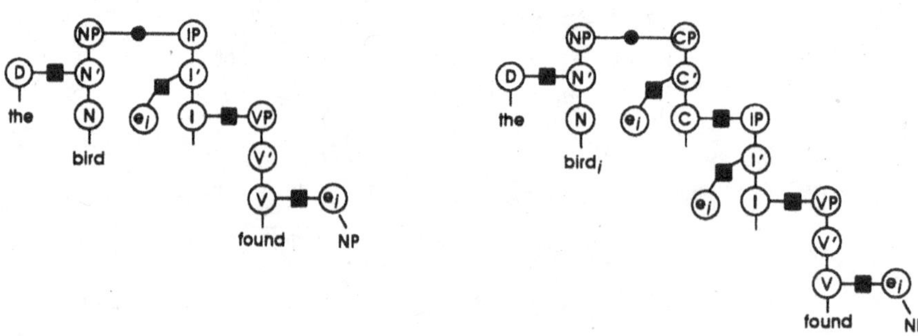

FIG. 17. The extended projections within the network corresponding to the reduced relative reading of *found*, and their attachment as modifier of *the bird*.

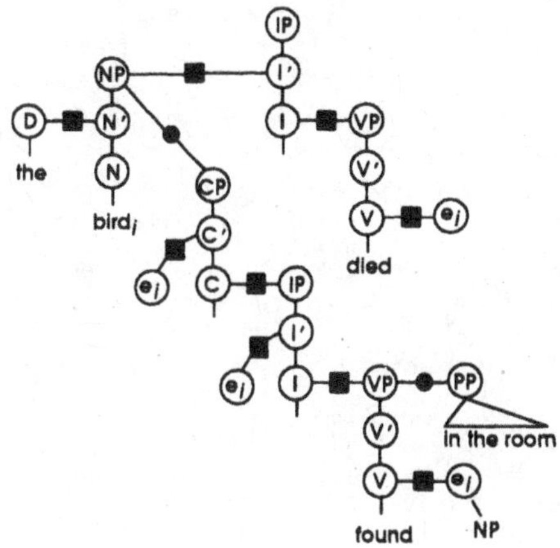

FIG. 18. The final network configuration for *The bird found in the room died.*

the external or internal theta role of *found*, and the lack of contextual bias, both structures will continue to remain active. When the final verb *died* is processed, the only grammatical alternative is for the NP *the bird*, which is modified by the reduced relative clause, to combine with the IP-VP extended projection of *died*, yielding the correct structure for the sentence, shown in Fig. 18.

Unergative Verbs

The ease of sentences like *The bird found in the room died*, which contains an obligatorily transitive verb in the reduced relative construction, has received much attention because of the stark contrast with the prototypical garden-path sentence, *The horse raced past the barn fell.* Figure 19(a) shows the syntactic structure of the latter sentence, under our analysis of the transitive alternative of *race* as an explicit syntactic causative. The proposed structure is clearly more complex than that of a reduced relative with a simple transitive verb such as *found*, repeated here as Fig. 19(b). The passive participle *raced* requires a VP complement with two traces. One is a trace of the NP-movement of the passive construction; it is in the [spec, VP] position and is bound by the empty operator, through the trace in [spec, IP]. The other is the trace of verb movement resulting from the syntactic incorporation of the verb with the CAUSE morpheme; it occurs in the embedded V and is bound by *raced*. Thus the structure not only contains an empty VP complement, but one which has internal structure with two traces.

We can now examine how this structural analysis affects the competitive attachment model in its processing of an MV/RR ambiguity with an

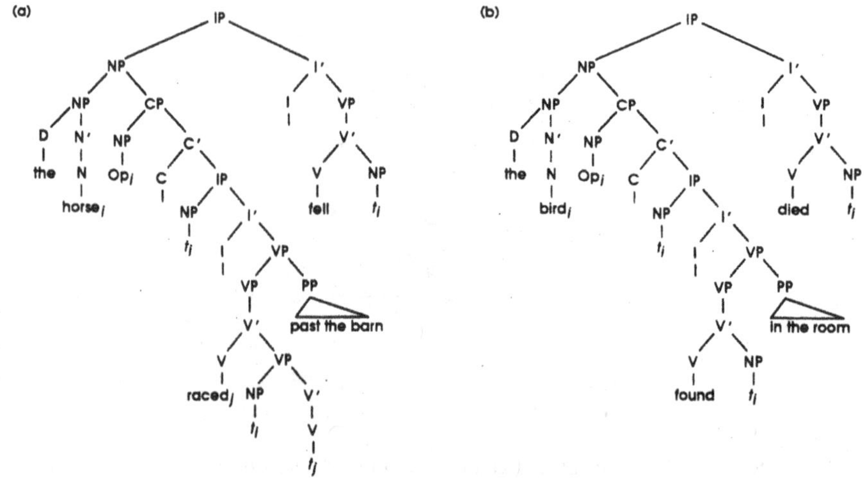

FIG. 19. (a) The syntactic structure for *The horse raced past the barn fell*; (b) the syntactic structure for *The bird found in the room died*, repeated here for comparison.

unergative verb. Like the unambiguous unergative verb *withdrew*, the verb *raced* has two main verb readings, the intransitive and the causative. For reasons analogous to those discussed above in relation to *withdrew*, the two best competitors of the possible extended projections of the main verb reading of *raced* are the two IP-VP forms corresponding to the intransitive reading and the causative reading; these are shown in Fig. 20. The empty node that is sister to V in the intransitive form, in contrast to the main verb reading of *found*, is specified to be empty, so all grammatical relations are satisfied in this structure. The causative form, however, is similar to the main verb reading of *found* in having a sister to the V node that cannot remain empty. Since the empty node is not bound, this structure has less activation and is less preferred.

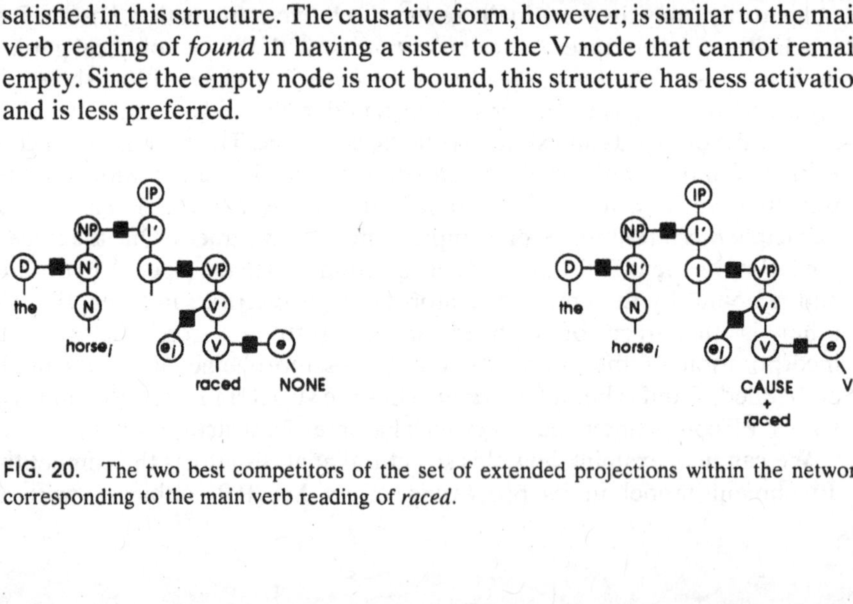

FIG. 20. The two best competitors of the set of extended projections within the network corresponding to the main verb reading of *raced*.

Extended projections are also activated based on the intransitive and causative forms of the past participle reading of *raced.* The intransitive past participle reading decreases in activation, since it can have neither a passive interpretation nor the complex perfect tense interpretation required. The causative past participle interpretation of *raced* yields the two initially activated projections of Fig. 21. As in the case with *found*, there is an empty node attached as the sister to the V node that must be bound. However, in the case of *raced*, the empty node is specified to be a VP, according to the CAUSE morpheme with which *raced* has been incorporated. This category specification leads to a situation in which neither of the extended projections can establish a valid grammatical structure. As with the verb *found*, the IP-VP projection has unbound traces and cannot participate in the appropriate predication relation with the noun modified by the relative clause. The CP-IP-VP projection, however, is very different when the verb is *raced* rather than *found*. In the current example, the empty node in [spec, IP] binds the complement of the verb, but this establishes a VP chain. To bind the empty node in [spec, IP], the empty operator in [spec, CP] would inherit the V category of the chain. But, to be in a predication relation with the noun being modified by the reduced relative clause, it is required to have category N. The empty node in [spec, CP] cannot participate in both relations, or an incompatible category specification will be made, as shown in Fig. 22(a) (compare the successful binding relations of Fig. 22(b), for the RR with *found*). Thus there is no way to establish grammatical binding relations among the empty nodes in this extended projection. The CP-IP-VP fails to become highly activated, since its $\overline{X}$ phrases have unlicensed empty nodes. Neither of the possible extended projections for the causative past participle can compete with the highly activated alternative, that of the main verb intransitive reading. The main verb IP-VP structure therefore wins the

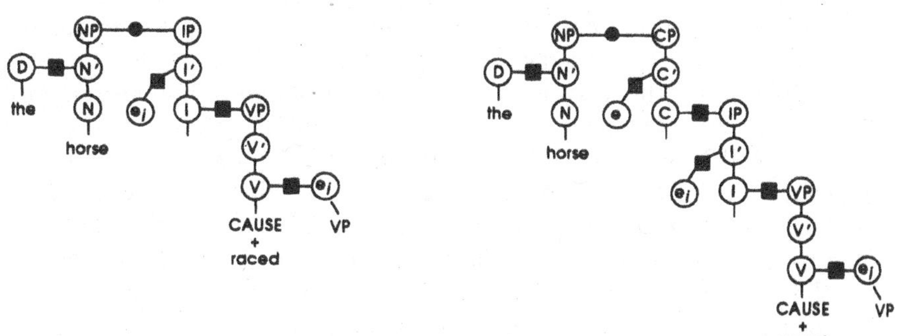

FIG. 21. The two extended projections within the network corresponding to the causative past participle reading of *raced*.

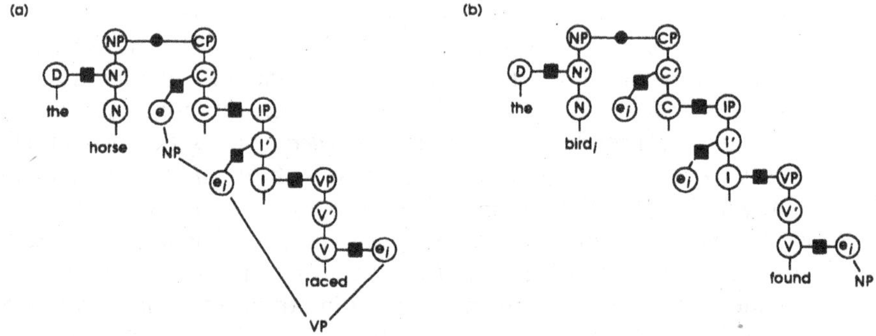

FIG. 22. (a) The invalid binding relations established in the reduced relative structure for *raced*. The [spec, CP] must be an NP, and the empty complement must be a VP. To be bound by the [spec, CP] and to bind the empty complement, the empty node in [spec, IP] would have an incompatible category specification—both NP and VP. (b) The successful network representation for the reduced relative structure for *found*, repeated here for comparison.

competition for activation, and the past participle structures become inactive.

It is crucial to note that the outcome for an unergative reduced relative construction in this account is far bleaker than one in which the structure just does not accumulate sufficient activation to compete effectively with the main verb structure. In fact, the parser is unable to activate the empty structure needed for a grammatical analysis of this sentence. Recall our observation that the reduced relative construction with an unergative verb requires that the verb take an empty VP complement, which must have articulated structure to support the right binding relations. This structural requirement arises from the fact that to be interpreted as a transitive verb, a syntactic operation is required to combine the unergative verb with the CAUSE morpheme. It is this fact of having an explicit causative structure in the syntax that causes the processing difficulty. The competitive attachment parser has limited abilities to activate empty structures, as explained on pp. 371–373. Here the parser can only activate a single empty node, attached to the V node for the incorporated verb, which stands in the position of the VP complement. The parser cannot activate a full projection for the empty embedded VP, which would be necessary to establish the correct empty nodes for the traces of the NP and V movements. Specifically, the parser is unable to activate an empty projection which has no overt elements or features to attach to it, which is precisely what is required in this case. The CP-IP-VP that it activates, as in Fig. 22, is as close as it can come. Thus it is not the case that the reduced relative structure merely loses the competition for activation. Rather, the model predicts a severe garden path, in which a grammatical structure for the reduced relative interpretation is unavailable to the parser within its normal parsing operation.

Unaccusative and Other Optionally Intransitive Verbs

This account differs from theories that attribute the distinction between easy and hard MV/RR ambiguities to the fact of a verb being obligatorily transitive (like *found*) and optionally intransitive (like *raced*) (e.g. Gibson, 1991; Pritchett, 1992). This distinction is not empirically adequate, as we noted earlier. For example, unaccusative verbs, such as *melt*, are also optionally intransitive, but are easily processed in the reduced relative construction, even when they have an MV/RR ambiguity. Furthermore, the distinction cannot be simply the fact that a transitive unergative verb is causative, since an unaccusative verb is also causative in its transitive alternation. The crucial distinction between the unergatives and unaccusatives is that the unaccusatives undergo causativisation in the lexicon, while the unergatives require a syntactic causative operation.

For example, consider *The witch melted in the movie deserved her fate.* Like *raced*, *melted* has both an intransitive reading and a transitive causative reading. Unlike *raced*, the two readings correspond to two different lexical entries for the verb, as shown in Fig. 3. When structure is activated based on the main verb entries, the parser ends up with the two competing IP-VP structures shown in Fig. 23: the intransitive form in which the verb has an empty node in the verb complement position bound by the subject NP *the witch*, and the causative from in which the V node has an empty complement that needs to be bound. The latter structure is somewhat less preferred because of the unbound trace. The past participle reading is only relevant for the causative form of the verb, since the intransitive form cannot be passivised. This lexical entry therefore leads to one extended projection, the CP-IP-VP shown in Fig. 24, which is exactly identical to the reduced relative structure for a simple transitive verb like *found*. This structure is also slightly less preferred than the main verb intransitive reading, because the NP *the witch* needs a predicate. Although there are incomplete relations, however, there is not the problem that arises in the unergative case, in which the parser is unable to complete the necessary structures at all, even with additional

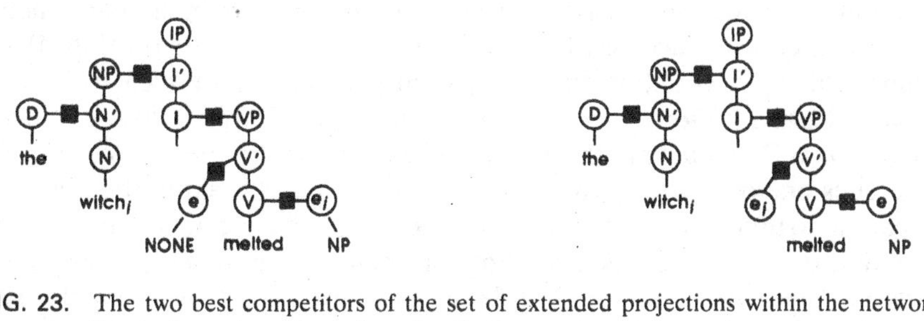

FIG. 23. The two best competitors of the set of extended projections within the network corresponding to the main verb reading of *melt*.

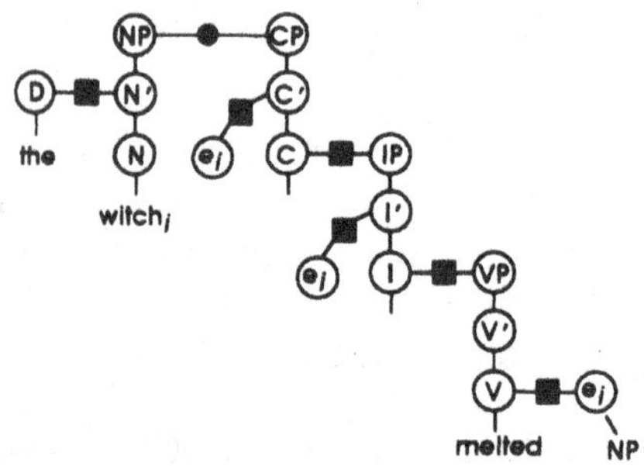

FIG. 24. The best competitor of the set of extended projections within the network corresponding to the causative past participle reading of *melt*.

input. For each of the unaccusative interpretations, the parser can activate and attach the structures it needs when given additional compatible input.

Although we will not go into the processing details here, this same result holds for other optionally intransitive verbs as well, apart from the unergative class. "Ordinary" (non-causative) optionally intransitive verbs have the same structure for the RR as the unaccusative verbs, and are therefore also relatively easy to process in the competitive attachment parser.

Discussion and Additional Consequences

We have shown that, together, our lexical structural analysis and the processing principles of the competitive attachment model account for the severe difficulty of reduced relatives with unergative verbs, as well as for the ease of interpretation of reduced relatives with verbs of any other class that support a transitive alternative. Thus the garden-path effect only arises in the very narrow class of unergative verbs with a transitive alternation. Table 3 summarises the main steps of the processing of the three classes of verbs seen so far.

In our account, the difficulty of an unergative reduced relative arises from the fact that the parser cannot activate the structure needed to represent a grammatical analysis of a syntactically causativised verb in this construction. Every alternative account of which we are aware focuses on the MV/RR ambiguity in accounting for the garden-path nature of such well-known examples as *The horse raced past the barn fell* and *The boat floated down the river sank*. Every approach relies on a basic main verb preference, and then pursues one of the following two strategies: that of making the main verb reading so much more preferred that the alternative cannot compete with it, or that of pruning the RR reading and making any reanalysis operations within the parser not applicable in this instance. Our account differs radically in asserting that the difficulty of these infamous garden paths is in

TABLE 3
Summary of Processing Steps for Different Kinds of Verbs (the Most Highly Activated Competitors are Underlined)

OBLIGATORILY TRANSITIVE: *found*					
The bird found		in the room		died	
MV	RR	MV	RR	MV	RR
VP IP-VP CP-IP-VP	VP IP-VP CP-IP-VP	IP-VP + PP	CP-IP-VP + PP		CP-IP-VP + PP + MV only one possible
		equally activated			

UNERGATIVE: *raced*					
The horse raced		past the barn		fell	
MV	RR	MV	RR	MV	RR
VP IP-VP$_{intr}$ IP-VP$_{caus}$ CP-IP-VP	VP$_{caus}$ IP-VP$_{caus}$ CP-IP-VP$_{caus}$	IP-VP$_{intr}$		no possible analysis	

UNACCUSATIVE: *melted*					
The witch melted		in the movie		deserved her fate	
MV	RR	MV	RR	MV	RR
VP IP-VP$_{intr}$ IP-VP$_{caus}$ CP-IP-VP	VP$_{caus}$ IP-VP$_{caus}$ CP-IP-VP$_{caus}$	IP-VP$_{intr}$ + PP IP-VP$_{caus}$ + PP	CP-IP-VP$_{caus}$ + PP		CP-IP-VP$_{caus}$ + PP + MV only one possible

fact not a result of a garden path at all, at least not in the usual sense of the term applied to this construction. That is because, in our model, the difficulty of the construction is not a result of the ambiguity.

Note that this explanation of difficulty with the MV/RR ambiguity for unergative verbs like *raced* has the following consequences. First, it predicts that even *unambiguous* reduced relative constructions will be very difficult with unergative verbs, because the structure of the embedded VP cannot be built under the restrictions of the competitive attachment model. Second, it predicts that passives of causative unergatives should also be difficult in this framework. Third, it predicts that unergative RRs should be hard in all contexts. Here we examine each of these potentially problematic issues in turn.

First, consider the prediction that even unambiguous unergative verbs will pose severe processing difficulty in the reduced relative construction. For example, when processing an unambiguous reduced relative, as in *The greyhound run around the track all day was tired*, the parser ends up with the same structure for the reduced relative clause as in the case for *raced*, as shown in Fig. 25. The parser also builds the main verb analysis. Agreement

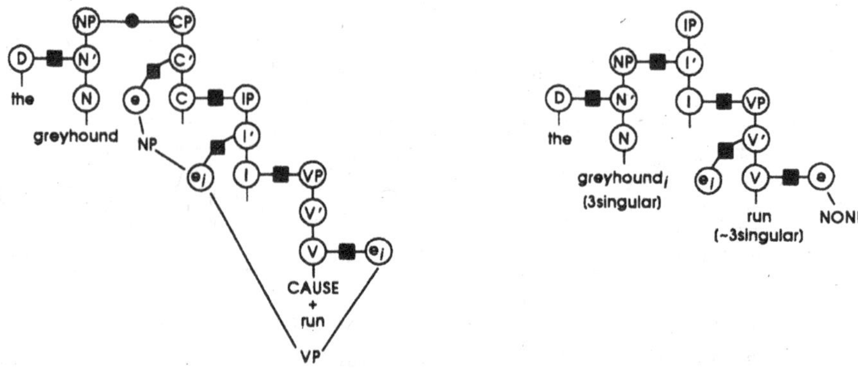

FIG. 25. The competing RR and main verb structures for the unambiguous unergative past participle *run*.

features are propagated by the feature passing mechanism from the NP and VP nodes to the attachment node between the NP and the I′, where it is found that the main verb structure has a person/number feature mismatch between the subject and the verb. However, the fact that there is no grammatical main verb alternative for *run* does not lessen the processing difficulty for the parser. Such an ungrammatical structure would "give way" to a valid grammatical structure, even if the latter were more complex. But there is no grammatical reduced relative alternative, so a main verb structure with a feature mismatch is better than none. This prediction is borne out by the intuitive judgements reported on pp. 353–355, where informants found this and other reduced relatives with an unambiguous unergative verb very difficult.

Thus this potential problem appears instead to be an advantage for the model. The same result of processing difficulty will also occur with ambiguous verbs in a disambiguating context. For example, like people, the competitive attachment model will also experience a garden path even when the RR construction occurs in a position that only licenses an NP and not a sentence, as in *Sara laughed at the horse raced past the barn*. It is not clear how other models that rely on there being an MV/RR ambiguity to explain the processing difficulty could account for these unambiguous data. Even a constraint-based account would be problematic, since it would have to propose that an ungrammatical main verb structure could be weighted sufficiently more than a perfectly grammatical RR structure to allow it to consistently win the competition between the two.

Now let us look at the syntactic structure of a passive unergative, as in *The horse was raced past the barn*, shown in Fig. 26. Here we see again the problematic empty articulated structure within the VP that is the complement to the syntactically incorporated verb *raced*. Turning to the

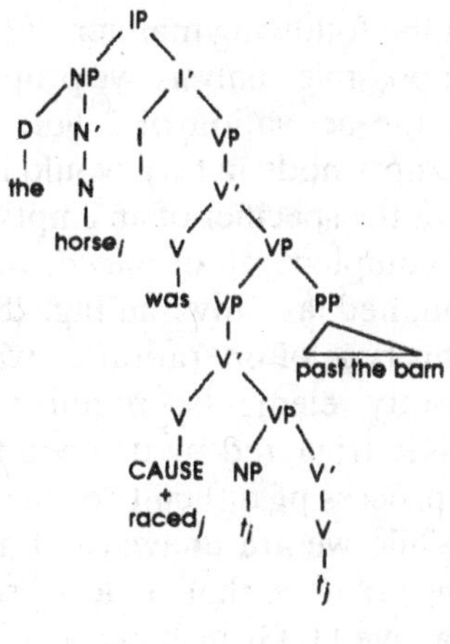

FIG. 26. The syntactic structure for a passive construction with an unergative verb.

processing model, Fig. 27 shows the competitive attachment parser at the point of processing the passive verb. Once again we see that the parser initially activates an empty node in the complement position of the VP, whose category is set to VP by the causative morpheme. The subject *the horse* does not receive a theta role and needs to bind an empty node which does, in order to form a grammatical chain. But it cannot bind the empty VP node. To this extent, the processing of the passive is similar to the processing of the reduced relative, and our model predicts processing difficulty here as well.

However, there is a difference between the network structure here and in the reduced relative construction. In the CP-IP-VP of the RR construction, there are only weak empty nodes which need to bind something or to be bound themselves. By contrast, in the passive, there is an *overt* NP that needs to bind an empty element within the VP. We speculate that this difference

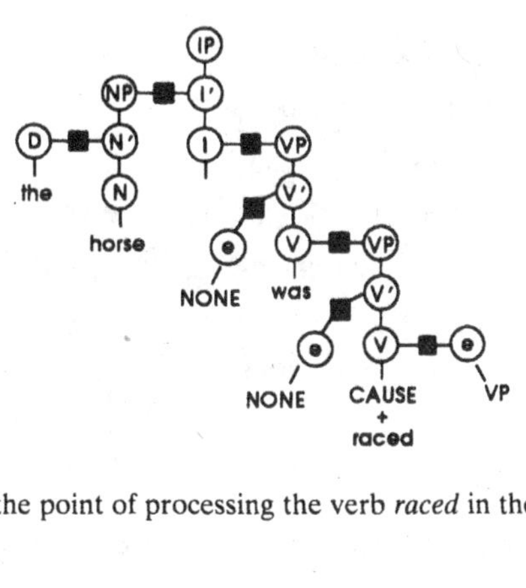

FIG. 27. The parser at the point of processing the verb *raced* in the sentence *The horse was raced past the barn.*

may come into play in the following manner. If the parser is in a position in which there is no other possible analysis, we propose that, as a last resort, the overt NP may trigger the activation of a *bound* empty node. Because it would be bound, this empty node in turn would have sufficient activation to initiate an attachment as the specifier of an empty phrase. This empty phrase would attach as the complement of *raced*, and a grammatical passive structure would be obtained, as shown in Fig. 28.

Clearly, however, this type of operation, in which a single overt element activates multiple empty elements, requires an unusual focusing of activation within the NP, triggered by its need to bind an empty element. Thus we predict some processing difficulty even with the "simple" passive of an unergative verb. While we are unaware of any experimental data that bear on this issue, we do note that at least some unergative verbs are unacceptable in the passive (J. Grimshaw, pers. comm.), so we believe this prediction is worth exploring further.

Finally, we turn to a class of apparent counterexamples to our claim that unergative RRs are unparsable, exemplified by the relative ease of sentence (21) (we thank an anonymous reviewer for pointing out this example):

21. The horse raced in the Kentucky Derby was faster than the one raced at Ascot.

This sentence poses a puzzle, given the observation that unergative RRs are generally not rescuable from a garden-path fate. Typically, unergative RRs in unambiguous contexts (e.g. *The stablehand groomed the horse raced past the barn*) or with unambiguous participles (e.g. *The greyhound run around the track all day was tired*) are as difficult as the traditional garden path *The horse raced past the barn fell*, indicating that even an unambiguous context is not sufficient to allay the difficulties inherent in this construction. First, we must point out that our claim is that unergative RRs are not parsable within

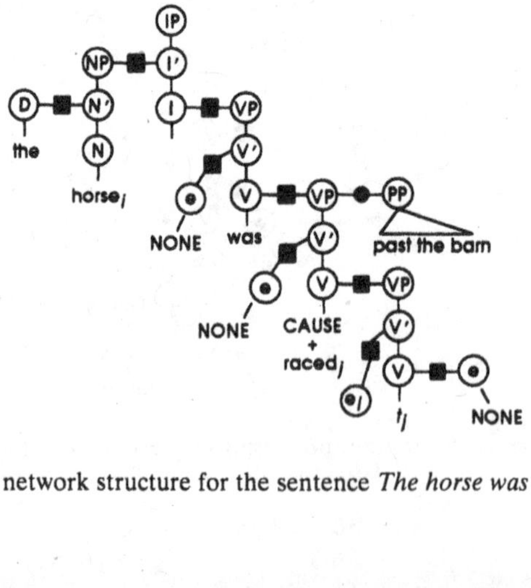

FIG. 28. The final network structure for the sentence *The horse was raced past the barn.*

the normal attachment operation of the parser. It is conceivable that there are special recovery routines that enable the parser to arrive at an interpretation under certain conditions, although it is clear from the empirical data that this ability is limited. One possibility is that a special routine similar to the "last resort" procedure described above for the unergative passive can be exploited.

The question, then, is why sentence (21) would be amenable to this procedure, whereas the other examples noted above would not. Since the precise nature of such a procedure awaits further research, we can only speculate here, but it is worth making two observations regarding which properties of example (21) may facilitate recovery. First, the use of "the one" construction is compatible only with a modifying phrase which is predicated of *the one*. This provides unambiguous evidence of a reduced relative (the only possible modifier headed by a verb) for the second occurrence of *raced* in the sentence and, by syntactic parallelism, for the first occurrence as well. Second, sentence (21) contains a lengthy disambiguating region (cf. *was faster than the one raced at Ascot* to *fell*). Although this phenomenon is not entirely understood, it has been noted that a lengthy disambiguating region appears to give the sentence processor the time it needs to revise a misanalysis that it might not otherwise be able to recover from (Frazier & Clifton, 1996). In the competitive attachment parser, the extra length may provide not only extra time but additional activation to lend towards triggering the necessary empty structure. However, the details of this approach are a matter for future research. We simply note in conclusion that, to our knowledge, no account of reduced relative difficulty can explain both the apparent contextual effects of this example, as well as the verb class distinction that we have explored in this paper.

GENERAL DISCUSSION

Our explanation of the difficulty of a subset of reduced relative clauses relies crucially on the interaction of processing effects and a different grammatical structure for easy and difficult cases. This proposal gives prominence to structural information stored in the lexicon, which determines the syntactic structure of verbal projections. Although it assumes that structure building is one of the causes of processing complexity, it contrasts with previous structure-based proposals which rely on general syntactic information only (e.g. Ferreira & Clifton, 1986; Frazier & Fodor, 1978; Frazier, 1978). The approach here also suggests a finer-grained lexical distinction than the simple obligatorily versus optionally transitive contrast called on by Gibson (1991) and Pritchett (1992).

Constraint-based models put forward to explain the differential difficulty of reduced relative clauses downplay the role of structure building as a source of complexity, and instead propose that several factors are simultaneously at play in the resolution of syntactic ambiguity (MacDonald, 1994; MacDonald et al., 1994; Trueswell et al., 1994; Trueswell, 1996). In analogy to word recognition, several competitors are activated corresponding to an ambiguous word (the *-ed* form of the verb, for instance, in the MV/RR ambiguity). Linguistic competence determines the number of competitors, depending on the subcategorisation frame of the verb and the syntactic constructions in which the ambiguous form of the verb can appear (for instance, active or passive). Frequency of usage of the linguistic features in the alternatives (voice, transitivity, tense, etc.) in the linguistic experience of the speaker determines the strength of the activation of each of these competitors. Probabilistic co-occurrence constraints of phrases can further increase or decrease the activation of the competitors. In these models, structural complexity comes into play indirectly, because the simpler representation usually corresponds to a global bias in the processing network, and it interacts with item-specific biases in the resolution of ambiguity. No constraint is, in principle, qualitatively different from the others. This approach, then, predicts that any difficulty posed by a constraint can be eliminated, if the opposing constraints are appropriately manipulated.

The current proposal shares the view of constraint-based models that several factors are at play in resolving ambiguity, and that the computation occurs in parallel and is activation-based. In fact, we specify a precise constraint-integration algorithm: We provide both a precise description of the representations that enter into the competition, and a numerical formulation of the constraint-integration mechanism, which is competition-based, as described above. In contrast to other approaches, however, we believe that not all constraints have the same importance. Structural complexity is given a special status by being defined implicitly in the architectural design, entailing that certain structures cannot be computed. In the current model, structural complexity alone can cause failure to interpret a sentence, even when all other factors would help its correct interpretation. This phenomenon is clearly observable when the sentence is not ambiguous. In general, the model predicts categorial processing effects, which are not predicted by other constraint-based models. Proposals that do not make crucial use of computational restrictions incur empirical inadequacies in that they do not readily explain the sharp difficulty for *unambiguous* reduced relatives with unergative verbs. As noted earlier, a constraint-based account, where the strength of activation of one analysis depends on the numbers and strength of competitors (MacDonald, 1994; MacDonald et al., 1994), would be problematic, since it would have to propose that an ungrammatical main verb structure could be weighted sufficiently more than a grammatical RR structure to allow it to consistently win the competition between the two.

A model that makes crucial use of architectural restrictions is a first attempt to provide an explanation for frequency differentials. In constraint-based processing, on the other hand, frequency is treated as if it were a primitive of the processing system, a predictor variable not reducible to other factors. Note that if frequency were a primitive—either in the perception or in the production system—one would expect it to vary independently of structural complexity and, in particular, independently of syntactic verb classes. One would expect, for instance, to see transitivity preference scattered across verb types. Corpus counts appear to contradict this position, and instead support the view put forth in Gibson and Pearlmutter (1994), where frequencies are taken to be an indicator of processing complexity. Processing complexity, then, has to be grounded elsewhere, to avoid circularity. We propose it to be grounded in structural complexity.[5]

Many other proposals that have discussed the resolution of MV/RR ambiguity are not equipped to explain the difference between verb classes *within* the same structural ambiguity. For example, referential theory (Altmann & Steedman, 1988; Crain & Steedman, 1985) proposes that RRs are particularly difficult because they require more presuppositions than the main verb alternative. This is due to the restrictive nature of the RR, which presupposes a set of elements in the discourse from which the RR picks one. The suggestion is that the human sentence processing mechanism follows a principle of referential parsimony in preferring the main verb interpretation, which carries fewer presuppositions. We simply note that this account needs to be extended to deal with the difference between verb classes found in this paper. The same conclusion is drawn regarding "construal theory" (Frazier & Clifton, 1996; Gilboy, Sopena, Clifton, & Frazier, 1995), which proposes an approach for the interpretation of adjuncts. Construal theory determines the timecourse of attachment of primary and non-primary (adjunct) relations. It assumes a delay in the attachment of adjuncts, which are "associated" with the current theta domain and interpreted using extragrammatical principles. The MV/RR ambiguity is a case of contrast between primary and non-primary relations, as the main verb role for the VP is primary, while a relative clause is not primary. A strong main verb bias in MV/RR ambiguities is then predicted, as the parser always tries to satisfy a primary relation if it can. No difference between different kinds of verbs

[5]It has been suggested to us by an anonymous reviewer that differential frequencies come from the production system—that is, people tend to avoid syntactically complex alternatives. The processing system, being a perception system, is sensitive to such differences. If such a preference exists in production, though, that shows that the linguistic processing faculties are sensitive to structural complexity in general. Simplicity of the theory would lead us to prefer an explanation where the language faculty were sensitive to the same factors both in production and in perception.

would be predicted, as in all cases the primary main verb relation would be preferred.

The current proposal highlights the role of the computation of syntactic structure, as projected from the lexicon. As the syntactic difference is derived from lexical structure, it accounts for differences across *classes* of lexical items and contrasts with those approaches that want to reduce or eliminate the syntactic level in processing. Within the framework of constraint-based processing, Spivey-Knowlton and Sedivy (1995) propose that PP attachment preferences rely on referential and verb-specific constraints, without any recourse to syntactic knowledge. Crucially, their study shows verb subclass effects (verbs of action *vs* psych/perception verbs), with preference for VP attachment for action verbs, and NP attachment for psych and perception verbs. They argue that lexical preferences account for the pattern, but it is never explained *why* action verbs, for instance, should favour an instrument interpretation over a manner interpretation of the ambiguously attached PP. More importantly, the conclusion of Spivey-Knowlton and Sedivy that syntactic distinctions are irrelevant to the pattern of attachment preferences seems too hasty, since verb classes are defined in terms of the content of theta roles. Although some researchers believe that theta roles constitute semantic information, there are well-attested syntactic corollaries of each different thematically defined subclass of verbs (unergatives, unaccusatives, perception verbs, psych verbs, etc.). In the absence of a precise formulation of the processing model and of the representation of linguistic knowledge, the evidence in Spivey-Knowlton and Sedivy (1995) is inconclusive between a semantic and syntactic account.

Although we propose that theta roles partially determine syntactic structure, they are not directly manipulated in our model. This position contrasts with the proposal put forth in Carlson and Tanenhaus (1988), where thematic roles are directly accessed by the processor, which uses them to integrate the incoming input incrementally into a discourse model. While our account does not address word sense ambiguity and discourse integration, an account in terms of the content of theta roles does not properly explain the difference in difficulty between unergative and unaccusative RRs. The crucial property proposed by Carlson and Tanenhaus to account for difficult RRs is that the role which is assigned to the subject of the intransitive is the same as the role of the object of the transitive. So, in both *the child hurried home* and *the father hurried the child home*, the argument *the child* receives a theme theta role. When the parser reaches the disambiguating portion of the sentence (the word *fell* in *the child hurried home fell*), the parser realises that it has incorrectly selected the intransitive theta grid, but it cannot reassign the theta role, since the theme theta role has already been assigned. The difficulty of these sentences contrasts with the ease of reanalysis of a sentence such as *The girl sent the flowers was pleased*, where *the girl* is at first assigned an agent theta role, which is then easily modified to "goal", a role that is still available at the point of disambiguation.

The account of Carlson and Tanenhaus (1988) thus predicts equal difficulty for unergatives and unaccusatives, as in both cases the thematic role that alternates between the subject of the intransitive and the object of the transitive is the same. Thus the prediction is that unaccusatives should also be hard. Indeed, Carlson and Tanenhaus list *the butter melted* as a difficult reduced relative. Our intuitions, supported by those of our informants, suggest that the difference in difficulty between the two subclasses of verbs is substantial. Our account of the difficulty of unergatives rests on the assumption that the object of the transitive variant is not a theme, but rather an agent. It might seem odd to have two agents in the same clause. To avoid this situation, it could be proposed that transitive unergative verbs assign two different roles, such as (agent, actor). But under this representation, unergatives would be easier than unaccusatives in the account of Carlson and Tanenhaus (1988), as a new theta role could be assigned to the subject of the RR at the point of disambiguation, namely the actor role. Our account achieves a better explanation of the data by mapping the difference in thematic role assignment in the two verb subclasses onto a structural difference, which in turn causes parsing difficulty in some cases. In this way, we are able to account for fine distinctions in the data without positing any parsing mechanism specific to the construction under study.

More recent discussions of the semantic and thematic constraints that affect the ease of resolution of the ambiguity under study can be found in Tabossi, Spivey-Knowlton, McRae and Tanenhaus (1994) and Trueswell et al. (1994). Studies have shown that animacy does not explain the difficulty in garden-path RRs (Ferreira & Clifton, 1986; Trueswell et al., 1994). The intuitive judgements reported here confirm the experimental results. Animacy of the modified NP is not necessary to make the sentence hard, since *The model planet rotated on the metal axis fell off the stand* is hard, although *the model planet* is clearly inanimate. Neither is animacy a sufficient condition for processing difficulty, since we found that *The witch melted in the Wizard of Oz was played by a famous actress* was easily understood.

In an attempt to find a better semantic predictor of processing difficulty of a reduced relative clause, Trueswell et al. (1994) suggest using the notion of "degree of semantic fit". The "degree of semantic fit" is a measure of the distance of a nominal lexical item from the prototypical recipient of a given theta role, in the context of a given verb. So, for instance, a *reporter* is a good agent for a verb like *interview* but a poor or unlikely patient. In the examples presented here, however, the "degree of semantic fit" of the initial NP with the main verb reading does not precisely correlate with the difficulty of the RR interpretation, as proposed by Trueswell et al. (1994). Trueswell et al. claim that if the mapping between thematic role and grammatical functions permits a main clause interpretation, then a garden-path effect will be found. But we observe that this incorrectly predicts a garden-path effect for unaccusative RRs, because the initial NP *necessarily* exhibits the same "degree of semantic fit" with either a main verb or RR reading, since the theta role of theme is equally suited to be an object or a subject in these verbs. Furthermore, although unergatives follow this same pattern of semantic fit, they behave very differently from unaccusatives.[6] In general, we can remark that the subclasses of verbs under study here differ from other classes because both the subject of the active voice and the subject of the passive voice can equally well be an agent in the case of unergatives, and a theme in the case of unaccusatives. The degree of semantic fit is not informative to resolve the MV/RR ambiguity for these classes of verbs. The manipulation of semantic content of the arguments of these verbs, then, will have to be studied differently.

In conclusion, we have proposed a lexical structural account for the differential difficulty of reduced relative clauses. We make the novel observation that extreme garden paths occur most of the time with manner of motion/sound emission verbs, a subclass of intransitive verbs with peculiar properties. We have proposed a lexical and syntactic analysis of these verbs that, in conjunction with a specific model of processing, produces the right description of the data. The processing model that is supported by the empirical evidence is the competitive attachment model (Stevenson, 1994b). This approach accounts for the sharp distinctions between unergative RR clauses and RR clauses with other verbs. The analysis achieves a better fit to the empirical data than those proposals which build the differences in parsing difficulty on the verb being optionally or obligatorily transitive (Gibson, 1991; Pritchett, 1992). Both unaccusatives and unergatives are preferentially intransitive verbs, but the difference in processing difficulty is remarkable.

The proposal achieves its account thanks to an independently justified linguistic analysis and independently justified properties of the processing model. In particular, the parser experiences difficulty in processing reduced

[6]Frequency effects are also not sufficiently strong to explain the difference. On the one hand, we find that unaccusative verbs have a strong preference to be used intransitively overall, thus favouring an association of the theta role theme with the grammatical function subject and making the wrong prediction if degree of semantic fit were the predominant factor. On the other hand, the reduced relative construction is equally rare for both classes of verbs, entailing that the relative frequency of main verb and past participle use can only be a weak factor in determining the preferred analysis of RRs with these verb classes. See Merlo and Stevenson (1996) for the relevant corpus analysis and discussion.

relative clauses of unergative verbs because of its limited ability to project empty nodes and to bind them in the structure. Our explanation does not rely on the fact that the RR participle is an ambiguous verb form, and thus it accounts for the observation that complexity effects persist even when there is no ambiguity, a fact not easily explained by other models. For other verbs, such as obligatorily transitive verbs or unaccusatives, where the lexical and syntactic competitors in the analysis are more evenly weighted, there is no processing breakdown, and the model can be influenced by pragmatic and semantic factors. The proposal thus reconciles results that point towards an architecture where several constraints are simultaneously at play, with results that indicate sharp and irrecoverable breakdown.

REFERENCES

Altmann, G., & Steedman, M. (1988). Interaction with context during human sentence processing. *Cognition*, *30*, 191–238.

Baker, M. (1988). *Incorporation*. Chicago, IL: University of Chicago Press.

Baković, E. (in press). Optimality and inversion in Spanish. In *Proceedings of the Optimality in Syntax Workshop*. MIT Working Papers in Linguistics. Cambridge, MA: MIT Press.

Belletti, A., & Rizzi, L. (1988). Psych verbs and θ theory. *Natural Language and Linguistic Theory*, *6*, 291–352.

Bever, T.G. (1970). The cognitive basis for linguistic structure. In J.R. Hayes (Ed.), *Cognition and the development of language*, pp. 278–352. New York: John Wiley.

Bresnan, J. (1982). The passive in lexical theory. In J. Bresnan (Ed.), *The mental representation of grammatical relations*, pp. 3–86. Cambridge, MA: MIT Press.

Brousseau, A.-M., & Ritter, E. (1991). A non-unified analysis of agentive verbs. In *West Coast Conference on Formal Linguistics*, *20*, 53–64.

Burzio, L. (1981). *Intransitive verbs and Italian auxiliaries*. PhD thesis, MIT, Cambridge, MA.

Burzio, L. (1986). *Italian syntax*. Dordrecht: Kluwer Academic.

Carlson, G.N., & Tanenhaus, M.K. (1988). Thematic roles and language comprehension. In W. Wilkins (Ed.), *Syntax and semantics*, Vol. 21, pp. 263–288. San Diego, CA: Academic Press.

Chomsky, N. (1981). *Lectures on Government and Binding*. Dordrecht: Foris.

Crain, S., & Steedman, M. (1985). On not being led up the garden path: The use of context by the psychological parser. In D.R. Dowty, L. Kartunnen, & A.M. Zwicky (Eds), *Natural language processing: Psychological, computational, and theoretical perspectives*, pp. 320–358. Cambridge: Cambridge University Press.

Cruse, D.A. (1972). A note on English causatives. *Linguistic Inquiry*, *3*, 520–528.

Dowty, D.R. (1979). *Word meaning and Montague grammar*. Dordrecht: Reidel.

Ferreira, F., & Clifton, C. (1986). The independence of syntactic processing. *Journal of Memory and Language*, *25*, 348–368.

Ford, M., Bresnan, J., & Kaplan, R. (1982). A competence-based theory of syntactic closure. In J. Bresnan (Ed.), *The mental representation of grammatical relations*, pp. 727–796. Cambridge, MA: MIT Press.

Frazier, L. (1978). *On comprehending sentences: Syntactic parsing strategies*. PhD thesis, University of Connecticut, Storrs, CT. Available through the Indiana University Linguistics Club, Bloomington, IN.

Frazier, L., & Clifton, C. (1996). *Construal.* Cambridge, MA: MIT Press.

Frazier, L., & Fodor, J.D. (1978). The sausage machine: A new two-stage parsing model. *Cognition, 6,* 291–325.

Gibson, E. (1991). *A computational theory of human linguistic processing: Memory limitations and processing breakdown.* PhD thesis, Carnegie Mellon University, Pittsburgh, PA.

Gibson, E., & Pearlmutter, N.J. (1994). A corpus-based analysis of psycholinguistic constraints on prepositional phrase attachment. In C. Clifton, L. Frazier, & K. Rayner (Eds), *Perspectives on sentence processing,* pp. 181–198. Hillsdale, NJ: Lawrence Erlbaum Associates Inc.

Gilboy, E., Sopena, J.-M., Clifton, C., & Frazier, L. (1995). Argument structure and association preferences in Spanish and English complex nps. *Cognition, 54,* 131–167.

Grimshaw, J. (1991). *Extended projection.* Waltham, MA: Brandeis University.

Grimshaw, J. (in press). Projection, heads and optimality. *Linguistic Inquiry.*

Hale, K., & Keyser, J. (1987). A view from the middle. *Lexicon Project Working Papers* No. 10. Cambridge, MA: MIT Press.

Hale, K., & Keyser, J. (1993). On argument structure and the lexical representation of syntactic relations. In K. Hale & J. Keyser (Eds), *The view from building 20,* pp. 53–110. Cambridge, MA: MIT Press.

Harley, H. (1995). *Subjects, events and licensing.* PhD thesis, MIT, Cambridge, MA.

Jackendoff, R. (1972). *Semantic interpretation in generative grammar.* Cambridge, MA: MIT Press.

Kaplan, R.M., & Bresnan, J. (1982). Lexical-functional grammar: A formal system for grammatical representation. In J. Bresnan (Ed.), *The mental representation of grammatical relations,* pp. 173–281. Cambridge, MA: MIT Press.

Koopman, H., & Sportiche, D. (1991). The position of subjects. *Lingua, 85,* 211–258.

Levin, B. (1993). *English verb classes and alternations.* Chicago, IL: University of Chicago Press.

Levin, B., & Rappaport, M. (1986). The formation of adjectival passives. *Linguistic Inquiry, 17,* 623–661.

Levin, B., & Rappaport Hovav, M. (1995). *Unaccusativity.* Cambridge, MA: MIT Press.

MacDonald, M.C. (1994). Probabilistic constraints and syntactic ambiguity resolution. *Language and Cognitive Processes, 9,* 157–201.

MacDonald, M., Pearlmutter, N., & Seidenberg, M. (1994). Lexical nature of syntactic ambiguity resolution. *Psychological Review, 101,* 676–703.

Merlo, P., & Stevenson, S. (1996). *Integrating statistical and structural information in a distributed architecture for syntactic disambiguation.* Technical Report TR-25, Rutgers Center for Cognitive Science, Rutgers University, New Brunswick, NJ.

Pritchett, B. (1988). Garden path phenomena and the grammatical basis of language processing. *Language, 64,* 539–576.

Pritchett, B. (1992). *Grammatical competence and parsing performance.* Chicago, IL: University of Chicago Press.

Reggia, J. (1987). Properties of a competition-based activation mechanism in neuromimetic network models. In *Proceedings of the First International Conference on Neural Networks,* pp. II-131–II-138. New York: IEEE.

Rizzi, L. (1990). *Relativized minimality.* Cambridge, MA: MIT Press.

Siloni, T. (1994). *Noun phrases and nominalizations.* PhD thesis, University of Geneva, Geneva.

Spivey-Knowlton, M., & Sedivy, J.C. (1995). Resolving attachment ambiguity with multiple constraints. *Cognition, 55,* 227–267.

Spivey-Knowlton, M.J., Trueswell, J.C., & Tanenhaus, M.K. (1993). Context effects in syntactic ambiguity resolution: Discourse and semantic influences in parsing reduced relative clauses. *Canadian Journal of Experimental Psychology*, *47*, 276–309.

Stevenson, S. (1993a). A competition-based explanation of syntactic attachment preferences and garden path phenomena. In *Proceedings of the 31st Annual Meeting of the Association for Computational Linguistics*, pp. 266–273. Morristown, NJ: ACL.

Stevenson, S. (1993b). Establishing long-distance dependencies in a hybrid network model of human parsing. In *Proceedings of the 15th Annual Conference of the Cognitive Science Society*, pp. 982–987. Hillsdale, NJ: Lawrence Erlbaum Associates Inc.

Stevenson, S. (1994a). Competition and recency in a hybrid network model of syntactic disambiguation. *Journal of Psycholinguistic Research*, *23*, 295–322.

Stevenson, S. (1994b). *A competitive attachment model for resolving syntactic ambiguities in natural languasge parsing*. PhD thesis, Department of Computer Science, University of Maryland. Available as Technical Report TR-18 from Rutgers Center for Cognitive Science, Rutgers University, New Brunswick, NJ.

Stevenson, S. (1995). Arguments and adjuncts: A computational explanation of asymmetries in attachment preferences. In *Proceedings of the 17th Annual Conference of the Cognitive Science Society*, pp. 748–753. Mahwah, NJ: Lawrence Erlbaum Associates Inc.

Sturt, P., & Crocker, M. (1996). Monotonic syntactic processing: A cross-linguistic study of attachment and reanalysis. *Language and Cognitive Processes*, *11*, 449–494.

Tabossi, P., Spivey-Knowlton, M.J., McRae, K., & Tanenhaus, M.K. (1994). Semantic effects on syntactic ambiguity resolution: Evidence for a constraint resolution process. In C. Umilta & M. Moscovitch (Eds), *Attention and performance XV*, pp. 589–615. Hillsdale, NJ: Lawrence Erlbaum Associates Inc.

Trueswell, J.C. (1996). The role of lexical frequency in syntactic ambiguity resolution. *Journal of Memory and Language*, *35*, 566–585.

Trueswell, J.C., Tanenhaus, M.K., & Garnsey, S.M. (1994). Semantic influences on parsing: Use of thematic role information in syntactic ambiguity resolution. *Journal of Memory and Language*, *33*, 285–318.

Subject Index